Born Again

Born Again
Evangelicalism in Korea

TIMOTHY S. LEE

University of Hawai'i Press
HONOLULU

15 14 13 12 11 10   6 5 4 3 2 1

Library of Congress Cataloging-in-Publication Data
Lee, Timothy S.
  Born again : evangelicalism in Korea / Timothy S. Lee.
    p. cm.
  Includes bibliographical references and index.
  ISBN 978-0-8248-3375-6 (hardcover : alk. paper)
  1. Evangelicalism—Korea (South)—History. 2.
Protestantism—Korea (South) 3. Korea (South)—
Church history—20th century. I. Title.
  BR1642.K6L44 2010
  280'.4095195—dc22

                                  2009028077

Designed by the University of Hawai'i Press production staff

Printed by The Maple-Vail Book Manufacturing Group

For Joseph, Esther, and Yeahwa

Contents

Acknowledgments

I t took a long time to complete this book, and I could not have done it without the guidance and support of a number of persons and institutions. I relish this opportunity to thank them.

First, my thanks go to scholars associated with the University of Chicago who helped me through the book's dissertation stage. This includes the late Jerald C. Brauer, who introduced me to the scholarship on evangelicalism and gave me an idea for the book. Apart from his encouragement and interest in my research, this book might not have seen the light of day. Martin E. Marty played a crucial role as dissertation director. He guided me till the end, helping me to refine the argument and instilling in me the importance of empathy in studying religion. And Bruce Cumings played a crucial role by encouraging me to be critical in studying East Asian history. Not a Chicagoan but also an important member of my dissertation committee is Yi Mahn-yol, at the time professor of Korean History at Sookmyung Women's University and director of the Institute of Korean Church History Studies in Seoul. He pointed me to key sources and shared keen insights about the history of Christianity in Korea. From each of these scholars I have learned a great deal, and I hope at least some of that learning shows through in this book.

I am also grateful to several institutions. The first two are the Social Science Research Council and Fulbright (Institute of International Education). Their grants enabled me to do research and interact with scholars in South Korea. Without them this book could not have been written. I am grateful to the Disciples Divinity House of the University of Chicago and its former dean W. Clark Gilpin and the current dean Kristine A. Culp. The DDH and the deans afforded me a supportive community while I was studying at Chicago. Thanks are also due to UCLA's Center for Korean Studies, where I served as Henry Luce Postdoctoral Fellow in Korean Christianity in 2001–2002. I am especially grateful to the then director Robert E. Buswell Jr., who trusted me to organize an international conference that resulted in a volume titled *Christianity in Korea*, published by the University of Hawai'i Press in 2006. My experiences at UCLA benefited this book. Brite Divinity School (Texas Christian University) provided me with a semester's leave in fall 2008 so that I could complete the major research and writing—thank you, Brite.

In publishing *Christianity in Korea*, Patricia Crosby, UHP's executive editor, played a crucial role. She has played the same role in the publication of this book. I am grateful to her—as I am to Rosemary Wetherold for her masterly copyediting, to the two anonymous readers who provided valuable suggestions for improvement, and to Minchung Kang of UCLA, who vetted the manuscript for McCune-Reischauer romanization. If errors remain, mea culpa.

Aspects of chapter 1 were published in *Criterion: A Publication of the Divinity School of the University of Chicago* (July 2002) and *Church History: Studies in Christianity and Culture* (March 2000); of chapter 3 in *Acta Koreana* (July 2002); of chapter 4 in *Religions of Korea in Practice*, edited by Robert E. Buswell Jr. (Princeton University Press, 2007); and of the epilogue in the above-mentioned *Christianity in Korea*.

While I was working on this book, Joseph and Esther grew up quite a bit, and Yeahwa became even lovelier. Without their support and understanding, I could not have conceived this book. To them this book is dedicated.

Introduction

Creatures always hope for salvation; that is their nature.
—*Joachim Wach*

In 1907, two years after it became a Japanese protectorate and three years before it was forcibly annexed to Japan, Korea was known in the West as a hermit nation, a backward and introverted country, unwilling to be assimilated into modernity.[1] For Korean Protestants, however, 1907 was a watershed year in which a great nationwide revival, under the auspices of foreign missionaries, swept through their churches, indelibly defining their religion's character.[2]

Eighty-one years later, something of a coming-out took place in Korea—South Korea—as it sponsored the twenty-fourth Summer Olympics, with the motto "Seoul to the World, the World to Seoul." In mid-August 1988, a few weeks before the games were to begin in modernistic stadiums that signified Korea's newly emerging status, hundreds of thousands of citizens gathered at the capacious Yŏŭido Plaza for what one revivalist called Soulympic, a four-day-long revival officially named the '88 World Evangelization Crusade—entirely under Korean auspices.[3]

The eight decades between the great revival of 1907 and the '88 World Evangelization Crusade were one of the most turbulent periods in Korean history. Politically, this was when Chosŏn (1392–1910), the half-millennial neo-Confucian dynasty, suffered its demise. In its stead, Korea's political fate was determined, in turns, by a Japanese colonialism that left a deep-seated anti-Japanese sentiment in the collective consciousness of Koreans;[4] occupational forces of the United States and the Soviet Union, both of which valued Korea mainly for its utility as a political buffer;[5] and the governments of North and South Korea, which waged against each other the most devastating war ever fought in the peninsula. Economically, this was the period when Koreans fully embraced a modern industrial economy, becoming quite proficient at it—especially in the South. Culturally, Korea was transformed from elitist Chosŏn, in which the mastery of classical Chinese—its official script—was the preserve of a privileged minority, to the mass societies of two Koreas, where the mastery of the native script *han'gŭl* was expected of every citizen.

Given these profound transformations, it would be peculiar if similarly significant change had not occurred in the nation's religious landscape. Such change was most apparent in the dislodgment of neo-Confucianism from its place as the regnant ideology and religion of the land.[6] Many Koreans, to be sure, still sought to practice Confucianism as their forefathers had done, and Confucianism's cultural legacies remained powerfully subjacent in Korea even in the late twentieth century. But as a worldview that oriented expectations of Koreans and an ethos that defined the sacred and structured their lives, Confucianism was all but a shadow of its former glory.[7]

If Confucianism waned in this period, two other traditional religions of Korea waxed. Buddhism had been suppressed by Confucians during the Chosŏn period as an ideological nemesis, but in the twentieth century, it rebounded and once again flourished.[8] Along with Buddhism, Shamanism also fared well, at least in prestige. Formerly disparaged as the crudest of all Korean religions, Shamanism was now in vogue among many educated Koreans as the most pristine of all their religions.[9]

Although Confucianism, Buddhism, and Shamanism underwent significant changes in Korea between 1907 and 1988, for a hundred years earlier they had been enduring terrains in the religious landscape. Nevertheless, two new phenomena had arisen and developed into veritable mountains in Korean religions. One was Kim-Il-Sungism, which towered over the North as a secular cult.[10] The other was Christianity, especially evangelical Protestantism, which became dominant in the South. This study focuses on the latter. More specifically, it is about the rise of evangelicalism in South Korea from the 1880s, when the faith was first introduced, to the late 1980s, when it reached its expansional peak. The study also examines the character of Korean evangelicalism and how it fared in the 1990s, when it became the most successful yet beleaguered religion in South Korea. Because evangelicals vastly predominate in Korean Protestantism, "evangelical" and "Protestant" will be used interchangeably in this study.[11]

Since Kim-Il-Sungism arose in the second half of the twentieth century, it has been practiced exclusively in the North. During the same period in Korea, Christianity was almost exclusively a southern religion, though this was scarcely the case before 1953. In 1900, Christianity—Catholicism and Protestantism—was a heterodox, foreign religion in Korea. Only since around

1890 had Christians been allowed to practice their faith openly, and they constituted less than one percent of the population.[12] After the turn of the century, Christianity—evangelical Protestantism in particular—grew phenomenally through the century, claiming around 21 percent of the population by 1985. In the 1990s the growth of evangelicalism stalled; even so, by 1995, evangelicals and Catholics constituted upwards of 26 percent of the South Korean population.[13] The stall in evangelicalism's growth in the 1990s is treated in the epilogue, but this book's focus is on the growth or rise of evangelical Protestantism in South Korea, from the turn of the twentieth century to the end of the 1980s.

Between 1885 and 1990, evangelical Protestantism rose to become the most influential religion of South Korea. This rise—this success—is curious and cries out for a good accounting. It is curious, for one thing, because evangelicalism outpaced Roman Catholicism even though the latter had arrived in Korea a hundred years earlier. For another, up until 1990, nowhere in East Asia was evangelicalism more successful than in Korea. Given that the other major nations in the region—China and Japan—had also been heavily shaped by Buddhism and Confucianism, one might suppose that evangelicalism would have adapted and spread in them as well as it did in South Korea. Also fueling the curiosity is that evangelicalism had arrived in China and Japan much earlier than it had in Korea: seventy-seven years earlier in China, and twenty-five in Japan.[14] Moreover, there is also the question of why it is only in South Korea that evangelicalism has succeeded—why not in the North? Questions such as these must be addressed in any account that seeks to understand evangelicalism's success in South Korea, a country that Paul Freston calls the "regional Protestant 'superpower.'"[15]

Since the early years of the missionary movement in Korea, many have sought to explain evangelicalism's success in Korea. To the early missionaries, who were delighted but also baffled by their unexpected success, the best answer lay in divine providence.[16] Less theologically, others have sought to puzzle out the problem by seeking some decisive causal factor that was present in Korea but absent in China and Japan. This search has elicited a number of candidates, including Koreans' allegedly affective temperament and receptive character, and a mode of evangelistic strategy—generally known as the Nevius method—which insisted that the proselytes take the initiative to govern and support their churches, as well to propagate their newfound faith. Other factors considered to be possibilities were homologies between certain aspects of evangelicalism and traditional Korean beliefs: for example, between the concept of God and Hanŭnim, the Korean high god; and structural similarities between the polity of the Presbyterian churches (which are especially strong in Korea) and the organization of traditional Korean society, which is oriented around the extended family. Reasons for Protestantism's success in Korea may even be found in the occasion of a missionary physician's nursing back to life an influential politician gravely wounded in a failed coup d'état, or in the yearning of a great many Koreans for a religion that was more credible and potent than Buddhism or Confucianism.

Each of these factors may be contributory, but in accounting for a complex historical development like the rise of evangelicalism in Korea, no single explanation will suffice. Any attempt to address this issue definitively must duly consider all of the major factors, like those mentioned above. Such an attempt, however, is not the object of our study. Our goal is more modest—more in line with what Paul Ricoeur has espoused in his *Hermeneutics and the Human Sciences*. In this treatise, Ricoeur rejects Carl Hempel's covering-law theory of historical explanations and posits that whether a historical account is adequate or not depends not so much on its predictability (as would be the case in the natural sciences, which informed Hempel's model) as on its acceptability. Ricoeur states, "Looking back from the conclusion towards the episodes which led up to it, we must be able to say that this end required those events and that chain of action. But this retrospective glance is made possible by the teleologically guided movement of our expectations when we follow the story. Such is the paradox of the contingency, 'acceptable after all', which characterises the understanding of any story."[17] Ricoeur goes on to say, "If history is thus rooted in our ability to follow a story, then the distinctive features of historical explanation must be regarded as developments at the service of the capacity of the basic story to be followed. In other words, *explanations have no other function than to help the reader to follow further. . . .* Explanations must therefore be woven into the narrative tissue."[18]

This book seeks to gain the reader's acceptance of the way it accounts for evangelicalism's rise in South Korea. To do so, it presents a tripartite thesis, each part intended to "help the reader to follow further"—that is, to help explain evangelicalism's cogent appeal to Koreans. The first subthesis is that evangelicalism succeeded in South Korea partly because it appealed powerfully to multitudes of Koreans as a religion of salvation. Having been disseminated at a time when Korea was engulfed in unprecedented crises—discrediting Koreans' traditional weltanschauung and social structures and imperiling their integrity as a people—evangelicalism attracted and empowered Koreans by offering them a more compelling worldview and a more meaningful basis for association. The second subthesis is that evangelicalism succeeded in South Korea partly because it interacted sympathetically with Korean nationalism and South Korean anticommunism. Such coalescence of interests was crucial, for it enabled evangelicalism to share in the aspirations and hardships of South Korean people and become legitimated in that society. And the third subthesis is that evangelicalism succeeded in South Korea partly owing to the relentless proselytization efforts it pursued throughout its history in the country, especially in the second part of the twentieth century when it implemented mammoth evangelistic campaigns that drew millions in attendance.

Using the framework afforded by these three arguments, the first three chapters narrate the rise of evangelicalism in Korea. The first chapter treats the period from the 1880s to the end of the 1910s, focusing on the spiritual revivals of 1903–1907 and the March First Independence Movement of 1919. Both these events were breakthrough moments for Protestantism in Korea, marking it indelibly as evangelical and fusing it with Korean nationalism. The second chapter treats the period from 1920 to 1953, from the aftermath of the March First Independence Movement to the end of the Korean War. During this period, evangelicalism underwent further annealing in Korea, particularly through its conflicts with Shintōism and communism, conflicts exemplified in the introversive spirituality of Kil Sŏnju, Kim Iktu, and Yi Yongdo—the leading revivalists of Korean evangelicalism. The third chapter focuses on a series of massive evangelistic campaigns that took place in the South between 1953 and 1988. These campaigns brought into focus the drive to proselytize that has always characterized evangelicalism in general and Korean evangelicalism in particular. The chapter also shows that as these campaigns proceeded, Korean evangelicals gained in numbers and confidence, such that by 1988 they saw themselves as standard-bearers of global evangelicalism.

If the first three chapters of this study befit what Ricoeur calls the "episodic dimension" of historical narrative, the fourth and fifth chapters befit his "configurational dimension"—the dimension that "constructs meaningful totalities out of scattered events."[19] The fourth chapter seeks to achieve two objectives: One is to reinforce a point that has been argued for in the narratives—that Korean Protestantism has been dominated by an evangelical ethos—by examining the beliefs and practices of Korean Protestants. This chapter, in other words, shows that Korean Protestantism, by and large, fits the commonly used definition of evangelicalism: a species of Protestantism (broadly defined to include movements more specifically known as Fundamentalism and Pentecostalism) whose hallmarks are a literalist bent in biblical interpretation, a high Christology grounded in the substitutionary theory of atonement, a soteriology that values the individual over society, and a fervent advocacy of evangelism. In evangelicalism, salvation is achieved typically through a conversion experience, wherein one accepts Jesus Christ as personal savior and resolves to live in accordance with the Gospel.[20]

The other objective of the fourth chapter is to answer this question: if evangelicalism has indeed dominated Korean Protestantism, what can be said about its character? For example, what common ground, if any, does Korean Protestantism have with its counterparts elsewhere, especially in the United States, whose missionaries played a crucial role in laying the basis of the faith in Korea? What is distinctive about Korean evangelicalism? How much of its character is attributable to evangelicalism's general disposition? Which of it is owed to the historical and cultural context of Korea? The chapter addresses these questions—again by examining the beliefs and practices of Korean evangelicalism—and argues that an intensely practical and devotional bent characterizes Korean evangelicalism.

Finally in the epilogue, the configurational dimension is presented in a sociologically oriented essay that examines Korean evangelicalism in the last decade of the twentieth century. In the 1990s, Korean evangelicalism found itself in an ambiguous state. On the one hand, it had become the most influential religion in South Korean society—in politics, the economy, and civil society. But the success had come with a cost: evangelicalism was beleaguered by a variety of problems—a stalemate in its growth, shortcomings of its leaders, and conflicts with other religions. The beleaguerment attested that evangelicalism not only had risen to dominance but also had become part of the establishment.

CHAPTER 1

Breakthrough for a New Moral Order, 1885–1919

Everywhere the first impulse to social action is given as a
rule by real interests, i.e., by political and economic interests.
Ideal interests lend wings to these real interests, give them a
spiritual meaning, and serve to justify them. Man does not
live by bread alone. He wants to have a good conscience as he
pursues his life-interests. And in pursuing them he develops
his capacities to the highest extent only if he believes that in
so doing he serves a higher rather than a purely egotistic
purpose. *Interests without such "spiritual wings" are lame; but
on the other hand, ideas can win out in history only if and
insofar as they are associated with real interests.*
—Otto Hintze

From a century or so before 1885, when Protestant evangelism began in
earnest in Korea, till the demise of the Chosŏn dynasty in 1910, Korea
experienced cultural distortion.[1] The roots of this distortion were varied and
cumulative. In part, it was caused by famines and epidemics that had dev-
astated the country with unusual frequency in the late eighteenth and early
nineteenth centuries.[2] The distortion was also caused by—and reflected in—
the corruption in the Chosŏn government, which rendered the government in
most Koreans' eyes more nearly an instrument of exploitation than an agent of
just order. In the midst of such distortion, most Koreans were oppressed and
alienated from the establishment; and the ideals of Zhu Xian Confucianism,
the state religion of the dynasty, incurred a loss in plausibility.[3] Faced with such
disorientation and suffering, multitudes of Koreans yearned for salvation, for a
new moral order wherein their spirits could be empowered and their integrity
as human beings reaffirmed.

The search for a new moral order has been a leading theme in modern Korean history, a search that has been expressed in numerous forms—in rebellions, in the founding of new religions, in the acceptance of foreign religions and ideologies. In this context, evangelicalism, too, appealed to Koreans as a means of satisfying their salvific desires. Of all the new salvific efforts that began in the late eighteenth century and throughout the nineteenth, evangelicalism has been one of the most successful, to the point of becoming the most dynamic institutional religion in South Korea in the last quarter of the twentieth century. Thus we begin our study with two theses: that evangelicalism satisfied the salvific needs of a great many Korean individuals during its hundred-year history in Korea, and that it successfully adapted to Korea's sociohistorical context.

Of the first two decades in the twentieth century, two dates are especially significant for this study: 1907 and 1919. The first date is meaningful primarily to Korean Protestants, for this was the year of the great revival of 1907, in which Korean Protestants experienced a nometic breakthrough and fulfillment of their search for personal salvation.[4] The second date is significant to all Koreans; this was the year of the March First Independence Movement, another kind of breakthrough—this one resulting in the birth of modern Korean nationalism.[5] Though its significance was national, encompassing Koreans of all walks of life, the March First Movement was especially meaningful to Korean Protestants. It was through this movement more than anything else—more specifically, through the Protestants' preponderant contribution to it—that evangelicalism successfully bonded with Korean nationalism and became legitimated in South Korean history.

SEARCHING FOR A NEW MORAL ORDER

A sign that a society is in the throes of cultural distortion is the appearance of millennial expressions, expressions that yearn for the end of the status quo and predict the establishment of a new and better order.[6] Such expressions were widespread in the latter years of Chosŏn. From the perspective of Chosŏn rulers, a startling prophecy was the one expressed in *Chŏnggam-nok*, an obscure and portentous text originating in the last quarter of the eighteenth century. This text predicted the imminent collapse of the Chosŏn dynasty and the emergence of a new kingdom based in Kyeryong Mountain and ruled by the Chŏng lineage.[7] In the end, neither a religious movement nor a political program crystallized around this text. But its diffused impact was considerable, as it helped to instigate many a popular uprising and influenced the rise of numerous new religions, including Tonghak, about which more will be said below.[8]

No less influential than *Chŏnggam-nok* was the movement of thought known as Sirhak, or Practical Learning. Initiated in the late seventeenth century, Sirhak had become by the mid-eighteenth century an influential intellectual trend in Chosŏn. Sirhak disavowed rituals and metaphysics, which were favored by neo-Confucian literati, and opted instead for practical methods to solve social and political problems. It was embraced by prominent scholars such as Yi Ik, who urged the redistribution of landed wealth, the abolition of slavery, and the end of a caste-like class system. Another was Chŏng Yakgyong, who advocated reform in central government, local administration, and penal institutions. Pak Chega and Yi Tŏngmu urged Koreans to embrace commerce and manufacturing, activities traditionally despised by *yangban*, the Yi gentry. Sirhak reformers were not of one mind. All of them, however, agreed that Chosŏn stood in need of a fundamental restructuring. In the end, they did not achieve their goals, despite their articulateness, as their ideas failed to develop into a concrete movement with popular support.[9]

Unable to restructure their society and disillusioned with the Zhu Xian weltanschauung, Sirhak reformers and others cast about for alternative ideologies. In the eighteenth century, some of them were taken with Wang Yang Ming's version of neo-Confucianism, long regarded as heretical.[10] More significant was the attraction many felt toward Sŏhak (Western Learning) or Roman Catholicism.

By the latter half of the seventeenth century, many Korean intellectuals had already been attracted to Catholic ideas, disseminated by writings such as Matteo Ricci's *Chŏnju sirŭi* (The True Meaning of the Lord of Heaven) and Diego de Pantoja's *Ch'ilgŭk* (The Seven Victories), which were brought into the country by Korean envoys returning from Beijing. Initially Catholicism was no more than an intellectual curiosity. But with the baptism of Yi Sŭnghun in Beijing in February 1784, it began to take root in Korea.[11]

Upon his return to Korea in March 1784, Yi Sŭnghun, a *yangban* with Sirhak leanings, baptized a number of like-minded *yangban*. They in turn baptized others, including many of the lower classes. Soon a protochurch was formed, with members holding worship without the benefit of a priest.[12] As Ki-baik Lee states:

> What they sought in Catholicism was the means to correct the distortions
> in the social and political order caused by concentration of political authority in the hands of a few powerful families. In an age beset by a host of social
> ills brought on by the oppression of the weak and the unbridled pursuit of
> personal gain by powerful families, wealthy farmers, and rich merchants,
> the Catholic doctrine of original sin, so unlike the dominant orthodoxy

of Neo-Confucianism, evoked a warm response from many out-of-power scholars critical of the existing order. One can well imagine that those reform-minded *Sirhak* thinkers, desperately searching for ways to improve the dismal conditions surrounding them, took fresh hope for creating a heavenly kingdom on earth through belief in the new religion.[13]

In 1785 when the *yangban*'s Catholic activities were discovered, the Korean court became alarmed. It declared the religion illegal and, in the following year, forbade the importation of Catholic literature.[14] In 1791 the court was scandalized when it was discovered that a *yangban* named Yun Chich'ung (Paul Yun), along with his cousin Kwŏn Sangyŏn (Jacob Kwŏn), had not only refused to bury his deceased mother according to the Zhu Xian ritual but had also burnt his ancestral tablets, an act tantamount to treason. The gravity of this incident was expressed by a government official:

What a tragedy! Nothing this bizarre has happened since time began. The laws of our land declare that the crime of destroying an ancestral tablet is as serious an offense as murder. The laws also say that anyone who destroys his father's ancestral tablet with his own hands should be treated exactly the same as someone who rebels against the throne. . . . They openly condemn the Way of our ancestors and embrace perversion without hesitation or restraint.[15]

For their heretical acts, Yun and Kwŏn were executed, and in the ensuing repression, many of the early *yangban* converts, including Yi Sŭnghun, suffered imprisonment and torture. Catholicism, however, persisted and grew, the leadership now in the hands of humbler classes. By 1800, five years after the arrival of Father Chu Munmo (Jacob Zhou Wenmo) of China, the first Catholic missionary to Korea, the number of the faithful swelled to about ten thousand, most of them women or of lower classes. The devotion of women and lower classes was profound, as attested in later persecutions, in which most of the martyrs were from these groups.[16] What was Catholicism's appeal to these oppressed folks? The answer is not difficult to grasp: the Catholic faith offered them not only a promise of eternal salvation but also membership in a moral order wherein they were valued. These were no small things in the highly patriarchal and stratified society of the late Chosŏn, in which the lives of women and lower classes were routinely disparaged. That in Catholic worship, everyone—even a despised butcher—was accorded equal honor and treatment must have deeply moved and empowered these people.[17]

As Catholics increased in number, they were seen as a threat by the powers that be. In 1801 the Chosŏn government was especially alarmed when it seized a secret letter intended for Western priests in China. The author of this letter, Hwang Sayŏng, asked the priests to invoke the aid of Western armed forces to demand that the Korean king allow Catholics to worship freely. For the government, Hwang's letter was conclusive evidence that Catholicism was a seditious sect, that its adherents were traitors bent on subverting the sociopolitical order. Subsequently, to eliminate the perceived threat, the government launched a series of violent persecutions. The bloodiest of these were the persecutions of 1801, in which Chu Munmo and many others were killed; of 1839, when three French missionaries were executed along with their Korean coreligionists;[18] of 1846, when Kim Taegŏn, the first Korean to be ordained into priesthood, was executed along with other converts; and of 1866–1873, the most severe of them all, in which 8,000 or more Catholics, including nine French missionaries, were executed.[19]

The frequency and ferocity of these persecutions indicated, on the one hand, the determined efforts of the powerful to preserve the traditional order and their interests embedded in it. On the other hand, they betrayed, in tragic terms, how unsatisfactory that order had become for the multitude of Koreans and how desperately they desired a new moral order.

However, even as the Catholics were being driven underground in the 1860s, a man named Ch'oe Cheu went about the country propagating a new way to salvation, which he claimed was based on a revelation he had received from the Ruler of Heaven. Thus Koreans came to know about Tonghak, or Eastern Learning.[20] Ch'oe, like most of the Catholics, came from a disprivileged stratum of society; he was the son of a remarried widow, a status that disqualified him from becoming a civil or military official.[21] But unlike the Catholics, Ch'oe was convinced that Eastern learning was superior to that of the West. And his religion incorporated Eastern assumptions—for example, the immanence of the divine—even though the imprint of his own genius upon it was indelible.

Tonghak, in brief, incorporated different strands of Korean religions—Shamanism, Confucianism, Taoism, Buddhism, and even (unwittingly, to be sure) Roman Catholicism.[22] Tonghaks believed that there is one supreme deity (Chŏnju) who is the creator of human beings. With Ch'oe Cheu, Chŏnju's transcendence and immanence were equally valorized; but in the interpretations of his successors such as Ch'oe Sihyŏng and Son Pyŏnghŭi, the deity's transcendence was eclipsed by immanence, such that Chŏnju and humans were believed to share the same nature.[23] This meant that it is not only possible but incumbent upon humans to become one with the deity by bringing their thoughts and actions in line with Chŏnju's will. Later Tonghaks held that since all humans partake of the divine, they are all equal, with service to others constituting service to the deity as well. They also held a millennial belief that humans have the capacity and responsibility to establish a heaven on earth. By 1888, Tonghak beliefs were formalized with the compilation of its canonical text, *Tonggyŏng taejŏn* (Eastern Scripture) and hymnal, *Yongdam yusa* (Songs of Yongdam).

Equipped with these beliefs and texts—along with sacred formulas and magical chants—Ch'oe readily found audiences, especially among rural people. As Benjamin Weems observes:

> In practical terms, Ch'oe's message was simply that any follower of Ch'ŏndogyo (or Tonghak, as it was then called), by exercising true faith, could acquire freedom from oppression and suffering. This message attracted large numbers of oppressed people of all economic and intellectual levels, including poor and unlettered farmers and also politically discredited members of the *yangban* class. Within three years after his "revelation," Ch'oe had acquired a large and devoted following throughout the provinces of southeastern and southwestern Korea.[24]

However, with Tonghak's egalitarian ideology and implicit criticism of the status quo, it was only a matter of time before Ch'oe and his followers ran afoul of the ruling elements. The decisive clash came in 1864, when the government, having arrested Ch'oe in the previous year, charged him of having held Sŏhak beliefs and hanged him.[25]

For many years after Ch'oe's death, Tonghaks kept a low profile and avoided confrontation with the authorities. But as their strength grew, they became emboldened to seek redress for their grievances. In 1892, after amassing their strength, Tonghaks initiated a drive to clear their founder's name and to petition the government to stop persecuting them. The government agreed to stop the persecution but refused to exonerate Ch'oe, further alienating and infuriating the Tonghaks. Finally, in 1894, sparked by a notorious incident of extortion by a government official in Chŏlla Province, in which some of their members were victimized, Tonghaks rose up in arms, starting a full-scale rebellion.

The course and aftermath of the Tonghak rebellion is peripheral to this study, but it is crucial to the development of modern Korean history. In order to suppress the rebellion, the panicky Chosŏn government requested the aid of China. As it turned out, the request was unnecessary, since Tonghaks agreed to lay down their arms upon learning that the government was willing to redress their grievances. But a fateful step had been taken. In response to the government's request, a contingent of Chinese troops arrived in Korea, and their arrival in turn provoked the arrival of Japanese troops. While in Korea, the Japanese peremptorily attacked the Chinese, defeating them in the Sino-Japanese War of 1894–1895, thereby establishing a hegemonic foothold in the peninsula.[26] Tonghaks concluded that the Japanese were now the main threat to their way of life and their land. Thus they once again took up arms, this time to expel the Japanese. But their forces, ill equipped and ill trained, fared badly against Japan's modern army, and the whole movement was soon crushed.

The spread of *Chŏnggam-nok*, Sirhak, Catholicism, and Tonghak is significant for two reasons. First, it showed that long before missionaries such as Henry G. Appenzeller and Horace G. Underwood arrived in Korea to espouse *their* vision the land, Koreans themselves were ardently searching for a new moral order.[27] Second, it showed that Korean reformers and religionists failed in their efforts, not because they lacked courage, conviction, or imagination, but because they were strenuously opposed by guardians of the traditional order, which was distorted, and by foreign powers that stood to gain by keeping Korea weak.

ARRIVAL OF THE FIRST PROTESTANT MISSIONARIES IN KOREA

Horace Underwood and Henry Appenzeller arrived in Korea in April 1885, nine years before the Tonghak uprising started. During the twenty-one years between the execution of Chʼoe Cheu and the arrival of the missionaries, social distortion remained unabated in Korea. In this period, however, Korea's internal problems were compounded by some new factors—foreign interests in, and incursions into, the country—which in the end led to the fall of Chosŏn.

Before the nineteenth century, Chosŏn had had contact with its neighbors China and Japan, much of it unpleasant. But now, in addition to this traditional company, Chosŏn had to deal with Western powers, with which it had no prior diplomatic relations. Initially, most of the contacts—or clashes—between Korea and Western nations were hostile. Among these clashes, one of the significant is the *General Sherman* incident, which occurred in August 1866. An armed merchant vessel of American origin, the *General Sherman* came up the Taedong River near Pʼyŏngyang, seeking to trade with Koreans. When the Koreans declined, the crew refused to relent, several of them even sortieing near the city wall. As the Koreans became angry and threatening, the crew took hostage of an official sent to negotiate with them and fired upon the crowd that had gathered on the shore, killing a number of them.[28] In time, the ship ran aground, owing to a sudden lowering of the water level. Korean soldiers attacked and burnt it, killing all its crew. Among the killed was Robert Jermain Thomas, a Welsh man who was aboard as a translator and hoped to work as a missionary in Korea. Thomas had been in Korea for a little over a month the previous year, distributing Chinese Bibles and picking up rudiments of the Korean language. His death is a matter of contention among historians of Korean church history, between those who see him as a martyr and those who see him as an intruder. Thomas was the second Protestant missionary to have reached Korea. His predecessor, Karl Gutzlaff, had been in Korea for several months in 1832 as part of the crew aboard the *Lord Amherst*, which belonged to the East India Company. Gutzlaff's party sought to negotiate a trade with Korea but failed; while in the country, Gutzlaff attempted to engage in evangelistic work, distributing Chinese-language scriptures.[29]

Not long after, in October of the same year, another significant clash occurred. This incident involved a squadron of a French fleet that had come to Korea to punish its government for executing French missionaries. In the month-long battle that ensued, the French initially made some headway, occupying Kanghwa Island near Seoul, but they were eventually repelled by the Koreans. In the end, the French left Korea, taking with them valuable Korean records and nineteen boxes of silver bullion that they had plundered from the Kanghwa fort. Five years later, in the spring of 1871, Koreans clashed again with Westerners. This time, the opposing force was a contingent of "the American Asiatic Squadron[, which] included the warships *Monocacy* and *Palos*, plus 'four steam launches, and twenty boats conveying a landing force of six hundred and fifty-one men, of whom one hundred and five were marines.'"[30] They had come to hold Korea accountable for the *General Sherman* incident and to force commercial relations with it. During this confrontation, the Americans also occupied Kanghwa Island and became embroiled in a month-long battle before they, too, withdrew.

As a result of these confrontations, Koreans became wary of Westerners. The government, under the regent Taewŏn'gun, now emboldened by its apparent success in fending off invaders, sought to protect the country by sealing off Korean shores and forbidding, on pain of death, any Korean from associating with Westerners. By the mid-1870s, however, Chosŏn could no longer withstand outside pressure to open its borders. Finally, in 1876, compelled by Japan's gunboat diplomacy, Chosŏn grudgingly signed a treaty with Japan, its first modern diplomatic treaty—in much the same way Japan had with the United States in 1854, under duress and guaranteeing extraterritoriality to the other party. Shortly, similar treaties followed suit with the United States (1882), Germany (1882), England (1884), Russia (1884), and France (1886).[31]

Thus a few years before the arrival of Underwood and Appenzeller, the Korean government had abandoned its xenophobic policy. Moreover, by that time, many *yangban* in the establishment had caught on to the realpolitik that their country was enmeshed in. This led them and the Korean court to appreciate the usefulness of Western know-how and technology. This appreciation, in turn, led the Korean court to countenance the arrival of the missionaries. And the missionaries were quite happy to offer to the court some perquisites of Western civilization, provided that at some point they would be allowed to engage in evangelistic work, for which the court gave its tacit consent.[32]

In addition to benefiting from changes in international circumstances, the Protestant missionary enterprise in Korea also gained from the struggles in Korea's domestic politics, the failed coup d'état of 1884, in which the nation's progressives attempted to force a reform on the government by eliminating their conservative rivals.[33] For the Protestant missionaries, it was a great stroke of luck (or, in their eyes, an act of providence) that in the midst of this coup, the fatally wounded Min Yŏngik, the queen's nephew and a powerful figure in the conservative camp, was nursed back to life by Horace N. Allen, a North Presbyterian physician-missionary to Korea and the first resident Protestant missionary to that country.[34] In the figure of a healthy and grateful Min, the missionaries had a powerful ally in the Korean court; and by restoring Min's health, Allen had demonstrated convincingly the effectiveness of Western medicine and technology. Soon, Allen was able to convince King Kojong to establish a Western-style hospital in the country. Thereafter, it was only a small step for him to arrange for the arrival of Appenzeller and Underwood, who came to Korea ostensibly as English teacher and hospital helper, respectively. So from the start—unlike that of Catholicism or Tonghak—Protestantism enjoyed the sanction, if not the blessing, of the establishment. As Everett N. Hunt noted, "The Protestant missionaries began with the court."[35]

PRELUDE TO THE GREAT REVIVAL: 1885–1903

The Korean court found Underwood and Appenzeller appealing, primarily for their usefulness as transmitters of Western knowledge and technology. Many ordinary Koreans, too, were interested in the missionaries mainly for the worldly benefits they could impart, as acknowledged by L. George Paik:

> The motives that actuated the early converts were partly selfish. A large proportion of the first Christians were household servants, language teachers, colporteurs, and teachers in schools who received compensation or salary. In order to get students, schools were, at the beginning, necessarily charitable institutions. It was natural that the missionaries should begin their work with those who were near to them. . . . We do not doubt that there were some among them that deserve the epithet, "rice Christians." Others

coveted the bait but avoided the hook. They were students who sought missionary teachers to learn English and Western science in order to get rank in the government service.[36]

Even so, from the beginning, the history of Korean Protestantism is characterized by many people who were attracted to the faith primarily for its message of salvation. Already in the spring of 1886, one year after his arrival, Underwood was sought out by a man known as No Tosa (probably a pseudonym for No Ch'un-gyŏng), who had become interested in the missionary's religion after reading a Chinese translation of the Gospels of Luke and Mark. He now came to Underwood for further instruction in the religion. On July 18, 1886, he was baptized by Underwood, with assistance from Appenzeller—a baptism the missionaries performed only after careful consideration, since the injunction against proselytizing was still in force.[37] As it turned out, No was not the only Korean who came to Underwood around that time seeking baptism, unsolicited. By the end of 1887, Underwood had baptized twenty-four more unsolicited Koreans.

How did this come about? Did these Koreans come to the missionary even though no one had reached out to them, even though they had not heard the Gospel? The fact of the matter is that they had heard the Gospel message several years earlier—delivered by converts of Scottish missionaries working in China, specifically Manchuria. Three missionaries figure importantly here: Alexander Williamson, John McIntyre, and especially John Ross—all affiliated with the Scottish Presbyterian Church. It was Williamson who persuaded Thomas to board the *General Sherman* for the fateful voyage of 1866 and persuaded McIntyre and Ross to come to Manchuria as missionaries.[38] In 1865 and again in 1867 Williamson visited a Manchurian border town called Korea Gate (Koryŏmun), the official gateway between China and Korea, evangelizing among Korean residents and sojourners there. Influenced by Williamson, Ross also visited Korea Gate in 1874 and 1876. During the latter visit he met Yi Ŭngch'an, who agreed to collaborate with him on a variety of translation works. Ross, with the help of Yi, published the *Corean Primer* (1877), *The Corean Language* (1878), *Yesu sŏnggyo mundap* (Bible Catechism; 1881), and *Yesu sŏnggyo yoryŏng* (Outline of the New Testament; 1881). In 1877 Ross and Yi began translating the New Testament, later aided by McIntyre and several other Koreans, including Sŏ Sangyun and Paek Hongjun. In 1882 Ross published the Gospels of Luke and John, the first Gospels to be translated into *han'gŭl*. This was two years before Mark was independently translated by Yi Sujŏng, a Korean sojourning in Japan, and published in Japan; copies of the translation were later brought to Korea by Underwood and Appenzeller. Then in 1887 under the initiative of Ross, the first complete translation of the New Testament was finally published in Korean.[39]

In 1879 Ross was on furlough in Scotland, where he published *History of Corea: Ancient and Modern with Description of Manners and Customs, Language and Geography; Maps and Illustrations*, the first history of Korea in English.[40] That same year, McIntyre, while supervising Ross' work in Manchuria, baptized four Koreans, who thereby became the first Koreans to receive Protestant baptism. Only two of these men's identities are known with certainty: Yi Ŭngch'an (Ross's collaborator) and Paek Hongjun (who, upon being baptized, returned immediately to his hometown in Ŭiju to evangelize).[41] In May 1881 Ross returned to Manchuria, initially to Newchwang (the next month, he would move to Mukden). There he met Sŏ Sangyun, an erstwhile ginseng peddler who had fallen deathly ill a couple of years earlier and was brought back to health owing to McIntyre's help. McIntyre sought to introduce Sŏ to the Christian faith, giving him a copy of the Chinese Bible, only to meet a polite rebuff—Sŏ had been steeped in Confucian learning. But becoming curious about the Bible, Sŏ read and reflected upon it for a year or so, before seeking out Ross for further instruction. Under Ross' guidance, Sŏ underwent conversion and was baptized in May 1881.[42]

After his conversion, Sŏ became an indefatigable evangelist, working closely with Ross as a colporteur. Between 1882 and 1885, Sŏ smuggled copies of the Bible into Korea, given to him by Ross, and distributed them in Sorae, his hometown in Hwanghae Province, and in Seoul. He was never just a seller of religious literature; he sought ardently to impart to his interlocutors the conviction of salvation he experienced in the Christian faith. Consequently, by the end of 1883 he was already able to report to Ross that he had thirteen persons ready to receive baptism.[43] A year later, the number of prospective baptizees Sŏ reported to Ross had climbed to seventy. By that time, his younger brother Sŏ Kyŏngjo (also known as Sangu) had converted and, with the help of Sangyun, had established a Protestant community in Sorae—that is, before the arrival of Allen.[44] In March 1885, Sŏ was back in Manchuria, in Mukden, asking Ross to come down to Korea and baptize the men he had led to the faith— a request Ross turned down reluctantly, owing to the inauspicious political circumstances. A month later Underwood and Appenzeller arrived in Korea. Near the end of 1886 Sŏ visited Underwood and asked him to go with him to Sorae to baptize the new believers. This request was also declined, since Underwood was prohibited from traveling inland. Consequently, in January 1887, Sŏ brought several of the believers from Sorae to Seoul, to be examined by Underwood for baptism.[45] Underwood recorded his recollection of this occasion:

I have also a matter of information that will rejoice you much, and will cause our churches at home to again thank the giver of all blessings for his having blessed the labors of a Korean among his countrymen. We are to have several baptisms on next Sunday, and the men who have applied appear to be thoroughly in earnest. They are some of the off-shoots as it were from some of Ross's work in the North.[46]

Others came from Sorae to visit Underwood; by the end of 1887 more than ten persons from Sorae had received baptism. In the fall of the same year, Underwood, ignoring the prohibition against Westerners' wandering beyond the capital, traveled north to Sorae, P'yŏngyang, and Ŭiju, baptizing more than twenty persons who had been prepared by Sŏ Sangyun, Paek Hongjun, and others. On September 27 of the same year a congregation was formally established at Underwood's house. Present at the gathering were Underwood, Ross, and fourteen baptized Koreans, thirteen of whom had been led to the faith by Sŏ and Paek. A colleague of Ross' described the scene that night:

They waited till dark. The laws against proselytism were still unrepealed. . . . The door was opened, and they found themselves in a room, where were fourteen men, bright, clean and intelligent-looking. A Congregation was formed, and two elders were chosen. Thirteen of the company were converts of the man Mr. Ross sent.[47]

By 1890, missionary works proceeded apace in Korea, both Underwood (representing the Northern Presbyterian Church) and Appenzeller (representing the Northern Methodist Church) having been joined by additional missionaries and the prohibition against evangelism having become all but a dead letter.[48] As indicated above, even in the early years, attracting the attention of Koreans was hardly a problem for the Protestant missionaries. Initially, however, the attraction was somewhat restrained, as Koreans' apprehension of foreigners and the missionaries' logistic problems could not be overcome at once. But as the missionaries increasingly gained the trust of the court and the people and as they made inroads into the countryside, more and more Koreans sought the church. More significantly, Protestant work in Korea was greatly facilitated by rapid deterioration of the nation's political fortunes. This was especially the case after the end of the Tonghak uprising and the outbreak of the Sino-Japanese War, as acknowledged by Arthur J. Brown of the Foreign Mission Board of the Northern Presbyterian Church:

After ten years of indefatigable labor on the part of Dr. Underwood and the few missionaries of our own and the Methodist Board who during that period had joined the little band, there were only one hundred and forty-one Christians in the whole country. The tide turned in 1895 when the missionaries in Pyeng Yang displayed such conspicuous fidelity, courage and devotion after the battle of Pyeng Yang in the China-Japan War and the missionaries in Seoul manifested equally conspicuous courage and devotion in dealing with an epidemic of cholera.[49]

The Sino-Japanese War was only the beginning of a series of disasters that befell Chosŏn. Ten years later, the country became the battle ground of another major war, the Russo-Japanese War. By the time this war was over, Chosŏn was no longer under Korean control. In November 1905, Japan, with the recognition of Britain and the United States, imposed a protectorate over the nation. The coup de grâce for Chosŏn came in 1910, when it was forcibly annexed to Japan.[50]

As one disaster after another befell Korea, the already distorted society became even more so. The number of the disoriented increased, and the intensity of their disorientation deepened. As a result, more and more Koreans suffered and searched desperately for salvation—from disorder, fear, hunger, and humiliation. One place where such salvation was promised was the Protestant Church, where a new life was offered to whoever would convert.[51] As Southern Methodist missionary J. R. Moose wrote: "The general unrest and lack of something to which they may cling is causing the people to turn to the Missionary and the message he has; and they are trying to find out if we have something which they can trust. On my last visit to the country I often heard the expression 'wei-chi hal kot tomochi oupso' (There is altogether no place to trust)."[52]

That many Koreans sought refuge in the church after 1895 was also reflected in the number of Koreans who were accepted as adherents in the years immediately following the Sino-Japanese War. In 1896, for example, the total figure for the number of adherents (the baptized and probationers) was 4,356. In the next year, the figure increased by more than 40 percent, to 6,164. By 1900 the number reached 20,914, nearly a fivefold increase. By 1907, the year of the great revival, the figure had increased to 106,287—a growth of more than twenty-four times over a period of eleven years.[53]

Though the circumstances in which many Koreans thronged to the church were tragic, for the missionaries—who regarded the main task of their calling to be saving souls—Korea was an evangelistic gold mine. Almost every issue of the *Korea Mission Field* published between 1905 and 1907 contained accounts of evangelistic success.[54] For example, in its first issue (November 1905), a missionary noted, "Sunday the church was crowded; people filled the spaces of the doors and many could not get in at all. Mr. Junkin preached almost continuously from about 9:30 till about 12, and the people would have listened much longer."[55] By July 1906 it was clear that the missionaries' main task was not so much seeking out new converts as accommodating all those who came to them without prompting. This development was highlighted in an article entitled "No Need to Seek an Audience," in which a missionary wrote:

> We found the country in a very ready condition and people everywhere who seemed simply waiting for an invitation to come into the church, and as never before ready to buy books and to listen to the preached Word. . . . It was not necessary to go out to seek an audience. All that we had to do was to stay quietly in our rooms at the inns and we would have a constant succession of inquirers coming to us. We often could not get the rest we needed on account of the large number of inquirers.[56]

Most missionaries were convinced that the increase in the number of believers signified that their work was progressing satisfactorily. On the other hand, they also believed that numbers alone were not conclusive evidence of how well they had been working. The missionaries wanted some qualitative proof that their labor was bearing authentic fruits, that the Koreans were truly being converted. Barring such evidence, they could not dispel the suspicion that the Korean believers, however numerous, were Christians in name only. On this matter, one missionary succinctly stated his and his colleagues' view:

> They [missionaries] feel it is one thing to gather into the churches and another thing to lead those gathered to a personal Savior. Korea's people are believing Christ in great numbers during these transition days and we missionaries feel that they should have a type of religion that goes to the bottom of heart and life and by almighty power makes a new man. We must have the "new man" experience in the Korean church. We have had it, we are having it, and more than ever must it be the battle cry of the coming year.[57]

Not having witnessed Koreans undergoing the "new man" experience, however, some missionaries even began to doubt Koreans' spiritual capabilities. Thus one of them wrote, "Among a people like the Koreans there is no definite and clear idea of sin, so that when first converted they are not prepared to manifest the deep and awful conviction that is found among those who have been taught what sin really is. This fact has led some into believing that the Koreans are incapable of deep feeling."[58] The missionaries, however, did not have to harbor their misgivings for long. In 1907 a truly great revival occurred in Korea, giving them plenty of occasions to witness among the Koreans the "new man experience," the evidence that would attest to the worthwhileness of their labor and the authenticity of Korean faith.

THE GREAT REVIVAL: 1903–1907

The great revival of 1907 was a watershed in the history of Korean Protestantism. It was, as L. George Paik states, "the spiritual rebirth of the Korean Church," which "gave to the Christian Church in Korea a character which is its own."[59] However, the great pan-Korean revival did not erupt out of the blue in 1907. Rather, it was the culmination of a series of local revivals that had started in 1903. Moreover, from beginning to end, the revival was very much a cooperative venture between the missionaries and Korean converts.

The beginning of the great revival can be traced back to a 1903 meeting of missionaries in a town called Wŏnsan in the Kangwŏn Province. Coming together for a week of Bible study and prayer, the small group of Methodist missionaries were moved by a confession made by one of their members, Robert A. Hardie. Agonizing over his failure to develop a church in that province, Hardie confessed his shortcomings to his colleagues.[60] Afterward he confessed similarly to some Korean believers, including those who were working as his servants. Hardie told them of feeling God's grace in his repentance and expressed the wish they too might be able to own the "actual and living experience" of grace. Hardie wrote:

> After I had entered upon a realization of the fullness of the Spirit and with shame and confusion of face confessed my pride, hardness of heart, and lack of faith, and also much that these had led to, they saw for the first time what conviction and repentance mean in actual experience. I told them of how by simple faith in God's promise I had claimed the gift of the Holy Spirit.[61]

In the following year, Hardie made a similar confession at a larger Bible conference held among the missionaries in Wŏnsan, greatly moving those present. Soon he became a sought-after speaker, invited to lead numerous prayer meetings and Bible conferences in the country. Influenced by Hardie's efforts, in September 1905 the General Council of Evangelical Missions in Korea decided to set aside a period of two weeks in 1906 for revivals, beginning on the first day of the lunar new year (January 26).[62]

In truth, the General Council's plan to hold revivals was influenced by more than piety. It was also affected by Korea's political circumstances. By planning to hold revivals at a time when the Russo-Japanese War was winding down, the missionaries wished to prevent any political unrest from developing within Korean churches. The war had greatly politicized the Korean populace and had caused multitudes to join the church. Most of them had joined in the hope of finding a personal haven, but some among them were more politically oriented and hoped that the church could serve as a vehicle to save not only their souls but also their nation.

Granted, at the time in Korea the concept of nation was not yet fully developed. Indeed the Korean word for "nation"—*minjok*—was a neologism adopted from the contemporary nationalist discourse in Japan and was perhaps used for the first time in Korea in an editorial published on January 12, 1900, in *Hwangsŏng sinmun*, one of the earliest Korean newspapers.[63] As Andrew Schmid notes, "Although the editorial marked one of the earliest appearances of *minjok*, the editors were still groping for a definition of a term whose conceptual bounds had yet to be fixed."[64] Consequently, the notion analogous to *minjok* at the turn of the century did not necessarily mean the ethnic Korean nation (centered on the mythical progenitor Tan'gun) that the term came to mean in the second half of the twentieth century. Even so, it can be said that by 1907 the evangelicals had a heightened sense of what John Duncan would call Korean protonationalism—the Koreans as "collectivity defined and symbolized by the state."[65]

Indeed, among educated evangelicals, such sentiment was strong even in the late nineteenth century.[66] At that time, this sense was called *ch'unggun aeguksim* (loyalty to the sovereign and patriotism to the state), and Protestants such as Yun Ch'iho, Sŏ Chaep'il, and Ch'oe Pyŏnghŏn believed that the best way to practice such national devotion was for Koreans to adopt a new way of life that would help their nation become strong and affluent (*pugang*), that would keep it from becoming a victim of East Asian realpolitik. To them, Christianity—that is, evangelical Protestantism—was that way of life. In thinking this way, they were subscribing to a social Darwinian notion that was widespread at the time, a notion whose validity seemed amply attested by the strength of Britain and the United States, nations believed to be grounded in Christian values and practices, a notion Hyaeweol Choi has aptly described as Christian modernity: "an ideology which advocates the inevitable historical movement toward modernity in material and technological aspects but which also places the moral and spiritual role of Christianity [evangelical Protestantism] at the core of that enterprise."[67]

After 1905, as Japan's political power became more pronounced in the peninsula, the nationalist leaders scrambled to marshal their resources to resist Japanese imposition, including the resources available in the Protestant

Church, by now composed of the best-educated and best-organized cohort of people in the country.[68] A politicized church, however, was anathema to the missionaries. They believed that such a church would invite abuse from its members as well as from those who opposed the members' politics.[69] The missionaries loathed the prospect of the church's resources being exploited by Korean nationalists. They also dreaded the prospect of the church being ransacked by opponents of Korean nationalism.

To prevent the church from being beset by either partisan, the missionaries sought to head off any nationalistic movement from arising within the church. They also attempted to sublimate whatever nationalistic fervor was already seething within the church. To accomplish these ends, the missionaries turned to revivals:

> At the meeting of the General Council in September a resolution, providing
> for a simultaneous revival movement in the church throughout Korea, was
> passed. . . . Perhaps, as never before in the history of the church in Korea,
> there is need for a manifestation of the power of God. The gospel has met
> with a cordial response as it has been preached here and the Church has
> steadily increased in numbers. A crisis has been reached. The political situa-
> tion brings the entire people to a state of unrest. The hope of the nation and
> the individuals that compose it lies not in agitation and discussion, but in
> God. The way to combat the unrest in the Church is to stress the hope that
> the Gospel offers.[70]

Thus the missionaries' motive for holding revivals was a conflation of two desires: the genuinely religious desire to see Korean churchgoers undergo born-again experiences, and the desire to prevent political agitation from developing in the church.

In their wish to deepen Korean Christians' faith, the missionaries turned to revivals almost instinctively. This was understandable, for having been raised and trained in the tradition of American evangelicalism, the missionaries were accustomed to revivals. And like Charles G. Finney, Dwight Moody, and Billy Sunday before them, the missionaries had no doubt that revivals were the best means of bringing about true conversion.[71] As one Southern Methodist missionary wrote:

> The church of God becomes strong in purity, character, and personal fel-
> lowship with Christ its Head only as it realizes in individual experience the
> touch of the divine life. The power of Christ to transform, regenerate, to give
> a new zeal and zest to life should be a matter of personal testimony with every

member of the church militant. One of the most effective ways by which these results can be obtained is the revival. The revival of genuine conviction for sin, deep repentance and complete surrender to the will and power of God.[72]

Another missionary, who stated the similar point more specifically with respect to the Korean church, seems prescient in retrospect:

We are now at a place in the history of the Church in Korea when the problem is not so much of getting people to hear and believe the Word; but it is how to properly care for and instruct those who are now coming to us and begging to be taught. Nothing will solve this like a genuine old fashioned revival of heart felt religion. Let people be saved and *know* they are *saved* and we shall have no trouble about having some one to testify for our Lord. . . . It is all right to have study classes. I have not a word to say against them. But I do believe that what the Church needs just now more than any thing else is REVIVAL. Let every worker in Korea pray as never before that the coming Korean New Year may be the time when this revival shall come and this be the real beginning of Korea's Pentecost.[73]

The desire expressed by the second writer—that the scheduled revivals focus not so much on attracting new believers as on deepening the faith of those already attending church—was more explicitly stated by a group of concerned missionaries in an open letter to *KMF*: "[Let] the first aim [of the revivals] be spiritual. Work within the church, rather than the enrollment of new names. Let the work first be *deep*, and *breadth* will naturally follow."[74]

When the lunar new year arrived, the revivals took place as scheduled. The results, especially in the Northern provinces and Seoul, were encouraging.[75] By and large, the revivals of 1906 had been fruitful; many souls had been saved. But these revivals had been local affairs and failed to appease political agitation within the church. They were not enough. The missionaries and Korean church leaders yearned for something bigger, something more immersing and more encompassing.

By the summer of 1906, missionaries in Korea became highly anxious as the possibility of their churches becoming engulfed in politics became more imminent. The anxiety was especially acute for the Presbyterian missions. Prior to the Russo-Japanese War, they had set upon September 1907 as the time when the first Presbytery of Korea—the foundation of the Korean Presbyterian Church—would be established.[76] There was a real chance that this presbytery would become a basis not for the Presbyterian Church but for Korean nationalism. The missionaries' concern was well expressed by William N. Blair, a Northern Presbyterian missionary who would play a key role in the great revival of 1907:

> All eyes were turned upon the Christian Church. Many Koreans saw in the Church the only hope of their country. There is no denying the intense loyalty of the Korean Church. Christianity gives men backbones. There were not lacking many hot-heads in the church itself who thought the church ought to enter the fight. The country wanted a leader and the Christian Church was the strongest, most influential single organization in Korea. Had she departed even a little from the strict principle of non-interference in politics, thousands would have welcomed her leadership and flocked to her banner. . . . Have I made the situation plain? We were about to turn over the authority of our Church to Korean hands, to establish an independent Korean Church. Suddenly we found ourselves in the dangerous situation described. How could we take so critical a step at such a time? Yet we had to do what we had promised to do or break faith with our Korean brethren. So it was that God compelled us to look to Him.[77]

In August 1906, Hardie was invited to P'yŏngyang to lead a week of Bible study and prayer, attended by both Methodist and Presbyterian missionaries. After this meeting, the Presbyterian missions in Seoul and P'yŏngyang were visited by Howard Agnew Johnson of New York, whose reports of the religious revivals that had taken place in Wales and India stirred both the missionaries and Korean believers to yearn for similar happenings in Korea.[78] By the latter part of 1906, the missionaries from both denominations and many Korean church leaders were anxious for an "outpouring of the Holy Spirit." The Presbyterians, in particular, prayed that such an outpouring would occur during the winter Bible study classes scheduled for January 1907.[79] On January 2 the Presbyterian lay leaders from all over the country converged on P'yŏngyang. Of the four Presbyterian churches that existed in P'yŏngyang at the time, they chose for their gathering the Central Church (Changdaehyŏn kyohoe), the oldest and largest, which could accommodate around 1,500 at a time.[80] The mission station's Bible study classes started as scheduled, and the missionaries and Korean church leaders such as Kil Sŏnju led the meetings with high hopes.[81] However, on this particular day, the participants did not evince any sign of heightened enthusiasm. This state of affairs continued for the next few days. Then, after the evening service on January 6, a prayer session was held, and during the session a powerful outpouring of the spirit began. A missionary who was present at that session reported: "Two or three most earnest prayers, one after another, were followed by such an outpouring of the Spirit as I had never before witnessed, great strong men, half a dozen at a time, pleading for forgiveness and confessing their sins in great agony of spirit. . . . From that day on there was not a day without some new proof of His presence with us individually and collectively."[82]

On Saturday, January 12, when Blair preached during the worship, another noticeable scene of repentance and renewal occurred. Significantly, in his sermon, Blair preached that it was unchristian for Koreans to hate the Japanese. His sermon had some effect, as he wrote, "A number with sorrow confessed lack of love for others, especially for the Japanese."[83]

As the second week of the Bible study session was coming to an end, it was clear that the revival was engrossing all the Presbyterians in P'yŏngyang. However, the climax of this particular revival was yet to come—on Monday, January 14. The account of what went on in P'yŏngyang Central Church that night was best described by the two missionaries who led the meetings, William N. Blair and Graham Lee. Blair wrote:

> After a short sermon, Dr. Lee took charge of the meeting and called for prayers. So many began praying that Dr. Lee said, "If you want to pray like that, all pray," and the whole audience began to pray out loud, all together. The effect was indescribable. Not confusion, but a vast harmony of sound and spirit, a mingling together of souls moved by an irresistible impulse to prayer. It sounded to me like the falling of many waters, an ocean of prayer beating against God's throne. It was not many, but one, born of one Spirit, lifted to one Father above. Just as on the Day of Pentecost they were all together in one place, of one accord praying, "and suddenly there came from heaven the sound as of the rushing of a might wind, and it filled all the house where they were sitting." God is not always in the whirlwind, neither does He always speak in a still small voice. He came to us in Pyongyang that night with the sound of weeping. As the prayer continued a spirit of heaviness and sorrow came down upon the audience. Over on one side someone began to weep and in a moment the whole congregation was weeping.[84]

Graham Lee recorded:

> After prayer, confessions were called for, and immediately the Spirit of God seemed to descend on that audience. Man after man would rise, confess his sins, break down and weep, and then throw himself to the floor and beat the floor with his fists in a perfect agony of conviction. . . . Sometimes after a confession the whole audience would break out in audible prayer, and the effect of that audience of hundreds of men praying together in audible prayer was something indescribable. Again after another confession they

would break out in uncontrollable weeping, and we would all weep, we couldn't help it. And so the meeting went on until two o' clock A.M. with confession and weeping and praying.[85]

After this climax, the P'yŏngyang Bible study class for the Presbyterian Church ended the next day. But what had happened during this class was only the beginning of the great revival. Upon leaving P'yŏngyang, the class participants initiated revivals in their own hometowns.[86] Also the revivalistic fervor that was ignited in the Central Church spread to other quarters of P'yŏngyang, at first mostly among the Presbyterians, then to the Methodists. On Wednesday, January 16, a revival swept through the Advanced School for Girls and Women, lasting till Friday. A revival also occurred in the boys' school at the Central Church, and another took place in a nearby high school, where it "continued until every student had felt its power and fully nine tenths had come into a conscious experience of being born again."[87] On Thursday the revival was evident among the primary school for girls. On Saturday it erupted among the Presbyterian women of P'yŏngyang, as they were worshiping in the Central Church; this was repeated on January 21 and 22.[88] The revival's influence was not limited to Koreans; the missionaries too were touched by it. Thus Lee wrote of a meeting among the missionaries, "The Spirit of God literally fell upon us, and we couldn't help but weep and confess our sins."[89]

In February the revival continued in P'yŏngyang's Union College and Academy, where both Presbyterian and Methodist students attended. Initially, only the Presbyterian students participated, but it soon erupted among the Methodist students as well. Mrs. W. M. Baird, a teacher of the school and an eyewitness of the revival, wrote:

All were prostrate on their faces, and all alike, with the exception of the few who had already received a blessing, were in an agony of repentance. Sometimes they beat their foreheads and hands against the floor, sometimes they literally writhed in anguish, roaring as if the very devils were tearing them, and then at last, when there seemed no more power of resistance left, they would spring to their feet and with terrible sobs and crying, pour out their confessions of sin. And such confessions! It was like hell uncovered. Everything from murder, adultery, and the most inconceivable abominations of uncleanness, through arson, drunkenness, robbery, thieving, lying, down to hatreds, spites, and envying, was emptied out, and with what shame and loathing! No human power could have dragged these confessions to light, and many of the Koreans themselves were horror-struck at what they heard.[90]

Having affected the Methodist students, the revival spread to P'yŏngyang's Methodist churches, which were hitherto untouched. Soon the entire Christian community in P'yŏngyang was engulfed in revivalistic fervor. Part of this fervor was shortly translated into a citywide evangelistic campaign, which was rewarded with some two thousand persons being converted.[91] When this campaign was over, P'yŏngyang was visited by the nation's Methodist lay leaders, who came to participate in the denomination's class for preachers and Christian workers. This class lasted for one month, and during its sessions a revival occurred with a result similar to that of the January Presbyterian Bible study classes.[92] On March 16, soon after the Methodists' departure, 550 leading women of the Presbyterian church arrived for their training class, which lasted for twelve days.[93] Predictably, they, too, were engulfed in a revival.

For the Presbyterian missionaries the most important group of people to arrive in P'yŏngyang in 1907 was the seventy-five seminarians who had come to attend Presbyterian Theological Seminary, whose spring term was to begin on the first of April. From these students, seven were to be selected for ordination in September. These seven students thus ordained were to be the backbone of the Korean presbytery, which was to be established in the same month. Because these seminarians, especially the seven, were crucial for the future of the Korean Presbyterian church, the missionaries were anxious that each one of them undergo a born-again experience. To ensure this, eight months before school began, a plan was set for the students to hold an hour of prayer meeting on each evening of the term. Once school started, all the missionaries' anxiety and planning proved superfluous, however, for the seminarians were at once infected with the revivalistic spirit that prevailed in the city. Wrote one missionary, "These, who are to be the pastors of Korean churches, experienced the fire of the Holy Spirit burning sin out of their lives."[94] Another missionary wrote, "We now feel assured that the first [Presbyterian] ministers who are to be ordained and take their place as pastors in the Korean church will be Holy Spirit filled men."[95]

In mid-January, with the end of the Presbyterian church's station Bible study classes, the evangelical contagion had begun to spread quickly into many parts of the country. Already in January, revivals were occurring in northern cities like Hamhŭng.[96] By February, revivals had spread to most of the major cities, such as Songdo, Taegu, and Seoul.[97] Indeed, by June of 1907, when the fervor had subsided, every Protestant mission in the country had been affected by the evangelism.[98]

Moreover, the impact of this revival was not limited to Korea. In May, news of the Korean revival was reported to a gathering of Chinese Christians in Manchuria. Seven years earlier, China had experienced the Boxer Uprising, and these Chinese Christians were still suffering from the spiritual depression that followed. In the hope of finding ways to overcome this depression, the Chinese sent two of their members to P'yŏngyang to investigate the revival. Upon arriving in P'yŏngyang in January 1908, these representatives participated in the city's Bible study classes and prayer sessions, where the spirit of the great revival still lingered. Deeply moved by their experiences, the Chinese Christians returned to Manchuria in February and started their own revival, using the methods they had learned in Korea. Soon this revival spread to other churches in Manchuria and elsewhere in China. As a result of this revival, "permanent moral and spiritual transformations were recorded and many accessions to the Church."[99]

THE MILLION MOVEMENT

As noted earlier, the missionaries purposed that in the revivals of 1906 and 1907 Korean churchgoers should undergo "new birth" experiences. Thus churchgoers were the main audience. However, as the revival proceeded and more and more believers experienced conversion, the focus inevitably shifted toward unbelievers. This shift was already apparent in February 1907, when, in the midst of revivalistic fervor, the Presbyterians and Methodists of the city joined their efforts to evangelize the whole of P'yŏngyang, the third-largest city in Korea at the time. As a result, 8,000 of the 50,000 citizens of P'yŏngyang had professed to be Christians by 1909, earning for their city the title "Jerusalem of Korea."[100]

The zeal that kindled during the great revival became a permanent feature of Korean evangelicalism. The citywide evangelism that took place in P'yŏngyang marked the beginning of a series of such activities that would take place in Korea. Indeed, after the great revival, the next noteworthy event that the Korean Protestants engaged in was a large evangelistic campaign called the Million Movement.

The impetus for this movement came in early 1909, when three missionaries from the Southern Methodist mission at Songdo began meeting for prayers, sensing that the spiritual fervor of 1907 had dissipated. Soon Koreans joined the meetings. Then one of the missionaries, M. B. Stokes, embarked on an itinerating tour through his two circuits, urging Korean believers to lead 50,000 additional souls to the church by the end of the year. Stokes' urging impressed other missionaries, such that during the Southern Methodist Mission's annual meeting in September of that year, the denomination adopted the watchword "Two Hundred Thousand Souls for Christ." The next month, in the annual meeting of the General Council of Evangelical Missions in Korea, another of the three missionaries, W. T. Reid, proposed that the entire evangelical body in Korea adopt a similar watchword. The proposal was sent to a committee, which Reid chaired, and the committee recommended "A Million Souls for Christ This Year."[101]

To the missionaries, this watchword, like another of the kind—"the evangelization of the world in this generation"—was more of a spur than a realistic goal. By the end of 1909, active missionaries in Korea numbered only about 200, and the total number of Protestants in the country was about 158,000—this achieved after twenty-five years of labor.[102] Thus, winning almost six times this number of converts in a single year would have been unrealistic even to the most pious of the missionaries. Once the watchword was adopted, however, the missionaries and Korean Protestants launched into the project with enthusiasm. And as was the case in the great revival, the all-out efforts of Korean Protestants greatly impressed the missionaries. One of them wrote,

> Poor and hard working Koreans were inspired to give at least 100,000 days of work in all, for 76,000 days of earnest personal work was done last winter, and this fall several hundreds of native workers gave a whole month to special service going from house to house, as well as dealing with men personally in great meetings. Many millions of tracts and 700,000 gospels of Mark were purchased by native Christians and given to unbelievers with prayer and earnest persuasions; nearly every home in Korea has been visited, and daily prayer has been offered for this by thousands of Koreans.[103]

Despite such efforts, when 1910 ended, new converts numbered only about 20,000—a considerable gain, yet no where near the million mark. But this result hardly discouraged the missionaries. Some of them took comfort in the thought that in the day of reckoning a million souls would surely date their salvation from this campaign. And nearly all the missionaries believed that the campaign justified itself in another way: it had fortuitously engrossed Korean Protestants when their country was in the throes of extinction, when powerful incentives existed for political agitation within the church.[104]

THE GREAT REVIVAL AS A BREAKTHROUGH

In his *Christians of Korea*, Samuel H. Moffett relates a conversation between missionaries and Korean Christians about the great revival. A Korean states, "Some of you go back to John Calvin, and some of you to John Wesley, but we can go back no further than 1907 when we first really knew the Lord Jesus Christ."[105] Truly, the great revival of 1907 was a paradigmatic event for the Korean Protestant Church, a breakthrough in which the church became grounded in the worldview and ethos of evangelicalism. With this event, Korean Protestants acquired the basis for a new normative order and a fulfilling way to orient themselves toward the sacred. Moreover, from 1907 on, leaders of the church would seek to live up to the example of the revival, by routinizing the beliefs and practices born of it.

Of the beliefs that came to be associated with the great revival, the most important was the doctrine of conversion: to be saved, one must have a felt experience of rebirth—one must be born again. This experience might be extraordinary, in which one encountered visions of the supernatural. But such was not the type that predominated the great revival, nor was it the kind that the church leaders advocated. A different type of conversion experience characterized the great revival, one in which persons became profoundly aware of their moral shortcomings and their inability to merit salvation, leading them to repent of their sins and accept Jesus Christ as their personal savior. To some, repenting was a painful process, in which the agony was so unbearable that they exhibited unusual physical behavior such as prostration and prolonged crying. But such behavior was epiphenomenal and, more often than not, discouraged. To be saved, what was crucial was the unflappable conviction that one was made anew in the blood of Jesus Christ.

The second most important belief driven home to Korean Protestants during the revival was a behavioral imperative. It held that born-again persons must be able to give proof of their change in their personal life, by incorporating into their lives certain behavior and practices by virtue of which they could be distinguished from nonbelievers. This behavioral imperative had both devotional and ethical dimensions, and when put into practice by serious Protestants, it had both integrative and disintegrative consequences.

One integrative consequence resulted from the insistence that born-again persons be diligent in devotional practices of the church. Devotional practices in Korean evangelicalism included Sunday worship, Bible study classes, and revival meetings. But they also included less traditional activities, some newly adopted during the great revival—for example, united vocal prayer (*t'ongsŏng kido*), daybreak prayer meetings (*saebyŏk kido*), and, in many areas during the early years of the church, obligatory evangelism.

From the start, the Korean church regarded these practices seriously. One could not claim to be a proper Christian, it was held, unless she regularly attended church and fervently prayed, studied the Bible and faithfully gave to the church, and actively participated in evangelism. During early years of the church, a person, as a rule, could not be baptized unless she mastered *han'gŭl*, so that she could read the Bible. And one could not be a full member of a church until she had led another soul to Christ.[106] Such an imperative tended to institutionalize evangelicalism's proclivity toward emotionalism: one might exuberate over one's rebirth, but such exuberance had to be expressed through established devotional practices, without neglecting the more mundane aspects of the faith.

In addition to the practical dimension, the behavioral imperative also had an ethical dimension that contributed to the community's integration. In large part, this dimension consisted of upholding personal morality, such as proscriptions against theft, smoking, drinking, and promiscuity. Since the Korean society at the turn of the century tended to be fairly loose against these vices—at least for men and except theft—they provided the converts with clear and demanding, yet feasible, means of distinguishing themselves from the rest of the society. The sense of separateness and uniqueness thus achieved helped integrate the church.

In Korea, upholding personal morality became associated with Protestantism early on, and this association became axiomatic, established in the minds of Christians and non-Christians alike. A born-again Christian, it was held, must be an honest teetotaler. He must be industrious, must refrain from smoking and gambling, and must be impeccable in sexual matters. In missionary literature on Korea, there is a plethora of stories that illustrate the importance of these virtues. One story, for example, tells of a Chinese merchant who was astonished to see a Korean convert walk into his store during the great revival and pay him compensation for some sum he had previously swindled from him.[107] Another tells of a Korean who was ridiculed and criticized by nonbelievers for claiming to be a Christian but not being able to refuse a bowl of rice wine.[108] Over the years, some of these prohibitions, mainly on smoking and drinking, became less strict; but they were still the general rule rather than the exception.[109]

Aside from insisting on devotional practices and personal morality, the behavioral imperative also required living out stipulations like "Love your neighbor" and "Love your enemies." These stipulations were usually interpreted in personalistic terms. Therefore, loving one's neighbor usually meant overcoming whatever grudges or vendettas one had against another. Often Korean evangelicals took these stipulations to heart, as was apparent during the great revival, when converts went from house to house seeking reconciliation.[110] In some cases, the evangelicals applied these stipulations to their literal limits. In this regard, the most famous case was that of Reverend Son Yangwŏn. In the late 1940s, during the Yŏsu rebellion in the South, Son's two sons were killed by communist youths. When the rebellion was put down and one of the killers was apprehended and sentenced to be executed, Son successfully interceded with the South Korean police to spare him. Not only that, he went on to adopt the youth.[111] During the great revival, it was this stipulation— "Love your enemies"—that the missionaries urged on the Korean evangelicals to have them stop hating the Japanese. To be sure, to Korean nationalists, such a stipulation sounded infuriatingly unjust (since it failed to take into account the evils of Japanese imperialism) and self-serving (since it seemed nothing more than a rhetoric aimed at keeping the missionaries in favor with the Japanese). On the whole, however, the sense of new morality engendered by such an imperative had an integrative effect upon the church.

The sense of integration engendered by the great revival spread beyond Korean circles. It was also apparent in the relations between Koreans and the missionaries, as well as among the missionaries themselves. As noted above, before the great revival some missionaries suspected Koreans' spiritual capabilities and the authenticity of their conversions. As the revival proceeded, however, it became obvious to them that Koreans were no less spiritual than they. This was the point made by a missionary who participated in a 1906 revival. She wrote, "I have heard it said that Koreans are *impossible*, one cannot lead them to 'Higher Ground!' They are so dark! If they get saved that is as far as one need expect them to go. Friends it isn't true. We have *seen*, and we *know* that we can pray them down to the depths and up to the heights."[112]

As the revival continued on to 1907 and its enthusiasm enveloped both the missionaries and Koreans, more and more missionaries found that they were being disabused of their prejudices toward Koreans and instead were developing a respect for them. Clearly, this was the case of John Z. Moore, one of the most eloquent recorders of the event:

> Until this year I was more or less bound by that contemptible notion that the East is East and the West, West, and that there can be no real affinity or common meeting ground between them. With others I had said the Korean would never have a religious experience such as the West has. These revivals have taught me two things: First, that though there may be a thousand things, on the surface, that are the direct opposite of the West, the Korean is at heart, and in all fundamental things, at one with his brother of the West. . . . In the second place these revivals have taught me, that in the matter of making all life religious, in prayer, and in a simple, child like trust, the East not only has many things, but profound things, to teach the West, and until we learn these things we will not know the full-orbed Gospel of Christ.[113]

In another context, Moore observed:

> For two years I had been living among them [Koreans], looking down upon them as something less than "white" and as though made of a lower grade of clay than myself. Now, for the first time I looked a Korean fully in the face and felt myself unworthy to call him brother. Not because he had been unworthy, but because I had been blind. Gentle reader with a white skin, is there not a strange feeling, as though some of the old prejudice about the yellow man was slipping away?[114]

Similarly, for Korean Christians the revivals provided an occasion to see a side of the missionaries they had not access to before. To begin with, it was something of a turning point in 1903 when Hardie humbly sought forgiveness from his Korean servants, greatly impressing the Koreans who hitherto had more or less regarded their relation with the missionary as one between superior and inferior. In the course of the revival, many missionaries followed Hardie's example and experienced their superiority complex toward the Koreans softening. On the other hand, Koreans, through hearing confessions, came to realize that the missionaries were just as human as they themselves were—a realization that probably drew them closer to the missionaries and made their Gospel more acceptable.[115]

In his *Gold in Korea*, William N. Blair offers a good example of the kind of reconciliation that occurred between the missionaries and Koreans during the great revival. Blair writes of a prayer meeting during which he surprisingly learned of a grudge one of his elders had been harboring against him:

> I never had a greater surprise in my life. To think that this man, my associate in the Men's Association, had been hating me without my knowing it! It seems that I had said something to him one day in the hurry of managing a school field-day exercise which gave offence, and he had not been able to forgive me. Turning to me, he said, "Can you forgive me, can you pray for me?" I stood up and began to pray, "Apa-ge, Apa-ge" ("Father, Father") and got no further. It seemed as if the roof was lifted from the building and the Spirit of God came down from heaven in a mighty avalanche of power upon us. I fell at Kim's side and wept and prayed as I had never prayed before.[116]

Worship, Evelyn Underhill once remarked, restrains "religious egoism and breaks down sociological and denominational differences."[117] During the great revival, worship also broke down a great many cultural and racial barriers that had existed between the Koreans and missionaries.

As the revival progressed, the missionary community itself was influenced by the unitive atmosphere, strengthening even more the solidarity that had already existed among the missionaries, who had been regularly relying on each other for mutual comfort and aid. Annie L. Baird attested to the power of this influence in her description of a group of missionaries who had been gathering for noon prayers: "I find it difficult to speak of the sacred times that we have here. All denominational lines seem wiped out, and we wonder that we could ever have attached importance to them, or have allowed ourselves to be cramped by them. Faults are freely acknowledged, and as freely forgiven, and all hearts are melted up together in a wonderful solvent of love such as we have never known before."[118]

Indeed, so centripetal was the solvent of love that it overrode the missionaries' denominational proprieties. A year after the revival, an American visitor to P'yŏngyang was puzzled that Graham Lee, a Northern Presbyterian, should have been so enwrapped in the enthusiasm of revival:

I said to him, "The one thing I cannot understand is how coolheaded, dispassionate Presbyterians like yourself, who do not believe in or allow the emotional to be stressed in your religion, could have led and participated for many weeks in meetings that were characterized by such tremendous upheavals of human feeling!" "Neither can we account for it," said he, with a solemn look of retrospection upon his face, in a memory of the strange scenes through which he had passed. "You are right when you say it is not our customary way, but you are wrong when you speak of it 'as human.' It came from God supernaturally, and we were utterly unable, if we had wanted to do it, to hold ourselves under ordinary conditions."[119]

The revival deepened the fellowship among the missionaries, and it fostered trust and sympathy between them and their Korean counterparts, which stood them both in good stead later, when they had to struggle against Japanese efforts to undermine their religion.

If the great revival had an integrative effect on the relation between missionaries and Korean evangelicals, the same was not true of its effect on the relation between Korean evangelicals and those Koreans who zealously held on to their traditional mores. Evangelicalism's impact on traditional ways of Korea was disruptive, and it was vis-à-vis Korean religions that the evangelicals and their more traditional countrymen conflicted most conspicuously.

To the missionaries in Korea, the religions of Korea were, at best, ersatz faiths useful only to the extent that they prepared Koreans for the "true" religion.[120] At worst, they were heathen superstitions consigning to eternal damnation all those believing in them. Thus when Koreans converted, they were expected to do away with not only their unseemly habits but also all of their former religious practices that might conflict with evangelicalism. As one missionary wrote, "When the Koreans become Christians they destroy the 'devil house' on the mountain sides and the booth for the evil spirits by their door-yard."[121]

To a newly converted evangelical, destroying the "devil house" and the "booth for the evil spirits" may well have been the most conspicuous way of announcing his religious breakthrough, of separating himself from his previous life pattern. However, to Koreans still attached to the traditional worldview, such were acts of sacrilege. To them, the objects destroyed were not a devil house and a booth for evil spirits but a shrine for a mountain spirit and an abode of household guardians. These were sacred entities, whose violations in former times would have incurred grave retribution. Times had changed, though, so that Christians no longer incurred immediate persecution for violating such taboos. Even so, it was inevitable that as evangelicalism consolidated in Korea, its adherents would clash bitterly with the traditionalists.

In the *Korea Mission Field* there are many reports of such clashes. We learn of villagers threatening to destroy a newly built church, thinking that the recent death of a couple of village boys was caused by the Protestants' use of some of the village's sacred stones to build the church.[122] Another report reads: "A certain clan was fixing up their ancestral worship house. A Christian member was approached for his share [of] three cents. He refused. The collector had him haled before the magistrate. The magistrate roundly abused him and ordered him to pay the money. He refused. The magistrate in a rage ordered him stripped, tied to the beating board and flogged till he paid it."[123] In one instance, a church leader attempted to build a new chapel on his land near his ancestral graves. He was opposed by his relatives, who protested that doing so would "pinch the tail of the dragon who had guarded the graves of their ancestors for centuries," and therefore "dire calamity would befall the whole family."[124] In Sinchŏn, new converts decided to renounce ancestral rites; as a result, "some of the older men [of the town] gathered with clubs and beat some of those who were gathering for worship."[125] When the son of a *yangban* family became a Christian, his mother tried to hang herself twice.[126] When a fifty-four-year-old *yangban* became a Christian, he burnt his ancestral tablets; in retaliation, "a crowd of relatives came, took the old gentleman out, tied his hands, kicked him, smashed his hat, tore his clothes, led him over to his ancestral graves and said they were going to kill him there to appease the spirits for his sacrilege."[127] One report relates that "a poor widow was beaten insensible by her drunken brother-in-law because she refused to allow her children to sacrifice to their father, the drunkard's brother."[128] A converted government official who "had been transformed by the study of the Word into a humble believer" gave up his office because it "hindered his faith." [129] In another instance, a polygamous *yangban*, after becoming converted, severed his relationship with his second wife. On the other hand, a woman gave up her home and went off to live by herself "because she realized that she could not be a consistent Christian and live as a man's second wife."[130]

These examples show that evangelicalism began its career in Korea as what Joachim Wach calls "a specifically religious group," a group that gathers and integrates those who share a common religious experience, while setting itself apart from the rest of the society that does not share in that experience.[131] These examples also show that even as Korea was entering the twentieth century, being a Christian in that country still entailed a measure of hardship. As a report in the *Korea Mission Field* puts it, "It costs something to be a Christian here."[132] That thousands of Koreans flocked to the church despite such costs attested to evangelicalism's appeal as a vehicle of salvation to the multitudes of Koreans.

As has been argued since the start of this chapter, with the traditional order in disrepair, the quest for salvation—the search for a new moral order— was a major concern for Koreans at the beginning of the twentieth century. It was this quest that had led a multitude of Koreans to Roman Catholicism, Tonghak, and evangelicalism. By 1910, when Japan annexed Chosŏn, these religions were in good shape, with Roman Catholicism claiming approximately 75,000 adherents; Tonghak, 750,000; and evangelicalism, 175,000.[133]

One reason for the comparatively low number of Catholic adherents was the negative associations that the church had acquired during the nineteenth century, associations that were not easily dislodged from the popular mind. Another reason was that, during this period, the Catholic Church did not engage in intensive proselytization, at least not nearly as intensively as the evangelicals did. The Catholic Church, nevertheless, did register steady growth, so that by 1920 its membership had increased to 90,000.[134]

By 1910 Tonghak had been renamed as Chŏndogyo (Religion of the Heavenly Way) and had recovered from the setbacks it had suffered during the 1894 rebellion. Also by this period, under the guidance of its Third Great Leader, Son Pyŏnghŭi, the church had purged itself of a pro-Japanese faction that had been giving it a bad reputation. Too, Tonghak had strengthened its grassroots organizations. All this enabled Tonghak's membership to increase to about 1.5 million by 1919.[135]

For the evangelical church, the most rapid growth occurred between 1900 and 1910. In 1900 its total membership was 39,217; by 1910 it was 177,692. The same, however, could not be said of the period between 1910 and 1919, when the membership actually declined, to 175,780, prompting historian Alfred W. Wasson to title his study of the 1911–1919 period "Nine Lean Years."[136]

MISSIONARIES AND KOREAN NATIONALISM

Why wasn't the evangelical church able to maintain its growth momentum of 1905–1910 into the subsequent years? Part of the answer is that, after 1910, evangelicals left Korea by the thousands to escape famine and political repression, migrating mostly to Manchuria. However, there is another, more significant reason for the church's languor in this period: the missionaries' efforts to depoliticize the church led the Koreans to believe that the church was indifferent to the fate of their nation.

As noted earlier, even before the arrival of missionaries, evangelicalism was winning converts among Koreans of the lower class in northern parts of the country. For the most part, these and other lower-class Koreans sought the church for apolitical reasons—personal salvation, ways to cope with personal stresses—as was the case with other lower-class Koreans who had become Roman Catholics and Tonghaks earlier. Indeed, even after the arrival of Appenzeller and Underwood in 1885, the bulk of those who sought the church were such people.

While it was attracting commoners, however, evangelicalism was also making inroads into the ranks of the politically minded *yangban*. Just as the commoners had done, *yangban* started to join the church in the 1880s, when the country was still under Korean sovereignty. These *yangban* evangelicals were largely from the disaffected portion of their class. To be sure, many of them, such as Kil Sŏnju, were attracted to the church primarily for religious reasons.[137] For a significant portion of them, however, politics played a role in their adoption and support of the religion. Such, for example, was the case with two of the first *yangban* to be converted to evangelicalism: Sŏ Chaep'il (Philip Jaisohn) and Yun Ch'iho, influential progressives linked with the failed coup d'état of 1884. Yun, Sŏ, and other *yangban* like them believed that evangelicalism could help reform their people and their nation. Thus they encouraged their countrymen to embrace the religion.[138] Moreover, after the Russo-Japanese War of 1904–1905, more traditional Korean officials who had discountenanced evangelicalism earlier came to recognize its reformative potential and to endorse it.[139]

In part influenced by such endorsements, many Korean nationalists turned to evangelicalism to find ways to ameliorate their nation's woes. Thus, a missionary wrote:

Many are realizing the failure of the ancient civilization of their fathers in the stress of the twentieth century. They see that the nations styled Christian are the ones that today possess the highest civilization and culture, and, turning from the old, they are now seeking the new. But with many of these Christianity means a kind of civilization only. They do not distinguish between Christianity and some of its results. These people are calling for schools and western learning and western culture.[140]

How important did Koreans, some of them at least, think Western education was for the survival of their nation? Another missionary addressed this question in an account of a Korean patriot:

The passing away of Korea's independence has served somewhat to stimulate the Koreans along the line of education. . . . On Kangwha the school established by Yi Dong-whai [Yi Tonghwi] is doing excellent work. . . . He has a very commendable scheme of education, and all is carried on without any expense to the church. In the last quarterly conference he arose and, with tears trickling down his face, pleaded for the parents to take more interest in the education of their children, as that was the only hope left for Korea; and he announced before the conference that the Christians all over the island [Kanghwa] could send their boys and rice to feed them—he would furnish them their rooms and instruction free.[141]

Faced with politically motivated seekers, the missionaries, on the one hand, did not quibble over the motives of the newcomers. They were glad to have as much raw material as they could for evangelism, as evidenced by the following sentiment: "While we regret that the people are coming from such low motives, we cannot but rejoice at such an opportunity to give them the Bread of Life."[142] On the other hand, with the nation's politics becoming increasingly volatile, the missionaries became alarmed lest the church turn into a hotbed of the independence movement. Consequently, they began to emphasize to the Koreans, especially the converts, their longstanding policy of disallowing political activities within the church.[143]

By disallowing political activities within the church, the missionaries believed that they were taking a nonpartisan stance.[144] In actual fact, such a stance was extremely difficult—if not impossible—to achieve in Korea at the time. Indeed, except in the minds of certain Koreans whom later generations stigmatized as collaborators, there was little, if any, middle ground between Japanese colonialism and Korean nationalism.[145] One had to choose a side. And if one refused to take a side—which was what the missionaries did with their declaration of political neutrality—it merely meant that one was accepting the status quo, which was just a passive way of accepting the Japanese rule.

Moreover, the missionaries did more than just disallow political activities from taking place in the church. They actively discouraged their flock from harboring nationalistic sentiments. Thus, in 1906, when twelve students from P'yŏngyang Academy participated in a rally against the imposition of the Japanese protectorate over Korea, they were promptly suspended.[146] It has already been mentioned that during the great revival, Korean believers were urged to repent of their hatred for the Japanese. It so happened that 1907 was also the year when the Japanese abolished the Korean army, prompting former Korean soldiers to lead guerrilla uprisings (ŭibyŏng, "righteous armies") all over the country. Many in the church were tempted to join the guerrillas, only to be dissuaded from doing so by the missionaries.[147] A similar development occurred in 1910 while the Million Movement was taking place; in the course of it, missionaries discouraged Koreans from protesting against Japan's annexation of their country.[148] That was not all. From 1910, when Japanese rule over Korea began in earnest, the missionaries made it clear they were willing not only to accept the status quo but also to regard the Japanese as a partner in their self-appointed task to enlighten Koreans. Thus in 1918 a KMF editorial welcomed the arrival of the second governor-general of Korea, Hasegawa Yoshimichi: "We are pleased thus to honor our Governor General; firstly because the Bible commands us to honor the Powers that be; . . . Thirdly, because the Governor General and the missionaries are both interested in the Koreans to improve their condition. Though methods employed are different they need not conflict, but, on the other hand, should be mutually helpful and complementary."[149]

The missionaries, to be sure, had good reasons to discountenance Korean nationalism. After 1905, to safeguard and continue their evangelistic work in Korea, it was crucial that they win Japanese toleration. And as was shown by the "Conspiracy Case" of 1911, the Japanese authorities were ever wary of the church's potential for subversion. In the Conspiracy Case, the Japanese arrested a large number of Korean Protestant leaders, falsely accusing them of having plotted to assassinate Governor-General Terauchi Masatake, and torturing many of them.[150] Thus it was clear to the missionaries that unless the Japanese could be assured that the church was "apolitical" and was not being used for the independence movement, their prime mission of preaching the Gospel would be imperiled.

Having led the church to accept the status quo of Japanese rule, however, the missionaries could not help but disappoint Korean nationalists within the church and alienate those outside it. Inevitably, many Koreans left the church—at least the church as institutionally conceived—and some of them violently expressed their disappointment as they left.[151] By the same token, fewer and fewer Koreans were attracted to the church. Thus, the missionaries' "apolitical" stance and the consequent depoliticization of the church were an important reason that church growth stagnated between 1910 and 1919.[152]

It is not a historian's task to speculate on what might have been had certain events transpired differently. But it is hard to resist considering what might have happened to Korean evangelicalism had it maintained its apolitical stance throughout the Japanese occupation, the period when, for most Koreans, anti-Japanese sentiment was intense. Had that been the case, the Korean church might have taken the path of the Protestant churches of Japan and China. In other words, it might never have become positively associated with Korean national interests and therefore might never have been more successful in Korea than the churches in Japan and China were.

In China and Japan, evangelicalism initially succeeded in becoming meaningful to thousands of individuals. In failing to make a meaningful contribution to their collective aspirations, however, it failed to bond with the Chinese and Japanese as nations. This appraisal denies neither that Protestantism had a powerful appeal to significant segments of the populations—such that they eventually developed into indigenous Chinese and Japanese churches— nor that it shared in the patriotism of a great many individual Chinese and Japanese Christians.[153] But on a more collective level—that of the nation rather than the individual or even the subnational group—Protestantism's interaction with China and Japan was antagonistic, precluding any chance for a positive identification between the religion and either nation.

The roots of such antagonism lay in the history of unhappy interactions between Protestantism and these two nations. In China, for example, Protestantism became identified with a Britain that inflicted the Opium War (1839–1842) on the Chinese. The Japanese identified Protestantism with an American commodore, Matthew C. Perry, whose gunboat diplomacy humiliated them and pried open their ports. As a result of such conflicts, Protestantism (and Christianity in general) appeared to the Chinese and Japanese as part and parcel of Western imperialism, bent on militarily and economically subjugating their nations. In China, such antagonism was clearly and violently expressed in events like the Boxer Uprising of 1900, student-led anti-Christian movements of the 1920s, and ultimately the Chinese communists' expulsion of the missionaries in the 1950s.[154] An aspect of this antagonism is documented by Kap-che Yip in his *Religion, Nationalism and Chinese Students: The Anti-Christian Movement of 1922–1927*, wherein he writes, "Indeed, by 1924 they [the Chinese intellectuals] viewed Christianity as not only unscientific and outdated, but also as a major obstacle to China's attainment of national independence. Many alleged that it was the vanguard of Western imperialism."[155] In Japan, similar antagonism was expressed in the so-called Uchimura Kanzo Lèse-Majesté Incident of 1891, the passage of the Religious Bodies Law of 1939, and the expulsion and imprisonment of Christian missionaries on the eve of Japan's entrance into the Second World War.[156] In view of such events in Japan, historian Winburn T. Thomas writes: "Anyone believing in Christianity was regarded as having lost his national spirit, for it was rumored that the growth of the foreign faith would endanger the future of the nation."[157] Given their histories of conflict, it is not surprising that Protestantism failed to flourish in China and Japan in the twentieth century.

Protestantism (or evangelicalism) in Korea, as it turned out, did not follow that path. Unlike its Japanese and Chinese counterparts, the church deeply shared in and contributed to Koreans' collective aspirations—despite the missionaries' efforts to depoliticize the church. How was this possible? Although the missionaries succeeded in depoliticizing the church qua an institution, they did not depoliticize it qua Korean men and women, as attested by the March First Independence Movement.

EVANGELICALISM AND THE MARCH
FIRST INDEPENDENCE MOVEMENT OF 1919

The March First Movement marked a turning point in modern Korean history.[158] It was a classic event, à la David Tracy, in which Koreans of different backgrounds came together en masse to defy their Japanese colonizers and to demonstrate to the world their fervent desire for independence.[159] In the end, the movement failed to achieve its objective of Korean independence, but it did succeed in galvanizing and uniting Koreans. As Michael E. Robinson observes, "The memory of this uprising plays a significant role in the narrative of modern Korea and the evolution of Korean nationalism."[160] The most concrete manifestation of that unity was the founding in April 1919 of the Shanghai Korean Provisional Government, which, despite its checkered history, was the most important nationalist organization for Koreans during the colonial period.[161]

Like all classic events, the March First Movement is pregnant with diverse meanings and interpretations.[162] Despite such diversity, consensus has emerged—at least among historians in South Korea and the United States—on the major factors that went into the making of the movement.[163] One such factor was Koreans' persistent desire for independence. That desire was fueled by their historical memory and imagination as one nation, whose history stretched back to 2333 BCE, when the mythical Tan'gun purportedly founded the earliest Korean kingdom, Old Chosŏn.[164] The second factor was the extremely repressive nature of the first ten years of Japan's rule in Korea. During this period, the colonial government employed racial discrimination, systematic terror, and torture as mainstays of its policy. A historian of this policy, Frank P. Baldwin Jr., wrote in 1969, "The political, social and educational disqualification imposed on Koreans from 1910 to 1918 resemble the plight of the American negro living a precarious, subservient existence in America."[165]

These two factors were deep-seated and fundamental to the March First Movement. A more immediate factor was the Fourteen Points speech made by President Woodrow Wilson of the United States. First delivered in January 1918, nine months after he had persuaded Americans to join the Allies in World War I, Wilson's speech seemed to promise the right of self-determination to colonized people everywhere.[166] Later, this ideal would turn hollow, as it was not applied to the colonies held by Allies, such as Japan. But when the speech was first aired, Korean nationalists embraced it as a clarion call to action. The first Koreans to act on it were those outside Korea, who were freer and had readier access to news than their counterparts in Korea.

Thus, when the war ended in November 1918, Korean émigrés in China and the United States scrambled to make their case for Korea in the Paris Peace Conference, which began in January 1919. In Shanghai the nationalist leaders agreed to send Kim Kyusik, an erstwhile Protestant educated by Underwood, as a delegate to Paris to plead for Korea. They also sent covert operatives to Korea to obtain financial and moral support for their efforts. The most successful of these was evangelical Sŏnu Hyŏk. Arriving in Korea, he called on a number of well-known evangelical leaders like Yi Sŭnghun and Kil Sŏnju and succeeded in obtaining a promise that they would hold a peaceful demonstration in support of Kim when he arrived in Paris. Their demonstration aimed to give the lie to Japanese propaganda that Koreans were content and well-off under Japan's rule and to proclaim the Korean desire for independence. At about the same time, late January 1919, leaders of Chŏndogyo also planned to hold a peaceful demonstration independently of the Protestants. The impetus for their plan came from a contact sent by a group of Korean students attending school in Japan who had been planning clandestinely to hold their own independence demonstration in Tokyo. These students were spurred on in their plan by a Japanese newspaper account of Korean émigrés in the United States who sought to enlist American aid to regain Korean independence.[167] Subsequently, on February 8, 1919, about four hundred Korean students assembled at the Tokyo YMCA and demonstrated, decrying Japanese repression in Korea and demanding independence for their homeland. The demonstration lasted about an hour, until it was broken up—and the leaders arrested—by the police.

This Tokyo student demonstration inspired Koreans in the peninsula and emboldened the evangelicals and Chŏndogyoists who were planning their separate demonstrations. The efforts of both were further filliped when Kojong died on January 23, a singularly advantageous circumstance since droves of people would converge on Seoul to participate in the monarch's funeral, scheduled for March 3. By February 22, realizing that they shared much the same objectives, the evangelicals and Chŏndogyoists joined forces. Five days later, they were joined by the Buddhists, completing the triumvirate of the religious leadership at the helm of the movement.[168] Then, as a last preparatory step, thirty-three of the top leaders of the triumvirate inscribed their names on a Declaration of Independence, drafted by Ch'oe Namsŏn, and copies of the document were to be distributed to people on the eventful day.

On March 1, 1919, evangelicalism's most potent encounter with Korean nationalism took place. On that day, in Seoul's Pagoda Park, thousands of Koreans—men and women, young and old—had been gathering since the morning. Many of them had come from the countryside for Kojong's funeral. At two o'clock in the afternoon, a young evangelical man mounted the platform in the middle of the park and stirred the crowd by reading the Declaration of Independence. As soon as he was finished, the crowd burst into deliriously resounding cheers: "Taehan tongnip manse!" (Long live Korean independence!) The scene was well captured in the following account:

> Soon from the East Gate to the West Gate and from the Bell Tower in the center of the city to the South Gate, a veritable pandemonium of enthusiasm and joy reigned. Students with books in one hand and uplifted cap in the other; stately white-robed old gentlemen with their hoary beards flowing and their wrinkled hands waving; young girls with their dark skirts streaming and upturned faces shining; elderly ladies with their characteristic green veils on top of the immaculate dress; mechanics with their rolled-up sleeves and some of them with tools still in hand; sons of the rich with their shimmering silk coats flying; rustic farmers with horny fingers and bony arms lifted toward the blue heavens; stocky-limbed cart-pullers with their long white cloth wound tightly round the head and hung loosely behind; staid and substantial-looking merchants and shopkeepers, some with their long pipes, and others with pen either in their hands or behind their ears; fat and plump youngsters with their baggy wadded pantaloons, some in wooden shoes, and some in silk slippers; smart-looking young men

dressed in European style and wearing rimless spectacles; and men and women of every and sundry description, age, and rank—one and all—were in a happy delirium, shouting, "*Mansei! Mansei! Tok-rip Mansei!*" [Long live! Long live! Long live Korean independence!][169]

Shortly after the Declaration of Independence was read in Pagoda Park, Koreans elsewhere in the city and in the country at large staged similar demonstrations. Within days, the movement for independence erupted in virtually every corner of the country and in nearly all segments of society, with upwards of two million people directly participating in more than 1,500 gatherings, occurring in all but seven of Korea's 281 county administrations.[170]

The March First Independence Movement was meant to be nonviolent and started out that way, but it failed to remain so. The leaders intended to appeal to the conscience of the Japanese colonizers and, more importantly, to the Wilson-led victors at the Paris Peace Conference by using peaceful demonstrations.[171] Instead of affecting the Japanese conscience, the demonstrations only galled the gendarmes, who, assisted by Japanese residents in Korea, indiscriminately beat and shot at the demonstrators. Some of the demonstrations then turned into riots. Police stations were attacked, and no Japanese was safe in the streets. [172] Riots continued sporadically through the summer. The situation came under full control only with the arrival of additional Japanese troops. By that time a great many casualties had been suffered by the Koreans: 7,645 killed and 15,961 injured—with 715 houses, 47 churches, and 2 schools burned or otherwise destroyed.[173]

Soon after the independence movement broke out and it became clear that it had not been spontaneous but was carefully planned, many Japanese—given their low opinion of Koreans—suspected the missionaries to be behind it and denounced them. One such denunciation was published on March 12 in *Chosen shimbun*, a Japanese daily in Korea:

> The stirring up of the mind of the Koreans is the sin of the American missionaries. This uprising is their work. . . . They take the statement of Wilson about the self-determination of nations and hide behind their religion and stir up the people. However, the missionaries have tried to apply the free customs of other nations to these Korean people who are not fully civilized. From the part that even girl students in Christian schools have taken it is very evident that this uprising has come from the missionaries.[174]

Despite this newspaper's contention, the truth was that the demonstrations surprised the missionaries no less than the Japanese. A position paper submitted by missionary representatives to the American consulate in Seoul voiced their reaction:

> Except for the admitted fact that they are propagators of a gospel which had more than once been accused of turning the world up side down missionaries have had no direct relation to this present movement. It was but natural that the charge should at once be made in the Japanese press that missionaries were the instigators of the uprising. This may be categorically denied. It arose without their knowledge. Their advice as to the inception and direction of the movement has not been sought.[175]

Accused of having abetted and aided the Koreans, the missionaries continued to vigorously deny the accusation and to proclaim their political neutrality. Eventually, in mid-March, influenced by protestations and pressure from the American consulate, the government-general publicly exonerated the missionaries.[176]

In hindsight, given their manifest disapproval of Korean nationalists' aspirations, it is understandable that the missionaries were not apprised of the movement. And if by keeping the missionaries in the dark the planners intended to minimize any hindrance to achieving their goal, subsequent developments proved them to have been prudent. When the demonstrations erupted, the immediate reaction of many missionaries was to dissuade their Korean converts from joining in. One particularly poignant example of such dissuasion is described in the journal of Methodist missionary Mattie Wilcox Noble, whose March 1 entry reads:

> Today has been a great day for Korea. How long their joy will last, who can say? At two P.M. all the schools, from grammar grades or middle schools up went on strike against Japan's governing Korea, and all started out on the streets in parade, hands thrown in air, caps swung, and Hurrahs ("Ten Thousand Years of Korea") shouted. People of the streets dropped in line with them; and such joyful shouting all over the city. I could see from our window one long procession filing past the corner around the palace wall. The Government School for Girls also paraded, and when a company of boys came past Ewa Haktang [a Methodist school for girls], they rushed into the compound and called to the girls to come on. The girls rushed out to go but Miss Walter in her kimono ran down to bolt the big gate and head off the girls. Mr. Tayler [Taylor] and Mr. Appenzeller went over to her assistance and they succeeded in keeping the Ewa girls from going. They cried, and some of the boys grew almost wild, but had to go on and leave them.[177]

On the one hand, missionaries such as Taylor and Appenzeller genuinely feared for the safety of Korean believers, even if much of that fear emanated from paternalism. On the other hand, the missionaries were alarmed lest their own apolitical stance be jeopardized by their converts' participation in the demonstrations. Despite their efforts, however, the missionaries could not stem the tide of nationalistic fervor that swept through their schools and churches. Nor could they prevent the violence perpetrated on the demonstrators by the Japanese.

Seeing Koreans brutalized, the missionaries could no longer remain aloof. They became actively involved in caring for the injured, and insisting on "no neutrality for brutality"—a slogan born of moral indignation—they urged Japanese authorities to desist from using brutal tactics against the demonstrators.[178] Failing to make much impact by a direct appeal, they drew on the resources of their overseas contacts. They documented clear cases of Japanese atrocities and, using unofficial channels, reported to mission boards and influential friends in Europe and America. About one thousand pages of such documents were compiled by the Commission on Relations with the Orient of the Federal Council of the Churches of Christ in America, and in July 1919 a select portion of them were published as a pamphlet under the title *The Korean Situation: Authentic Accounts of Recent Events by Eye Witnesses.* Among the numerous accounts cited in the pamphlet are these:

On March 4th, about 12:30 noon, loud cheering was again participated in by the Koreans. With this cheer the Japanese fire brigade was let loose among the crowds with clubs; some carried pickax handles; others their long lance fir-hooks, some iron bars, others hardwood and pine clubs, some with short-handled club hooks. They rushed into the crowds, clubbing them over the heads, hooking them here and there with their lance-hooks, until in a short time many had been seriously wounded, and with blood streaming down their faces were dragged to the police station by the fire brigade.

Chung Yung Hui, aged 34, lives in the county of Paiju. On March 28th, at one o'clock in the afternoon, a crowd of 400, yelling "Mansay," were met by Japanese gendarmes, who fired. Eight men were killed. They had done no violence, and were not even armed with rocks. This man was shot through the neck.

At Maungsan: During the first part of the March after the people at this place had shouted for independence, fifty-six people were asked by the gendarmes to come to the gendarme station, which they did. When they were all inside the gendarmerie compound the gates were closed, gendarmes climbed up on the wall and shot all the people down. Then they went in among them and bayoneted all who still lived. Of the fifty-six, fifty-three were killed and three were able later to crawl out of the heap of dead. Whether they lived or not is not known. A Christian woman in whom we have confidence made her way to foreign friends after several days' travel and made the above statement. Undoubtedly it is true.[179]

Accounts such as these proved to be a public relations nightmare for the Japanese government, as they provoked international outcries and in the United States provided ammunition to senatorial critics of Japan.[180] Consequently, the Japanese government was compelled not only to renounce using such violence against the demonstrators but also to overhaul its colonial policy in Korea. As part of this policy change, Japan recalled the heavy-handed Hasegawa and installed in his place the more diplomatic but no less imperious Saitō Makoto in September 1919.

The moral courage the missionaries displayed in the face of colonial brutality proved crucial for evangelicalism. Their humanitarian treatment of the injured, and their publicizing of the Korean plight, went a long way toward redeeming them—and their religion—in the eyes of many Koreans. Subsequently, from 1919 on, no Korean could blindly accuse the missionaries of being self-serving or of having no sympathy for the Korean people, without provoking a loud cry of dissent from their more discerning countrymen.[181]

A year after the demonstrations, a book titled *The Rebirth of Korea: The Awakening of the People, Its Causes, and the Outlook* was published in the United States. By "rebirth," the author, a Korean Methodist educator named Hugh Heung-Woo Cynn [Sin Hŭngu], did not mean a religious awakening. Rather, Cynn was referring specifically to the March First Movement: "In the midst of mighty shouts the Korea that had been 'dead and buried' for eight and a half years 'rose from the dead' at two o'clock in the afternoon of the first day of March, 1919."[182] Cynn's purpose in writing the book was to publicize the March First Movement and to argue that the movement was the Koreans' breakthrough for a democratic order, the starting point of Korea's evolution toward full democracy, which, he wishfully opined, would culminate in Japan's granting independence to the country.[183] Cynn also posited that Christianity (by which he seemed to have had in mind mainly Protestantism) must take a large share of credit for this breakthrough. He argued that the movement, having been an expression of democracy, could not have occurred except for the influence of Christianity, since, he premised, democracy was possible if and only if Christianity (Protestantism) was possible.[184]

It is debatable as to what extent, if at all, the fate of democracy is linked with that of Protestantism, but as to the role Korean Protestants played in the March First Movement, there cannot be any doubt. It is true that the initiative for cooperation among the religionists came from Chŏndogyo. Indeed, the March First Movement was a pan-Korean phenomenon to which no single group could lay an exclusive claim. From the top leadership that signed the Declaration of Independence down to the peasants pounced on by the gendarmes, solidarity prevailed. And among the religionists who were at the forefront of the movement, ecumenism was the order of the day. Nevertheless, it must be noted that once the movement got under way, the contributions rendered by Korean evangelicals—roles played and sufferings borne—stood out. Of the thirty-three signers of the Declaration of Independence, for example, about half (sixteen) were evangelicals; the others were two Buddhists and fifteen Chŏndogyoists.[185] For the movement to have spread so quickly and cohesively, communication and organization were key. Here too the church's national network and local leadership played crucial parts.

How significantly evangelicalism contributed to the March First Movement can also be gauged by analyzing some figures concerning those arrested during the demonstrations. According to a report issued near the end of 1919 by the Japanese military police, 19,525 persons were arrested in connection with the demonstrations. Of these, 6,310 were religionists, including 3,371 evangelicals. The evangelicals alone amounted to more than 17 percent of the total arrested—an impressive proportion, considering that by 1919 they constituted a little over 1 percent of the total population of Korea.[186] Furthermore, of the arrested, 489 were clergy; nearly half of them (244) were evangelicals, with 120 Buddhists and 125 Chŏndogyoists making up the remainder. Finally, of the 471 women arrested, evangelicals accounted for more than 65 percent (309), attesting to the empowering effect the religion had on Korean women.[187]

As a result of its in-depth involvement, evangelicalism came to be linked with some of the most potent symbols of the movement. One such symbol was the little village of Cheamni, near the city of Suwŏn. On April 15, 1919, a unit of Japanese gendarmes descended on this village. They rounded up all the village men who had been demonstrating in previous days (mostly Methodists and Chŏndogyoists), placed them in the village church, locked the door, and set the church on fire. Some tried to claw their way out, only to be cut down by awaiting bullets and bayonets.[188] In the end, twenty-nine villagers were massacred, the church burnt to the ground together with the entire village. Reprehensible as the Cheamni massacre was, it was not an isolated incident. Quite a number of other villages met similar fates. Thanks mainly to the publicity the missionaries gave to the incident, Cheamni became a symbol for all those villages as well as a symbol of Japanese atrocities and Korean suffering under Japanese rule.[189]

Another potent symbol of the March First Movement was Yu Kwansun. When the independence movement began, Yu was a seventeen-year-old student at Ewha haktang, a mission school for girls (and the predecessor of Ewha Womans University). Arrested and imprisoned for taking a leading role in demonstrations, Yu refused to abjure her passion for Korean independence. To make it more galling for the Japanese police, she and others in the prison instigated a commemorative demonstration on the anniversary of the movement.[190] Brutally tortured, she died in prison.

In the twenty-five years after the March First Movement, during which Japan continued to rule Korea, Cheamni and Yu Kwansun persisted in the underground of Korean memory. Then, with Japan's defeat in World War II and the subsequent liberation of Korea on August 15, 1945, they emerged as nationalist icons. In 1959 a commemorative monument emblazoned with the words of President Syngman Rhee was set over the site of the burnt church in Cheamni. Cheamni has become a pilgrimage destination not only for Korean Christians and nationalists but also for repentant Japanese Christians, a group of whom donated funds that enabled a new chapel to be constructed in the village in 1969. As for Yu Kwansun, she has become the epitome of patriotism, venerably referred to as *yŏlsa* (patriot) or, more affectionately, Sister Yu Kwansun. To honor her, a museum was built in her name, and her statue erected in Seoul's conspicuous Namsan (South Mountain) Park and elsewhere. A prestigious medal was conferred on her posthumously, and the song "Sister Yu Kwansun" is taught to schoolchildren all over South Korea, who sing it on March 1.

Yu Kwansun and Cheamni are two vivid symbols of the March First Movement that live on in the collective memory of the Korean people, primarily in the South, where March 1 is celebrated as a national holiday—as well as being a fixture in the church calendar. In annual March First commemorations, as these and other symbols of the movement are recalled and celebrated, believers and nonbelievers alike acknowledge the inextricable association established between evangelicalism and their nation in 1919.

The March First Independence Movement was yet another manifestation of Koreans' search for a new moral order. In that respect, participants of the movement expressed the same salvific aspirations of the adherents of *Chŏnggam-nok,* Sirhak, Tonghak, and Roman Catholicism: freedom from oppression and the construction of a more meaningful, more humane moral order. On the other hand, because of the movement's immense scope and intensity, because nearly all Koreans were on the side of the oppressed, and because the oppressor was an alien nation bent on extirpating Korean cultural entity, the March First Movement towered over all previous searches for order.

By taking a leading role in the March First Movement, evangelicalism stood to gain greatly. It recouped the appeal it had lost among the Korean populace. A new upturn in its membership enrollment concretely reflected this gain, as noted by Wasson:

> Since 1910 the curve representing the total number of Southern Methodist members and probationers had been steadily going downward; in 1920 the curve turned sharply upward again, and within five years there was a net gain of 102 percent. In each of the other churches in Korea also the year 1920 marks the beginning of a period of growth. . . . This period of rapid growth was ushered in by the Independence Movement.[191]

Also important, though difficult to quantify, were the renewed trust and acceptance the missionaries came to enjoy among the Koreans. Regarding this gain, Wasson states, "The charges against the missionaries [that they instigated the uprising], instead of discrediting them in the minds of the people, put them in greater favor. They were looked upon as comrades in spirit even though they remained neutral in political action."[192]

In addition, evangelicalism gained something much more enduring—its right to be considered a legitimate religion of Korea. By virtue of having contributed so passionately and manifestly to Korea's struggle for political freedom, evangelicalism acquired nationalist credentials few Koreans could gainsay. Thus evangelicalism had become indigenized in Korean history. And by the time the March First Movement ended as an event and began to emerge as a towering national monument, the spiritual interests of evangelicalism had become well associated with the real interests of the Korean nation.

CHAPTER 2

Conflict, Introversion, and a Tradition of Korean Revivalists, 1920–1953

> The renunciation of individual activity in social matters, and
> submission to the world domination of the Empire, drove the
> individual into his own inner life, and forced him to concen-
> trate his energies on the effort to elevate private and personal
> morality; meanwhile both individuals, and groups composed
> of individuals on a voluntary basis, found comfort in religious
> exaltation as a compensation for the hopelessness of the tem-
> poral outlook. . . . In reality, however, all impartial religious
> research reveals the fact that, to some extent at least, religious
> thought is independent; it has its own inner dialectic and its
> own power of development; it is therefore precisely during
> these periods of a total bankruptcy of human hope and effort
> that it is able to step in and fill the vacant space with its own
> ideas and its own sentiment.
>
> —Ernst Troeltsch

Though the March First Movement failed to bring national independence to Koreans, it did bring an end to the so-called Dark Period of
the Japanese rule in Korea.[1] For evangelicalism and Korean people in general,
however, this did not mean that the remainder of the Japanese rule would
change for the better. Indeed, perhaps except for Saitō Makoto's governor-
generalship from 1920 to 1925, known as Cultural Rule, the remainder of the
Japanese rule in Korea was, if anything, harsher. The introduction of a new
land tenure system that caused hundreds of thousands of Korean farmers to
lose their livelihoods, compelling them to drift in search of jobs; large-scale
exportation of Korean rice to Japan, causing serious rice shortages in Korea
itself; the domination and exploitation of Korean commerce and industry by

Japanese entrepreneurs; the prohibition against using the Korean language in schools and official transactions; forcing all Koreans to pay obeisance to the Shintō shrine; shutting down all Korean newspapers except for that of the governor-general; conscripting Korean men to work as laborers and soldiers; dragooning young Korean women into the sexual slavery called the comfort corps; compelling Koreans to abandon their ancestral names and adopt Japanese ones—such circumstances meant that Japanese rule in Korea from 1920 to 1945 hardly afforded light or joy to Koreans.[2]

When Korea was finally liberated from Japanese rule on August 15, 1945, all Koreans, except those who had intimately collaborated with the colonizers, looked forward to their future with great expectations.[3] But their expectations were cruelly dashed. Five years later, instead of becoming the site of renewal and reconstruction, the Korean peninsula became the site of the horrific destruction known as the Korean War.

When North Korean tanks blitzed through the thirty-eighth parallel on June 25, 1950, South Korea, as well as most of the world, was unprepared for an all-out civil war in the peninsula. In hindsight, however, such an event seems all but predictable. Intense disagreements about how Korea was to be reordered had been simmering among Koreans since the end of the March First Movement and boiled over soon after liberation. Indeed, as Bruce Cumings observes, "the emergence of nationalist and communist groups dates back to the 1920s; it is really in this period that the left-right splits of postwar Korea began."[4] On the one hand, a great many Koreans (called leftists, *chwaikp'a*), especially of the underprivileged class (in the South as well as in the North), wanted to change Korea along a socialist or communist model. They called for measures to drastically overhaul the nation's social and economic structures and to purge the elements that had collaborated closely with the Japanese. On the other hand, a great many others (rightists, *uikp'a*), especially the propertied class, sought to change the nation gradually, seeking ultimately to achieve some kind of representative government.

At first, efforts were made to compromise the demands of these two main ideological blocs. This compromise was best reflected in the formation of the Korean People's Republic (KPR), Chosŏn inmin konghwaguk, whose aim was to keep the sovereignty of the country in Korean hands. The KPR had evolved from an antecedent organization called the Committee for the Preparation of Korean Independence (Chosŏn kŏn'guk chunbi wiwŏnhoe), a nationwide grassroots organization. The KPR was purely Korean, established soon after the Japanese surrender; and in it, most important leaders from Korea's main ideological camps were at least nominally represented.[5] This organization, however, was never given a chance to prove itself. Though found acceptable to the North (by Korean communists and their Soviet backers), it was rejected in the South by the United States Army Military Government in Korea (USAMGIK, which ruled Korea from September 1945 to mid-August 1948) and by Korean rightists, who regarded it to be overly tinged with the "red" influence.[6]

With the dissolution of the KPR, also dissolved was the only credible forum in which Koreans from the two ideological blocs could work out their differences. The lack of such a forum, however, did not diminish the eagerness of Koreans in either bloc to unify Korea under their particular form of government. By then, however, since bilateral negotiation was ruled out, the only viable recourse for reunifying Korea seemed to be a unilateral one—in which the stronger of the two blocs would forcibly impose its plan of Korea on the other. Both ideological camps resorted to this approach. In the South, the police—with the backing of the USAMGIK—began rooting out the leftists in their midst, forcing many of them to flee to the North. In the North, the communists—with the blessing of the Soviets—began persecuting Christians, who refused to be assimilated into the emerging communist structure, prompting a massive exodus of Christians to the South. By the end of September 1948, this conflict assumed an official form, as two separate Korean states were established in the peninsula: the Republic of Korea in the South and the Democratic People's Republic of Korea in the North.[7] By the end of 1948, Koreans were more or less left to themselves, as all the Soviet troops and all but a couple of hundred American military advisers had withdrawn from the peninsula. But the conflict between the two ideological camps continued. Border skirmishes near the thirty-eighth parallel continued. Syngman Rhee, president of the southern state, made postures of invading the North.[8] In November 1948, in the southwestern portion of the peninsula, leftists rose up in arms, briefly taking over Yŏsu and Sunch'ŏn, only to be crushed. Finally, North Koreans launched their attack of June 25, 1950, to settle the issue once and for all.

By then, however, Korea had become a crucial node in the East Asian phase of the cold war. Any serious conflict in Korea would involve not only Koreans but also the main rivals of this global confrontation—the Soviets and Chinese on the one hand and the Americans and their allies on the other. Thus, after North Korean forces took Seoul in three days and, in less than two months, had cornered the southern forces in the southeastern tip of the peninsula that came to be known as the Pusan Perimeter, it became incumbent upon the Americans and their allies to react. So came MacArthur's amphibious landing in Incheon on September 15, 1950, and the United Nations' thrust all the way up to the Yalu River, which in turn provoked hundreds of thousands of Chinese troops to flow into the peninsula, beginning in October of the same year. Eventually, the war was stalemated near where it started, the thirty-eighth parallel, and on July 27, 1953, a truce was signed.[9]

For all the devastation and tragedies it perpetrated, the war accomplished nothing, leaving only harsh legacies. Millions of Koreans from both sides were killed, wounded, or reported missing, and even more were separated from their families.[10] The partitioning at the thirty-eighth parallel, which was to have been temporary, still remains precarious. Also remaining are the bitter memories of the war. North Koreans recollected how their cities were laid waste by American bombs, giving plausibility to their regime's hate-filled propaganda against the United States.[11] South Koreans recollected how they, their relatives, and friends had suffered atrocities at the hands of communists, giving rise to genuine anticommunist sentiments in the South, as well as providing a rationale for their government's oppressive "national security laws."[12]

Despite the turbulent events that took place in Korea between 1920 and 1953, evangelicalism persisted; conversion was continually emphasized, and revivals were regularly held throughout the country. On the other hand, it was hardly possible for evangelicalism to carry on without being affected by the sociopolitical circumstances of the period. How did evangelicalism interact with the societal forces that dominated Korea in this period? What impact did that interaction have on the way evangelicalism related to the collective and individual experiences of the Korean people? What impact did it have on the mood of the revivals of the period? To deal with these questions, we need to examine three themes: conflict, introversion, and a tradition of Korean revivalists.

EVANGELICALISM IN CONFLICT

Conflict best characterizes the interaction between evangelicalism and societal forces of Korea in this period—conflict that subjected Korean Protestants to a great deal of hardship. Owing partly to such conflict, evangelicalism would undergo two significant developments. First, its place in Korean—that is, South Korean—society would be further legitimated, since the conflict and attendant hardships were shared by the population at large. Second, a change of mood would occur in evangelicalism: the hopeful, reformative mood of the earlier decades would give way to one that was more passive, otherworldly, and introversive.

Conflict would be a barren generalization were it applied to the development of the Korean society in general from 1920 to 1953. Well before 1920, at least since 1866, when the *General Sherman* was sunk and burnt, conflict had been a predominant theme in modern Korean history, the Korean War merely being its most destructive form. Conflict, however, had not been a pronounced theme in these years with respect to the history of evangelicalism. To be sure, as evangelicalism was being propagated, it did conflict with certain aspects of Korean tradition, and disagreements occurred between missionaries and some Koreans with regard to the church's stance toward Korean nationalism. And in the March First Movement—the most significant national conflict of the period, along with the Korean War—Korean Protestants did take the lion's share of leadership. However, the fact remains that, as far as evangelicalism was concerned, these instances of conflict were eclipsed by instances of unity. The conflict between evangelicalism and Korean tradition, for example, was overshadowed by the harmony engendered among the Christians by the great revival of 1907. Though disagreement existed between the missionaries and some Korean Christians over the church's position on nationalism, it was muffled by the general consensus that prevailed within the church. As to the March First Movement, it had more to do with the patriotism of individual Korean evangelicals than with evangelicalism itself.

In the decades before 1920, evangelicalism was not embroiled in serious conflict, in part because it did not become directly entangled in major political issues of the day. Between 1920 and 1953, however, evangelicalism could not avoid such entanglement. In this period, whether they liked it or not, Korean evangelicals were directly challenged by certain societal forces that espoused values sharply contrasting to theirs. There were three such forces that saw evangelicalism as their nemesis. The most abstract yet pervasive was modernity; more concrete and menacing were State Shintōism and communism.[13]

EVANGELICALISM VERSUS MODERNITY

With the opening of Korean ports to Japan in 1876 and to Western nations in the 1880s, it was inevitable that modern modes of thought and practice would make their way into Korea. Koreans came in contact with modernity most palpably by seeing and using modern inventions such as the telegraph (first built in Korea in 1885), electrical power services (1898), and the railroad (1900). Koreans also became aware of modernity through the reform activities of their younger countrymen, such as Yun Ch'iho and Sŏ Chaep'il, who had returned to Korea after years of study overseas. While overseas, these young men studied not only modern sciences but also Western political theories, and their attempt to apply such theories in Korea often proved unsettling to the status quo.[14]

After the annexation in 1910, Koreans experienced the impact of modernity even more disturbingly, as the government-general initiated a series of modern programs to rationalize Korean society to suit its colonial purposes. One such modern program was a series of land surveys and reform that took place between 1910 and 1919. As a result of this measure, the positions of Japanese settlers and wealthy Korean landowners were bolstered; but a great many peasants were deprived of their livelihood, not least because the reform eroded traditional mores that governed the owning and cultivation of land.[15] Another modern project was the establishment of public schools shortly after the annexation. As a result, large numbers of Korean youth were exposed to secular values and Japanese ideology, both of which were baneful to Korea's tradition.[16] In the 1930s, as Korea figured importantly as a base for Japan's military thrust into Northeast Asia, the Japanese intensified modernizing their heavy industries and railroad system in Korea. They extended the railroad networks and constructed numerous dams, mines, and factories, especially in the northern regions.[17] In the process, they disfigured the landscape and uprooted masses of Koreans, a great many of whom were exploited as industrial fodder.

In the modernization of Korean society, the missionaries, too, played a part. Their modern hospitals, for example, could not help but discredit traditional Korean medicine, whose philosophical underpinnings were based on much of the same beliefs that informed Korean weltanschauung.[18] Their schools could not help but inculcate in young Koreans the beliefs that contradicted the values that had dominated the Korean society for centuries, such as strict discrimination between the sexes and social classes.

At first, most missionaries were favorably disposed to the modernization of Korea. They believed, for example, that Korean womanhood stood in need of modernity—Christian modernity. During a celebration of the Presbyterian mission's fifty years of service in Korea, a missionary reflected on the church's contribution to Korean womanhood, proudly and justifiably:

> If you ask Korean Christians, what the Gospel has done for Christian women, they will say first of all that it has brought them salvation from the guilt and power of sin. Then will come a long list of blessings, social, moral, educational and religious, sometimes quaintly expressed in English like the following: "It broke the door that kept them in houses." It gave them liberty to believe in Jesus Christ. It gave them rights to become members of their own families and not merely necessary and useful appendages. It gave them names. It gave them liberty of soul and action.[19]

This remark essentially seconded one made nine years earlier. In 1925 Chŏn Samdŏk, one of the first Korean Bible women, said at a celebration of her thirtieth year as an evangelist: "I had eyes but could not see, had ears but could not hear, and had a mouth but could not speak. But once I came to know Jesus I became an independent human being."[20]

But by the mid-1920s, Chŏn already no longer represented the forefront of Korean womanhood. The cutting edge had moved more toward the secular, represented by avant-garde women of Korea known as *sinyŏsŏng* (literally, new women). They were less Victorian matrons and more American flappers, giving many a missionary cause for concern. One such a missionary was Ella Sue Wagner, who wrote numerous missionary novels set in Korea, including an unpublished novel titled "The Concubine." In that work she introduces a twist to the notion of an oriental concubine, in that the "concubine" in the story is a white American flapper who is a foil for a Victorianized Christian Korean woman. Contemplating this manuscript, Hyaeweol Choi observes:

> Wagner's novel is highly suggestive of what constitutes true "modern" womanhood in missionary discourse and how the missionary vision for modern womanhood was in tension with the phenomenon of the New Woman and the feminist movement. In a significant way, the novel illustrates both the anxiety and ambivalence felt by missionaries in the face of growing challenges to the "cult of true womanhood," in which religious piety and domesticity were the core of a woman's virtue. [21]

Indeed, in the 1920s some missionaries wondered whether modernization in Korea had not gone out of control. Modern thoughts were leading Koreans (especially the young and educated) to doubt not only their traditional culture but also all nonsecular traditions, including evangelicalism. The fundamentalist leanings of most missionaries in Korea only heightened the discomfiture they felt about the new development.[22] The missionaries' disquietude was well expressed by M. B. Stokes, a Southern Methodist missionary who had played a leading role in the Million Movement:

> It has become difficult to hold revival meetings. It has never been easy, but in recent years it has become more difficult. World-wide currents of thought have tended to increase the difficulty here, as elsewhere. A very insufficient broadcasting of modern scientific knowledge among the youth of the land has already brought forth a great harvest of doubt and unbelief toward fundamental truths, that has created a situation in which it has become difficult for the Spirit of God to work upon souls. . . . It has been nearly twelve years since I was first shocked to find that a young student in one of our mission high schools for girls was doubting the existence of God. It was a very serious matter with her. Later I discovered that this has

become very common in the thinking of our youth. Now I expect to meet it as a problem to be dealt with wherever I go to hold meetings.[23]

To Stokes and kindred spirits in Korea, dealing with the modernity problem mainly meant shielding the church from the onslaught of secular worldview. Nevertheless, as modern thought began to permeate the Korean society, it was only a matter of time before the more inquisitive and receptive of the faithful would seek to accommodate at least some aspects of their faith to modern sensibilities. But whenever these accommodationists sought to make the desired adjustments, they were invariably opposed by the conservatism of the church (especially in the Presbyterian Church) and failed.

This was the case with three controversies that originated in 1934. The first occurred in August of that year when Kim Ch'unbae, a Presbyterian minister who had attended a seminary in Japan, wrote an article in the Christian newspaper *Kidoksinbo*, arguing that the Korean Presbyterian Church should allow women to be ordained as elders. The Presbyterian Church not only denounced this view—contending that what Paul stated about women in First Corinthians and Second Timothy was valid for all times—but also questioned the soundness of Kim's theology: Kim was forced to retract his offending remarks.[24] In the same year, another Presbyterian minister, Kim Yongju, wrote an article anonymously for a different Christian newspaper. This article, which cast doubt on Moses' authorship of the Pentateuch, proved just as controversial. In response, the Presbyterian Church, without specifically mentioning Kim, declared that anyone espousing such a view not only violated the first creed of the Korean Presbyterian Church but also should be barred from the ministry.[25] The third controversy started in December 1934, with the publication of the Korean translation of the *Abingdon Bible Commentary*, a popular American work that incorporated higher criticism of the Bible. This commentary was translated by a group of young Korean churchmen, several of whom had been trained in American seminaries and divinity schools.[26] When the translated commentary was published, it did not cause much stir in the Methodist Church, which tended to be tolerant theologically. But it did cause quite a stir in the Presbyterian Church, some of whose leaders, such as Kil Sŏnju, denounced it as heretical. Like the other two incidents, this conflict also ended with the conservative victory. The Presbyterian ministers who had participated in the translation work were compelled to issue a statement of apology for their role in the affair.[27]

As the conservatives consistently gained the upper hand in their conflicts with the accommodationists, evangelicalism failed to interest those Koreans who were taken with modernity, especially the young and educated. This much was admitted by a missionary who condescendingly stated, "It cannot be denied that we are not reaching what for want of a better term I will call the intellectual classes."[28] One particular Korean intellectual whom evangelicalism failed to reach was the leading novelist Yi Kwangsu. In February 1918 the *Korea Mission Field* published an article by Yi, in which he highly praised evangelicalism for the contributions it had made to the modernization of Korea.[29] By December of the same year, however, Yi had a second thought, which he expressed in another *KMF* article: "In spite of the fact that the component elements of civilization are politics, law, industry, science, philosophy, literature and arts, religion being no more than one of the elements, the Korean Church despises learning and arts[,] considering all civilizing forces, except religion, profane, having no zeal for progress and enlightenment."[30]

Even after liberation and the Korean War, conflict over modernity continued in the Korean Protestant Church. One instance of the conflict occurred in June 1953 when a group of accommodationists, led by Kim Chaejun, were forced to secede from the conservative-dominated Presbyterian Church and established their own denomination and seminary: the Presbyterian Church in the Republic of Korea (Han'guk kidokkyo changnohoe) and Hanshin University.[31] These would become the only avowedly liberal (or "mainstream," in the American sense) Protestant denomination and seminary in Korea—perhaps with the addition of the Episcopal Church (Sŏnggonghoe) and its seminary. In comparison with the evangelicals, the liberals have always been in the minority in Korean Protestantism, both in numbers of supporters and in the theological impact they have had on the church; but their influence on the larger society has been considerable, especially during the 1970s and 1980s when they were at the forefront of democratization movement in South Korea.[32]

Evangelicalism versus State Shintōism

In evangelicalism's conflict with modernity, its nemesis was a secular worldview, which was corrosive of the beliefs that the evangelicals held dear. Though modernity's threats were real enough, its challenge was limited mainly to the realm of ideas. So long as evangelicalism remained alert, it stood a fair chance of repulsing modernity. In contrast, the challenges that evangelicalism received from two other nemeses—Shintōism and communism—went beyond the realm of ideas. In these cases, the nemeses were outright hostile, bent on subduing and denaturing evangelicalism. Thus in the confrontation with State Shintōism and communism, what was at stake was the very survival of evangelicalism.

State Shintōism was a form of Japan's traditional Shintōism especially valorized by the founders of Meiji Japan, who sought to make it the ideological underpinning of their state.[33] At first, State Shintōism was a phenomenon confined solely to Japan. But as their empire expanded, the Japanese imposed it also on the peoples they colonized, such as Taiwanese and Koreans, to further integrate their empire. When such imposition came to bear on evangelicalism, conflict was inevitable.

It was in the 1930s, the decade when Japan seized Manchuria (1931) and invaded China (1937), that the governor-general clashed head-on with evangelicalism over Shintō ceremony. The initial occasion of this clash was a conference of educators in the northern province of P'yŏngnam, called forth by the provincial governor. No doubt in adherence to the governor-general's policy, the provincial governor sought to impose Shintō ceremony on school pupils. At the outset of this conference, held on November 11, 1935, the governor asked all the participants to join him in paying obeisance to P'yŏngyang's Shintō shrine. At this request, most participants obliged, but three Christian principals balked.[34] Thereupon, the governor, who had probably expected such a response, affected a great show of indignation and ordered the three objectors to submit to him in sixty days a report of their personal views and their schools' policies regarding the Shintō ritual. He added the caveat that should the principals fail to submit a satisfactory report, they would risk the revocation of their teaching credentials and the closure of their schools. Eventually, one of the objectors—a Seventh-Day Adventist missionary—submitted to the Japanese demand. But the other two—both Presbyterian missionaries—refused; they lost their teaching licenses and were harried out of the country.

Soon, whether or not to observe Shintō ceremony in Christian schools became an acute controversy among Christians in Korea. At first, most Christians—missionaries and Koreans alike—opposed the imposition, especially the Koreans, to whom the ceremony did not seem to differ much from the ancestor worship that they had to relinquish in order to become Christians.[35] As the controversy evolved, however, the community became divided over the issue. On the one hand, many thought it better to suffer the closure of their schools rather than submit to what they felt was idolatry. On the other hand, many others thought it better to accept at face value what the governor-general had claimed about the Shintō ceremony—that it was merely a patriotic act—and submit rather than to close the schools, since, they argued, Christian influence was a desideratum at a time when unwholesome forces inundated Korean society.[36]

In the end, these contrasting views played themselves out to their logical conclusions, with the denominations either submitting to Shintō worship or closing their schools. For the Catholics, the matter was taken out of their hands, as, on March 25, 1936, the Vatican declared that the Shintō ceremony was a civic act, not a religious one.[37] The Methodist Church also went along with the governor-general's demand; in June 1936, J. S. Ryang (Yang Chusam), general superintendent of the Korean Methodist Church, made known his desire to comply with the governor-general's policy.[38] The Episcopal Church, the Holiness Church, the Seventh-day Adventist Church, the Salvation Army, and the United Church of Canada also complied.[39]

In this conflict, it was the Presbyterians who most vigorously opposed Shintō worship and consequently suffered most of the closures. When the controversy first arose, the leaders of the Northern Presbyterian mission attempted to work out a compromise with the governor-general. But when that failed, in May 1938 they settled on closing all their schools. The Southern Presbyterian mission was even more adamant about noncompliance, having begun to close all its schools in July 1937. The third Presbyterian mission in Korea, that of Australians, also closed all its schools in January 1939. By the beginning of 1939, all schools that remained open in Korea adhered to the governor-general's policy.

Confident that it had the schools under its control, the governor-general sought to further strengthen its Shintō policy by wresting from the Presbyterian Church—the lone institutional recalcitrant and by far the largest Protestant group—the official sanction for the Shintō ceremony.[40] Conflict was inevitable. The governor-general chose the twenty-seventh general assembly of the Korean Presbyterian Church—to be held on September 10, 1938, in P'yŏngyang's West Gate Church—for his showdown with the denomination. Even before the general assembly was held, however, the governor-general had made some headway, since by that time, seventeen of the twenty-three Korean presbyteries had already agreed to allow certain forms of Shintō ceremony for their members. But since nothing less than absolute compliance was satisfactory, the governor-general resorted to a variety of stratagems to ensure that the forthcoming Presbyterian assembly would not render any resolution in opposition to Shintō worship. First, well before the date of the assembly, the governor-general directed the police to summon each Korean delegate to the assembly. Brought to the police station, the delegate was told to make one of three choices: (1) attend the assembly and vote for Shintō worship, (2) attend the assembly and remain silent when the motion came up, or (3) not attend the assembly.[41] Some commissioners refused all three and sought to attend the assembly anyway, but they were arrested en route and jailed till the assembly was over.[42] The missionaries, too, were not neglected. On the day before the assembly, the government-general assembled all the missionary representatives at the P'yŏngyang police station. There the police warned them against interfering in the scripted procedure of the assembly, insisting that the assembly was a Korean affair in which the missionary had no proper role.

On September 10, 1938, the day of the general assembly, the meeting room was packed. One hundred ninety-three representatives attended, but there were twice as many policemen. At the conference table, on either side of the delegate sat a plainclothesman. Fifty or so policemen—uniformed and armed with a sword—stood guard at the rear and sides of the room.[43] When the motion to validate Shintō ceremonies was proposed, the moderator, following the script, attempted to ram it through, refusing any discussion. Some missionaries rose to challenge the legality of such a move, only to be shouted down by the police. When one of them, Bruce F. Hunt, became insistent, he was unceremoniously pushed out of the room. Finally, the proposal was passed with a lame voice vote, the voice for objection not even mentioned.[44] This way the proud Presbyterian Church, too, was bludgeoned into accepting Shintō worship.

Soon after the twenty-seventh assembly, the governor-general gained additional leverage over the Korean church by virtue of the Religious Bodies Law, which the Japanese Diet enacted in March 1939. This enactment gave the government-general the authority, among other things, to decide when and where religious bodies could assemble and what religious beliefs could be propagated.[45] After the enactment of these laws, the governor-general made detailed demands on the Korean church. Korean Christians were forced to sever their relations with international organizations. Thus, in 1938 the Korean YMCA, the Korean YWCA, and the Korean Sunday School Association terminated relations with their respective international bodies.[46] In 1940 the Japanese army seized the Methodist Seminary in Seoul and billeted its troops on it; in 1943, they did the same with Chosen Christian College (formerly operated by the Northern Presbyterian mission), declaring it an enemy property.[47]

Under these circumstances, it was scarcely possible for the Koreans and missionaries to maintain a normal relationship. As Donald N. Clark writes, "The kindest thing a Westerner could do for his Korean friends in 1940 was to avoid them. Police surveillance was intense, and many foreigners had full-time detectives assigned to report on their every move. These detectives made themselves conspicuous at the gates of foreigners' houses explicitly to discourage Koreans from coming to visit."[48] By the time Japan launched into a full-scale war with the United States by bombing Pearl Harbor on December 7, 1941, most missionaries had left Korea; the few who remained were imprisoned and then traded for Japanese nationals in an exchange of civilians.[49] In 1942 the Korean church fully under its grips, the governor-general compelled the outright closure of the three denominations known for their emphasis on the second coming of Christ: the Holiness Church, the Seventh-day Adventists, and Tonga Christian Church (precursor of Korean Baptists). Then, to cap it all, on June 25, 1945, the governor-general abolished all Korean Protestant denominations and reduced the Korean Protestant churches to the Korea division of the Japanese Christian Church (Ilbon kidokkyo Chosŏn kyodan).[50]

The period from September 1938 (the month of the twenty-seventh general assembly of the Presbyterian Church), to August 15, 1945 (Korea's liberation from Japan), was the harshest that evangelicalism endured under the Japanese rule. During this time the government-general set about systematically perverting the religion. It abolished all holidays, including Sunday, allowing only an hour or two for worship. Hymnals were bowdlerized to remove any reference to spiritual freedom or mention of Jesus as the "king of kings," since that would amount to lèse majesté against the emperor.[51] It disallowed portions of the Bible, especially the prophetic books such as Daniel and Revelation. It outlawed key Christian beliefs like the final judgment and the second coming of Christ.[52] Every church worship had to open with a Shintōistic ritual, which included singing the Japanese national anthem, giving a pledge of allegiance (kokumin seisi), bowing to the emperor's palace (kyujo yohai), and praying to the Sun Goddess (mokto). In this latter phase of the Japanese captivity of the church, every Christian church was compelled to install within it a small Shintō shrine (kamidana).[53]

With the institutional church now reduced to an instrument of Japanese colonial policy, if Korean church leaders retained their positions, they could not escape from doing at least some amount of collaborative work with the Japanese. Many church leaders did retain their positions and were adroitly used by the government-general. They were forced, for example, to renounce their ties with the missionaries, by making statements like, "We are resolved to set ourselves free from the past principle of reliance on Europe and America and establish a purely Japanese Christianity."[54] They were also exploited for a variety of war efforts, such as helping to collect church bells to be melted down for scrap metal, raising funds to purchase fighter planes for the Japanese navy, and urging young Korean men and women to fight and die for the Japanese emperor.[55]

On the other hand, even as there were collaborators, there were others—though fewer—who resisted the Japanese imposition till the end. When the Shintō shrine issue arose in the 1930s, Christians all over the country resisted the Japanese demand. These resisters came from both the leadership and the rank-and-file of the church. Though found in just about every denomination in Korea, they were especially numerous in the Presbyterian Church. Among them, the most famous was Chu Kich'ŏl, minister of the Sanjŏnghyŏn (Presbyterian) Church in P'yŏngyang.[56] At the time of the controversy, Chu was a noted preacher. This made him a special target of the Japanese police. Chu, however, refused to submit and, in the end, died in prison of the torture wounds he had received there.[57] Two other prominent resisters were Pak Kwanjun, a Presbyterian elder, and An Isuk, a dismissed woman schoolteacher. In February 1939, Pak and An went to Japan to lobby government officials to reverse the Shintō worship policy. When their efforts failed, they, along with Pak's son Yongch'ang, managed to sneak into the meeting of the Japanese Diet on March 22, 1939. When the diet passed the fateful Religious Bodies Law, Pak shouted, "This is the great message of Jehovah God" and threw onto the floor an envelope containing a letter that warned of the grave judgment that Jehovah would bring upon Japan if the government did not repeal its Shintō worship policy.[58] Their action caused a pandemonium in the diet and became a cause célèbre in Japan and Korea. The elder Pak and An were immediately arrested, taken to Korea, and imprisoned. An survived to rejoice in liberation, but Pak died soon after his release, owing to the torture he had undergone in prison.

In addition to individual acts of resistance, there was also organized resistance against Shintō worship, especially among Christians in the South Kyŏngsang Province, under the leadership of Han Sangdong. and among the Korean Christians in Manchuria, under the guidance of Pak Ŭihŭm and Bruce F. Hunt.[59] In both of these cases, the resisters formed pacts not only to oppose Shintō worship but also to undermine church bodies controlled by compliers. All these resisters, however, were relentlessly pursued and persecuted by the Japanese police. When liberation came, some two thousand of them were languishing in prison and more than fifty others had died.[60]

The Japanese occupation of Korea was costly for evangelicalism. Not only did it sully the church's integrity and lead to the death of many of its best leaders, but it also engendered a deep dissension among Korean evangelicals. By oppressing and exploiting the church, the Japanese had divided the Korean evangelicals, especially the leaders. In the years immediately following the liberation, in a development reminiscent of what occurred in North Africa in the aftermath of the Decian and Diocletian persecutions, the surviving resisters—the confessors—insisted on a purification of the church.[61] They demanded that the "lapsed" clergy undergo a period of atonement before continuing their pastoral roles. The compliers, however, rebuffed them, insisting that they had endured hardship to keep the church open under the oppressive regime.[62] In the end this issue failed to achieve a satisfactory resolution, partly owing to the eruption of the Korean War. One of its results was the formation of a new denomination: the Koryŏ Presbyterian Church, established on September 11, 1952, mainly by resisters who refused to unite with the compliers.[63]

Consequently, the South Korean Protestant Church—like other institutions of the society—remains conflicted over the legacy of collaboration.

From the perspective of Korean nationalists, evangelicalism's record during the last decade of Japanese rule was at best ambiguous. To be sure, through the defiance of resisters such as Chu Kichŏl, Han Sangdong, and others, evangelicalism had stood up against the Japanese Empire. On the other hand, many Christians not only blemished their faith but went out of their way to collaborate with the oppressor.[64] All things considered, however, even this ambiguous record was something of an achievement. When it came to openly facing up to the oppressor in Korea at that time, no other institution or group of people (comparable to evangelicalism) had even an ambiguous record; they all had prostrated before the military might of the Shintōist nation.

After liberation, Korean preachers tendentiously retrieved their history under the Japanese. In their sermons, they played up the heroic deeds of their confessors and martyrs—hardly mentioning those who had collaborated with the Japanese rule. In the North, the evangelicals' more-nationalistic-than-thou attitude could be (and was) challenged by the communists, many of whom had waged guerrilla warfare against the Japanese.[65] But in the South, where communism had become something of a bugbear, not many were in a position to confront such an attitude. There evangelicalism's nationalistic credentials could only be strengthened.

EVANGELICALS VERSUS COMMUNISTS

It was already mentioned that in the late 1940s a large number of Christians in northern Korea were forced to flee their homes to escape communist repression. Though the period preceding and during the Korean War was the most violent phase in evangelicals' conflict with communists and leftists in general, the origin of this conflict traces back to the 1920s.

Korean communism was born of economic and political causes. During the Japanese occupation, Korea's traditional socioeconomic division between landowners and peasants worsened. In large part owing to the new Land Reform Act, more and more wealth fell into the ownership of a small portion of the population, and an increasing proportion of the masses was reduced to peonage.[66] This, coupled with the political deprivation and wrenching economic depression that had prevailed for most of this period, rendered Korea a fertile ground for the socialist ideas brought to Korea by exiles returning from Russia and Manchuria and by Japanese migrants, especially students.[67] Moreover the great powers that met in Versailles in June 1919 to end World War I had ignored the March First Movement and refused to recognize the Shanghai Provisional

Government. These developments disappointed many Korean independence leaders and persuaded them to turn away from capitalist powers and toward the new communist power that was emerging in Russia.[68] Among a number of socialist groups that sprouted up in Korea during this period, one developed into the Chosŏn Communist Party in 1925.[69] This party, along with kindred leftist groups, vigorously reached out to the Korean populace. By 1930 it had made significant inroads into Korean society, especially among the youth. This trend was noted by a missionary who stated, "From every source I hear of socialistic thinking among the young people. Next to the desire for education, socialism takes the greatest place in their thought. . . . The names of Marx and Lenin are on every tongue."[70]

In the 1920s and 1930s the relationship between evangelicals and leftists was more complex than it might have appeared when seen through the anti-communist lenses of post-1953 South Korea. For one thing, socialism appealed to a number of important church leaders. One of them was Yi Tonghwi (whom we met in chapter 1, imploring parents to send their children to Protestant schools in Kanghwa Island). He worked closely with missionary Robert Grierson as a revivalist itinerating northern parts of the country. Yi was famous as much for his passionate advocacy of Korean independence as for his emotional preaching. Another was Yŏ Unhyŏng, onetime assistant to missionary Charles Allen Clark and well-regarded evangelist (*chŏndosa*)of Sŭngdong Presbyterian Church in Seoul.[71] By 1917 both of them had left Korea. In 1918 Yŏ was in Shanghai, carrying on independence activities among Koreans in the city; Yi was in Khabarovsk, Russia, where on June 25 he founded the first Korean Socialist Party (Hanin sahoedang).[72] After the March First Movement in 1919, both men were present at the founding of the Shanghai Provisional Government and assumed important roles, especially Yi, who was elected prime minister. By January 1921, Yi had changed the name of his group to Korean (Koryŏ) Communist Party.[73] For a time Yi and Yŏ may have collaborated as leaders of the Korean Communist Party. In 1922 Yŏ attended the Congress of Far Eastern Laborers in Moscow. In the 1920s and 1930s the two men continued their independence activities, moving mainly among communist circles. Though never completely cut off from Christian groups, the two men more and more drifted away from Christianity toward communism; however, it is not clear whether either of them had renounced his Christian faith.[74] Another point worth noting is that in the 1920s and 1930s, evangelicals did not deem communists to be entirely incompatible with them, if their mutual goal was working toward achieving Korean independence. This was attested in 1927 in the formation of the Sin'ganhoe (New Shoot Society), a broad independence-movement organization that included both leftists and rightists. Until it was dissolved in 1931, owing to the communists' reluctance to continue it, many an evangelical played a key role in it, including Yi Sŭnghun, Cho Mansik, and Yi Sangjae, who served as the organization's first president.[75]

Though the relationship between evangelicals and leftists in the 1920s and 1930s was somewhat ambiguous, persons such as Yŏ Unhyŏng and Yi Tonghwi were exceptions, as was the short-lived cooperation between evangelicals and communists in the Sin'ganhoe. Most evangelical Koreans and missionaries had a low opinion of communists; "infected with the Communistic, anti-Christian virus" was the way a missionary principal characterized a student who had written scurrilous remarks about his Korean Christian teacher.[76] The communists generally reciprocated in kind. Most of them, in keeping with Marxism-Leninism, viewed religion as superstition (at best) and an opiate of the people, and missionaries as forerunners of imperialism.[77] They felt duty-bound to attack religious establishments and their proponents, and evangelicalism was their prime target. They had at least two specific reasons to attack evangelicalism. First, evangelicalism tended to be politically conservative: as long as the ruling power did not infringe on its religious activities, evangelicalism supported it. Second, there was an indisputable link between Korean evangelicalism and religious establishments in America; the communists saw that link as a channel through which the United States, an imperial power, sought to delay the liberation of the Korean proletariat.[78]

During the Japanese occupation the governor-general had harshly suppressed communism, so a large-scale conflict between communists and evangelicals did not erupt. Nevertheless, conflicts that did occur in this period engendered a great deal of antagonism between the two groups and lay the groundwork for the larger conflicts that would flare up after liberation. Before liberation, much of this antagonism was found in schools, where leftist youths often acted as provocateurs. As one missionary wrote, "The general secretary of the Christian Endeavor Society tells me the opposition to Christianity increases markedly during the high school course; by the third year they are hard to reach. The reason he assigns for this is the influence of socialist students among their classmates."[79] Outside schools, the leftists' attacks on evangelicals were more overt. They included the disruption of revival meetings—especially those led by Kil Sŏnju and Kim Iktu—and the 1925 killing of Korean ministers itinerating in Manchuria.[80]

The conflict between evangelicals and leftists continued unabated during the interim between liberation and the Korean War. It was especially fierce in northern Korea, where the communists, backed by the Soviets, were in control. Early conflicts erupted when northern Christians attempted to establish their own political parties to counter the emerging communist regime. A case in point is the conflict surrounding the Christian Socialist Democratic Party (Kidokkyo sahoe minjudang). It was in September 1945 that this first Christian political party was founded in Sinŭiju, northern Korea, on the initiative of Yun Hayŏng and Han Kyŏngjik (Han Kyung-Chik). Although it was initially called the Christian Socialist Democratic Party, it soon changed its name to the Socialist Democratic Party (Sahoe minjudang), or SDP, to have a broader appeal. With northern P'yŏngan Province as its base, the SDP rapidly spread to other areas of northern Korea, with a church in each district serving as its headquarters.

As the SDP expanded, however, it was seen as a threat and attacked by the communists. On November 16, 1945, for example, evangelicals were holding a rally in the town of Yongamp'o, near Sinŭiju, to celebrate the founding of an SDP branch. In the middle of the celebration, they were attacked by hundreds of communist-instigated metalworkers from a nearby plant. SDP's headquarters in Yongamp'o (Cheil Church) was wrecked, a church elder was beaten to death, and twelve other Christians were seriously injured.[81] A week later, enraged by the Yongamp'o incident, five thousand evangelical youths of Sinŭiju attacked the communist headquarters in their town. The youths were quickly put on the defensive, as they were fired upon by machine-gun-wielding soldiers on the ground and a Soviet fighter plane from above. When the melee subsided, about twenty to fifty of the instigators, mostly teenagers, lay dead. Alarmed by the incident, the Soviet commander of northern Korea quickly imposed martial law on the city and arrested SDP leaders, thus sounding the death knell of the party.[82]

On November 19, 1946, Kim Hwasik and several other Christian leaders attempted to found another Christian political party, known as the Christian Freedom Party (Kidokkyo chayudang), but the party never got off the ground. Communist authorities arrested the planners the night before the party's inaugural day.[83]

The political party most widely known to be affiliated with evangelicals during this period was the Chosŏn Democratic Party (Chosŏn minjudang), or CDP, founded on November 3, 1945, under the leadership of Cho Mansik, an evangelical Christian with strong nationalistic credentials, having served as head of the southern P'yŏngan branch of the Committee for the Preparation of Korean Independence.[84] This party was favored by the propertied and professional classes in northern Korea. According to Bruce Cumings, "Christians joined the CDP exclusively, and most of them were from landed backgrounds."[85] The party, however, was no real competitor to the Korean Workers' Party (Chosŏn nodongdang). Founded in August 1945, it soon fell under the control of Kim Il Sung, who enjoyed the backing of the Soviet army. Kim saw Cho's

CDP more as a tool than a competitor and sought to use it to help implement and legitimate his policies. But Cho was hardly a pushover. In January 1946, he opposed a plan to place Korea under a five-year foreign trusteeship before it was granted full independence—a plan favored by Kim and the communists. Cho was summarily sacked and replaced by Ch'oe Yonggŏn, a Kim supporter.

Such turns of events led many evangelicals to drop out of the CDP and migrate to the South. The evangelicals' southern exodus increased after March 1946, when the regime carried out land reform that allowed landowners to keep only a limited tract that they themselves could farm. The rest was confiscated and distributed among former tenant farmers.[86] The law also forbade churches to own properties or collect offerings; by 1949, all the Christian schools had been nationalized.[87] These measures infuriated most evangelicals. On the other hand, a minority of evangelicals embraced them. Charles K. Armstrong notes that in 1946 they "organized into a North Korean Christian League (Puk Chosŏn kidokkyo yŏnmaeng)" led by a Presbyterian minister, Kang Yanguk, "who (not coincidentally) was the cousin of Kim Il Sung's mother, Kang Pangsŏk [sic]."[88] This league was supported by the northern regime, and the Protestants who did not join it were barred from participating in important meetings of the church. At the time of its formation, about one-third of the Protestants joined it, but by March 1950, owing to appeasement, coercion, and the endorsement of a few prominent ministers such as Kim Iktu, most northern Protestants had joined it.[89]

Given the communists' resolve to revamp the northern society, and the evangelicals' largely middle-class background and equally adamant resolve to secure the fundamental points of their religion, it is not surprising that additional clashes occurred between these two groups in the North. One such incident, involving a Christian praxis, revealed the ideological nature of the conflict. In 1946 the regime announced an election of regional committee representatives, to be held on November 3, a Sunday. It demanded that Christians participate. This insistence posed a dilemma to the church. For as long as Korean evangelicals controlled church affairs, they practiced Sabbatarianism, eschewing secular activities on Sundays. Thus for them to yield to the communist demand meant violating this cherished practice, an important mark of their identity. They also saw the demand as a direct challenge to their authority. To deal with the problem, evangelical leaders of the North submitted a special appeal to the regime, asking it to either reschedule the election or exempt the Christians from participating. Part of the appeal read:

> Our 2,000 churches and 300,000 Christians, for the preservation of the faith
> and the progress of the church, have approved the following five principles

for the governance of the church and as rules for Christian living, and wish to inform the People's Committee of them, hoping for their kind cooperation: (1) keeping the Sabbath holy is vital to the church; the church cannot participate in activities other than worship on the Lord's Day; (2) politics and religion must be kept separate; (3) maintaining holiness in the chapel is a natural duty of the church; a chapel cannot be used for any purpose other than worship; (4) if an acting minister enters politics, he must resign his office in the church; (5) the church maintains its freedom for faith and assembly.[90]

The petition failed to change the regime's plan, and the election proceeded as scheduled. On election day, despite their attempts at refusal, many Christians were forced to vote, often under physical threat.[91]

As the communists solidified their control of the North, it became increasingly difficult for evangelicals to live there. Consequently thousands of them fled to the South, constituting a significant portion of those who left the North between 1945 and 1953. Figures on the southward migrants are at best estimates, especially with respect to evangelicals. The number of all Koreans who migrated southward between 1945 and 1953 is estimated at between 1,014,000 and 1,386,000—about 10.7 to 14.7 percent of the average population (9,440,000) in northern Korea between 1946 and 1949.[92] Kang Inch'ŏl estimates that in 1945 the number of northern Protestants was around 200,000, about 2.1 percent of the population.[93] Of them, he estimates that 70,000 to 80,000 might have migrated to the South, constituting 35 to 40 percent of the Protestant population in the North and 6 to 7 percent of all northerners who migrated.[94]

In the South, northern evangelical refugees became a force to reckon with. They zealously evangelized and built churches. In 1950 alone, they were responsible for 90 percent of the two thousand or so newly established churches in the South.[95] Especially zealous were the Presbyterians. Their stronghold had always been in the North, in P'yŏngyang, but by the end of the Korean War a great many of them had migrated, constituting one of every four Presbyterians in the South.[96] The northern Presbyterian refugees went on to build some of the largest and most influential churches in the country—including the Yŏngnak (Youngnak) Presbyterian Church (which in 1971 had a membership of twelve thousand, making it the largest Presbyterian church in the world) and the Ch'unghyŏn (Choonghyun) Presbyterian Church (one of whose elders, Kim Young Sam, became president of South Korea in 1992). From the 1950s to the 1970s, northerners led the church growth movement in the South, not only in the Presbyterian Church but in all the churches of evangelicalism.[97] In the process, they assiduously espoused their anticommunist sentiments, widening and deepening a sentiment that had already found a home among the southerners.[98]

Between 1945 and 1950, South Korea was also a scene of conflict between leftists and evangelicalism. In the South, however, it was the Christians who had the upper hand. There the occupying force was the United States Army Military Government in Korea, which was anticommunist and favorably disposed toward Christians. The evangelicals' position was also strengthened by the USAMGIK's support of the rightist faction of Syngman Rhee, a Methodist elder who on August 15, 1948, became the first president of the Republic of Korea. Backed by the USAMGIK and the rightist regime, southern evangelicals became active in national politics. On October 5, 1945, the USAMGIK appointed eleven Koreans as administrative advisers; of these, six were evangelicals. Of the thirteen bureau chiefs appointed by the military government between December 1946 and August of the following year, seven were evangelicals, all of whom had studied in the United States. And of the fifty Koreans appointed to the highest positions in the USAMGIK in 1946, thirty-five were evangelicals. Throughout the American military government's rule in Korea (September 1945–August 1948), around 10 percent of the key posts were assumed by Korean evangelicals. Moreover, Kang Inch'ŏl finds that during the Syngman Rhee administration (August 1948–May 1960) over 39 percent of the top posts were held by Protestants.[99] These figures, as Kang notes, are extraordinary, given that after liberation the number of Protestants in the South was about 100,000, or about 0.6 percent of the southern population in 1945, which was estimated to be around 16,136,000.[100]

In the South, evangelicals also took the lead in campaigns against communists. They staged rallies denouncing communism and used force when necessary to undermine leftist activities. Evangelicals, indeed, were deeply implicated in rightist terror that took place on both sides of the thirty-eighth parallel. Among the most notorious rightist groups was the Northwest Youth Association (Sŏbuk chŏngnyŏndan), named for the area where most of its members hailed from, which happened to be the center of Korean evangelicalism. The association was formed in November 1946 and dissolved in December 1948. On February 24, 1947, when the North Korean Christian League sought to establish a southern branch, three hundred youth led by the Northwest Youth Association made sure the meeting was broken up and the leaders arrested.[101] This was probably one of the milder activities carried out by the association. According to Bruce Cumings,

> The Northwest or *Sŏbuk* Youth . . .was a nasty but classic example of terrorist reaction, pure and simple. Most of its members were recruited from

dispossessed refugee families fleeing the northern revolution, it was purely negative in its direction, and it shamed the Korean people. It was the main shock force in the slaughter of thousands of people on Cheju island [when residents rose up in April 1948 to oppose the South-only election by which Syngman Rhee became president] . . . and was hardly less constrained in other parts of southern Korea.[102]

Chang Pyŏngwuk—who is favorably disposed toward the association in his book 6.25 Kongsan namch'im kwa kyohoe [The Church and the June 25th Communist Invasion of the South]—states that the organization was formed in the Seoul YMCA.[103] And Kang Inch'ŏl, in a careful analysis of the group, shows that evangelicals dominated the organization's leadership.[104]

During the war, one of the most infamous incidents of rightist violence occurred in the town of Sinch'ŏn, an evangelical stronghold in the Hwang-hae Province in northern Korea. After achieving the famous Incheon landing on September 15, 1950, General Douglas MacArthur and his United Nations troops began rolling back communist forces. Taking advantage of this reversal, evangelicals who had been lying low in Sinch'ŏn rose up on October 10, taking their revenge on the communists who had been delayed in evacuating. In a rampage that lasted for fifty-five days, they avenged the deaths of their relatives and friends who had been slain earlier by communists. It is not clear how many died in the carnage, though an estimate of thirty-five thousand has been suggested.[105] What is certain is that the lion's share of the killings was perpetrated by evangelicals, causing Chang Pyŏngwuk to lament,

> The problem is that in this process [of rising up,] Christian youth, who made up a significant part of the commando group, played an enormous role, making us doubt our own eyes and ears. . . . At this time, we must once again raise the theological question of whether war and faith are separate things. In other words, could a believer offer death to an imprisoned person simply because he possessed a counter ideology?[106]

This tragedy will not easily be forgotten, thanks in part to Hwang So-kyong's novel Sonnim (The Guest)—the guests being Marxism and Christianity.[107]

The leftists committed their share of atrocities against Christians. One of their victims was Ethel Underwood, a missionary to Korea and wife of Horace H. Underwood (son of the famous pioneer missionary). She was shot to death on March 17, 1949, by a communist youth who used to attend the mission school where she had taught. Earlier, in October 1948, a leftist rebellion occurred in southern cities of Yŏsu and Sunch'ŏn, led by renegade officers of a

South Korean army regiment based in Yŏsu.[108] The leftists, most of whom were indigenous to the region and not under Kim Il Sung, were dissatisfied with the southern regime for its failure to make land reforms and purge the government—especially the police—of colonial remnants. For about a week they took control of the region around the two towns and attempted to institute a socialist regime. In the process, they carried out a bloody purge against whomever they suspected of standing in their way. Christians and South Korean officials became their prime targets. By the time the uprising was quelled, three thousand or so had been killed, many of them evangelicals.[109]

Two years after the Yŏsu rebellion, the peninsula was engulfed in a full-blown war, intensifying the conflict between communists and Christians. When the Korean War was over, 1.5 to 4 million Koreans from both sides had perished, and 4.83 million were estimated to have been injured or to be missing, making it one of the most destructive wars of the twentieth century.[110] Though their own hands were not free of blood, Christians incurred great losses. Chang Pyŏngwuk, using data gathered by various Christian organizations, approximates that in the South the war totally destroyed 263 churches and partially destroyed another 700. In terms of human losses, at least 202 Protestant ministers and seminarians were verified to have been killed or kidnapped to the North.[111] The total number of Christians who perished in this war is hard to come by, but it is certain to run into many thousands.

The unavailability of such information, however, has not deterred Korean evangelicals from harboring strong antagonism toward communists. There were enough authenticated cases of communist atrocities in which Christians—along with others (typically South Korean government officials)—suffered cruelly. In the county of Okku in North Chŏlla Province, for example, seventy-three of seventy-five members of the Wŏndang Church were massacred by communists.[112] In P'yŏngyang, communists dug cavernous holes in the ground and buried alive ministers, elders, deacons, and other Christians along with hundreds of other citizens.[113] In Hamhŭng, Christians and other civilians were dumped into three wells, which were then covered with lids, causing all of them to drown.[114] In Wŏnsan, about five hundred people, including city officials and Christians, were put in a bomb shelter, shot, and buried.[115] There were many more of such instances.

By the time the war ceased, upwards of 40 percent of northern evangelicals, or 80,000 of them, had fled southward.[116] The remaining evangelical community was at the mercy of a hostile communist regime. It is difficult to tell what exactly happened to that community after 1953. By all accounts, it seems to have been thoroughly repressed.[117] In the 1980s the North Korean regime adopted a new policy toward Christians in particular and religions in general. As a result, in 1988 the Pongsu (Protestant) Church and the Changch'ung (Catholic) Church were constructed in P'yŏngyang, with the state providing the land and northern Christians providing a collected offering. In 1992 another Protestant church, the Ch'ilgol Church, was constructed, largely to commemorate the memory of Kim Il Sung's mother and maternal grandmother, who were evangelical Protestants.[118] As for North Korea's religious population, *Wŏlgan choguk* (Monthly Fatherland), a pro–North Korea journal based in Japan reports that as of August 2004 around 40,000 belonged to recognized churches. These were Protestants (13,000), Tonghak adherents (13,000), Buddhists (1,000), and Roman Catholics (3,000).[119] With the construction of a Russian Orthodox church in P'yŏngyang in 2006, there is now also a handful of Orthodox Christians in North Korea.

Korean Christians used to call P'yŏngyang the Jerusalem of Korea. After the war, that was no longer possible. P'yŏngyang now became the center of another kind of religion—centering on Kim Il Sung, the son of an evangelical woman.[120] Thus, since the Korean War and the bifurcation of Korea, to speak of evangelicalism in Korea is to speak of evangelicalism in South Korea.

Like the Japanese occupation of Korea, the Korean War was a traumatic and epochal event for the Korean people. The war led to the formation of North Korea and South Korea. It also led to the development in each Korea of a collective sentiment that distinguished it from the other. In North Korea, anti-imperialism (more specifically, anti-Americanism) has become a prominent part of that sentiment.[121] In South Korea, at least till the middle of the 1980s, anticommunism was the predominant ideology. Since North Korea is a totalitarian society, it is difficult to ascertain to what extent its anti-imperialism is based on genuine popular sentiment and to what extent it has been manufactured through the state propaganda. Much of the anticommunist sentiment in South Korea, to be sure, came about due to state propaganda.[122] Nevertheless, a great deal of it is deeply and genuinely rooted in the collective sentiments of the South Korean populace—at least among the generation that had experienced the war, the generation that would fill the megachurches and crowd the revival meetings of the 1960s onward.[123] And evangelicalism, by virtue of having opposed communism and suffered preponderantly at its hands, coalesced with these sentiments, enabling it to emerge after the war as a preeminently South Korean religion.

Introversion and a Tradition of Korean Revivalists

Between 1920 and 1953, as sociopolitical conflicts engulfed Korea, it was inevitable that they would affect the development of evangelicalism in some qualitative way. Before 1920, evangelicalism was best characterized by its activist mood, the spirit to reform individuals and through these reformed individuals to remake society and reclaim the nation's political independence.[124] Even after 1920, with the evident failure of the March First Movement to free Korea, this public-minded spirit was not entirely spent. Vestiges of it lived on into the 1920s and early 1930s in various temperance, educational, and economic self-sufficiency movements that the Protestants led and in which they partook. By then, however, there was a shift in the emphasis of these movements. With the possibility of achieving political independence remote at best, these public activities now focused more on strengthening the moral and cultural prowess of the Korean nation—now conceived mainly in cultural rather than political terms.[125]

But even with such a change in orientation, these public movements could not proceed far before they were stifled by the totalitarian powers that held sway over the country. The Japanese (and later the North Korean communists) had no intention of allowing evangelicals or any other group to cultivate an autonomous public space. Prevented from meaningfully engaging in the nation's public life—in its social and political spheres—evangelicalism perforce turned inward, giving rise to a highly private and introversive mood.

Many a missionary understood and empathized with what the Koreans were going through. Thus one of them wrote: "Other avenues for national expression, such as politics and commerce, are largely closed to them. The people of Korea are reaching inward and upward to satisfy the craving of the soul."[126] Another noted, "There is a general feeling of pessimism even among many of the staunchest and most faithful Korean Christians." Yet another missionary, in an article on Korean farmers, observed:

> The study of Korean village life is not a cheerful business. From whatever angle we look the prospect seems hopeless. This is not on account of any world depression, it is a chronic condition. The farmer is proverbially a growler, but few farmers can have such cause to complain as the Korean, who is often so poor that he can't afford to eat even the rice he grows. He sells it and buys cheaper and coarser grain, eking them out with wild grasses and roots. Starvation is never very far from the door. Few farmers work their own land, prices are so unfairly high that independent farmers are becoming fewer every year. Rent, taxes, seed, tools, and labour take more than half the yield from each tiny farm. . . . Even the pride of nationhood is denied, and every year thousands leave their native land to seek a better fortune as farmers in Manchuria or as labourers in Japan. . . . Is the situation, then, utterly hopeless? Some villagers will tell you that they have been given a new hope in recent years. "Are rents, then, coming down? Is there

some new and cheap kind of fertiliser to improve the crops? Have you found a remedy for smallpox or measles?" we ask; but they reply, "No, there is still no hope for any of us in this evil world; but we have learnt that if we believe in Christ we shall be saved from our sins and shall receive everlasting life when we die, and in Heaven with Jesus we shall be compensated for all our present miseries. This is even likely to happen before we die, for isn't Jesus coming again soon?" This is the implicit hope of many a simple Christian in the Korean villages. For them Christianity offers no real hope for this life, whatever the missionaries may teach; their eyes are on the beyond. Experience has taught them that any hopes for this life are vain.[127]

If introversion was the general mood of Korean evangelicalism in the second quarter of the twentieth century, it follows that this mood would be reflected in the revivals of the period. Revivals continued to be a significant and regular aspect of the church life in this period—that is, at least till 1939, before the passage of the Religious Bodies Law and the restriction of the church's activities. In the planning and implementation of these revivals, the missionaries continued to play a significant role. By 1920, however, more than a generation had passed since evangelicalism was brought to Korea, and a sufficient number of Koreans had risen to the leadership of the church, assuming its day-to-day operations.[128] Thus in matters pertaining to revivals, too, Koreans figured in prominently.

Among many Koreans who actively evangelized in this period, three stood out: Kil Sŏnju (1869–1935), Kim Iktu (1874–1950), and Yi Yongdo (1901–1933). At the time, these three were the most famous and influential preachers in Korea. Moreover, they were the first big-time Korean revivalists, whose combined achievements laid the groundwork for the rise of an indigenous revivalist tradition in Korea. Among the three, Kil and Kim—both Presbyterians—were first-generation Korean Protestants, their heyday as revivalists coming in the early and mid-1920s. Yi, a Methodist, was a generation younger, and his peak years stretched from 1928 until his death in 1933, due to illness. To understand the mood of Korean revivals of the 1920s and 1930s, it is by and large sufficient to examine the piety and works of Kil, Kim, and Yi, because of their predominant influence in the period.

As products of their time, all three men shared in the conflicts and mood of the period. Each of them came into conflict with one or more of the nemeses of evangelicalism: modernity, Japanese colonialism, and communism. In addition, they all shared in the introversive mood that pervaded Korean evangelicalism at the time. They all regarded the world as a wicked place, to be endured rather than transformed. And they all concentrated their efforts to foster private dimensions of the faith. Given this common ground, they nevertheless differed in the way they reflected or expressed the introversive mood. In Kil, this mood was most distinctively expressed in his millenarianism. In Kim and Yi, it was just as distinctively expressed in the former's faith healing and the latter's bent toward spiritualistic mysticism.

Kil Sŏnju: The Millenarian

In one of his posthumously published works, Kil Sŏnju summed up the gist of his piety: "The second advent of Christ is the target of our faith and the province of our hope."[129] Like William Miller and other revivalists of the millenarian bent, Kil set little store by the things of this world. What was real and meaningful to him was the Parousia that would wipe away the wrongs of the present world and establish in its stead a new heaven and a new earth. Kil's millenarianism (premillenarianism, to be exact) derived from varied sources. One was the inherently millennial disposition of his religion; another was the pessimistic reality of the Korean society of his time.[130] Yet another was certain events in his early life.[131]

Born on March 15, 1869, in Anju, southern P'yŏngan Province, in what is now North Korea, Kil was the second son of a military official, a *yangban* in the dilapidating Chosŏn dynasty. A precocious child, Kil began learning classical Chinese from his mother at the age of four, and at eleven, in accordance with the *yangban* custom of the period, he married an older girl (by five years). In his early teens, because he was perceptive, Kil held some minor bureaucratic positions.

In 1885, when Kil was sixteen years old, the home of his extended family in Anju was viciously attacked by three brothers of another family who had been harboring a grudge against Kil's older brother. This attack proved traumatic to Kil; he was almost killed in it, and whatever idealistic, if not naïve, notions he had about life and the world were shattered. Shortly, Kil developed a strong loathing toward the world, becoming quite withdrawn and pessimistic.

This state of affairs worsened a year later when he experienced a failure in business. Upon the suggestion of his wife, Kil sought healing in a variety of religious and quasi-religious practices (most of them stemming from Buddhism, Taoism, and Shamanism). Eventually, he became adept at these practices and succeeded in putting his trauma behind him. By this time, Kil had become deeply immersed in religiomagical activities and was searching for some extraordinary means to deal with the corruption and confusion within his society. His pessimism toward the world, however, remained.

Given such a disposition, when Samuel A. Moffett arrived in P'yŏngyang in 1893 to preach the gospel, Kil was naturally attracted to him. Kil consulted the missionary about the new doctrine he was propagating; he also introduced the missionary to some of his friends. At this stage, Kil's interest in Christianity was merely intellectual; when a friend of his, Kim Chongsŏp, converted and suggested that Kil convert too, Kil became angry. Kim's conversion had a deep impact on Kil, however, motivating him to read a variety of Christian literature, including a Korean translation of John Bunyan's *Pilgrim's Progress*. In 1896, at the age of twenty-eight, Kil underwent a deep conversion experience, in which he thrice heard the voice of God calling him.[132]

After conversion, Kil became a new man. He cut off his topknot, a daring thing to do in the still-Confucianist Korea of the 1890s; received formal baptism (1897); and actively helped establish churches in P'yŏngyang and elsewhere. In 1901 he was elected one of the first Presbyterian elders in Korea, and in 1903 he began studying for the ministry. In 1905 he and his friend Pak Ch'irok initiated daybreak prayer meetings, which soon became a hallmark of Korean evangelicalism. During the great revival in 1907, Kil served as an active lay evangelist, working closely with Lee and Blair, and in July of that year he was ordained one of the first seven Korean Presbyterian ministers. When the Independence Movement broke out in 1919, Kil was a signatory to the Declaration of Independence along with fifteen other evangelicals, and he spent two and a half years in prison for it.

In his forty or so years of ministry, Kil was a preeminent revivalist and church leader who often became embroiled in conflict with accommodationists and leftists. He is estimated to have preached about twenty thousand times to a total of about 3.8 million people, baptized more than three thousand people, and founded more than sixty churches.[133] Kil was also an avid Bible reader. A missionary friend of his noted, "He read the Old Testament through from Gen. to Mal. thirty times and from Gen. to Esther more than five hundred times. He read the entire New Testament more than a hundred times and he memorized the Revelation and recited it several thousand times."[134]

For Kil the millenarian, his involvement in the Independence Movement was pivotal. Though his otherworldly disposition was clear before March 1, 1919, it was during his imprisonment for having taken part in this movement that he solidified and systematized his millennial views, which were published in his posthumous collection.[135] A few years after his release from prison, Kil resigned from his pastorate and devoted the rest of his life to being a revivalist.

In Kil's preaching and revivals, the Parousia and the millennium became central. This was especially the case during the fourteen years of his itinerancy after being released from prison, when he devoted about 90 percent of his preaching in daybreak services and morning Bible studies to the suffering of

Christ and the eschaton.[136] In his revivals, Kil told the audiences that though it was not possible to date the return of Christ exactly, one could validly make an approximation of it by reading signs of the times. And that return, Kil warned—based on his own reading of the signs—was not far off. He calculated, without claiming certainty, that the Parousia would occur in 1974.[137] To Kil, the March First uprising itself was a sign of the impending end, for how could such a massive movement take place right under the eyes of the Japanese unless it was God's way of warning the world of the impending doom that awaited it?[138]

Kil's enthusiasm for the Parousia was not shared by the Japanese, who discountenanced anything that smacked of subversion against their this-worldly empire. Ineluctably, Kil conflicted with the police. One account, for example, describes an incident that occurred after his imprisonment for taking part in the independence movement: "He was holding an evangelistic service in Andong in 1929, teaching the Scriptures relative to the end of the age and telling of the sufferings that were due to come on the world at that time; he was arrested by the police and locked up for twenty days as a disturber of the minds of the people."[139] Imprisonment, however, hardly deterred Kil from preaching about the impending doom. He continued to do so until November 26, 1935, when he died of a stroke after giving a benediction in a revival service.

Kim Iktu: The Faith Healer

The belief in the millennium, like that of Kil's, is one that is ultimately grounded in the Bible, especially in the books of Daniel and Revelation. This belief has had a special appeal to the adherents of evangelicalism, since they have tended to be biblical literalists and since the homology between the conversion of the individual and the millennium (the conversion of the world) is apparent to them.[140] Moreover, like any deeply held belief, millenarianism has an independent dynamic that cannot be reduced to a set of socioeconomic factors. Thus throughout the history of evangelicalism, there have been numerous instances of believers professing ardent millenarian views even in relatively undisturbed times, often to the extent of selling their worldly possessions in preparation.[141] On the other hand, it is also true that the millenarian impulse of a religion gains more currency when the adherents of the religion are alienated from the establishment, when they feel unjustly repressed and prevented from meaningfully participating in the larger society—as was the case with the Korean evangelicals of the 1920s and 1930s.

Much the same could be said about faith healing. Like millenarianism, faith healing also has a biblical warrant—for example, the healing acts of

Jesus in the Gospels. And those who practice faith healing are not limited to a particular socioeconomic stratum, just as its beliefs and practices cannot be reduced to a set of sociohistorical circumstances.[142] On the other hand, faith healing is especially valorized by those for whom the supernatural is real, for whom the sacred is just as meaningful as the secular, if not more so; and this was the outlook of most Koreans of the 1920s and 1930s. With regard to a religious community, faith healing becomes particularly significant when that community is forced to turn inward, to focus its attention on the individual rather than the public. This was true of the Korean evangelical community of the 1920s, when—even as Kil was pronouncing his millennial prophecies—Kim Iktu attracted thousands of men and women into his revivals, whose most distinctive feature was faith healing.

Kim was born on March 1, 1874, in the village of P'yŏngch'o, in the Hwanghae Province of northern Korea, to a déclassé *yangban* parentage. His father set him up at an early age to be trained in classical Chinese literature, in preparation for the traditional civil examination. But Kim's father died when he was thirteen years old. Nevertheless, in 1890, at the age of sixteen, Kim set out to Seoul and took the examination along with hundreds of other scholars, most of whom were much older than he was. He failed the examination. Though deeply disappointed, Kim promptly returned home and began a new career as a merchant, marrying at the age of eighteen. Like Kil, however, business was not his forte; he failed as a merchant, losing most of the capital he had started out with.

This second failure drove Kim into despair, leading him to contemplate life's meaning and death. In his existential search, Kim for a while became involved in Taoism and Ch'ŏndogyo, neither of which ultimately satisfied him. Unable to shake off his angst, he became dissolute, attempting—unsuccessfully—to find contentment in the stupor of a drink or the company of *kisaeng* (entertaining women). In January 1900, hearing that an exotic Westerner, W. L. Swallen, was going to preach in Korean about a new religion at a church in Anak, Kim attended the service. Moved by Swallen's preaching on eternal life, Kim decided to become a Christian.

After making this decision, Kim felt that his faith was not strong enough to resist the temptations present in his native village, so he moved with his family to another village. While visiting another town, however, Kim ran into some of his old drinking friends and could not refuse their offers of drink. In the midst of drunken merriment for old times' sake, he was overwhelmed by a strong compunction and bolted out of the party. After walking more than ten miles in tears and ashamed repentance, Kim arrived home and fell on the floor of his room, whereupon, in a half-conscious state, he experienced a ball of fire falling upon his chest.[143] Later, Kim pointed to the experiences of that night as the true turning point—the conversion—of his life.[144]

After this experience, Kim became a resolute believer. In July 1901 he was baptized by Swallen and went to Chaeryŏng to teach at a church-run school and to work as an evangelist. There he experienced his first instance of faith healing, by restoring to health through prayer a woman who had lost her conscience.[145] In October of the same year, hired as Swallen's colporteur, he went to Sinchŏn and founded a church. There he performed another act of healing by restoring through a weeklong prayer a woman who was believed to have been possessed by a shamanistic spirit. In 1906 Kim enrolled in the Presbyterian Theological Seminary, graduating in 1910. Shortly thereafter he was ordained a Presbyterian minister and formally installed in a Sinchŏn church in 1913. While serving this church, Kim also itinerated as a successful revivalist. In October 1919, while leading a Bible-study revival, he was deeply moved by the words of Mark 16:17—"And these signs will accompany those who believe"—and concluded that the miracle of healing was possible even in his (i.e., post-apostolic) times.[146] To verify this for himself, upon his return to Sinchŏn, Kim—by prayer and the laying on of hands—sought the healing of a woman who was suffering from a grave illness. When she was healed, Kim became even more convinced of his conclusion.

In comparison with Kil, who was a magisterial preacher, Kim was somewhat unpolished. Yet he was so effective an evangelist, especially to the lower classes, that the missionaries dubbed him "the Billy Sunday of Korea."[147] Kim's success as a revivalist began in the latter half of 1910s and continued throughout the 1920s. His peak year came in 1920, when he was elected moderator of the Presbyterian assembly and also led series of revivals in some of the major cities in Korea, each of which attracted thousands of people. Harry A. Rhodes, a Presbyterian missionary, captured the atmosphere of one such meeting in Seoul:

> In accepting an invitation to come to Seoul in 1920, he was undertaking something more difficult than for Billy Sunday to go to New York or Chicago. Mr. Kim is a homely man, and sometimes uncouth in manner and speech. . . . And yet he conducted the most largely-attended series of evangelistic meetings ever held in the capital. The meetings began in the auditorium of the Central (Seungdong) Presbyterian Church, but soon the pulpit was moved outside to the steps of the church. It was estimated that the crowd inside and out often numbered from six to seven thousand people, and there was no loud speaker except the evangelist's voice which soon became husky. Each morning six hundred and more attended the day-

break prayer meetings. A still larger number attended the prayer service and Bible study hour each day. At one evening meeting an offering of seventeen hundred and fifty yen was received. (At that time a yen was equivalent to about fifty cents.) The offering included two hundred finger rings, twenty silver watches, two gold watches, two hundred silver hairpins, suits of clothes, bridal ornaments, etc.[148]

In all of his revivals, Kim's chief goal was the same as that of any other revivalist: saving souls. On the other hand, there was no question that the most conspicuous and magnetic aspect of his revivals was faith healing. Thus Rhodes wrote, "One reason why the 'Kim Ik Tu Meetings' throughout the country attracted attention was because of his custom of praying for the sick and for the demon-possessed. The report went out that he was performing miracles. For several years large numbers of the sick and demon-possessed were taken to his meetings."[149]

Many, perhaps most, of the sick whom Kim prayed for were not cured. This led some missionaries and Koreans to question his claims of healing.[150] Despite such skepticism, Kim had healed enough of the sick that his reputation as a healer held. In fact, during his heyday as a revivalist, some believers became so taken with his healing ministry that they formed an Association to Verify Miracles (Ijŏk chŭngmyŏng-hoe). This association was composed of 167 ministers and laymen from all over the country, including a well-known doctor, and it set out to authenticate Kim's healings by interviewing and examining those who claimed to have been healed by him. The result of their investigation was published in 1927 as Ijŏk chŭngmyŏng-sŏ (Record of Verified Miracles).[151]

Despite the support Kim received from this association and others, he never lacked critics. They came not only from the ranks of skeptics within the church but also from the secularists. On May 9, 1922, for example, the influential newspaper Donga ilbo (Tonga ilbo), which once had expressed wonderment at Kim's healing, accused him of spreading superstition.[152] But his harshest and sometimes violent critics came from the political left, which regarded him as epitomizing the superstitious mentality that impeded Korea from moving forward to a more rational society. In February 1926, for example, while he was leading a revival in Kando (the Manchurian region near the northern border of Korea), Kim and other Christians, including a missionary, were clubbed by a group of leftist youth. And on May 21 of the same year, in a series of lectures sponsored by a group of leftist intellectuals, Kim was severely castigated as being nothing more than a high-class shaman.[153] Perhaps because of these controversies, in his revivals from 1930 onward Kim did not emphasize faith healing.

In the last decade of his life, Kim became mired in additional controversies. In 1940, while in Sinŭiju for a revival, he and his company were arrested and made to pay obeisance to a Shintō shrine. After liberation, in November 1946, Kim joined the procommunist Christian Alliance, perhaps coerced and cajoled, and in 1949 he became its assembly chairman. His inability to resist the Japanese and the communists, irrespective of the circumstances, derogated from his reputation, causing Korean evangelicals to feel ambivalent about him. This ambivalence remained unabated by October 14, 1950, when, while worshiping in his church in Sinchŏn, Kim was shot to death by a retreating communist soldier.[154]

Yi Yongdo: The Revivalist with a Mystical Bent

Despite the controversies that followed him, Kim Iktu was a popular revivalist well into the 1930s, as was Kil Sŏnju. Moreover, by the late 1920s, both Kim and Kil—and the beliefs and practices associated with them—had become a well-established presence in Korean evangelicalism. Despite their prominence, however, during the five years from 1928 to 1933, neither Kim nor Kil had pride of place in Korean evangelicalism. In that period, that status belonged to another revivalist, Yi Yongdo.

Yi represents yet another type of introversive piety that came to the fore in Korean evangelicalism in the second quarter of the twentieth century. Like Kil, Yi believed in and longed for the millennium, and also like Kim, though to a much lesser extent, Yi was known to have a healing touch. Yet it was neither millenarianism nor faith healing that distinguished Yi from his senior revivalists. His distinctiveness lay in having a piety that decidedly tended toward spiritualistic mysticism.

Yi was born on April 6, 1901, to poor peasant parents in a village in Hwanghae Province in northern Korea. Yi's mother was a devout believer, but his father was not and often became drunk and persecuted his family for their faith. (Later in his life, however, he too converted.) Under his mother's influence, Yi became a faithful churchgoer and attended mission schools.

While Yi was in secondary school, the March First Independence Movement erupted, and at once he became an ardent participant. Apprehended by the police in 1919, he endured two months of imprisonment. Despite this, he did not desist from engaging in independence activities. On three other occasions, he was captured and incarcerated, spending a total of more than three years in prison. By the time Yi had graduated from secondary school in 1924, nine years had passed, and he was already married.

After graduation, upon the suggestion of A. W. Wasson, a Methodist missionary and the principal of the secondary school, Yi enrolled in the

Methodist Theological Seminary. In his second year at the seminary, however, Yi contracted tuberculosis. In the winter of 1925, to nurse this disease, he and his friend Yi Hwansin visited the latter's hometown in Kangdong in southern P'yŏngan Province. Upon their arrival, Yi and his friend were asked to hold a revival by local believers who were unaware of Yi's illness. Though reluctant, and mainly because they felt inadequate, the two seminarians could not decline the request. To prepare themselves for the revival, Yi and the friend spent nearly two days in prayer on the frozen surface of the nearby Taedong River.

On the first night of the revival, it was decided that Yi Hwansin would preach, with Yi Yongdo presiding. But before the sermon could be delivered, Yi, while presiding, was overwhelmed by emotion and began weeping uncontrollably. Seeing this, and touched by it, the rest of the congregation also wept. Throughout that night and the following night, when Yi Yongdo led the meeting, the revival was characterized by tears, united vocal prayer, and repentance. To Yi, what he experienced in that revival was a turning point. Until then, though he had considered himself a faithful Christian and had enrolled in the seminary, he had lacked the burning baptism of the Holy Spirit. With the Kangdong experience—bolstered by the knowledge that his tuberculosis had gone into remission there—all that changed. Yi was now certain not only of his salvation but also of his calling as God's minster.[155]

Upon graduation from the seminary in 1928, Yi was sent to a small church in T'ongch'ŏn, in Kangwŏn Province. After nearly one year of ministry there, he had a spiritual experience in which he saw supernatural visions; he had another visionary experience in the following year, and still more were to come. In part empowered by these experiences, Yi became a potent preacher. His church of fifty to sixty people tripled in membership, and his reputation as a preacher spread. He now received constant invitations to lead revivals throughout Korea and Manchuria.

For five years, from 1928 to shortly before his death in 1933, no other revivalist in Korea equaled Yi in the ability to draw and move people. Partly this appeal was due to his reputation for living a Francisesque life—he often gave away his belongings to the needy and lamented his inability to give more.[156] But there was no doubt that the chief reason for Yi's success as a revivalist was his highly emotional yet penetrating preaching. When Yi was on the pulpit, he frequently would simply break down and weep—as he had done in Kangdong—causing the others to weep also. When he was in control of his emotions, he preached powerfully, as was observed by his missionary friend and admirer Victor Wellington Peters:

He was now at his zenith [in 1931]. To have followed him to all his meetings would have been more than human flesh could stand. Even to write
an account is impossible. He was like lightning over the thirteen provinces
of Korea and even into Manchuria, and he burned a deep impression upon
the hearts of the people everywhere. There was something magnetic about
his preaching that never failed to draw crowds. Admirers followed him
sometimes hundreds of miles. I remember well a dramatic scene in one of
the Seoul city churches. It was a Sunday morning, the closing of a pro-
tracted meeting in the spring of 1932. Simeon [Yi's pen name] read from
the Scripture the account of Jesus' triumphal entry into Jerusalem, and then
preached a sermon that for mingled pathos and glory was unforgettable.
"This was the first time in all their lives," he began with touching sympathy,
"that these people had a chance to cry, 'Hosanna to their king.' They were
wrong; His was not an earthly kingdom. Yet we cannot despise them for
their enthusiasm. If I had been there, I, too, would have cast my coat under
His feet and waved my palm branch and shouted, 'Hallelujah.' The English
and French and Americans have their countries to love, and even away from
their native land, can meet at their legations and stand on a bit of their soil
under their own flag. The Japanese have their armies to rally about." . . .
"Yes," he lifted his voice in climactic power, "yes, and we Christians, too,
have a flag, a war. When I am up till midnight or later and rise again at
three, I have no time for taking off my belt; I am always girded for the
battle." Then catching the sight of the collection bags lying in front of the
pulpit, he exclaimed, "They are a pitiful people who have never paid taxes
into the treasury of their own country. In time past we were not a people,
but are now the people of God, a holy nation called out of darkness into
His marvelous light. Ignorant country people do not understand what their
taxes go for; but we know ours are in gratitude, unspeakable gratitude and
thanksgiving, for salvation and life and love. Oh, how happy we! To have a
heavenly kingdom and here to pour out our offerings to our King."[157]

If this was a sermon born of political deprivation and if Yi's heavenly
country was functional compensation for the Korea that no longer belonged
to Koreans, Yi's commitment to his faith was genuine enough. Upon ordination, not only did Yi withdraw from political involvement and become an
active revivalist, but he also leaned toward mysticism. In attempts to define
mysticism, a number of salient attributes have been adduced.[158] Of these, with
respect to Yi's piety, it is that of nuptial unity that was most clearly discernible.
The nuptial aspect of his piety, for example, could be discerned in the following entry from his diary:

I am the bride and the Lord is my groom; I find no joy in anyone but him. Most desirable are the face and the words of the Lord. Sometimes the Lord's words are sternly pointed, yet I prefer it to the sweet and soft words of the worldly. There may be fragrance in the hand of the worldly and a switch in the hand of the Lord, yet I will go to the bosom of the Lord.[159]

And the unity aspect of Yi's piety could be detected in another of his entries:

Thus I was attracted to the Lord, the Lord to me; and we formed one. I came to swallow the Lord's love, and the Lord came to swallow my faith; and, in the end, I came to be in the Lord's love, and the Lord came to be in my faith. Oh, how profound is the way of unity! Oh, my eyes, look at the Lord, single-mindedly look at the Lord. Glancing aside not even for a moment, look only at the Lord. The Lord who is captured in my sight will settle within me. Oh, my eyes, look at the Lord single-mindedly. Will the Lord move away? So that He will not move away, let us look only at him.[160]

As Yi became more mystical and charismatic, his piety evolved beyond what was conventional in Korean evangelicalism, exhibiting spiritualistic tendencies. That is, Yi increasingly preferred the authority of his own inner experiences over that of the creeds or ecclesiastical norms. Moreover, finding the institutional church to be soulless, divisive, and worldly, he castigated it.[161] Also going beyond the pale of convention was Yi's concept of spiritual indwelling, his belief that God might dwell in just about anything—man, woman, even a cloud or a donkey—in which case the words originating from it should be adored.[162] This unconventional tendency of Yi's was noted by Peters: "Here was the very marrow of his mysticism. With an unbounded faith in the power and leadership of the Holy Spirit, he was ready to credit any manifestation. He would not presume to curb or guide; the Spirit must be given free rein, he felt. Hence, he was apt to see even prudence as a frustration of the Spirit."[163]

Given Yi's spiritualistic inclination and Korean evangelicalism's structural orientation—in which enthusiasm was valued only if it did not contravene the church order—it was inevitable that Yi would clash with the established church. Thus just as Yi accused the church of being soulless, the church accused Yi of being irregular—for holding prayers in the dark, impugning other ministers, promoting Non-Church Christianity (which Yi denied), freely corresponding with female believers, and disrupting affairs of some churches where he led revivals.[164]

In October 1932 an incident occurred that gravely damaged Yi's reputation, relegating him—in the eyes of the church leaders—from the category of the "irregular" to that of the "heretical." Yi for some time had been associating with a group of Christians who were deeply immersed in Swedenborgianism and were even more spiritualistic than he was. This group, which church authorities had suspected of heresy, included some noteworthy individuals such as Paek Namju, a theologian, and Han Chunmyŏng, a linguist; it also included a number of women who claimed to be spiritual mediums. In one of their gatherings, a medium by the name of Yu Myŏnghwa fell into a trance, and through her, a voice, claiming to be divine, spoke to Yi, insisting that he pay obeisance to it. Though hesitant at first, Yi succumbed to the voice and dropped to his knees.

When this incident became known, the church leaders were scandalized. For though Yi insisted that it was the divine voice, not the woman, that he had paid homage to, what had occurred was all too shamanistic to most church leaders. Yi was roundly denounced; many of his friends abandoned him. In November 1932, Yi, along with Han, Yu, and other spiritualists, were judged as heretics by the P'yŏngyang Presbytery of the Presbyterian Church, and in the following month one of the leading Christian newspapers *Kidoksinbo* condemned him as a modern-day Jezebel. In March 1933, Yi was suspended from ministry by the Korean Methodist Church.[165]

Alienated from the church as a heretic in the eyes of most church leaders, Yi was courted by his spiritualistic friends in January 1933, as they planned to establish a church of their own. Though reluctant at first—he loathed to be divisive—he eventually joined them in forming the Jesus Church (Yesu kyohoe), becoming its first superintendent on June 6 of that year. Within several months, however, Yi had become exhausted. The controversies and grueling itinerancy had taken their toll, and his tuberculosis relapsed. His condition worsened, and on October 2, amid his family, Yi breathed his last, at the age of thirty-two.

More than sixty years after his death, Yi Yongdo remains an enigmatic figure. Through research and interpretations by scholars such as Min Kyŏngbae (Min Kyoung-bae) and especially Pyŏn Chongho, Yi's contributions to Korean evangelicalism have been acknowledged.[166] However, though it is unlikely that a Korean evangelical of the twenty-first century would call Yi a Jezebel, he may yet balk at Yi's absorption in spiritualism. Yi thus remains a Janus-faced figure, on the boundary between orthodoxy and heterodoxy in Korean evangelicalism, a boundary fraught with conflict.[167]

Korea between 1920 and 1953 was a crucible of conflict in which evangelicalism intermixed with modernity, Japanese imperialism, and the Korean War. In the end, however, when the conflict abated, evangelicalism survived. Not only that, the conflict had remolded evangelicalism, rendering it more introversive in mood and firmer in its bond with Korean society. Another significant development in this period was that the leadership of the church was transferred from the missionaries to Koreans. A vivid indication of this transfer was the prominence of Korean leadership in the planning and implementing of revivals, giving rise to a Korean tradition of revivalists. The beginnings of this tradition could be traced to the great revival of 1907, when native exhorters worked with the missionaries to fan revival fires. Even in this period, Kil Sŏnju was an outstanding evangelist. But it was during the 1920s and 1930s that Kil, Kim Iktu, and Yi Yongdo (despite his later estrangement) firmly established it. These three revivalists flourished at the time when evangelicalism was forced to renounce its activity in the larger society. They still made the religion meaningful to the faithful—by directing them to see its power and glory in the millennium, in the miracle of healing, and in the indwelling of the spirit.

Even after 1953, the influence of these three revivalists would persist. By then, however, there would be some crucial changes in the scene. In South Korea at least, the restraints that had prevented evangelicalism from participating in public life were removed. Evangelicalism could again be active in public. But it would not be active in the way it was at the turn of the century. Now the key word would not be "reform" or "introversion." It would instead be "growth"—growth in the number of saved souls and in the size of churches.

CHAPTER 3

Evangelicalism Takes Off in South Korea, 1953–1988

> The success of the revivalists could be made very tangible and
> nicely measured merely by counting ministers, churches, and
> converts. . . . Dwight L. Moody was to declare that it makes no
> difference how you got a man to God, just so you got him there.
> —Sidney E. Mead

From the great revival of 1907 till the onset of Japanese repression, the rapid growth of evangelicalism in Korea had continually elicited enthusiasm from the international Protestant community. The first non-Koreans to express such enthusiasm were the Korea missionaries themselves, whose success could rarely be matched by other missionaries anywhere, anytime. Thus if David Brainerd, an eighteenth-century missionary to Native Americans—in his moment of anguish for lack of success—could not refrain from belittling the Indians as "brutishly stupid and ignorant of divine things," James S. Gale, a Northern Presbyterian missionary and one of Brainerd's spiritual descendants in Korea, incisively stated, "Politically she [Korea] is nil, but in the missionary circle she is a first-rate power."[1] Elsewhere, the rapid growth of evangelicalism in Korea was eagerly touted by the "missionary statesmen" who were at the forefront of the "evangelization of the world in this generation" movement.[2] Thus even as early as 1897 Robert E. Speer, secretary of the Board of Foreign Missions, Presbyterian Church in the U.S.A., commented on the missionary development in northern Korea: "In the North, the church has spread and penetrated, as we saw nothing to surpass anywhere else in the world. The churches are crowded; the opportunities are unlimited." In 1907 John R. Mott, winner of the Nobel Peace Prize in 1946 and head of the Student Volunteer Movement for Foreign Missions for thirty-one years, stated, "I know of no mission field where larger or more substantial results have been secured, in proportion to the expenditure, than in Korea." Two years later another influential mission leader, Arthur J. Brown, of the Foreign Mission Board of the Northern Presbyterian Church, reported glowingly on the growth of evangelicalism in Korea: "Every year it has seemed that the movement must have reached its climax and that there would certainly be a reaction; but every year has seen the movement broadening and deepening until it now looks as if Korea would be the first of the non-Christian nations to become evangelized."[3]

To evangelize Korea—to make Korean evangelicalism yield results by converting each and every Korean—had been the aim of foreign missionaries like Underwood and Appenzeller, as it had been the dream of native evangelists like Kil Sŏnju, Kim Iktu, and Yi Yongdo. To be sure, as long as North Korea remained communist, this dream had to remain just that, a dream. But if not all of the peninsula could be saved (at least not yet), then surely those who were "free" could and must be saved—not only for the sake of their souls, which would otherwise be lost forever, but also for the benefits that would accrue to a nation composed entirely of born-again Christians, such as prosperity, moral harmony, international recognition, and security against communism.

After the Korean War, such, in brief, were some of the assumptions and goals held by many Korean Protestant leaders.[4] During the three and a half decades that followed the Korean War, these leaders worked diligently to attain their goals. As historian Sidney E. Mead observed with regard to the revivalists in the United States, Korean evangelicals too usually expressed their success in numbers.[5] Judging by this criterion, they had done quite well, proving themselves to be worthy legatees of the great revival of 1907.

From 1950 to 1988, Korean evangelicalism underwent remarkable growth. In 1950 it claimed at most 600,000 adherents (2.9 percent of the total population). By 1960 that figure had increased to 1,257,000 (5 percent); by 1970, to 2,197,000 (7 percent); and by 1979, to 4,868,000 (13 percent). By 1985 the number of evangelical adherents had risen to 6,489,000 (16 percent).[6] This meant that from 1950 to 1980 the number of Protestants in Korea roughly doubled just about every decade, and from 1950 to 1985 the growth was more than tenfold. Moreover, by the middle of the 1980s, Korean evangelicalism had become a record holder in a number of categories of church growth. As of 1981, for example, according to church growth expert Peter Wagner, it had the fastest-growing congregation in the history of evangelicalism as a whole: the Hallelujah Church in Seoul, whose congregation shot up in six months from 6 people to 700.[7] By 1984, Korean evangelicalism not only had the world's largest single church—Yoido Full Gospel Church (Yŏŭido sunbogŭm kyohoe), with 350,000 members—but also had the world's first- and second-largest

Presbyterian churches—Yŏngnak Presbyterian Church (60,000 members) and Ch'unghyŏn Presbyterian Church (19,730). By 1985, Korean evangelicalism also had the world's largest Baptist church—Sŏngnak (Sungrak) Church (24,000).[8] The growth of these megachurches continued, and new ones shot up, so that by the end of 1992, according to the Christian magazine *World*, twenty-three of the fifty largest churches in the world were located in Korea—including the largest (Yoido Full Gospel Church, 600,000 members), the second-largest (Nambu Full Gospel Church in Anyang, 105,000 members), and the seventh-, ninth-, and tenth-largest churches.[9]

That is not all. In this three and a half decades after the Korean War, Korean evangelicalism staged some of the largest evangelistic gatherings that had ever taken place in the history of the Christian church. Seven massive assemblies took place in this period. Though more will be said about them later, five of these assemblies reached the 3 million mark in total attendance; five of them had a single-day attendance of 1 million or more people; and in the largest single gathering, more than 2.5 million people turned out. Given such astronomical figures, it is little wonder that Korean evangelicalism continued to evoke enthusiasm from conservative Protestants around the world—such as Billy Graham, who in an evangelistic assembly in Amsterdam in 1986 echoed Gale seventy-seven years before him by referring to Korea as a great spiritual power—and has regularly hosted American conservative Protestants of all stripes, from hard-core fundamentalist Carl MacIntyre to neo-evangelical Carl Henry, from televangelist Robert Schuller to campus crusader Bill R. Bright, from church-growth pundit Donald McGavran to the ever-returning Billy Graham himself.[10]

Such development naturally gives rise to the question of how it all came about. What caused Korean evangelicalism to grow phenomenally in the years following the Korean War? To be sure, this question can be treated fully only after considering how evangelicalism became implanted and legitimated in Korean society before the end of the war. Having learned how evangelicalism contributed to both Korean nationalism and South Korean anticommunism in the preceding chapters, we are now in a position to examine more directly the political, socioeconomic, and especially religious factors pertinent to evangelicalism's rise in post-1953 Korea.

POLITICAL AND SOCIOECONOMIC CONTEXT OF EVANGELICALISM'S GROWTH, 1953–1988

However casually one surveys the development of South Korean politics from 1953 to 1988, two observations are inevitable. One is that during this period the nation's political development was extremely unstable and democracy had a difficult time anchoring in the country. This was apparent from the First Republic (1948–1960) of Syngman Rhee, whose political manipulations and autocratic ways finally provoked a student revolt on April 19, 1960, exiling him to Hawai`i; to the Second Republic (1960–1961) of Yun Posŏn and Chang Myŏn, whose inability to maintain public order provoked a military coup in May 1961; to the Third and the Fourth Republics (1963–1972, 1972–1979) of Park Chung Hee, who set the country on the path to economic prosperity but in the process subverted democracy and perpetrated severe human rights violations; and to the Fifth Republic (1981–1988) of Chun Doo Hwan, who came to power by another military coup and whose name will always be linked with the Kwangju Uprising of May 1980, in which his troops massacred citizens of Kwangju who opposed his dictatorship.[11]

A second ready observation that can be made about Korean politics in this period is that all of the five republics made anticommunism their official ideology and assiduously exploited it.[12] A glaring embodiment of such exploitation was the National Security Law. This vaguely worded law was passed in November 1948 in the wake of the leftist-led sedition in Yŏsu and Sunchŏn, and in the hands of Rhee and all his successors down to Chun, it became a hot iron by which anyone opposing their politics was branded a communist and deprived of civil liberties. In their exploitation of the fear of communism, these leaders were unwittingly aided by the northern communists themselves, who intermittently terrorized the South, for example, by kidnapping fishermen, hijacking an airplane, sending commandos to assassinate the southern president, and digging tunnels under the thirty-eighth parallel.[13]

In sum, political instability, oppressive government, and fear of communism combined to create in South Korea a tense atmosphere of unpredictability, insecurity, and stress, an atmosphere that provoked religious—more specifically, salvific—impulses. Moreover, at the time in South Korea, politics was not the only source that provoked such an impulse. As unsettling as it was, this political unease was exacerbated by the disorientation that attended a massive transformation of the nation's economic and societal structures.

In the decades following the Korean War, the South Korean economy underwent extraordinary growth. In just one generation the South was transformed from the impoverished nation familiar to many Americans as the uninviting backdrop of the *M*A*S*H* television series to a model of economic development. As Carter J. Eckert and his coauthors point out, this transformation is "a tale whose drama is heightened by breathtaking contrasts":

A per capita GNP of about $100 in 1963 versus a figure of nearly $5,000 as
the year 1990 began; a war-ravaged Seoul of gutted buildings, rubble, beg-
gars, and orphans in 1953 versus the proud, bustling city of the 1988 Summer Olympics with its skyscrapers, subways, plush restaurants, boutiques,
first-class hotels, and prosperous middle class; a country abjectly dependent
on foreign aid in the 1950s versus a 1980s economic powerhouse—a factory
to the world for everything from clothes, shoes, and electronic goods to
steel, ships, and now even automobiles and semiconductors.[14]

An economic transformation of such magnitude could not have taken
place in South Korea without significant rearrangements occurring simultaneously in the nation's societal structures. Of these structural rearrangements, one
of the most consequential was a change in the nation's demographics. Between
1960 and 1990, South Korea's rapid industrialization was accompanied by an
equally rapid urbanization. Whereas in 1960 only 28 percent of the population
was considered urban, 74.4 percent was considered so by 1990. The administrative regions considered as cities rose from 27 to 73. During this thirty-year
period, South Korea's total population grew from 25 million to 43.4 million, a
74 percent increase. But the urban population in the same period more than
quadrupled, rising from 7 million to 32.3 million.[15] As would be expected, this
urban population growth was most significantly influenced by migration from
the country, which accounted for 46.3 percent of the total increase; the next
most important factor was birth rate, which accounted for 41.4 percent of the
increase.[16]

Migrants from the countryside tended to concentrate heavily in a few
major metropolitan areas, such as Seoul, Pusan, and Taegu. Seoul and its environs were especially affected by this in-migration. In 1960, for example, the
population of Seoul was 2.6 million. By 1970, it had more than doubled, reaching 5.5 million. In this decade-long period, especially noteworthy were the
years from 1966 to 1970. During that time, Seoul's population grew by 1.73 million, which amounted to 77 percent of the population increase for the nation
as a whole. And significantly, 80 percent of Seoul's increase in population was
composed of migrants.[17] After 1970, migration to Seoul was less drastic but
nevertheless continued, so that by 1990, Seoul by itself claimed 24.4 percent
(10.61 million) of the national population. When combined with the rest of its
metropolitan region, which included the city of Incheon and the province of
Kyŏnggi, Seoul claimed 42.8 percent of the nation's total population.[18]

Such a rapid and massive urbanization had grave repercussions in Korean
society. In the countryside, it created serious shortage of able-bodied men and
women to farm the land, as Korea's rural population shrunk from 18 million to

11 million between 1960 and 1980.[19] In the cities, it led to overcrowding, traffic congestion, a housing shortage (with the attendant skyrocketing of real estate values), and a superabundance of unskilled and uprooted people in search of work. In both settings, traditional values and communal structures eroded.[20]

Thus during the three and a half decades following the Korean War, South Koreans—especially the urban dwellers—were under a great deal of stress, caused by political instability, fear of communist invasion, and societal restructuring. To deal with this stress, they needed new meaningful structures and communities for orienting themselves existentially and socially. In short, they needed salvation. According to some observers, such salvific need among so many individuals by and large explains why, for example, all of the ten largest megachurches in Korea are located in metropolitan Seoul and why Korean evangelicalism grew so rapidly after the Korean War.[21]

It is difficult to dispute the claim that people tend to become more religious in times of political turmoil, societal restructuring, and value confusion, for evidence in support of it can be readily adduced. After all, wasn't that the situation in Korea at the turn of the century when Koreans flocked to the Protestant missions?[22] The plausibility of such an assertion is bolstered by the fact that, in the aftermath of the Korean War, South Korea was a hotbed of new religious movements, including Pak T'aesŏn's Chŏndogwan (more popularly known as the Olive Tree Church) and Mun Sŏnmyŏng's Unification Church.[23]

Though societal stress in the wake of the Korean War undoubtedly stimulated the rise of religious interest in Korea, that fact alone is not sufficient to explain why evangelicalism—and not just any religion—grew exponentially in that period. In other words, it does not explain why in this period evangelicalism grew so much more than, say, Roman Catholicism—especially since the Catholic Church (or, for that matter, any other religious group) was no longer under persecution the way it had been in the nineteenth century. After the Korean War, the Catholic Church did grow significantly, but at nowhere near the rate that evangelicalism did.[24]

Thus, to puzzle out the rapid growth of Korean evangelicalism since 1953, we need to consider more than the contextual factors conducive to the rise of religious interests in general. What must also be considered are the factors inherent to evangelicalism itself that may have made the difference. In other words, we must also consider some religious proclivity unique to evangelicalism—at least in Korea in this period—that may have played the pivotal role in evangelicalism's outpacing other religions. A number of suggestions have been proffered. Some of the oft-suggested ones are Korean Protestants' diligence in prayer (especially the daybreak prayer, *saebyŏk kido*), their diligence in Bible study, the comprehensive visitations (*taesimbang*) that most Korean churches undertook annually, and the effective use of highly organized cell groups to which everyone in a church belonged.[25]

There is no denying that each of these factors played a role in the growth of evangelicalism in Korea. On the other hand, it is clear that to posit these as the main factors in the growth of Korean evangelicalism would be to set the cart before the horse, for it is apparent that these are mainly nurturing practices meaningful only to those who are already part of the church. Normally, one would attend *saebyŏk kido*, be visited by a pastor, participate in Bible study, or belong to a cell group only if one was already a believer or had at least been led to the church. Thus, more relevant for our examination of the growth of Korean evangelicalism after the Korean War are not nurturing practices but evangelistic practices, practices geared toward proselytizing.

In their effort to proselytize unbelievers, Korean evangelicals of this period relied on a variety of strategies. Some of these were time-honored ones that dated back to the great revival of 1907 and beyond—such as handing out tracts, visiting homes of unbelievers (especially those related to the believers), and holding seasonal revivals. But some other strategies were quite new. These included establishing chaplaincies in the armed forces, police departments, and prisons and using them to proselytize troops, police officers, and inmates, as well as using modern communication media such as the radio to reach the homes of unbelievers.[26] But of all these strategies, old and new, what undoubtedly stood out was the series of evangelistic campaigns—especially the massive ones—that took place in South Korea from the 1950s to the end of the 1980s.

From 1953 to 1988, especially after the mid-1960s, South Korea was the site of intensive evangelistic campaigns. To be sure, South Korea had seen evangelistic campaigns before, but only a few of those in the past had been as sustained and comprehensive as many that took place after 1953. Some of these post-1953 campaigns were merely expanded versions of traditional revivals, and some were regional in aim, seeking, for example, to proselytize the residents of a city or province. Many of the campaigns were undertaken by various denominations in efforts to expand their memberships by the centenary of the Korean Protestant Church (1984). But mixed with the traditional revivals and regional campaigns were the new massive evangelistic campaigns, national in scope and attended by millions, with an aim to evangelize not only South Korea but beyond.

These massive campaigns, being unique to evangelicalism at the time in Korea, constituted one conspicuous difference from the practices of other Korean religions of the period. They, along with smaller campaigns, played a decisive role in evangelicalism's outpacing other Korean religions in this period. Consequently, to understand the rise of evangelicalism in the post-Korean War period, it is essential that we survey and analyze these campaigns. Moreover, examining them will also afford us a window into three related developments during this period: intensification of tension between conservatives and liberals in the Korean Protestant Church, a symbiotic relationship that existed between Korean evangelicalism and Korean government, and Korean evangelicalism's decreasing tendency to depend on foreign revivalists and increasing tendency to regard itself as a chosen group.

MASSIVE EVANGELISTIC CAMPAIGNS IN SOUTH KOREA

1953-1969: "Thirty Million to Christ"

Efforts to evangelize Korea were in progress even before the Korean War ended. During the war and the years immediately following it, American revivalists—both missionaries and peripatetic preachers from the United States—played an active role. In December 1952, for example, even as the war was going on, Billy Graham held his first Korean revival in Pusan. After the war, from October 13 to 19, 1953, another Baptist preacher from America, Bob Pierce, held revivals in Taegu, to which people "swarmed like clouds." Pierce, the founder of World Vision, was one of the most active American revivalists in Korea in this period, holding his first revival in Korea in 1949 and many more after 1954.[27]

A third American Baptist active in Korea at this time was Everette E. Swanson, who took part in the most successful Korean revival of the 1950s. It was held in Seoul from March 26 to April 5, 1955, in Namsan Park Plaza. Swanson was billed as the main preacher, but it was his partner—then reputable Elder Pak T'aesŏn, with his acts of healing and claims to supernatural visions—who was the main factor in chalking up a total attendance of 600,000. The *Han'guk kidok kongbo* (Christian News) described Pak's appeal:

> These people who have gone through the Korean War have a strong will to live. And they seek to rebuild their altars even if they have to do it on top of ashes. . . . In this juncture, all over the place numerous revivalists, famous and nameless, are leading revivals and are raising the church's concern. . . . In this revival, he [Pak] reportedly healed the deaf, the lame, etc. People from just about every denomination came to Namsan and pitched tents to be part of the event.[28]

Despite his popularity, Pak was one of the revivalists who had raised the church's concern. Shortly after this revival, because Pak did not desist from flaunting his paranormal inclinations and making unorthodox claims, he was castigated as a heretic, leading him to found his own church, Chŏndogwan.[29]

After the Namsan revival, some Protestants expressed apprehensions about emotional excesses such revivals generated.[30] Yet Koreans continued to flock to revivals led by Americans and Koreans. In a revival held in Taegu from June 2 to 9, 1955, for example, a total attendance of 150,000 was recorded. This revival was led by Swanson, a second American, and a few Koreans, and it was the first revival sponsored by the newly formed Presbyterian Revivalist Organization (Ch'onghoe Puhŭngdan). In June of the same year, the organization held another series of revivals in Taejŏn, in which at least 74,000 attended.[31] On February 2, 1956, Billy Graham, en route to Southeast Asia, visited Korea for a second time. At a revival in Seoul, saying that he loved Korea as he did his own home and that only God could solve the problems of the world, Graham preached for one and a half hours, with Han Kyŏngjik translating. Graham's short revival was attended by some 80,000 people, including Syngman Rhee and his officials.[32] The 1960s began in South Korea with a violent if hopeful note as the April 19 student revolt brought down Rhee's government. It was replaced by a government led by titular president Yun Posŏn and prime minister Chang Myŏn, only to be followed by a coup d'état of May 16, 1961, that placed Park Chung Hee in power for eighteen years. During this decade, American revivalists continued to be active in Korea, as could be seen in the return of Bob Pierce for another revival in 1960.[33] Korean revivalists were also active. For example, a group of revivalists from different denominations held a unity revival on the sands of the Han River from August 11 to 20, 1961, which drew more than ten thousand people on its first night.[34] Park Chung Hee's coup was a milestone that distinguished the 1950s from the 1960s. But for evangelicalism another milestone differentiated the two decades: Korea's first massive evangelistic campaign.

"Thirty Million to Christ" was the title of this first massive evangelistic campaign held in Korea. Since the "thirty million" represented the total population of South Korea at the time, this slogan (even more so than the "One Million Movement" of 1910) represented not a realistic goal but an evangelistic spur. The idea for the campaign originated with Helen Kim, president of Ewha Womans University, but it was made possible by the cooperation of Korea's major Protestant denominations. Under the supervision of these denominations, various phases of the Thirty Million to Christ campaign were implemented in the 2,239 meetings that took place all over the country.[35]

The campaign was held for the greater part of 1965, but the main event took place in May and June of that year with the arrival of Hong Kong revivalist Timothy S. K. Chao (Cho Segwang in Korean). At the time, Chao was unknown to most Koreans, yet he had something of international repute, having been invited by the publishers of *Christianity Today* to lead a revival in West Germany with Billy Graham. Arriving in Seoul on May 1, Chao remained for forty-six days, leading more than one hundred revivals in various cities. After Chao's departure, the campaign continued for four more months, until it culminated on November 5 in a massive rally held at Seoul Stadium. In the end, the Thirty Million campaign recorded a total attendance of 2,294,159 people and resulted in 40,000 people making a commitment to believe in Jesus Christ.[36] In addition to these new believers, the campaign—coming at the time when Korean Protestantism was riven with schisms—benefited the church by promoting cooperation among the denominations.[37]

In the remainder of the 1960s, revivals continued on a smaller scale. In 1967 and 1969 Chao returned to Korea for two more revivals. In 1967 the so-called Big City Saturation campaign took place in the city of Chŏngju, with the presumed aim of reaching every citizen in the city with the Gospel message. In August 1969 a revival organized by the Nazarene Church was held at a *kidowŏn* (prayer house) in Samgaksan (Mount Samgak), with two thousand participants from various denominations.[38]

1970-1979: Billy Graham Crusade, Explo '74, and '77 Holy Assembly

The South Korea of the 1970s was characterized by intensive economic development and Park Chung Hee's dictatorial *yusin* regime. The negative consequences of these two circumstances—for example, exploitation of laborers and human rights violations—not only provoked ceaseless clashes between the riot police and student demonstrators but also stirred socially conscious members of the church into acts of protest. Many evangelicals partook in such protest, but it was chiefly led by the liberal wing of the Korean Protestant Church.[39] Though relatively small in number, these liberals worked indefatigably, organizing labor unions and protesting against the Park regime's human rights violations, and many of them suffered imprisonment and torture for their efforts.[40] Social and political activism of liberal and other Protestants constituted one of the two main characteristics of the Korean Protestant Church in the seventies. The other characteristic was a series of massive evangelistic campaigns. And if social activism was pursued most actively by the liberal wing of Korean Protestantism, these evangelistic campaigns were pursued most enthusiastically by the evangelicals, by far the larger of the two wings of the Korean Protestant Church.

For Korean evangelicalism the 1970s began as usual, with revivals. In May 1970, for example, a large revival was held in Namsan under the slogan "Return to Pentecost"; and as this revival was going on, another large one took place in Pusan. Between August 10 and 16, the Christian Association of the

City of Chŏnju held a revival on the campus of a local high school, under the slogan "Going to Jesus Christ Is Our Only Way to Survive; Let's Return to the Pentecost; Let's Evangelize the Fatherland; Let's Drive Out Communists"; 35,000 attended this event. In the same month, in Samgaksan the Men's Association of the Korean Holiness Church (Sŏng'gyŏl kyohoe) held a revival, in which more than 11,000 people participated during its first two days.[41] For the soul reapers in the Korean armed forces, 1972 was a banner year; in April, 3,127 Korean soldiers were baptized in a united baptismal ceremony.[42]

As 1972 wore on, many Korean church leaders looked forward to the next year with anticipation. For some time, these leaders, led by Han Kyŏngjik, had been planning for what they hoped would be a shot in the arm for Korean evangelicalism: a Billy Graham revival. In early 1971 some of these leaders and the staff of the Billy Graham Crusade (BGC) had held a preparatory meeting. At that time they had made important decisions regarding the upcoming crusade; for example, expenses for the event would be shared by the BGC and the Korean sponsors, with the former assuming all the expenses related to inviting and boarding Graham and other visiting speakers and the latter assuming the remaining expenses, such as renting the necessary equipment and facilities.

The official title of this event was "Korea '73 Billy Graham Crusade," but it was also called Fifty Million to Christ. Its theme was "Find a New Life in Jesus Christ." In 1973 the crusade took place in Korea in two phases. In the first phase, between May 16 and 27, a team of BGC revivalists (except Graham) held preparatory revivals in Pusan, Taegu, Incheon, Taejŏn, Kwangju, Chŏngju, Ch'unchŏn, and Cheju—Korea's largest cities after Seoul. In the second phase, from May 30 to June 3, Billy Graham himself led evangelistic gatherings at the huge Yŏŭido Plaza.

Given Graham's prominence and the success of the Thirty Million to Christ campaign, the organizers of this crusade had reason to expect a high turnout. Yet probably few of them expected the kind of turnout the crusade actually generated. In the regional campaigns alone, the crusade drew 1.36 million people, 37,000 of whom made the decision to believe for the first time.[43] But even this regional campaign was superseded by the second phase of the crusade.

The Yŏŭido Plaza at the time was a huge tract of open area (slightly larger than one and a half square miles) in Yŏŭido, a Han River islet near the heart of Seoul. Even in densely populated Seoul, this area was kept off-limits from developers so that it could be turned into an airfield in the event of war.[44] Despite its size, however, from May 30 to June 3, 1973, the plaza became the most densely populated area in Seoul, serving as the site of the most successful Billy Graham Crusade to date.

To make this crusade a success, just about all the Protestant denominations in Korea cooperated.[45] Even Park Chung Hee's government helped out, giving permission to hold the event in the plaza, temporarily rescheduling the bus routes near it, and sending its army construction corps to build a choir section big enough to accommodate a 6,000-interdenominational chorus.[46]

On the first night, the crusade drew an audience of 510,000. Impressed by the turnout and the preparatory work that had gone into the crusade, Graham predicted that the evening would be the first assembly of the largest evangelistic rally in the history of the church. The turnouts of following nights bore out Graham's prediction. On each of the first four evenings of this five-evening crusade, the turnout averaged about 526,000, and the last night's service was attended by 1.1 million people. In addition, during each night of the revival, about 4,000 people stayed up all night to pray. In all, 44,000 of the participants made the decision to believe for the first time.[47]

In this crusade, Graham delivered typical revivalistic messages, emphasizing the sinners' need to repent, to be born again, and to gain true freedom by accepting God as the sovereign of their lives. By and large, his message found a receptive audience. On the other hand, it did run into some criticism. Most liberals, for example, dismissed Graham's sermons as being too simplistic and formulaic. They concurred with L. George Paik, not a liberal himself, who opined that Graham delivered what amounted to an "Apostles'-Creed" type of sermon. Some of them also criticized Graham for failing to take a more prophetic stance—that is, for not addressing issues like democracy and freedom in Korea.[48]

In contrast to the liberals, evangelicals found no problem in Graham's messages. But they did feel dissatisfied that the whole crusade had been conducted under the leadership of foreign revivalists. They felt that Korean evangelicals should have been able to conduct such an event on their own, with their own resources, addressing their own evangelistic needs in their own tongue.[49] These two developments—liberals' criticism of evangelistic campaigns for ignoring sociopolitical issues and the evangelicals' desire to Koreanize them—and the tension created between them would surface again in subsequent evangelistic campaigns.

After the Billy Graham Crusade, the next massive evangelistic campaign to take place in Korea was Explo '74, held at the Yŏŭido Plaza from August 13 to 18, 1974. But in the fourteen-month interim between the Billy Graham Crusade and Explo '74, smaller evangelistic efforts continued. Two months after the BGC, for example, the Tenth World Pentecostal Conference was held in Seoul, with participation by more than 2,000 representatives from thirty-six nations.[50] In November of the same year, another united baptism was held in the Korean army, this time more that 1,300 soldiers receiving the sacrament.[51] And from May 29 to June 2, 1974, rallies were held in the Chŏngju Public Stadium to evangelize 1.5 million residents of Ch'ungbuk Province. Thirty thousand participated in this event daily, and 3,700 of them made the decision to believe.[52]

Explo '74 was an event sponsored and funded mainly by Campus Crusade for Christ (CCC), an American evangelistic agency founded by Bill R. Bright and devoted primarily to evangelism among college students. In Korea, CCC was established in 1958 under the leadership of Kim Chun'gon. It was during the last night of another Explo—Explo '72, held in Dallas, Texas—that Korea was proclaimed as the venue of the 1974 Explo.[53]

The theme of Explo '74 was "Jesus Revolution, the Holy Spirit's Third Explosion." The name "Explo" referred to the explosion—or dissemination—of the Holy Spirit, which the organizers believed was the only hope of the world. It was called the "third" explosion because Explo '74 would follow Pentecost and the Reformation.[54]

Explo '74 differed from its American counterpart in that it targeted not only collegians but also the general public. Moreover, Explo '74 differed from an evangelistic event like the Billy Graham Crusade in that its main goal was not only to convert unbelievers but also to train current churchgoers, so that they could be effective disciple-evangelists and, through them, individual churches could be strengthened.[55] To achieve this goal, on each day of the event the Yŏŭido Plaza was turned into a massive study camp. There participants received systematic training in the method of evangelism, which they were then expected to apply upon returning to their own churches. Despite such studiousness, however, Explo '74 hardly lacked a revivalistic atmosphere, for the nights were wholly given over to preaching and prayer sessions.

Like the Billy Graham Crusade, Explo '74's main event was preceded by series of preparatory activities. First, there were weeklong regional gatherings, in which a half million people participated. Then, on the eve of the main event, an ancillary service was held at the Yŏŭido Plaza. In it a 4,000-member united choir sang hymns, and Cho Yonggi of the Yoido Full Gospel Church preached. After the service, 100,000 women from 15,500 churches stayed up till 4:00 a.m. to pray.[56]

The next day, on August 13, the main event—a series of training sessions and evening services—started in earnest. For the training sessions, collegians and other laypeople attended classes in hundreds of tents pitched on the Yŏŭido Plaza, many of which were borrowed from the Korean army, and over three thousand classrooms that were rented from eighty or so nearby schools. During the evening services, Bright, Han Kyŏngjik, Kim Chun'gon, and other conservative luminaries preached before audiences of hundreds of thousands. Every night, 30,000 people stayed up late into the night for prayer. And a police force of 8,000 kept order throughout the event.[57]

Again, like the Billy Graham Crusade, Explo '74 was an unparalleled success. The total attendance for the six days of training sessions was 3,400 registrants from eighty-four countries and 320,000 Koreans. The daily attendance for training sessions and evening services combined averaged 1,090,000, and the total attendance for the entire event was 6,550,000. Moreover, as something unique to this event, on August 17, the penultimate day, 200,000 of the participants spread out into metropolitan Seoul to evangelize, chalking up 272,000 new believers.[58]

Though Explo '74 ended successfully, it did have its share of controversy. For one thing, unlike the Billy Graham Crusades, the Explo '74 sponsor CCC was unfamiliar to most ministers in Korea, so initially many of them hesitated to cooperate. Thus, even though Han Kyŏngjik had lent the prestige of his name to the event by agreeing to become the honorary chairman of its planning committee and openly vouched for Bright and CCC, many Korean Presbyterians were skeptical about the wisdom of "evangelizing" college students who were already churchgoers. They also feared that the event would bring confusion to local churches because the organizers had not coordinated their activities with the major denominations. Those associated with the fundamentalist International Council of Christian Churches (ICCC) were especially uncooperative, criticizing the event as a way of promoting indiscriminate commingling of strict fundamentalists with allegedly communist-influenced ecumenicals.[59]

Explo '74 was also criticized by liberals, such as those affiliated with the Presbyterian Church in the Republic of Korea and the Korean National Council of Churches, but for different reasons. For the liberals, and others who had opposed Park's dictatorial regime, 1974 had been a difficult year—many of their numbers had been arrested and imprisoned.[60] They viewed Explo '74 as a great distraction. It diverted Korean Protestants' attention away from the nation's sociopolitical ills, which they felt were the most pressing issues facing the church. Moreover, many of the liberals found some of the theological implications of Explo '74 questionable. They also regarded Explo organizers' conservatism toward social activism deplorable. Thus, for example, Mun Tonghwan, a theologian at the liberal Hanshin Theological Seminary, decried the Explo organizers' audacity to "explode" the Holy Spirit. He also castigated some of them for denouncing the civil rights movement among black students in the United States.[61]

Furthermore, for some liberals the very idea of evangelization espoused by the conservatives, and under which an event like Explo '74 was being held, was problematic. To them, evangelization, as defined by the conservatives, was not only small-minded but also irresponsible. One such a liberal, Kim Chongnyŏl, wrote:

> Even more important is the question of evangelization. I want to know the content of the Gospel that has been proclaimed in the evangelistic gatherings held thus far. I want to know what it means for an individual, a group, or a nation that has heard the Gospel, to be evangelized. What does it mean to evangelize a nation? Does that happen if every single person in the nation believes in Christ? . . . Do we succeed in evangelization if we actually succeed in turning "Thirty Million to Christ" or "Fifty Million to Christ"? Regardless of what goes on in politics, how society operates, what the economic situations are, whether or not there is corruption, whether organized forces of evil are tyrannically trampling on human rights . . . regardless of what happens to our neighbors, society, and nation if we only believe in Jesus—so that our souls are saved—has evangelization been realized? Is social justice going to be realized if we, whenever possible, compromise with the powers that be in order that we can spread the Gospel and convince a great many people to believe in Jesus? Is evangelization different from humanization? Truly, what does evangelization mean?[62]

These, to be sure, were rhetorical questions. Kim, having his own theological axe to grind, had a definite idea as to what evangelization meant or should have meant. To him, evangelization was another word for humanization. Thus he stated,

> I do not wish to think of evangelization and humanization separately. . . . Christ came to this world (i.e., he became humanized, a true human) in order to enable each individual and all of humanity to live in a manner worthy of human beings. Therefore it was while he was eradicating those factors (diseases, poverty, hatred, prejudice) that prevented human beings from living as human beings[,] . . . and while he was leading a movement to liberate human beings, that Christ was crucified.[63]

For Kim Chongnyŏl, then, to evangelize was to change society, to eliminate the structures that created and perpetuated social and economic injustice.

Obviously, no conservatives worth their salt would agree with either Kim's characterization of their concept of evangelization or Kim's own concept of it. To charge that they did not care about society—the conservatives would assert—was either to distort their position or to misunderstand how they proposed to do it. The heart of the matter, they would say, was that people, not structures, created injustice. Therefore the point of evangelization was not to change society but to change people. The typical conservative view on this matter was expressed by Kim Chun'gon: "There is the internal human revolution and social revolution; we believe that social revolution is possible [only] through human revolution." He continued, "This one thing is clear: social action does not constitute evangelism. No matter how important it is, how urgent it is, and how pleasing it is to God, it cannot constitute evangelism; that is my viewpoint, my way of interpreting the Bible on this matter."[64]

Just as the evangelicals did not agree with the liberals on the issue of social activism versus personal evangelism, they also disagreed in how they regarded the government. How far apart they were from the liberals on this matter could be surmised from the fact that even as the liberal leaders were being imprisoned for criticizing the government, the conservative leaders were regularly participating in annual presidential prayer breakfasts sponsored by the government. Indeed, in Explo '74's ancillary prayer session, one of the intercessory prayer topics was the well-being of President Park Chung Hee.[65]

By openly supporting the authoritarian government, organizers of Explo '74—and other evangelicals—appeared to be ingratiating themselves with the government. The reality, however, was more complicated than that. For one thing, between the leaders of the church and the government, much affinity existed. That the conservative leaders condoned authoritarianism in government, for example, was scarcely due to any coercion applied against them by the government. Having been grafted onto a culture that lacked a democratic tradition—on top of the inclination of a charisma-oriented religion like evangelicalism toward the authoritarian—Korean evangelicalism itself was hardly democratic.[66] Thus an author who had studied eleven rapidly growing Protestant churches in Korea observed, "A common characteristic of the successful churches is that almost none of them are so-called democratized churches."[67] Most leaders of Korean evangelicalism, in other words, tended to empathize with authoritarian leaders in the government. In addition to being similar in their authoritarianism, Korean evangelicalism and the Korean government shared a common enemy: communism. During the Korean War, as they both opposed and were opposed by communists, evangelicalism and the Korean government formed a bond, and in the years following the war, this bond was strengthened by the intermittent acts of terrorism that the communists carried out in the South. Just a few months before Explo '74, for example, North Koreans had kidnapped a number of southern fishermen off the coast, triggering fifty thousand Christians to gather at Namsan to condemn the North. And less than one week after Explo '74, on August 24, Park's highly respected wife, Yuk Yŏngsu, was killed by an assassin's bullet that was meant for Park himself. The assassin was a communist-instigated Korean living in Japan.[68]

Among evangelicals, anticommunist sentiment was pervasive. The more conservative they were, the more anticommunist and pro-government they tended to be. Thus it was a group of fundamentalists linked with ICCC that openly slandered the liberal-controlled Korean National Council of Churches, calling it a communist organization and advertising in a major American newspaper that despite what liberals had asserted, there was freedom of religion in South Korea.[69] Many more-moderate evangelicals also were not reluctant to openly express their hardened distrust toward communists. Han Kyŏngjik, the quintessential moderate, for example, noted, "Kim Il-sung, the dictator of North Korea, wants to unite South Korea [sic] under Communism. It is absolutely useless to attempt to communicate with this man. . . . [P]eaceful unification would be impossible under Communism as the ideology of South and North Korea is quite different. We want North Korea to be a nation like ours. If we want peaceful unification, we must evangelize our fellow North Koreans."[70]

Korean evangelicals' unequivocal opposition to communism and their deference to the government put them on a good footing with authoritarian leaders of the Korean government. That Park Chung Hee, for one, expected the church leaders to stay out of politics—in other words, to fall in line with his politics—was evidenced in a remark he made at the seventh presidential prayer breakfast held in May 1974. In that gathering, a minister rose to say a prayer, in which he stated, among other things, that the nation should unite around the president. When his turn came, Park spoke and warned the religionists present that they should be wary of the communists' attempt to infiltrate into their circles. He then added that there was no function as clean as a religious one, for a religious function was one in which the participants did not seek to further their self-interests or pursue political agendas—a wryly ironical remark, intended or not, since the religionists' very participation in a function like the presidential prayer breakfast was a political act that would help legitimate the government.[71]

Though the conservatives deferred to the government, the government could scarcely take them for granted. The conservatives' deference to the government was always conditional. They deferred to the government only so long as the government did not encroach on their religious prerogatives. And whenever the conservatives felt that this premise had been violated, they did not hesitate to confront the government. Thus in September 1956, when the mayor of Pusan decided to hold an election for minor city posts on a Sunday, thousands of evangelicals joined in a demonstration to change the election date.[72] And in February 1966, when a proposal was made to erect in Namsan a statue of Tan'gun, the legendary founder of the Korean nation, the conservatives mobilized their forces to oppose it, on the grounds that their taxes should not be used to build an idolatrous monument.[73] Similarly, in April 1972, when the government proposed an image of the Buddha for its new ten-thousand-won note design, the evangelicals mounted a vigorous protest to scuttle the proposal.[74]

After Explo '74, the next massive evangelistic campaign to take place in Korea was the '77 Holy Assembly for the Evangelization of the Nation. But between 1974 and 1977, smaller evangelistic gatherings continued. Partly reflecting the turbulent sociopolitical circumstances of the time, evangelistic gatherings during this interim were interspersed with church-sponsored meetings that were more political in nature.[75] From September 8 to 12, 1974, for example, Yŏngnak Presbyterian Church held a nightlong prayer for the security of the nation, attended by 3,000 people. On October 26 of the same year, Saemunan (Saemoonan) Presbyterian Church was the site of another prayer session, in which 400 youths prayed for the nation's political prisoners. On the other hand, at the Yoido Full Gospel Church, thousands of youth gathered on November 9 for the start of a five-day revival.[76] On January 4, 1975, at Chŏngdong Cheil Methodist Church a prayer gathering was held for the imprisoned ministers and for George E. Ogle, a Methodist missionary deported in December 1974 for allegedly engaging in subversive activities.[77] On January 6, 1975, the T'onghap Presbyterian Church formed its own revivalist organization.[78] On June 22 of that same year the Yŏŭido Plaza was filled with over one million Christians who had come to hold a united prayer meeting for the country.[79] From September 11 to 14, 1975, a campaign to evangelize Tajŏn city was held; it recorded a total attendance of 80,000, including 7,000 new believers.[80] From September 22 to 27 the Yu Kwansun Hall at Ewha Womans University held a revival in which 2,000 people participated nightly, and from November 5 to 8 the Sinch'ŏn Holiness Church hosted a revival in which 5,000 youths took part.[81] From July 5 to 8, 1976, the Yoido Full Gospel Church held a Korean Church Growth workshop featuring seventy leading ministers in the field; one of the main speakers was Donald McGavran of Fuller Theological Seminary.[82] On August 18, a team of forty evangelists from the United States visited the city of Kangnŭng for several days of evangelism; their revivals recorded an attendance of 50,000 and 300 new believers.[83] On August 29 a weeklong series of evangelistic activities ended at the city of Masan, with the total of 80,000 attendance and 2,000 new believers. On September 4 an article in the *K'ŭrisŭch'yan sinmun* asked, "Why are there so many revivalists in Korea?"

And from October 25 to 28, 1976, Korean Methodists held a unity revival in the Yu Kwansun Hall, with 5,000 people participating daily.[84]

Of these revivals, many were held as part of various denominations' plans to expand their memberships by 1984, the centennial of Korean Protestantism. The Korean Methodist Church, for example, planned to increase in size to 5,000 churches and 1 million members by that year; the T'onghap Presbyterian Church, to 5,000 churches and 1.5 million members; the Haptong Presbyterian Church, to 10,000 churches and 4 million members; the Kijang Presbyterian Church, to 2,000 churches; and the Korean Holiness Church, to 2,000 churches and a doubling of its existing membership of 231,000.[85]

It was between August 15 to 18, 1976, that the '77 Holy Assembly for the Evangelization of the Nation took place in the Yŏŭido Plaza.[86] Like the Billy Graham Crusade and Explo '74, this was also a massive evangelistic campaign, but it differed from the previous revivals in at least two respects. First, this campaign was explicitly intended and held as a Korean-sponsored and Korean-led affair—it was to be a coming-of-age for Korean evangelicalism. What led to this assembly was explained by Sin Hyŏnggyun, a prominent revivalist and the preparatory committee chairman for the '77 Holy Assembly:

> While leading nightly prayers and meetings for the CCC- sponsored Explo '74, I was asked by participants whether it would be possible to have Korean speakers instead of foreign ones, whose messages needed to be translated into Korean. Shortly thereafter, I began to wonder if we must always have foreign speakers whenever we hold mammoth gatherings. Then, in an officers' meeting of the Korean Revivalists' Association in November, it was decided to hold the '77 Holy Assembly. We chose this year because it is seventy years since the great revival of 1907, and we chose August 15 because it is Independence Day, which makes it special, as well as being in summer vacation period. The special aspects of this gathering are, first, that all of the activities are to be planned and carried out by ourselves with our own financial resources; and, second, that from the sixteenth we will fast and pray for three days for the country and the Korean people.[87]

Sin's view was echoed by Kim Chinhwan, head of the planning committee:

> It is very important that the speakers for this event be Koreans. Billy Graham [in his 1973 Korea crusade] did not address any of the issues that directly concerned Koreans. . . . This was a big problem. This revival, which is being held on the seventieth anniversary of the Changdaehyŏn revival,

must deal with issues that matter to Koreans, issues like the withdrawal of American troops and peaceful unification.[88]

The views of both of these men were reflected in the event's slogan: "To Evangelize the Nation, by Koreans and Only through the Holy Spirit."

The second difference from the previous revivals was that, aside from being a mammoth campaign to be led and financed solely by Koreans, the '77 Holy Assembly was also presented as an event seeking to address a matter keenly felt by the South Koreans of the time: the sense of national insecurity. This concern, to be sure, derived mainly from the precarious political situation that prevailed in the peninsula. On the other hand, the intensity of this sense of insecurity was heightened by at least two factors that were beyond Koreans' control. One was that by 1977, Vietnam had fallen into communist hands. During the Vietnam War, South Korea had been an important ally of the United States, having contributed 300,000 troops between 1965 and 1973.[89] The Korean participation in the war had been supported by most Korean evangelicals as a way to combat their "natural" enemy, communists. Consequently, when the communists emerged victorious in that war, it heightened the fear among evangelicals and South Koreans in general that a communist invasion of their country was possible. The other factor feeding the sense of insecurity was that 1977 was the year when Jimmy Carter seriously considered withdrawing American forces stationed in South Korea. If that were to happen, many South Koreans believed, their country would be bereft of one sure deterrent against a communist invasion. This possibility greatly worried the evangelicals and South Koreans in general, prompting them to issue statements of protest and hold rallies to oppose withdrawal.[90]

What did all this fear of communism and sense of national insecurity have to do with the claims made by the organizers of the '77 Holy Assembly? The answer to that question is that if communism was the greatest threat to national security (of which there was no doubt), then the best way to combat it—insisted the organizers—was to fill the land with its antidote: born-again Christians. "If Vietnam became communist because it failed to be evangelized," premised one of them, "then evangelization is an absolute factor in the nation's security."[91] Kim Chinhwan noted, "This Holy Assembly for the Evangelization of the Nation is a movement not only for Christians; it is a movement to find a way to save the whole nation."[92] At least for the assembly's organizers, the '77 Holy Assembly was viewed as a patriotic event as well as a religious one. Therefore, every Korean, they urged, should attend for their country, if not for their souls.

As with the Billy Graham Crusade, the '77 Holy Assembly was preceded by a preparatory phase—this one even longer, from November 1974 to June 1977. During this phase, revivals were held not only in Korea but also among Koreans living overseas. And they produced considerable total results: 1,150,000 in total attendance (1,120,000 in Korea; 30,000 overseas) and 20,510 decision makers (19,327 in Korea; 1,183 in overseas).[93]

The '77 Holy Assembly proper began with a service held in the evening of August 15. After a chorale sung by a united choir of ten thousand members, Sin Hyŏnggyun, who had fasted forty days to prepare for the event, delivered the keynote sermon, entitled "Why Did We Gather?" Sin preached that the purpose of the assembly was to carry out God's word, drive out communists from the country, and evangelize the nation. He also expressed his desire to bring the second Pentecost to Korea through repentance and fasting. The first night's service was attended by 800,000 people, including 3,000 Koreans from overseas and 600 foreign guests from fifteen countries. After the service, 250,000 participants spread their blankets on the plaza and stayed for a night-long prayer.

During the four days of its proceedings, the '77 Holy Assembly did quite well in the numbers game. In total attendance, it recorded the new high of 7 million, which meant that each day's activities averaged 1.75 million in attendance. The event also produced 80,000 new converts, making it second only to Explo '74 in this regard among all the massive evangelistic campaigns held thus far. In addition, the '77 Holy Assembly distinguished itself from the previous campaigns in that over 1 million people participated in a three-day fast.[94]

On the last night of the '77 Holy Assembly, the organizers presented a four-point declaration: "(1) We will continue to be the standard-bearers of evangelization, (2) Kim Il Sung and the Northern puppet regime must give up their ambition to invade [the South] and cooperate with the South's effort to unify the country, (3) the United States should stop withdrawing [its troops] from Korea and keep its trust as an ally, and (4) the Korean church will work to fulfill its evangelistic mission to the world."[95]

Aside from its emphasis on patriotism and the Korean church's self-sufficiency, the '77 Holy Assembly also differed from previous massive campaigns in one other way. As was hinted in the last item of its four-point declaration, the '77 Holy Assembly was a turning point for Korean evangelicalism vis-à-vis the evangelization-of-the-world movement. Up to that point, despite its limited missionary work in China, Thailand, and Bangladesh, Korea had been regarded more often than not as a nation where foreign missionaries and revivalists came to evangelize. However, with the success of the '77 Holy Assembly—and with the seemingly unstoppable growth in their church memberships—leaders of Korean evangelicalism now regarded Korea less as a nation that got evangelized than as a nation that did evangelize.

One manifestation of this coming-of-age was detectable in the increasing frequency with which Korean revivalists spoke of Korea as one of God's chosen nations—indeed, as the last redeemer nation. Thus a month before the '77 Holy Assembly, Sin Hyŏnggyun wrote, "I am certain that we Koreans are the people who, from Asia, have the mission to restore God's glory at the end of the time, and I earnestly pray that God's glory will be amply revealed through the '77 Holy Assembly for the Evangelization of the Nation."[96] As Korean churches continued to grow and the next massive campaign—the '80 World Evangelization Crusade—approached, the intensity of such rhetoric would only increase.

In the interim between the '77 Holy Assembly and the '80 World Evangelization Crusade, ordinary evangelistic efforts continued in Korea. From June 5 to 9, 1978, Chŏngju was again the site of a revival to evangelize Ch'ungbuk Province: an attendance of 150,000 was recorded.[97] In July of that year the Yoido Full Gospel Church held another seminar on church growth. This time the speaker was Robert Schuller, who commented that the Korean church, with its enthusiasm, was the most outstanding national church in the world. In the coming century, he added, the Korean church could change the world.[98] Also in July, the public stadium in Incheon hosted a revival to evangelize that city, with 50,000 people participating. In the following August, Yŏngnak Presbyterian Church held the '78 World Evangelization Conference, attended by 50,000, to help it send ten or more missionaries abroad in the 1980s.[99] On October 17 yet another North Korean tunnel was discovered under the thirty-eighth parallel, prompting 2 million citizens to gather at the Yŏŭido Plaza and condemn the North.[100] From October 30 to November 3, the Yoido Full Gospel Church held a revival called the '78 Holy Assembly for the Evangelization of the Nation, with 2,500 people in attendance. In the following December, 1,800 soldiers were baptized, and on April 14, 1979, another 850 were added to the number.[101] From June 18 to 21, 1979, church leaders gathered at the Hanŭl kidowon (the Heavens Prayer House) in the city of Chŏngp'yŏng, in Kyŏnggi Province, for fasting and revival. The theme of the gathering was "The Minister Must Live for the Church to Live and the Church Must Live for the Nation to Live." Three thousand ministers, including 5 Japanese and 30 Taiwanese, and 3,000 laypeople attended.[102] In July 1979 the government released a number of activist ministers from prison, including Pak Hyŏnggyu, the minister of Cheil Church in Seoul. But many still remained there, including the poet Kim Chiha and the Presbyterian minister Mun Ikhwan, one of the three prisoners of conscience highlighted that August by Amnesty International.[103] From September 27 to 30 a united evangelistic campaign in which 150,000 people participated was held in Taegu. On November 4 the Yoido Full Gospel Church celebrated reaching 100,000 in membership. To help it celebrate, Pat Robertson of the United States came as a special speaker.[104]

1980–1988: World Evangelization Crusades of 1980 and 1988 and the '88 Olympics

For South Korea, the transition from the 1970s to the 1980s was marked by especially volatile political circumstances. Park Chung Hee was gunned down on October 26, 1979, triggering a bloody coup d'état that culminated in the ascendancy of Chun Doo Hwan as president in February 1981. Chun ruled the South till 1988, but his tenure was characterized by ceaseless demonstrations, led by Koreans who deemed his government to be illegitimate. His regime lacked credibility partly because in late May 1980 he deployed special troops to Kwangju, a major city in South Chŏlla Province, to brutally suppress citizens who were peacefully demonstrating against martial law and other dictatorial measures he had imposed; at least 240 citizens of the city were killed.[105] Arnold A. Peterson, a Southern Baptist missionary who happened to be in Kwangju at the time, recalled the tragedy:

> The soldiers who appeared on the streets of Kwangju on Sunday, May 18, and Monday, May 19, were black beret paratroopers who had been transferred from the Pusan area to Kwangju on Saturday, May 17. . . . They were the best trained combat paratroopers in the Korean military. Their unit had served in Viet Nam. They were trained for "kill and destroy" type of combat mission. . . . What occurred in Kwangju was not an unfortunate case of over-reaction by the military as they tried to deal with student demonstrations. Quite the contrary is true. On May 18, the Korean military in Kwangju began to commit unprovoked atrocities against people who were not involved in demonstrations. The Kwangju Incident did not occur because demonstrations went out of control. It occurred because the military committed unprovoked atrocities against the people.[106]

The military's brutal behavior in Kwangju caused Chun's opponents to be more aggressive in their demonstrations: throwing of rocks and Molotov cocktails became de rigueur, the riot police responding with rounds of tear gas canisters. In the spring of 1987 the demonstrations reached fever pitch, as Chun outlawed any discussion of a constitutional revision that would allow for a direct presidential election in December. Unexpectedly, however, Roh Tae Woo, tapped by Chun to be his successor, proclaimed that he would run only if Chun would, among other things, agree to a constitutional amendment allowing for a direct presidential election. With Chun backing down, a direct presidential election was held in December 1987. Roh won by a plurality vote (37 percent of the cast vote), beating out Kim Young Sam (28 percent) and Kim Dae Jung (27 percent). With his election deemed legitimate, Roh was inaugurated in February 1988 and governed the Republic of Korea till 1993.[107]

Even in such a political maelstrom, the work of soul saving continued. From May 18 to June 18, 1980, for example, the Korean Baptist Church held an evangelistic drive in five major cities (Seoul, Pusan, Taegu, Kwangju, and Taejŏn), gaining more than 20,000 new converts. The drive in Kwangju, in which Arnold A. Peterson was involved, coincided with and was aborted by the bloody massacre.[108] From July 28 to August 1, 1980, Taejŏn was the site of yet another large revival, this time led by Ch'oe Chasil (Choi Jashil) of the Yoido Full Gospel Church; 12,500 people attended and 300 made the decision to convert.[109]

"Evangelization of the Nation Today Leads to the Evangelization of the World Tomorrow" was the theme of the '80 World Evangelization Crusade. It was the first massive evangelistic campaign in which Koreans showed an explicit and substantive concern for world evangelism. For the organizers, however, the '80 Crusade was to be more than simply Korea's contribution to world evangelism. They had a distinct epiphenomenal objective: this crusade was to be Korean evangelicalism's big step toward assuming the leadership of the evangelization-of-the-world movement. Thus if, in the '77 Holy Assembly, Korean revivalists had urged their countrymen to attend and convert for the sake of national security (aside from the salvation of soul, which was always held primary), in the '80 Crusade they urged the same, so that Korea could become the preeminent leader and model in world evangelism. This much was clearly implied by Kim Chun'gon, chairman of the '80 Crusade's preparatory committee, who waxed sanguine:

> Our first goal in this campaign is to achieve most speedily and efficiently the supreme goal of carrying out evangelism. To do so, we are mobilizing all the resources and mass media necessary to create an atmosphere conducive to evangelism. . . . Moreover to achieve this goal, we are intensively organizing and disciplining all the believers in the churches, so that when the centennial of Protestant missions arrives in 1984 and 80 percent or more of the total population [of South Korea] becomes evangelized, we can earnestly start a Korea-modeled and Korea-led missionary movement in which the world and all peoples become our working unit.[110]

The '80 Crusade took place in the Yŏŭido Plaza from August 12 to 15, 1980. Its elaborate plans, however, had been well under way since April 1979.

During this preparatory period, the organizers formed a district committee in each of the 213 counties outside Seoul and in each of the 203 areas in Seoul, with each area consisting of ten churches. They conducted warm-up revivals in many of these districts and areas. They also intensively advertised the crusade, using secular media such as national newspapers, radio, television, and billboards and featuring slogans like "I Found It!"; "New Life in Jesus!"; and "You Too Can Find It!"[111]

As the date of the event approached, the island of Yŏŭido was turned into an urban revival camp. To lodge the participants from faraway places, the organizers rented 1,000 classrooms from nearby schools and pitched over 3,000 tents in Yŏŭido. To feed them, the organizers set up a facility in which a rice lunch for 100,000 to 150,000 people could be cooked and boxed in two hours. In the Yŏŭido Plaza itself, the organizers set up 120 giant high-powered speakers, 250 portable lavatories, 20 telephone booths, and 3 movable post offices. They also had on-site an emergency medical team composed of 300 or so doctors and nurses.[112]

Initially, the organizers of the '80 Crusade hoped to achieve a total attendance of 10 million in all their activities, including the main services and nightly prayer sessions held in the plaza, as well as seminars and Bible study sessions that were to be held in the churches throughout Seoul and its environs.[113] The actual turnout of the event, however, far surpassed this goal. The event in fact would make history as the largest evangelistic assembly to have taken place in Korea (and perhaps in the world) up to that time.

The '80 Crusade started in earnest with its opening service on the evening of August 12. But as with previous campaigns, this main event was preceded by a series of preliminary activities. First, on the night of August 11, a prayer session attended by 1 million people was held on the Yŏŭido Plaza. The next day, from 9:00 a.m. to 5:00 p.m., twelve series of seminars were held separately in twelve sections of Seoul. These seminars took place throughout the crusade, with each geared toward a particular audience, such as ministers, teenagers, or Sunday school teachers, and there was also a popular seminar on evolution and creationism. While these seminars were going on, Bible study classes were held at fifty designated churches in Seoul and nearby cities .

In the evening of August 12, when these preliminaries were over, people began arriving at the Yŏŭido Plaza in droves. By 6:00 p.m., they swarmed over the sidewalks leading to the Map'o bridge, which connected Yŏŭido to central Seoul—by this time the auto traffic around the plaza was completely proscribed and the traffic on the roads near Yŏŭido was heavily congested. By around 7:30 p.m. when the opening service started, 2 million had gathered at the plaza; by 8:00 p.m., the crowd had swollen by a half million more.[114]

Because the '80 Crusade was oriented toward global evangelism, the organizers had invited many foreign evangelical speakers, mainly Americans. Thus in the opening service both Korean and foreign speakers shared the podium. Kim Ch'angin, senior minister of Ch'unghyŏn Presbyterian Church, delivered the opening remarks. He was followed by John Wright, head of the Southern Baptists' home ministries, who preached a sermon entitled "The Mystery and Method of Rebirth," in which he stated that, without experiencing rebirth, no one could be saved. After Wright, another American, astronaut James Irwin, gave a testimony entitled "God's Love I Felt on the Moon."

Throughout the event, efforts to internationalize the event were evident. At all the main services, for example, the 5,000 foreign participants from sixty or so countries were provided with instant translations in English, Japanese, Chinese, and Spanish. Among them, 70 or so took leading roles in the crusade as preachers or seminar leaders—the more prominent of them included Bill Bright, Donald McGavran, Carl Henry, and Peter Beyerhaus (from West Germany).[115]

In the final service, held on August 15, Han Kyŏngjik, honorary president of the crusade, delivered a sermon entitled "Evangelization of the Nation and National Unification." He preached that if Korean churchgoers desire to evangelize and unify their country, they should have the experience of rebirth and give their all to the task of proselytizing. Kim Chun'gon also delivered a sermon that night, entitled "A Nation without a Vision Will Perish." He stressed that Koreans should believe in God if they desired democracy to settle in their country and that evangelizing the nation would be the quickest way to peacefully reunify the North and the South.[116]

Except for a few that were rained out, on each of the four days of the '80 Crusade three services were held on the Yŏŭido Plaza: a morning service, a main evening service, and an all-night prayer service (lasting till 5:00 a.m. the next day). The following is a breakdown of the attendance on each day:

August 12: morning, 100,000; evening, 2.5 million; all-night, 1.2 million
August 13: morning, 50,000; evening, 2 million; all-night, rained out
August 14: morning, rained out; evening, 2.7 million; all-night,
    2 million
August 15: morning, 1 million; evening, 2.3 million; all-night,
    1.8 million

In addition, the twelve seminars attracted 160,000 participants; the local Bible study classes drew 240,000; and the ancillary prayer night was attended by 1.2 million people. The grand total attendance for this four-day crusade was 17.25 million. On top of this, during the crusade a total of 700,000 made their commitment to believe for the first time; 2 million reported having experienced the fullness of the Holy Spirit; and 100,000 volunteered to serve for some limited time in foreign missions. Of course, all these activities could not have been possible without the government's cooperation, which included the lifting of the martial law curfew from 12:00 to 4:00 a.m. specifically for the Yŏŭido Plaza, to allow people to stay overnight for prayer.[117]

With the '80 Crusade, massive evangelistic campaigns in Korea had reached their peak—at least for the period leading up to 1988. Two more massive gatherings took place at the Yŏŭido Plaza in the remainder of the 1980s, but neither came close to the '80 Crusade in scope and total attendance. Nevertheless, both drew millions of participants and had symbolic significance. The first of these two gatherings took place from August 15 to 19, 1984, in celebration of the centennial of Korean Protestantism. Korean Methodists and Presbyterians had already separately celebrated their denominational centennial in April, with William B. Underwood reenacting the landing of his great-grandfather for the Presbyterians. But the massive centennial held in the Yŏŭido Plaza was different from, say, the '80 Crusade in that its main goal was not to evangelize but to express gratitude to God for the country and the church, as well as to repent of the church's past sins.[118] The centennial was a cooperative venture, as the nation's twenty major denominations and twenty-five Christian organizations worked together to make it possible. The whole event was held under Korean auspices, with Billy Graham being the only foreign guest invited to preach. Also noteworthy was that among the audience were 722 Japanese Christians. The centennial recorded a total attendance of more than 3 million people, with the last service drawing 1 million or so.[119]

Four years later, Seoul was the site of the twenty-fourth Summer Olympic Games. That same year, the city was also the venue of the last massive evangelistic gathering to take place in Korea in the 1980s: the '88 World Evangelization Crusade. Also called the Soulympics, the crusade took place in the Yŏŭido Plaza from August 15 to 18.

The '88 Crusade had as its slogan "Spread the Fire of the Holy Spirit throughout the World." And it was clear that the Summer Olympics—with its motto "Seoul to the World, and the World to Seoul"—provided the impetus for the event. On the one hand, with a total attendance of only 1.5 million, the '88 Crusade was nowhere near the '80 Crusade in scope. On the other hand, no previous evangelistic campaign surpassed the '88 Crusade in one category: the rhetoric of Korea the chosen nation.[120]

In the '88 Crusade, leaders of Korean evangelicalism unabashedly pounded on the jingoistic notion that theirs was not only a chosen nation but also the final redeemer nation—the nation that would redeem for Christ as much of the heathendom that God would allow to be redeemed before the end of time. These leaders asserted, moreover, that the Olympics were the means by which God sought to make this point. This they hinted at in the prospectus of the crusade:

> In 1988 the Olympic Games will be held in Seoul. This is a happy and proud occasion since it shows that our nation's strength has grown [enough to host an event of this magnitude]. But seen through faith's eyes, we feel there is another providential will for such an epochal event taking place in Korea. We believe that God seeks to accelerate the evangelization of the world by enabling visitors from Asia and all over the world to be challenged and influenced by the Gospel [in Korea]. To be sure, all the activities of the Olympics . . . must be carried out in an orderly manner; but just as important . . . the Korean church has the duty to implant in the minds of visitors from all over the world the image of a Gospel Korea.[121]

The Olympics were a boon to the South Korean government because they brought the nation recognition. They were a windfall to Korean conglomerates by providing them with an unparalleled opportunity to advertise their products. But to the leaders of Korean evangelicalism, the Olympics were a clear signal from God that the Korean church had now taken over the mantle of leadership of the evangelization-of-the-world movement.

Korea as the final redeemer nation was a prominent theme in many of the sermons during the crusade. In the first evening, for example, Cho Yonggi preached, "The reason God has made the whole world recognize Korea by reviving its economy and arranging for the Olympics to take place here is that he wants us to use them [the Olympics] as an opportunity to range all over the world and give witness to the Gospel. . . . Therefore Korea, as a nation in this world, as the nation that offers sacrifices at this end of time, must spread Christ throughout the world."[122]

From whom did Korea take over the responsibility of being God's final redeemer nation, of running his final errand? Such a question was not even an issue for the crusade's preachers, because the answer—the secularized and liberalized West—was a foregone conclusion. This point was rather facetiously illustrated by one of the preachers:

> I heard this interesting story. A tourist who was traveling the world went to Europe and looked for Jesus. He was told that Jesus had left that place a long time ago. He went to America and looked for Jesus. He was told that Jesus had left there just a short while ago. When he came to Seoul's Kimpo

airport, however, he learned that Jesus himself had arrived there just a short time ago.[123]

The same point was also clearly assumed in the following rhetorical question raised by another preacher: "The period of Euro-American missions is over. Now Korea must assume the responsibility of evangelizing the Third World—this kind of mission is increasingly demanded of us these days; what can we the believers do to take part in missionary work?"[124] The preacher's own answer to this question—that if the believers themselves could not be missionaries, it behooved them to support the missionaries who were already in the field with prayer, money, and whatever else—echoed what Speer, Mott, and Brown might have said to their constituents at the heyday of their nation's foreign missions at the turn of the twentieth century.

Another aspect of this crusade—indeed, of all the previous massive gatherings—was also reminiscent of American evangelicalism at the turn of the century: emphasis on rebirth. Rebirth by the power of the Holy Spirit, for example, was the key theme of a sermon by Sin Hyŏnggyun, a Presbyterian and one of the key leaders of the '88 Crusade:

What Jesus wants most of all is for us to receive the fire of the Holy Spirit. It is important that we receive the baptism of water and formally become official members of churches, but [Jesus] wants us to become Christians by fundamentally receiving the Holy Spirit's baptism of fire. A number of them who had received [only] the formal baptism have fallen. But those who receive the Holy Spirit's baptism of fire will not fall even till the end of time.[125]

Another preacher, from a Holiness background, expressed the same point a bit more earthily:

What is the ultimate purpose of those who believe in Jesus? To be saved, of course. To go to heaven. . . . However, we cannot go to heaven unless we are saved. In other words, if we do not undergo rebirth, if we are not born again, that is impossible. . . . You cannot go to heaven even if you build a church entirely by yourself. It is absolutely impossible. Even if you offer one million won, you cannot go to heaven. Even if you offer ten million won, that is impossible. Then how can you go to heaven? You can go to heaven only if you are born again—through the experience of rebirth.[126]

The importance of rebirth had been seared into the core of Korean Protestantism at the great revival of 1907. The fact that Korean ministers of 1988 preached about rebirth in much the same vein as the missionaries of 1907 underscored the sturdiness and staying power of evangelicalism as a vehicle of salvation. On the other hand, it also underscored the Korean evangelicals' faithfulness in keeping up the tradition. Had the sermons of Cho, Sin, and others at the '88 Crusade been heard by J. R. Moose—the Southern Methodist missionary who in 1906 passionately urged Koreans to experience "a genuine old fashioned revival"—they would have warmed the cockles of his heart.[127]

From the great revival of 1903–1907 to the '88 Crusade, Protestantism in Korea was predominantly evangelical; that is, throughout this period the church's main dynamic was the will to save souls. In practical terms, the will to save souls meant the will to proselytize the bodies that embodied those souls. Once the souls were saved, the church insisted, all the ills of society would be taken care of naturally, at least to the extent allowed by fallen human nature. This view of social change was criticized by others as naïve and irresponsible from the time of the great revival of 1907 to the late 1980s. Undaunted, the evangelicals held to the mission to save souls, consistently and profitably turning to a propagative strategy that had no parallel in other Korean religions of the period: revivals and evangelistic campaigns.

The consistency with which the church turned to this strategy can be gathered from the continuity of revivals and evangelistic campaigns that, except for the period when Japanese repression was harshest, characterized the history of Korean evangelicalism. This string of revivals began with the citywide evangelism in P'yŏngyang in 1907 and the Million Movement of 1910. During the Japanese occupation—before and especially after the March First Independence Movement—the continuity of the revivals was kept alive by itinerant evangelists such as Kil Sŏnju, Kim Iktu, and Yi Yongdo. After the Korean War, it resurged with a vengeance, especially in the form of massive evangelistic campaigns that culminated in the World Evangelization Crusades of 1980 and 1988.

That these revivals and evangelistic campaigns played a significant role in the growth and rise of Korean evangelicalism is clear. Taking a cue from Mead's revivalists and just counting the number of people reported to have been saved in the first five massive evangelistic campaigns, for example, yields a total of 1,166,510. On the other hand, that these evangelistic campaigns were successful and instrumental in the rise of Korean evangelicalism invites a further question. Why did they appeal so powerfully to South Koreans in the first place—especially since such was not the case in, say, Japan?

This question has two answers. The first answer lies in the turbulent course of modern Korean history, in which traditional religions were discredited and individual Koreans were often driven to despair and disorientation, arousing their salvific impulse and motivating them to search for a new moral order, such as the one offered by evangelicalism. A second, more decisive answer lies in the way evangelicalism became positively identified with the Korean nation and participated in Koreans' collective aspirations and sentiments. It participated in Korean nationalism, especially during the dark years under Japanese colonialism, and in South Korean anticommunism, which became the entrenched ideology in the South well into the 1980s, the latter participation leading to the legitimization of evangelicalism in South Korea. Together, these three factors—unusually active proselytization efforts, appeal as a means of individual salvation, and identification with collective aspirations and sentiments of the South Korean people—go a long way toward explaining the rise of evangelicalism in South Korea.

With the end of the 1988 Seoul Olympics, Korean evangelicals looked forward to the 1990s. They believed that in the last decade of the second millennium, their churches would continue to advance, along with their country's advancement in its economy and in democracy. The reality, however, would be different. But before that reality is described in the epilogue, we will take a detour from the narrative to examine the character of Korean evangelicalism.

CHAPTER 4

The Intensely Practical and Devotional Character of Korean Evangelicalism

Intensity rather than breadth characterizes the typical Korean
Christian. Intense in advocacy of the truth, some say; intense
in advocacy of only a part of the truth, others say.
—Arthur Judson Brown

In 1990 Harold L. Willmington, vice president of the fundamentalist Liberty University in Virginia, visited South Korea. During his visit, Willmington observed various aspects of the Korean Protestant Church. Apparently impressed by what he saw, he lauded the church for the central role it plays in its adherents' lives, the strong leadership of its ministers, and especially the ardent prayer life of its laypersons and their diligent participation in church activities.[1]

Willmington's observations provide a starting place for delineating the character of Korean evangelicalism. They allude to two important points that can be made about it. The first, indirectly attested by the fundamentalist's praise of the Korean church, is that Korean evangelicalism shares much in common with its American counterpart, however they may differ from each other. That is not surprising, given that it was the revivalistic missionaries from America who sowed the seeds of Korean evangelicalism.

The second point concerns two specific traits that Willmington found to be noteworthy about Korean evangelicalism: the believers' fervency in prayer and active participation in church life. This observation, echoed by other foreign observers, points to a more general characteristic in Korean evangelicalism: its intensely practical bent.[2] Korean evangelicalism, in other words, is practical both in the sense that it is much more enterprising in devotional practices than in theological ideas, and in the sense that it tends to set great store by concrete criteria such as strict observance of the Sabbath, fervent prayer, regular tithing, this-worldly blessings, and the size of church membership.

Before proceeding any further, however, a disclaimer is in order. Regarded as a form of Protestantism whose chief characteristics are, among others, the doctrine of rebirth via felt experience and literalist biblical hermeneutics, evangelicalism is readily distinguishable from liberal and high church groups in Korea.[3] This commonality, however, should not be taken to infer that Korean evangelicalism is monolithic and lacks variety and differences within its ranks. Such is hardly the case. Within Korean evangelicalism, there is not only a great deal of denominational difference, for example, but also a fair amount of conflict as well.[4] This means that any generalization about Korean evangelicalism is likely to have an exception and that what is offered here is not a detailed map but a general sketch of the character of Korean evangelicalism. That being said, let us reiterate our thesis: though Korean evangelicalism shares many characteristics with its counterparts elsewhere, especially in the United States, it is distinguishable from others by its intensely practical and devotional disposition. This chapter examines these characteristics as they have been manifested in the beliefs and especially the practices of Korean evangelicalism.

Beliefs in Korean Evangelicalism

Throughout the first hundred years of Korean evangelicalism's history, American missionaries and Korean churchmen who had been trained by conservative American theologians set the terms of orthodoxy in Korean Protestantism.[5] Thus it comes as no surprise that it is in the realm of beliefs rather than practice that Korean evangelicalism shares most with its American counterpart. For ascertaining the beliefs of Korean evangelicalism, the findings of two major surveys on various aspects of Korean Protestant faith are helpful. One is *Han'guk kyohoe 100-yŏn chonghap chosa yŏn'gu* (Centennial Comprehensive Study of the Korean [Protestant] Church, or CCSKC), conducted by the Christian Institute for the Study of Justice and Development. The other is *Hyŏndae kyohoe sŏngjang kwa sinang yangt'ae e kwanhan chosa yŏn'gu* (Investigation into the Growth and Religiosity of the Korean [Protestant] Church, or IGRKC), conducted by the Institute for the Study of Modern Society.[6] Both surveys were published in 1982, and both directed their questions to two sample populations: Korean clergy and laity from all over South Korea.[7] Their findings, in the main, reveal that Korean Protestants hold beliefs that are quite conservative, that is, fundamentalistic and practical.

Conversion Experience

It is a key premise of this study that at the heart of Korean Protestantism is conversion experience. The results of the IGRKC and CCSKC surveys bear out this premise. Of the two surveys, the IGRKC's is more concerned with this issue. Among its many pertinent questions, one is especially relevant, one that asks the clergy and laity whether having the experience of the Holy Spirit is essential, presumably, for salvation—which is another way of asking if conversion experience is necessary for salvation, since a Holy Spirit experience either entails or presupposes a conversion experience.[8]

To this question, the response was overwhelmingly in the affirmative. First, in IGRKC's sample of 160 clergy, 73 percent affirmed the absolute necessity of conversion experience; 26.4 percent, its desirability; and 0.06 percent (one minister), its nonnecessity. In the other sample, of 1,257 laypersons, 58.5 percent affirmed the absolute necessity conversion; 35.9 percent, its desirability; and 5.5 percent, its nonnecessity or their uncertainty about the answer. Thus, to extrapolate from these findings, the majority of the laity and even a larger majority of the clergy in Korean Protestantism regard the Holy Spirit experience—conversion experience—as absolutely necessary, and almost all of them regard such experience to be either essential or desirable.

As might be expected, the IGRKC's findings on this issue were corroborated by the CCSKC. One of the CCSKC's questions asked whether the respondents had the felt certainty of their salvation. Of 787 clergy members, 773 (98.2 percent) answered in the affirmative, as did 1,854 (93.1 percent) of the 1,991 laypersons.[9] Since it is the certainty of salvation that is sought in conversion experience, the evidential value of this result is clear.

Inerrancy of the Bible and Its Corollaries

One of the key doctrines in evangelicalism is the inerrancy of the Bible. In Korea this doctrine has been vigorously disseminated and inflexibly held by missionaries and Korean church leaders alike. In chapter 2, we saw how Korean leaders such as Kil Sŏnju battled against any attempt to modify the literal interpretation of the Bible. In such a battle Kil was hardly alone, since he was overwhelmingly supported by his missionary friends, such as the one who wrote the following:

> The missionary body of Korea has as a whole been characterized by an unreserved acceptance of the Bible as the truth of God, believing the poetical parts are divinely inspired songs; the historical parts are [an] accurate account of what happened to actual persons, not relegating Adam to the myths and Abraham to the shades, nor putting Job and Jonah in a class with

Jack and Jill. . . . In spite of the strong tide of destructive criticism there has been little wavering in the teaching of the Word in Korea. The Korea missions consider that the Bible is to be accepted as a whole, and is not like a moth-eaten bolt of cloth, from which may be cut, according to human will and judgment, here and there, a usable remnant.[10]

Largely due to the efforts of church leaders like Kil and the above-quoted missionary, biblical inerrancy has continued to prevail in Korean Protestantism. This prevalence was reflected in the CCSKC survey, in which 84.9 percent of the clergy and 92.3 percent of the laity answered affirmatively the question of whether they believed every word of the Bible to be God-inspired—and, presumably, unerring.

Since most Korean Protestants believe in the inerrancy of the Bible, it follows that most of them would also believe in the corollaries thereof. Thus on the matter of the virgin birth of Christ, 97.0 percent of the clergy and 95.6 percent of the laity answered affirmatively in the CCSKC survey. On biblical miracles, 94.5 percent of the clergy and 95.6 of the laity gave their assent in the same survey; on the same matter, IGRKC found 89.3 percent of the clergy and 84.5 percent of the laity in agreement. On the existence of an afterlife, the CCSKC found 98.4 percent of the clergy and 91.6 percent of the laity believing in it. As to the resurrection of Jesus, according to CCSKC, 91.5 percent of the clergy and 70.5 percent of the laity held it to mean that Jesus' dead body had come back to life. Interestingly, 18.3 percent of the laity (and 3.6 percent of the clergy) regarded the resurrection to mean that though Jesus' body remained dead, his spirit went up to heaven. Why would so many laypersons hold such a spiritualistic understanding of the resurrection? One reason may be that many Korean Protestants unwittingly hold to a Monophysite Christology, as attested by a CCSKC finding that 31.0 percent of the laity (and 20.3 percent of the clergy) believed the nature of Christ to be divine only, whereas 65.8 percent of the laity (and 76.5 percent of the clergy) professed the orthodox two-natured Christology. Why the Monophysite tendency? For a possible clue, we may look to the traditional Korean view about what follows after death—that the deceased's body dissolves into earth while his or her soul joins the realm of spirits.[11]

Eschatology

Since the days of Horace G. Underwood and Henry G. Appenzeller, premillennialism has been axiomatic in Korean evangelicalism. This brand of eschatology holds that the millennial reign of Christ predicted in Revelation would be preceded by a catastrophic confrontation between good and evil, culminating in the return of Christ himself to bind the forces of Satan. During the Japanese occupation, premillennialism took on an urgent note, especially in the dooms-day preaching of Kil Sŏnju.[12] The Korean War only fueled this tendency, and premillennialism remains strong even in the twenty-first century. Two findings by the CCSKC bear out Korean Protestants' widespread belief in premillennialism and the imminence of Christ's return. In the CCSKC survey, 98.3 percent of the clergy and 94.8 percent of the laity affirmed a belief in Christ's return, and 95.4 percent of the clergy and 89.1 percent of the laity expressed a belief in its imminence.

Personal Morality

On matters regarding personal morality, too, the CCSKC confirms the conservative tendency of Korean evangelicalism. This can be seen in the following breakdown on some of the issues thought to be immoral by the survey respondents.

	CLERGY (%)	LAITY (%)
Abortion	80.9	72.4
Premarital sex	95.6	88.4
Adultery	97.2	72.4
Smoking	89.7	80.6
Drinking	90.8	84.6
Gambling	97.2	94.1
Social dance	87.6	80.7

Church and Politics

On the church's relation to politics, Korean Protestants were found to be ambivalent in surveys. For example, they appeared to be jealous of defending

	CLERGY (%)	LAITY (%)
If they go against the faith, they should be condemned.	70.9	72.9
Christians must unquestionably submit to secular authorities.	1.8	3.0
It is desirable for Christians to submit to secular authorities.	22.7	20.1

their religious rights, as indicated in the affirmative responses to the CCSKC question "What kind of attitude should Christians have toward secular authorities?"

On the other hand, despite their opposition to governmental infringement on their religious rights, when it came to active political participation, the majority of Korean Protestants balked, as indicated in their responses to the question "Do you feel that the church should participate in politics?"

	CLERGY (%)	LAITY (%)
The church should not do so.	17.0	17.8
It is better if the church did not.	42.4	34.5
It is acceptable if circumstances warrant it.	33.2	38.4
The church should do so.	5.1	7.0

These CCSKC findings are seconded by the IGRKC survey. The following summarizes the responses when Protestants were asked what the church should do about corruption and human rights violations in their society.

	CLERGY (%)	LAITY (%)
The church should actively and collectively oppose them.	7.1	5.5
The church should deal with them through criticism and evangelism.	48.1	32.6
Prayer meetings against them are the best approach.	24.4	43.1
The decision should be left with each individual.	18.6	13.1
The church should simply ignore them.	1.9	5.7

Views on Other Religions

South Korean society is ethnically homogeneous but religiously pluralistic. Indeed, South Korea is probably the only country in the world that officially celebrates holidays rooted in Buddhism, Christianity, and Shamanism.[13] Living in such a society, Korean Protestants must sooner or later come to terms with other religions. What do the Protestants think of the others?

In chapter 1, we saw that the missionaries' attitude toward Korea's traditional religions was one of triumphalism, seeking to supplant—or at best co-opt—native Korean religions. Throughout evangelicalism's hundred-year history in Korea, such an attitude persisted and was variously expressed. In chapter 2, we saw some of the ways in which this hostility toward other religions was expressed. But perhaps its starkest expression came from the pen of Pak Hyŏngnyong, a well-known fundamentalist theologian who had studied under the fundamentalist New Testament scholar J. Gresham Machen at Princeton Theological Seminary. Pak asserted, "Christianity's most appropriate relation to other religions is not compromise but conquest. . . . The attitude of the religion that bears the name of Jesus Christ is not compromise but clash and conquest."[14]

The CCSKC survey results indicate that the general attitude of Korean Protestants toward other religions is not as overtly or thoroughly hostile as Pak's. On the whole, however, theirs is hostile enough. To the CCSKC question "What do you think of other religions?" the pluralistic option (their truth is just as valid as Christianity's) garnered the smallest percentages of affirmative responses: 4.7 percent of the clergy and 8.8 percent of the laity. The percentages were higher for the somewhat inclusive response (Christianity's truth is most superior)—20.7 percent of the clergy and 25.0 percent of the laity. The majority of respondents selected the exclusivistic answer (only Christianity's truth is valid): 70.9 percent of the clergy and 62.6 percent of the laity.

Thus in South Korea, despite the reality of religious plurality, evangelicals have held an antagonistic stance toward other religions. Such antagonism has tended to make life difficult for Korean theologians who have refused to fall into line with the exclusivistic orthodoxy. This, for example, was the case with Methodist theologian Pyŏn Sŏnhwan, who was accused of heresy for espousing an inclusive soteriology.[15]

Another vilified theologian is Chŏng Hyŏngyŏng (Chung Hyung Kyung). Dubbed a "survival-syncretist" by the *Christian Century*, she was denounced and harassed by conservative Protestants in Korea after she openly expressed pluralistic sentiments in her controversial address at the 1991 World Council of Churches conference held in Canberra, Australia.[16] The experiences of Pyŏn and Chŏng underscore how unrepresentative their views are in Korea. At the same time, these experiences betray that, even after becoming legitimated in Korea, evangelicalism remains a disintegrative force vis-à-vis the traditional culture of Korea.

This-Worldly Blessings

One aspect of Korean evangelicalism that has evoked much suspicion has to do with what is commonly called *kibok* (this-worldly blessings) in Korean.

Held by a significant portion of Korean Protestants, *kibok* is the belief that one's faith—once properly lived out—will enable one to obtain not only otherworldly blessings but also this-worldly blessings, such as material wealth, cure from diseases, and resolution of personal problems. To be sure, as Mary Douglas asserts, "it is human and natural to hope for material benefits from the enactment of cosmic symbols."[17] Didn't Jesus himself teach that if believers would only ask, seek, and knock, their needs will be satisfied?[18] What then is peculiar about the desire of Korean evangelicals—or at least a great many of them—for this-worldly blessings? The peculiarity, in short, lies not in that they seek such blessings but that they seek them with gusto.

More than anyone else, the person who has exemplified this practical spirit in Korea (and around the globe) is Cho Yonggi, who has made the quest for blessings of spirit, wealth, and health a hermeneutical principle.[19] Cho writes of it in his book entitled *Salvation, Health, and Prosperity: Our Threefold Blessings in Christ*:

> When I started my ministry at a tent in Pulkwang-dong twenty years ago, I had such complicated feelings that I could hardly bear it. The people to whom I tried to preach the gospel were living in a spiritually barren state, facing a wall of despair, and were so destitute that they had difficulty finding enough to eat. While preaching the Word to them and feeding them, I found myself involved in gross self-contradiction, for the God I had learned about at the seminary seemed to be merely the God of the future. I could not find the God of the present to show Him to people who were living in such desolation and poverty. Where was the God of the present in Korea? This question stirred in my heart. . . .
>
> I cried and prayed with tears day in and day out, earnestly seeking. After I spent much time in supplication, God finally spoke to my heart. His words, warm and full of hope, were a revelation to me. The word from God contained the truth of the threefold blessings of salvation, health and prosperity written in 3 John 2: "Beloved, I wish above all things that thou mayest prosper and be in health, even as thy soul prospereth." Since that time this truth has been the foundation of all my sermons, and I have laid the foundation of my ministry on this scripture. When I interpreted all Scripture in light of the truth of this particular portion, God began to manifest himself not only as God of the past and future, but as the God of the present. . . . When we understand the threefold blessings fully, we can interpret Scripture from Genesis to Revelation on the basis of the passages that speak these truths. After that the truth in the Bible revives and shines in the light of new life, and that truth becomes clearer to us.[20]

Cho's message has found a receptive audience in Korea, as evidenced by the success of his church. Even outside Korea, there have been many who took to his message. One such non-Korean is Oral Roberts. In the foreword to Cho's book, Roberts wrote, "Cho has taught these people to practice seed faith, to believe God and to put Him first in their lives. God is now blessing and prospering them—the same people of whom most were poverty-stricken when they came under his ministry. . . . I love this man of God. His God-ordained and anointed ministry means much to me personally—and to millions around the world."[21]

Despite Roberts' recommendation of Cho and his ministry, it is hardly the case that Cho lacks critics in Korea.[22] Some complain that he neglects the suffering aspect of Christian faith.[23] Some criticize him (and other health-and-prosperity ministers) for being influenced by Korea's Shamanistic ethos. One of the latter critics asserts:

> Shamanism is the oldest religion in Korea, brought to the peninsula by the first settlers. . . . Innumerable demons are believed to bless and curse men according to the demon's whims. Neither blessings nor curses are morally deserved. The demons are believed to be manipulated by Shamans using special occult techniques and offerings which amount to briberies. Both the blessings and curses are entirely worldly. Blessings include wealth, health, power and honor. Curses include disease, poverty, failure in business, etc. . . .
>
> Some Shamanistic elements are very effectively used by the Christian churches, most without fully realizing their origin, in order to attract more people. Most apparent is the excessive emphasis in sermons on the believers' earthly blessings. The Full Gospel Central Church in Seoul . . . uses as a church slogan 3 John verse 2. . . . The church teaches that all believers will be rich in possessions, healthy in body, and prosperous in spiritual life. They call this "the triple meter faith." . . .
>
> With little emphasis on Christian social responsibilities or daily Christian living, they loudly promise earthly blessings as rewards of faith, prayer, and sacrifices in form of offerings and services to the church. . . . The majority of the Korean churches, mostly Presbyterian, Methodist, and Korean Evangelical, remain rather sound, but very few remain totally unaffected by this Shamanistic mysticism.[24]

Cho denies that his theology is tainted by Shamanism.[25] He denies that seeking blessings should be the prime goal of a Christian, just as he denies the possibility of true happiness with godless wealth. On the other hand, Cho does not believe there is any Christian virtue in poverty or sickness as such.[26] He, in fact, states, "We have an important responsibility: to receive the prosperous life, a life flowing with all the provision you and I will ever need."[27] According to Cho, when Christ died on the cross, he redeemed sinners not only from spiritual abyss but also from poverty and sickness. Christ's sacrifice, in other words, enabled the born-again to revert to the prelapsarian state, in which humans were entitled to the blessings of spirit, health, and material. Therefore, Cho says:

> If we do not live a life of poverty without a special reason . . . we are insulting Jesus. Here the legitimate "special reason" could be that we volunteer to become poor by giving all we have to the work of God, or that under a great persecution we become poor to give glory to God. Other than these reasons, if we do not enjoy the prosperity provided for us by Jesus Christ, but we live in poverty, we bring shame to the name of Christ who became poor so that we might become rich.[28]

Moreover, Cho asserts,

> Sickness, which came upon man as the consequence of sin, must be included in the redeeming grace of the cross. If this grace had not been included in the redeeming work at the cross, however wonderful and full of tenderness and compassion Jesus' healing of the sick may have been, and though He spent two-thirds of His public ministry in this work, it would have ended merely as the compassion and work of a certain period.[29]

If the born-again are indeed redeemed from poverty and sickness, why are so many of them still poor and sick? The reason for this, according to Cho, lies with the Devil and the believers themselves. It lies with the Devil because he always seeks to prevent Christians from enjoying the full benefits of Christ's sacrifice on the cross. And it lies with the believers because they do not adequately resist the Devil and thus they fall into sins such as challenging God's authority—for example, by not fully tithing—and harboring negative sentiments like hatred, anger, covetousness, and guilt, in addition to being insufficiently penitent, forgiving, and faithful.

To criticize Cho's theology as being nothing more than Korean Shamanism in a Christian cloak is to caricature it. Whatever one thinks about his beliefs, they are made in a context that assumes the traditional tenets of evangelicalism—especially those represented by the Assemblies of God, to which his mammoth church belongs. The extent to which, if at all, his beliefs—and those of Korean evangelicalism in general—are influenced by Shamanism is not a simple matter to decide. To be sure, one may easily point to apparent similarities between Shamanism and Korean evangelicalism (particularly the portion of Korean evangelicalism that shares in the ethos of Cho's church), such as the emphasis on healing, exorcism, emotionality, and this-worldly blessings. But such similarities hardly warrant the inference of a causal relationship between the two. For practices that are often impressionistically regarded as "Shamanistic" in Korean evangelicalism in general and in Cho's religiosity in particular are readily paralleled in evangelicalism elsewhere, even in cultures not known for Shamanism. Thus Allan Anderson, the author of *An Introduction to Pentecostalism: Global Charismatic Christianity*, observes:

> I have attended three Sunday morning services in Yoido, and apart from the content of the sermon they were much the same. Korean Pentecostalism is generally more formal than most other Pentecostal types I am familiar with. Their liturgy is influenced by the Presbyterian churches in Korea, by far the largest group of churches in the country, who in turn have been influenced by the "Korean Pentecost," the Korean Revivals of 1903–10. Hymns born in the revivals and the USA Holiness movements of the late nineteenth century are easily recognized in their Korean translations used by all Protestant and Pentecostal churches.[30]

On the issue of the relationship between evangelicalism and Korean Shamanism, it is best to avoid facile generalizations and to err on the side of prudence. Such prudence would lead us to assert no more than this: evangelicalism's inclination toward the literal interpretation of the Bible has encouraged its adherents to conceive of biblical blessings in concrete, practical terms—and this practical tendency, along with evangelicalism's generally emotional disposition, has been thrown into high relief by the practical and affective character of the people attracted to the churches, a character also expressed in the affective and this-worldly ethos of Shamanism.

VARIETIES OF DEVOTIONAL PRACTICES IN KOREAN EVANGELICALISM

In the realm of beliefs, as we have seen, Korean Protestants are staunchly conservative, reluctant to contravene the views transmitted to them by the first missionaries. In the realm of practice, too, much of the tradition that the missionaries originally disseminated persist. Most generally, this persistence is evident in the low-church character of Korean Protestants' devotional practices. This means that the practices that are important and prevalent in Korean evangelicalism, like those of low churches elsewhere, are not elaborate liturgy, absorbing sacraments, or social activism but intense Bible study and fervent devotional activities. It is in these devotional activities that Korean evangelicalism excels, showing an unsurpassed fervency and developing practices that lack parallels elsewhere in the Protestant world.

The intensity of devotion in Korean evangelicalism is attested partly by the variety and frequency of devotional services that a typical Korean Protestant church holds each week. It is not unusual for a Korean Protestant church to engage in five kinds of congregational services weekly: the main Sunday worship, Sunday evening worship, Wednesday worship, Friday nightlong prayer worship, and daily—including Sunday—daybreak prayer worship. In addition, most churches have a system of weekly cell meetings, in which members meet in small groups, or cells, typically on Friday evenings for prayer and Bible study. Moreover, if to this fixed schedule are added intermittent ancillary activities such as missionary society meetings—which usually start with hymn singing and prayer and may be held in a prayer house (*kidowŏn*) on some out-of-the-way hill or mountain—it is easy to see that to be an active Protestant in Korea is to engage in some mode of church devotion daily or nearly so.

Main Sunday Worship

As in Protestant churches elsewhere, the main Sunday service is the largest and most formal worship in the Korean Protestant church. This service is usually held at 11:00 a.m., though in the megachurches the distinction implied by "main" is hardly meaningful, for most of their multiple services tend to be filled to capacity.[31] Regardless of the church size, however, the typical Sunday worship in Korean Protestantism is permeated by a low-church ethos. There is no lectionary reading, and liturgy is pared down to bare essentials. Emphasis is placed on hymn singing and prayer, and pride of place is given to preaching, which usually takes up half the worship time. This low-church ethos is typified by the following service schedule from the Yŏngnak Presbyterian Church, one of the more magisterial Protestant churches in Korea.

Silent prayer/chime
Call to worship/Psalm reading
Hymn singing
The Lord's Prayer
Hymn singing
Representative prayer/usually by an elder
Hymn singing
Bible reading
Anthem/by choir

Sermon
Prayer by the preacher
Hymn singing
Offertory/hymn singing during offering
Offertory prayer
Hymn singing
Benediction by preacher

Certainly there are variations to this more or less basic schedule. The representative prayer, for example, may be followed by a unified vocal prayer (*t'ongsŏng kido*), in which the worshipers simultaneously say their individual prayers aloud—usually one to three minutes. The unified vocal prayer is not uniformly practiced in Korean Protestant churches. However, as a product of the great revival of 1907, it has since that time been a regular feature of worship in a significant number of Korean Protestant churches, irrespective of their denominational affiliations. The popularity of this feature is reflected in the CCSKC study, which shows that of the surveyed population, 46.5 percent of the ministers and 49.8 percent of the laypersons favored including unified vocal prayer in their services (and presumably did so), whereas 50.8 percent and 48.3 percent of the ministers and laypersons, respectively, opposed it.[32]

Another service that may be incorporated into the basic schedule is healing prayer. This practice is characteristic of Holiness and Pentecostal churches, such as the Yoido Full Gospel Church. At the appropriate time in the service, usually right after the sermon, the minister asks the worshipers to place their hands on the part of their body that needs to be healed. He then asks them to join him in *t'ongsŏng kido* for healing. Often this request evokes the loudest and most poignant of the prayers.

Yet another practice may be added to the basic schedule: reading names of tithers and other noteworthy contributors. Well into the third quarter of the twentieth century, this practice was a standard part of offertory prayer in just about all Korean Protestant churches. Recently, however, most churches shun it, largely due to the criticism that it is ostentatious and demeans the act of giving. The origin of this practice is obscure, though it may have something to do with the early church leaders' desire to see the Korean church speedily become self-sufficient financially. Although offerings are voluntary in Korean evangelicalism, there is a very strong presumption that one cannot be a devout believer without faithfully supporting the church financially. The tithe, especially, is emphasized as an absolute obligation of all believers.[33]

Most Christians dislike hearing too much preachment about giving tithes or other offerings. In this, Korean Protestants are no exception, as one of their running complaints is that their ministers preach too much about offering. Despite such complaints, surveys find that most Korean Protestants are quite compliant in giving. One study, for example, found that of its sample population in metropolitan Seoul, 84.5 percent held that the tithe must be given, though only 72.2% of the same population reported actually doing so.[34] In another survey, conducted by Korea Gallup and the K'ŭrisŭch'yan sinmun (Christian Press), 86.5 percent of the respondents reported being regular tithers.[35]

Being low-church, most Korean Protestant churches do not relish sacramental contemplation. The Protestant tradition recognizes two sacraments, the Eucharist and baptism. That Korean Protestants highly value the Eucharist is attested by the CCSKC survey, which found that 92.4 percent of the clergy and 87.8 percent of the laity regarded it as absolutely necessary for Christian faith. However, despite this survey finding, most Korean Protestants partake of the Eucharist only about two to four times a year, suggesting that the Eucharist is not really at the heart of their piety. An exception here is the several hundred congregations identified with the Stone-Campbell (or Restoration) Movement, more specifically known as Churches of Christ or Christian Churches/Churches of Christ, for whom the weekly Eucharist is central.[36] Baptism is also regarded as important by Korean Protestants. Even so, a significant number of them do not regard it absolutely essential for their faith—the CCSKC survey found that only 64.4 percent of the clergy and 68.9 percent of the laity regarded baptism as an absolute requirement for becoming Christian.[37]

In interpreting the above survey response regarding baptism, caution is needed, for it is not entirely clear as to what the term "Christian" means here. Does it refer to a churchgoer or to one who is saved? In other words, whether the percentage of the affirmative response would increase or decrease if the question was linked more clearly to soteriology is unknown. Lacking better data on this issue, we can only guess at the possible response. Given Korean Protestants' belief in the soteriological sufficiency of the rebirth experience, it is likely that fewer people would respond affirmatively if the question linked baptism more clearly with salvation. That this guess is credible is evidenced by a faith-counseling column called Q&A in the K'ŭrisŭch'yan sinmun, a respected Christian weekly in Korea. On January 10, 1994, the Q&A column dealt with the following query from one of its readers: would the reader's mother, a devout believer who had died in an auto accident before receiving baptism, be saved? The counselor's answer was clear: the reader's mother would indeed be saved, if prior to the accident she had repented of her sins, had experienced rebirth, and was certain of her salvation. Baptism, as such, he added, was unimportant here, for it was merely an outward sign of one's inner rebirth.

One more item related to Sunday worship is Sabbath keeping. Along with tithing, Sabbath keeping is regarded as an absolute requirement for all believers. In the early days of the Korean church, when believers usually lived amid people hostile to the religion, Sabbath-keeping required a certain amount of determination. This could be seen in the following anecdote recorded by a missionary:

> Osi's mother-in-law is not a Christian and her father-in-law, mildly-speaking, has no sympathy whatever with the Jesus doctrine in which the son and his wife are trusting. According to the old custom, some times when a Korean girl is married she becomes little more than a slave in her mother-in-law's house. Osi's mother-in-law is very much worried because in spite of all her threats and scoldings Osi will not work on what she calls the Lord's Day.[38]

In contemporary Korea, a Christian is less likely to encounter this kind of difficulty, though it is not totally absent. By the same token, nowadays the idea of Sabbath keeping has become diluted, meaning more or less that one simply has to attend a Sunday service—after which one may, say, return to his shop or go on an outing with his family. But if Sabbath keeping is equated with church attendance on Sunday, most Korean Protestants are faithfully observant of it. That this is the case is shown by the response to the CCSKC survey question "How often do you attend church?" To this, 43.1 percent of those sampled responded that they attended four or more times a week; 41.7 percent, two or three times a week; 11.7 percent, once a week; 1.9 percent, two or three times a month; and 0.6 percent, once in a while. Hence, according to this study—and if those who responded that they attended church once or more weekly attend a Sunday service—we may surmise that 96.5 percent of Korean Protestants keep the Sabbath. As noted before, the CCSKC study was published in 1982, and it appears that since then Sabbath-keeping among Korean Protestants has slackened somewhat. In a 1995 government study, 80 percent of the believers responded that they attended church at least once a week, and 40 percent, two or more times a week.[39]

Daybreak Prayer Devotional

Of all its devotional practices, Korean evangelicalism is probably best known for *saebyŏk kido-hoe* (literally, "daybreak prayer gathering"), or simply *saebyŏk kido*. Daybreak devotional is not unique to Korean Christianity, nor were Koreans the first to practice it. Indeed, the historical record shows that the devotional was practiced (most likely weekly) at least as early as 112 CE.[40] But it is only in Korean evangelicalism that daybreak devotional is observed so assiduously by the vast majority of the congregations.

Like the unified vocal prayer, daybreak devotional also traces its origin to the great revival of 1907. The persons credited with introducing it are Kil Sŏnju and Pak Ch'irok. During the charged atmosphere of the great revival, these two men met daily for prayer at 4:00 a.m. in their church. Soon their prayer activity became known, and others desired to join them. Kil thereupon told them to come to church at 4:30 a.m. The next day, people began to arrive as early as 1:00 a.m.; by 4:30 a.m., a crowd of four hundred was waiting to enter the church. From this time onward, daybreak devotional became a regular feature in revivals and seasonal Bible study gatherings. Then during the Korean War, exigencies of the war prompted the churches to engage in this devotional daily. By the time the war ended, daybreak devotional had become a fixed practice in Korean evangelicalism.[41]

Daybreak devotional is a regular practice in most evangelical churches of Korea. In some of them it may be held once or twice a week, but in most it is a daily ritual, held usually at 5:00 or 5:30 a.m. The structure of the devotional is simple. Its main part, corporate worship, typically consists of hymn singing, scriptural reading, short (usually exegetical) preaching, more hymn singing, and unified vocal prayer. The corporate worship lasts about thirty minutes. Afterward, however, the participants may remain as long as they wish for private prayer. In most churches, during private prayer, participants (especially those suffering from illness or stress) may ask the pastor for a laying-on-of-hands prayer (*ansu kido*), which is believed to be especially effective.

For an average Protestant church in Korea, attendance at daybreak devotional is about 10 percent of its typical Sunday attendance. But there are occasions when daybreak attendance can equal or even surpass Sunday attendance. That usually happens during times set aside for special daybreak devotionals. Such special devotionals—titled, for example, Forty-Day Daybreak Prayer Meeting (or Seven-Day Daybreak Prayer Meeting) to Conquer the Walls of Jericho—are usually preceded by weeks or months of preparation. During this preparatory period the minister impresses upon the congregation the importance of attending the devotional and exhorts them to invite guests—the goal being to invigorate the congregation and attract new members. It is not surprising, then, that such a gathering engenders a revivalistic atmosphere.

In Seoul there is a church famous for its unusually fervent daybreak devotionals: Myŏngsŏng (Presbyterian) Church. Every day the Myŏngsŏng Church holds two daybreak devotionals, one at 4:30 a.m. and the other at 5:30 a.m., each of which is attended by thousands. Furthermore, every March and September, the Myŏngsŏng Church holds special monthlong daybreak devotionals, which draw even greater numbers. In late March 1989, for example, the church caused a stir by successfully attracting ten thousand people a day to its special daybreak devotionals.[42]

Participating in daybreak devotionals is a mark of religious zeal. Thus in the CCSKC study, 83.5 percent of the ministers and 82.8 percent of the laypersons surveyed affirmed that if one is faithful, one must attend them. In Korean evangelicalism, church leaders—ministers, elders, and deacons—are presumed to be more zealous than ordinary laypersons. This means that for them attendance at the devotionals is almost mandatory, to the extent of risking scorn if they fail to do so. Thus in the Christian newspaper *Kidok kongbo* (Christian News), one church leader declared,

> Elders and deacons are priests whose importance is superseded only by that of the minister. . . . [I]f they do not regularly participate in daybreak devotionals, are they qualified to be church leaders? Can they be examples in the churches? . . . Therefore, church leaders must take the lead—even if for the sake of formality—in all aspects of religious life. They must especially reserve time for daybreak prayer so that their inner person can be renewed daily.[43]

Nightlong Devotional

Though less familiar than daybreak devotional, nightlong devotional (*chŏrya kido-hoe*) is another ritual that is commonly practiced in Korean Protestant churches. Like daybreak prayer, this practice has its origin in the great revival of 1907 and seems to have become a fixed practice sometime after the Korean War. Unlike daybreak prayer, however, a nightlong devotional is normally not a daily practice. In many churches it is held once a month, but in most cases it is a weekly affair. Usually held on Fridays, the devotional starts anytime from 9:30 to 11:30 p.m. and lasts till between 2:00 and 4:00 a.m. the following morning. A nightlong devotional usually draws more attendance than a daybreak devotional, attracting about 10 to 20 percent of Sunday attendees.[44] A nightlong devotional is also lengthier and more elaborate than a daybreak devotional.

One of the simpler nightlong devotionals is that of the Ch'unghyŏn Presbyterian Church, as it was practiced in the 1980s. This church's devotional lasted from 11:30 p.m. to 3:30 a.m. During the first hour and half, the participants held a corporate worship, centered on preaching. This was followed by a thirty-minute snack time. Then, from 1:30 a.m. to the end of the devotional at 3:30 a.m., the participants engaged in prayer, which might include private as well as intercessory prayers.[45]

By contrast, the Sungŭi (Methodist) Church's nightlong devotional, also from the 1980s, had to be one of the most elaborate in Korea. Sungŭi Church started its nightlong devotional at 10:00 p.m. with an hour of gospel singing, led by a group of musicians playing the piano and guitars. Then, from 11:00 p.m. till midnight, the participants hold a corporate worship, rounded off by a short period of individual prayer. This was followed by a coffee break, lasting thirty to forty minutes. Then the second part of the devotional began with twenty minutes of hymn singing. Afterward, at around 1:00 a.m., the body-rhythm (*yuldong*) singers appear and led the participants in twenty minutes of callisthenic gospel singing. Next appeared a twelve-member orchestra, which played more-traditional hymns to set the mood for a thirty-minute prayer session that followed. In addition to private prayers in this session, the participants said intercessory prayers for the country, the church, and unwell members. Then came a period of part-song performed by a group of church men or women. This program was the main event: two hours of inspirational testimony by a layperson. After this, at about 4:00 a.m., there was one more round of private prayer. Afterward, the participants finally went home—unless they wished to linger for the daybreak devotional.[46]

Fasting-Prayer

In addition to daybreak and nightlong devotionals, another practice that is widespread in Korea and underscores Korean evangelicalism's practical bent, is fasting-prayer (*kŭmsik kido*). In his book *San'koltchak esŏ on p'yŏnji* (Letters from a Mountain Valley), Reuben A. Torrey, a Western Episcopalian priest residing in Korea, makes the following observation about fasting-prayer in the Korean church:

> Among the spiritual practices observed in the Korean church, yet another that shocks foreigners is fasting. Jesus taught us specifically that a fast should be done secretly so that no one could detect our doing it. I have frequently had Korean ministers ask me, "Father, what was the maximum number of days that you fasted?" I was shocked that they, by asking such a question, not only sought to show off their own experiences of fasting but also disdained Jesus' warning by trying to dig out the secret that should lie only between Jesus and me. I do not believe the missionaries had engaged in such behavior. I tend to think that this is a small piece of influence coming from Shamanism. As I think about it, I am shocked as to how the Korean church could have fallen into such a snare. In other words, the assumption is that if one applies pain to oneself, God will sympathize with him—if only reluctantly—and that if that pain is made known to others so that one could be praised, that in itself could prove to be a great consolation.[47]

Torrey's observation is problematic yet indicative of the practice in some respects. It is problematic because it gives the impression that Korean ministers in general are ostentatious about their fasting. This is not the case, as attested by articles in journals such as *Kido* (Prayer) and *Wŏlgan mokhoe* (Pastoral Monthly), where such behavior is routinely denounced—though, of course, the very existence of these articles implies that at least some of them do engage in the ostentatious behavior.[48] Also, Torrey's conjecture that the alleged problem of ostentatious fasting derives from Shamanism is invidious, reflecting a common tendency that prevails among Christians in Korea: caricaturing Shamanism and attributing to it just about everything bad and "unsophisticated" about their religion. This tendency is directly linked to the early missionaries' haughty contempt toward Shamanism.[49]

Nevertheless, Torrey's comment is still suggestive of aspects of the practice. First, it rightly suggests that Korean Protestants are less prudish about fasting (than fastidious Episcopalians, at least—to invoke a stereotype); that is, Korean Protestants fast commonly and, sometimes, quite openly. All this, in turn, presupposes that among Korean Protestants there is a belief that fasting-prayer is an especially effective means of approaching the divine, for unless this is presupposed, it is difficult to understand their ardent practice of it, not to mention the reams of writing recommending its virtues. Such a recommendation, for example, is offered by Yoido Full Gospel Church co-founder Ch'oe Chasil, known as the "Hallelujah Mama":

> Christianity is a religion of personal experience. It is a spiritual movement, not a lot of theories or "isms." It is a movement of life, truth, the Holy Spirit, and love. The important thing is to have a personal, real experience. Through the right relationship with God we can recognize and understand the Lord's will. There are many ways in which we can experience God's blessings. I recommend fasting and prayer as the most powerful of these. . . . The secret of successful Christian living is to have a personal, working faith. There is a desire in each of us to attain a high level in faith. Even in difficult situations there is a burning desire to be aware of God's love, His grace, His presence, and His guidance in our lives. This can be attained through fasting and prayer.[50]

Thus to Ch'oe, and others like her, fasting-prayer is a practice that would bring benefits to all aspects of one's spiritual life. But it is typical of Korean evangelicalism that most of its adherents would not rest content with just general benefits. So from the belief in general benefits of fasting-prayer, inferences and claims regarding its concrete benefits are made. Thus a minister asserts,

"According to the advice of many ministers, if [a minister] proclaims fasting-prayer prior to holding a revival meeting, that meeting will bring about a great revival. Moreover, even for the revival of a family, fasting-prayer is absolutely required."[51] Even a prominent Presbyterian such as Kim Chun'gon exhibited no squeamishness in assenting to the efficacy of fasting-prayer; in an article he wrote, he related how he and his college students, through fasting and prayer, obtained the funds necessary to build their Campus Crusade for Christ hall.[52] Ch'oe herself affirms the concrete efficacy of fasting when she states in her book, *Korean Miracles*, "As faith builds in fasting and prayer, we receive healing for our bodies as well as healing for our spirit and soul."[53] The bulk of her book, in fact, is but a collection of testimonies of once gravely unwell persons who were healed through fasting-prayer.

Cell-Group Devotional

A cell group in Korean evangelicalism consists of a small number of believers who come together for the purpose of devotion and fellowship. In Protestant history, cell groups trace their origins back at least to the beginning of German Pietism, to Philip Jacob Spener's *ecclesiolae in ecclesia* (little churches within the church) in the seventeenth century.[54] In Korea, cell groups are usually called *sokhoe* (class meetings) by the Methodists and *kuyŏkhoe* (zone meetings) by members of other denominations. They were used from early on by the Protestant churches and have been a ubiquitous feature of just about every Protestant church in the country, regardless of its denominational affiliation.

In large churches, cell groups form an elaborate network of parachurch communities. This, for example, is the case with the Chuan Methodist Church in Incheon. To use its 1978 figures, the church's one thousand active members in that year were divided into six cell-group areas.[55] Four of these areas each contained eight cell groups, the other two areas having nine each, for a total of fifty. Each cell group, in turn, was composed of eight to ten households, and every year, each cell was reorganized with one-half its households combining with one-half of another cell group, to promote more thoroughgoing fellowship within the church.

As an extracongregational worship service, a cell-group devotional is usually a weekly affair, held typically on Friday evenings in the home of one of the members. Each cell usually has two leaders. One is the cell coordinator, usually a deaconess, whose responsibility is to organize the meetings and be in close touch with her cell members. She is also in charge of presiding over the devotional. The other is the Bible study leader, usually an elder, a senior deacon, or an evangelist.[56]

The devotional itself lasts about an hour. Typically it starts with psalm reading, followed by hymn singing, opening prayer, scripture reading, Bible study, leader's prayer, offertory and prayer, announcements, more hymn singing, and, finally, the Lord's Prayer. After the devotional, there is usually a simple meal, provided by the hostess, during which time the members engage in fellowship. Relative to a Sunday service or to any other service, a cell-group devotional is much more intimate and informal. This is understandable, for a cell group is where believers engage in long and meaningful relationships, sharing each others' emotional, spiritual, and even material needs.

The system of cell groups may in fact be a chief reason why seemingly impersonal megachurches are able to thrive in Korea. Although a member of such a church might worship on Sunday with thousands of strangers, on Friday of the same week she could count on interacting with familiar faces in her cell group. It is no wonder then that there is hardly a sizable church—let alone a megachurch—in Korea that lacks an elaborate system of cell devotion.

The Prayer House
Another characteristic of devotional practice in Korean evangelicalism is the institution of the prayer house (*kidowŏn*), usually located on a mountain, where believers come to engage in concentrated devotion for hours, days, or even weeks. Like daybreak prayer and nightlong devotional, the prayer house became institutionalized in earnest only after the Korean War. Since the early days of their church, Korean Protestants have been known to retire to a mountain for concentrated prayer—resembling, incidentally, their Buddhist countrymen, who for hundreds of years frequented mountain shrines to meditate. Though some nondescript prayer houses may have existed in Korea during the years of Japanese occupation, the first noteworthy one was built in October 1945 in Chŏrwŏn, a town slightly to the north of the thirty-eighth parallel.[57] In the years immediately following the Korean War, many more were built all over South Korea, such that 210 of them were in operation by 1981, and by 1987 the total had increased to around 400.[58]

The Korean prayer house is distinct from its parallels in the West. For one thing, it differs from Protestant resorts in that it is not primarily a place for relaxation or fellowship, and it differs from a Catholic monastery in that it has no religious permanently residing in it. But corporate worship does take place in a prayer house. Every day, most prayer houses hold services that may be joined by visitors wishing to take respite from their private devotion. A prayer house may be owned by an individual, but more often than not it is operated by a church. In either case, its facilities are normally available to any individual or group for a nominal fee.

Prayer and devotion are the raison d'être of any prayer house, but there are some variations in the size and kinds of devotional activities that take place in it. There are, for example, small prayer houses, where one cannot engage in much more than private prayer or small group devotionals. Then there are bigger, specialized prayer houses, where one may, in addition to private prayer, engage in healing services sponsored by the house. In addition, there are huge prayer complexes operated by megachurches.[59] In this kind of prayer house, multiple devotional activities may take place at the same time. In the main hall of the complex, for example, tens, if not hundreds, of visitors might participate in a revivalistic service sponsored by the owner church. In a smaller hall in another part of the complex, a women's group might hold an overnight prayer meeting. Somewhat distant from both halls, there might be a row of prayer cells, in one of which a college-bound student might be engaged in intensive prayer regarding his upcoming college entrance examination. And not far from him might be a small room, wherein a pastor would be writing a sermon or fasting in prayer.

Bible Study

As is the case with other low-church traditions, the Bible and the study of it are central to Korean evangelicalism. From the very beginning, the missionaries and Korean church leaders were determined to make the Bible the basis of their church. Operating in a Confucian culture that prized and revered the written text and at a time when classical learning was in disrepute and vernacular literature was scarce, the missionaries found a people eager to embrace the Bible. Thus one missionary wrote, "Generally speaking the Korean Christian is a Bible loving soul. Often he has no other Book in the world but the Bible; 'twas the first book he ever had or ever read. . . . He never thinks of going to church without it, and *reads it probably much more than does the average Christian at home.*"[60]

In part, the church leaders' emphasis on the Bible was reflected in their determined efforts to translate it into Korean. Thus, as was noted earlier, in 1882, three years before the arrival of Underwood and Appenzeller, John Ross—with the help of Yi Ŭngch'an, Sŏ Sangyun, and other Korean collaborators—managed to publish the first Korean translation of Luke and John. This was followed by the translation of the entire New Testament in 1887. In 1900 a more refined translation of the New Testament was published by a committee of missionaries residing in Korea. In April 1911 the same committee translated and published all of the Old Testament, thereby making the entire Bible available in Korean.[61]

Another way in which early leaders of the church emphasized the importance of the Bible was by making the ability to read the *han'gŭl* Bible a requirement for baptism. Exceptions undoubtedly were made to this rule—for example, for those who were impaired in vision or too old to learn to read. Otherwise, this rule seemed to have been enforced quite consistently with good results. As a missionary observed:

> The refusal to give baptism to women who are able to learn to read and do not, has been very helpful. Those blind, shortsighted and over sixty should be excepted, if necessary. We have one woman with actually only half an eye left and yet she holds up her book against it and reads so well that she can teach a class. Another, an old lady of over seventy, has learned to read though her Korean friends discouraged her and told her that she was entitled to admission to heaven on her faith. She wanted more than admission. She wanted the comfort of the scriptures and has it every day through her old squinting eyes.[62]

A requirement such as this had an impact that went beyond the realm of the church. It produced not only biblically literate Christians but Koreans who were literate enough to read *han'gŭl* newspapers and journals, enabling them to participate in their nation's collective discourse.[63] Indeed, the Protestant Church, along with the Roman Catholic Church, must receive the credit of having taken the lead in popularizing *han'gŭl*, a script that is easy to learn yet was formerly disdained as inferior to the Chinese script.

Another way early leaders of Korean evangelicalism sought to valorize the Bible was through annual Bible study classes. The practice of holding such classes was a distinctive feature of Korean missionary work. It was an important evangelistic strategy employed by all the denominations in Korea.[64] The classes had different levels. At the lowest level were those held in individual congregations, which lasted for a week or longer. Above that, each district (or circuit) of the missions held classes, which might last longer than the congregational Bible study. Lastly, each of the mission stations held Bible study classes for church leaders, often in winter—when the farmers were off from their work—and lasting one to two months. These Bible study classes were valued by the missionaries, who carefully structured them, as noted in a *Korea Mission Field* editorial:

> It [Bible study] is of vital interest in Korea where so large a portion of time and strength is expended in the study of the Sacred Scriptures, which effort has developed three or four differing grades of Bible classes, leading up to Bible Institutes and finally culminating in the Theological Seminary. These different Bible classes are being correlated with one another and with the Bible Institutes . . . and [with] the very weeks and months of the Korean

year being new-calendared to attain an efficiency which shall attune them to the rhythm of seasons, harvests and heavens.[65]

Moreover, these early Bible study classes, especially the larger ones, had sociological import, functioning somewhat as camp meetings had functioned for early nineteenth-century frontier communities in America. Often participants came from long distances, at considerable personal expense and trouble. Once arrived, they studied the Bible and participated in revivals and evangelistic activities. They also held workshops—on farming or hygiene, for example—and socialized with each other. The atmosphere of such Bible study classes is well captured in an open letter by a missionary:

> Classes like the one I am now attending are the best means for getting results in Korea. "Class" is not the word, in fact there is no word for it. If you would move one of the Northfield meetings to Syracuse and hold it in Park church, and along with it have a meeting of Presbytery and get in all the ministers and elders from the nearby churches, and add a series of popular meetings in the evening that would pack the church, and if this was the main social and religious event of the year, then you would have a good idea of the way a Korean church looks at a "circuit class" like this one and the one I attended in Tong Ch'ang last week and the one Mrs. Koons and I will go to the last of this month. We have sun-rise prayer-meeting as I have described, prayers at 9:20, study the Bible in divisions according to the age and experience of the persons attending, for the rest of the forenoon and part of the afternoon, then go preaching and calling and *pass the time any way we like till evening*, when there is another general meeting. . . . This will last a week, and for two months of the Winter is going on all the time. In nearly every one of my churches such a class is held, with the helper taking the leading position, and men from other places helping him as he and the others have helped me here.[66]

After the Korean War, such Bible study classes were rarely organized. Bible study now tended to be separated from revival meetings and other activities not directly related to it. More and more, Bible study was integrated into Sunday school programs. Study or devotional activities surrounding the Bible became annual events in churches— activities such as monthlong Bible reading contests (whoever read the most pages winning) or, at intercongregational levels, intensive competitions like Special Training for Reading and Memorizing the Bible. In such a competition, believers gathered in a large indoor facility to spend three or more days under rigorous supervision to read the entire Bible and memorize certain passages. The one who was able to accurately memorize the most passages won.[67]

Epilogue
The Beleaguered Success of Korean Evangelicalism in the 1990s

We have to understand the situational character of religious
experience, that is, we must conceive of it in its particular
context. When seen historically, culturally, sociologically,
and religiously, our experience and its forms are always
conditioned.

—Joachim Wach

At the beginning of the twentieth century, Christians constituted less
than 1 percent of the Korean population.[1] Near the end of the century,
according to a 1995 survey by the South Korean National Statistics Office,
Christians constituted 26.3 percent of the population, surpassing Buddhists,
the next-largest religious group, with 23.3 percent of the population. Among
the Christians, Protestants predominated, accounting for 75 percent of the
entire Christian population (and 19.7 percent of the general population),
and Catholics constituted the remainder, save two to three thousand Eastern
Orthodox Christians.[2] These numbers reveal that Christianity—especially
Protestantism—rose to the status of a major religion in South Korea in the
past century. What these numbers obscure, however, is that within Korean
Protestantism itself there exist two main subgroups—evangelicals and, for
lack of a better term, non-evangelicals—and that, between them, evangelicals
predominate.

Throughout Korean Christian history, non-evangelical Protestants
have played and continue to play vital roles. This was the case especially
during the 1970s and 1980s when liberal Protestants created Minjung theology and took the lead in opposing political dictatorships.[3] Even so, in terms
of numbers and churchly influence, evangelicals overshadow their non-
evangelical counterparts. In fact, evangelicalism has so predominated the

Korean church that evangelicalism and Protestantism are often synonymous in Korea.

The rise of Korean evangelicalism has been discussed in earlier chapters. In light of this discussion, one might suppose that such success would have persisted through the end of the century, that the 1990s, no less than the previous decades, would have been a triumphant one for Korean evangelicalism. But such a hypothesis would be incorrect. Rather, Korean evangelicalism underwent a much more ambiguous and troubling development in the 1990s. Indeed, in that period, Korean evangelicalism—despite enjoying significant successes in politics, the economy, and civil society—was beleaguered by stalemated growth, scandals involving its prominent members, and challenges posed by other religions of Korea.

EVANGELICAL PREDOMINANCE IN KOREAN PROTESTANTISM

We have seen in earlier chapters that Korean Protestantism was imbued with an evangelical ethos from the beginning, especially after the great revival of 1907. Chapter 4, with its focus on the beliefs and practices of the evangelicals, confirms this generalization, making use of two 1982 surveys on Korean Protestant religiosity: the Centennial Comprehensive Study of the Korean (Protestant) Church (CCSKC) and the Investigation into the Growth and Religiosity of the Korean (Protestant) Church (IGRKC).[4] Unfortunately, these surveys were not replicated in the 1990s.

Another major study on Korean Protestant religiosity was conducted by Gallup Korea in 1997, however: *Han'guk kaesin'gyoin ŭi kyohoe hwaltong kwa sinang ŭisik* (Korean Protestants' Churchly Activities and Religious Consciousness).[5] This survey took up broader issues than those of the CCSKC and the IGRKC and did not ask some of the significant questions posed in the earlier studies, such as those concerning the inerrancy of the Bible or the essentiality of the Holy Spirit (born-again) experience. Still, some of its questions were revealing. Some of the more telling ones asked whether the respondents had accepted Jesus Christ as their personal savior (73.2 percent said yes); had experienced the Holy Spirit (52 percent, yes); were certain of their salvation (67.9 percent, yes); and believed in the imminent end of the world (68.9 percent, yes), the return of Jesus (80.7 percent, yes), and the possibility of salvation in other religions (24.5 percent, yes).[6]

These findings, when compared with those of the 1980s studies, suggest that Korean evangelicalism became diluted somewhat in the 1990s. Granted, one should not read too much into some of these figures, such as those relating to the Holy Spirit experience and the certainty of salvation, since even a respondent who had not experienced them might nonetheless have considered them essential, in which case she might still qualify as an evangelical. Overall, it is clear that even while evangelical religiosity became diluted somewhat in the 1990s, the evangelical ethos for the most part continued to predominate in the Korean Protestant Church.

But what percentage of Korean Protestants and their churches is evangelical? To my knowledge, no survey exists that directly addresses this question.[7] Therefore an answer must be estimated. One way to arrive at such an estimation is by determining the percentage of respondents in similar surveys who embrace attributes deemed evangelical. Extrapolating from the results of the IGRKC and the CCSKC surveys, one can thus estimate that in the early 1980s well over 90 percent of Korean Protestants were solidly evangelical; and an extrapolation from the Gallup Korea survey indicates that near the end of the 1990s at least 75 percent of all Korean Protestants were solidly evangelical.[8]

Also in need of estimation is the percentage of Korean Protestant churches that are evangelical, for no study addresses this question directly. One tack is to take a hint from the churches' denominational affiliations. Even if the religiosity of individual churches is difficult to determine, the ethos of the denominations they belong to is well known, and that information can be used to estimate how many of the churches are evangelical or non-evangelical. In South Korea there are three non-evangelical Protestant denominations: the Episcopal Church, the Lutheran Church, and the openly liberal Presbyterian denomination, Han'guk kidokkyo changnohoe ch'onghoe (the Presbyterian Church in the Republic of Korea). It is fairly safe to say that all the other Protestant denominations are evangelical. According to the 1991 *Christian Yearbook of Korea*, these three non-evangelical churches possessed 1,359 churches in 1990—about 4 percent of the total.[9] This figure is in line with the estimate of over 90 percent for the evangelicals based on the earlier IGRKC and CCSKC findings.

The *Christian Yearbook* ceased publication after the 1991 edition, but according to a figure cited in the Gallup Korea survey, 1,565 churches belonged to these three denominations in 1997, or about 5 percent of all the Protestant churches in Korea.[10] Conversely, this indicates that toward the end of the 1990s, 95 percent of all Korean Protestant churches were evangelical. This figure appears to conflict with the estimate above, based on the Gallup Korea survey, that suggested a figure as low as 75 percent for the proportion of evangelicals in the Korean Protestant church in the 1990s. It is not necessary to draw such a conclusion, however; a church may espouse a certain orientation even if some of its members do not. Either way, it is clear that with regard to both institutions and their members, Korean Protestantism in the 1990s was predominantly evangelical.

Evangelicalism as South Korea's Most Successful Religion in the 1990s

South Korea is a religiously pluralistic society, in which no single religion absolutely dominates. Still, if success is defined as "the attainment of wealth, position, honors, or the like," there is no denying that some religions succeed more than others.[11] In 1990s South Korea, evangelicalism was that religion. An initial case for this assertion can be made on the basis of a finding from the 1997 Gallup Korea survey: 53.2 percent of the nonbelievers surveyed stated that the Protestant Church's influence on society was on the increase, whereas their responses regarding Buddhism and Catholicism were 40.6 percent and 43.0 percent, respectively.[12] Of course, such a finding alone is not persuasive enough. But a much stronger, even indisputable, case can be made for this assertion if we examine how much influence the Protestant Church, or evangelicalism, wielded in some key areas of Korean society during the decade—namely, civil society, politics, and the economy—especially in comparison with other religions.

Civil society as a historical category has meant a series of societal developments, nongovernmental and noncommercial in nature, that occurred in the West accompanying the rise of capitalism and the bourgeoisie. As a substantive category, the term has little meaning outside the West. The term, however, also has an analytical meaning—for instance, as "the realm of organized social life that is voluntary, self-generating, [largely] self-supporting, autonomous from the state, and bound by a legal order or a set of shared rules."[13] In this sense, the concept has applicability in South Korea—and in evangelicalism. It also admits of the claim that, in the 1990s, evangelicalism constituted a significant portion of the South Korean civil society and that evangelicalism wielded more influence than any other Korean religions in this realm.

The assertion that evangelicalism was the most successful religion in South Korea in the 1990s finds support in the reach and sheer size of the evangelical establishment, which undoubtedly is an "organized social life that is voluntary, self-generating, [largely] self-supporting, [and] autonomous from the state." As noted, the 1995 census found Buddhists surpassing Protestants as a percentage of the general population: 23.3 percent to 19.7 percent. When it comes to the number of churches, however, the Protestants outpaced the Buddhists (and Catholics) much earlier and by a much larger margin. In 1990 the Protestants owned 34,407 churches—compared to 9,231 belonging to the Buddhists and 844 belonging to the Catholics. In the same year, the Protestant clergy numbered 58,288, whereas the Buddhist and Catholic clergy numbered 25,205 and 7,640, respectively.[14] Six years later, the gap had widened: Protestant churches numbered 58,046, to the Buddhists' 11, 561 and the Catholics' 1,019. Protestant clergy numbered 98,905, whereas the Buddhist and Catholic clergies numbered 26,037 and 10,151, respectively.[15]

Protestants predominated in less churchly institutions as well. In 1995, Protestants had 174 incorporated foundations and associations in South Korea, to Buddhists' 75 and Catholics' 70.[16] In 1996, Protestants possessed 69 institutions of higher education (colleges, universities, seminaries, and junior colleges), whereas Buddhists had a mere 2 and Catholics, 12. In the same year, Protestants published 111 periodicals, to Buddhists' 27 and Catholics' 71.[17] One study finds that, in 1985, Protestants ran 391 (61 percent) of the 637 faith-based welfare agencies in South Korea—elderly homes, orphanages, medical centers, vocational centers, and the like. Another study finds that 225 of the 440 social work agencies (66 percent) in 2001 were Protestant.[18] Evangelicals therefore must have operated 61 to 66 percent of all faith-based welfare agencies in South Korea in the 1990s. More specifically, in 1991 a movement to donate organs began in South Korea. Ten years and 570 transplants later, 65.4 percent of the donors were Protestants, 7.8 percent were Buddhists, and 7.3 percent were Catholics.[19] Finally, when the North Korean famine spread in the 1990s, it was the Protestants who formed the first civilian relief organizations in South Korea, sending aid worth approximately US$59.2 million, between 1997 and 2003.[20]

During the 1990s, politics was another arena where South Korean evangelicals, for better or worse, exerted a disproportionately large share of influence. The decade, in fact, saw the entire Christian community gaining in political influence: the Catholics also garnered considerable political clout, as evidenced by the presidency of Kim Dae Jung (1998–2003), a devout Catholic. Even so, the lion's share of political influence lay with the Protestants, as attested most notably by the presidency of Kim Young Sam, an elder from Ch'unghyŏn Presbyterian Church, who served from 1993 to 1998. Protestants preponderated in Kim's administration: of 175 ministers and vice-ministers, 76 (43 percent) were Protestants, 27 (15 percent) were Buddhists, 47 (29 percent) were Catholics, and 25 (about 14 percent) were nonbelievers.[21]

During Kim Young Sam's term as president, Protestants enjoyed plurality not only in the executive branch but also in the legislative branch, the National Assembly. Protestants constituted about half of the members of the assembly.[22] Even in Kim Dae Jung's administration, Protestants were well represented. For one thing, though Kim himself was a Catholic, his influential wife, Lee Hee Ho, was a Methodist. Moreover, a study conducted by Buddhists in 2000 found that of the top one hundred governmental positions of that year, Protestants occupied 42, Buddhists 9, Catholics 20, members of other religions 3, and nonbelievers 26.[23] Another study in 2000 found that 207 of the 273 National Assembly representatives professed a religion: of these 107 (39 percent of the entire assembly) professed to be Protestants, surpassing the number of Buddhists (30, or 11 percent) and Catholics (69, or 25 percent).[24]

In 1998 South Koreans held a nationwide election of regional officials such as governors and mayors. The results countered the Protestants' ascendance in politics, as more Buddhists were elected than Protestants. Of a total of 228 officials, 82 (35 percent) were Buddhists, and 58 (25 percent) Protestants; Catholics and nonbelievers garnered, respectively, 28 (12 percent) and 60 (26 percent).[25]

All in all, these figures suffice to make the point that evangelicals were the most influential religious group in South Korean politics in the 1990s. But that point becomes even more apparent when we examine the influence they displayed in the presidential elections of 1992 and 1997. In the 1992 election, none of the three top candidates—Kim Young Sam, Kim Dae Jung, and Chŏng Chuyŏng (the founder of Hyundai Corporation)—received a majority of the votes.[26] Considering that regionalism was a factor in this election (as in all elections in South Korea) and that Kim Young Sam's home base, South Kyŏngsang Province, is one of the least Christianized regions in the country, there is little doubt that his being an elder of the Ch'unghyŏn Presbyterian Church, the flagship church of the largest Presbyterian denomination (Haptong) in Korea, was a decisive factor in his attracting evangelical votes from all over the country and winning the election.[27] Indeed, during this election, evangelicals quite consciously mobilized on behalf of their favorite son. The Ch'unghyŏn Presbyterian Church, for example, formed a group of elders to canvass for Kim, and evangelical churches all over the country held prayer meetings to pray for the election of an elder as president.[28] In response, Kim promised that if he was elected, he would see to it that "hymns would continuously ring out from the Blue House."[29] Consequently according to K'ŭrisŭch'yan sinmun (Christian Press), over 90 percent of the evangelicals voted for Kim Young Sam in that election.[30]

The evangelical prowess displayed in the 1992 election was not lost on the candidates running in the 1997 presidential election. The contenders included Kim Chongpil, an archconservative and a Methodist deacon. In his case, though, religious affiliation did not help; he repulsed even the evangelicals, in light of his infamous political opportunism and sordid ties with past dictators. The two main contenders were Kim Dae Jung and Yi Hwoech'ang, both Catholics. Given these choices, evangelicals did not gravitate toward a particular candidate, as they had in the previous election.[31] Yi and both Kims, however, made a point of courting evangelicals by canvassing churches and visiting with the pastors. They paid special attention to the so-called king-makers like Cho Yonggi, minister of the Yoido Full Gospel Church, and Kim "Billy" Changhwan, president of the influential evangelical broadcast network Kŭktong pangsong (Far Eastern Broadcasting Company).[32] In their interviews at the Kŭktong pangsong, for example, the candidates took care to make appropriate comments about their faith. Kim Chongpil opined, "There aren't many countries that are more earnest than ours in believing in God and seek-ing to share the Gospel. I hope we will live out this spirit and faith in all our lives"; Yi Hwoech'ang recited his favorite biblical verses, Isaiah 43:1–3, from memory and stated that whenever he faced difficulties, he depended on God; and Kim Dae Jung trumped them both by saying that in his life thus far he had experienced five near-death incidents, six years of imprisonment, and ten years of exile, and in the midst of it all he had personally experienced and seen God twice.[33] In the end, the Asian currency crisis probably had more to do with Kim Dae Jung's election than his ability to play to Protestant sensibilities. Nevertheless, that Kim continued to hold the Protestants in high regard was displayed at a prayer gathering he attended before he left for the Blue House. With three hundred or so Protestant leaders in attendance, he asked for Chris-tians to pray for the nation and to "display the Puritan spirit in particular so as to overcome the collapsed economy."[34]

In addition to civil society and politics, the economy is another aspect of South Korean society that has been influenced by evangelism. In the 1990s, however, evangelicalism's influence appears to have been less pronounced than it was in civil society and politics. Nevertheless, it was still strong enough to surpass the influence of the other religions. A prima facie case for this claim can be made in this way: South Korea is an urban society, with most of the wealth concentrated in the cities, where most Protestants live. According to the South Korean National Statistics Office, in 1995 Protestants constituted more than 25 percent of the population in the Seoul metropolitan region. Moreover, they made up more than 30 percent of the population in the wealthiest districts of Seoul, Kangnam-gu, and Sŏch'o-gu.[35] Thus it is plausible to infer that, in the 1990s, Protestants possessed more wealth and wielded more influence in the economy than other religionists in South Korea.

Additional, more concrete pieces of evidence buttress this argument. A 1995 study by a research affiliate of the leading daily *Chungang ilbo* (Joong ang ilbo; Joong ang Daily) analyzed the religions of 4,903 chief executive officers of 4,076 private enterprises in South Korea and found that 34 percent (1,667) pro-fessed a religion. Of these religious CEOs, 43 percent (713) were Protestant, 38 percent (638) Buddhist, 17 percent (280) Catholic, and 2 percent (36) of other religions.[36] This study also listed the denominations of the presidents of the top 10 *chaeböl* (conglomerates) of 1995; there were 3 Protestants (including an Episcopalian), 3 Buddhists, 1 Confucian, and 3 nonbelievers.[37] Another study reported that in 1999 the presidents of the top one hundred Korean businesses included 31 Protestants, 23 Buddhists, 11 Catholics, and 29 nonbelievers.[38]

A BELEAGUERED EVANGELICALISM

The picture should now be clear: evangelicalism was South Korea's most successful religion in the 1990s. This picture, however, tells only half the story, and the other half is not very pretty. For if the decade was one of preponderant (though not quite hegemonic) sway for the evangelicals, it was also one of troubles for them: the growth of their churches slowed, scandals involving some of their high-profile members shocked the public, and open conflict arose between them and other religious groups.

Analyzing census figures collected by the National Statistics Office, sociologist of religion Lee Won Gue observed that, between 1991 and 1995, membership in the Korean Protestant Church increased from 8,037,464 to 8,760,336—a gain of 9 percent.[39] No Ch'ijun, another leading sociologist of religion, estimated a 4 percent growth rate between 1990 and 1995.[40] He also noted that growth rates in 1994 and 1995 for the two largest denominations—Taehan yesugyo changnohoe ch'onghoe (Haptong, or General Assembly of the Presbyterian Church in Korea) and Taehan yesugyo changnohoe ch'onghoe (T'onghap, or the Presbyterian Church of Korea), whose combined memberships constitute about half of the total Protestant membership in South Korea—was less than 1 percent.

Had this kind of development been noted with regard to the Protestant churches in Europe or the United States, where membership has been sliding for decades, not much alarm would have been sounded. However, it did arouse concern in South Korea—home to twenty-three of the fifty largest churches in the world. The slowdown represented a departure from earlier trends. Between 1960 and 1970 the membership in evangelical churches had grown by 412 percent (from 623,072 to 3,192,621), by 57 percent between 1970 and 1977, by 29.7 percent between 1977 and 1985, and by 23.9 percent between 1985 and 1991.[41]

The stalemate continued, and by the turn of the twenty-first century it had become clear that membership growth was no longer merely slowing but declining. A national census published in 2005 found that between 1995 and 2005 the Protestant numbers had decreased by 1.6 percent (150,000). This trend has caused considerable consternation among evangelical leaders.[42]

These doldrums have exacerbated some long-standing problems in Korean evangelicalism. One of them has been the diminishment of respect for evangelical ministers, especially new seminary graduates in search of pastorates. This diminishment of respect has occurred, in part, because the seminaries produced too many graduates, many of whom were ill-prepared for the role of church leader and in any case could not have been absorbed by either existing congregations or newly established ones. Even well-established seminaries, such as those belonging to the two largest Presbyterian denominations, tended to recruit more students than their congregations actually needed. The seminaries carried out this excessive recruitment partly for financial reasons, since student tuition was their main source of revenue. But a more serious reason for the lessening of respect for the clergy stemmed from the overabundance of nonaccredited and poorly equipped theological institutions that produced a slew of inferiorly trained graduates annually. In 1995, for example, more than 310 theological institutions existed in Korea. Of these, the Ministry of Education accredited only 38.[43] In total, these theological institutions produced about 8,000 graduates every year in the 1990s. Since only about 1,000 of them graduated from seminaries of six well-established denominations, the majority were products of either accredited but poorly equipped seminaries or, worse, nonaccredited institutions and lacked the knowledge and skills to minister to a highly educated society.

Much of the church growth in South Korea before 1990 was due to new seminary graduates striking out on their own and starting new congregations in unevangelized areas. By 1990, however, churches saturated the country, and it became increasingly difficult for new ministers to find pastorates. Many seminarians, as a result, opted for overseas work as missionaries, swelling the missionary ranks to more than 10,000 at the end of the decade, putting the Korean church second only to the American church in the number of missionaries it sent abroad.[44] Those seminarians that did not go overseas had no choice but to compete in the domestic religious marketplace, jostling with those already ensconced in churches for members.[45]

The behavior the clergy displayed in such competition was often unedifying. Such behavior probably had much to do with a trend revealed by a 1997 Gallup Korea study: 71.1 percent of the respondents thought that the Protestant Church was more interested in increasing its size and influence than in seeking truth, whereas only 33.8 percent thought this was true for the Buddhists and 32.1 percent for the Catholics. The competitive behavior among the clergy might also have contributed to the results of a 1995 Gallup Korea poll on the "honesty and professional ethics of Korean professionals": Protestant ministers came in fifth place, behind Catholic priests, university professors, Buddhist monks, and television reporters/announcers. In a similar survey conducted in 1993, Protestant ministers were not even in the top five.[46]

In the 1990s the ministers' lack of proper theological education and their preoccupation with membership growth were not the only problems the South Korean evangelical church faced. The church was also bedeviled by a series of scandals involving some of its high-profile clergy. The first of these involved a millenarian, or rapture, controversy that culminated in late 1992. At the center of it was Yi Changnim, the leader of a community called Tami Ministries (Tami sŏngyohoe). Since the 1980s Yi had been predicting that the world would come to an end on October 28, 1992, and that only those who adhered to his teachings would be saved—that is, would be lifted up to heaven and met by the returning Christ. To the utter bewilderment of most Koreans, including the evangelicals, 1,500 or so of his followers acted on his prophecy. They prepared to abandon the world, selling their property and severing ties with unbelieving family members. Most evangelical leaders promptly dissociated themselves from Yi and branded him a heretic, but whether the public was as quick to dissociate them from Yi is questionable, since they were all much more alike than different, theologically speaking. The rapture, of course, never came, and Yi was arrested for committing fraud. The police had discovered that he had been collecting money from his followers—resorting to extortion in some cases—and investing some of it in a bond that would not mature until well after October 28, 1992.[47]

Other scandals followed. On June 29, 1995, the upscale, five-story Samp'ung department store, in Seoul's posh Kangnam district collapsed, killing 502 and injuring more than 1,000. Seoul residents had witnessed the collapse of shoddy buildings before, but never one of this magnitude and with so many casualties.[48] Residents later became angry upon learning that the owner of the building—a deacon at Yŏngnak Presbyterian Church—had allowed it to remain in use despite obvious signs of imminent collapse.

Another scandal involved a company, Hanbo Steel. The company filed for bankruptcy in January 1997, and it was revealed that it had been bribing numerous public officials in an attempt to maintain the appearance of solvency. In the course of the subsequent investigation, President Kim Young Sam's evangelical son Hyŏnchŏl was implicated. Soon after, it came to light that even though he had no official authority, the son had been deeply involved in policy decisions at the Blue House and in influence peddling. This abuse of power at the highest level of government enraged the public, which supported the judge who sentenced Kim's son to two years in prison.[49] The "Hanbo Incident" proved to be a nightmare for Kim Young Sam in other ways as well. It ushered in a series of economic woes that ultimately resulted in a financial meltdown of the nation—the Korean component of the 1997 Asian Financial Crisis. And the president's inability to handle this crisis completely undermined his reputation, to the point that he found himself persona non grata even in his own church.[50]

Then there was a scheme concocted by Kwŏn Yŏnghae, Kim Young Sam's director of the Agency for National Security Planning (NSP, formerly the Korean Central Intelligence Agency). He loathed Kim Dae Jung's politics, and during the 1997 election attempted to smear Kim by falsely portraying him as being under the influence of the North.[51] When the scheme was exposed, Kwŏn attempted to commit hara-kiri. Although the Korean general public knows of this conspiracy as the Northern Wind Operation (*pukp'ung chakchŏn*), Kwŏn himself preferred to call it the Amalek Strategy, seeing himself as the Moses who would vanquish the evil Amalekites who stood in the way of God's people. It was not surprising that he would pick such a Hebrew Bible reference, for he, like the president, was an evangelical elder and an avid Bible reader.[52]

Finally there came the "Dress Lobby" (*ot robi*), a bribery scandal involving three avowedly evangelical women, who attended Bible study at the same church, and their clothier. Two of the evangelical women were wives of high government officials; the third was wife of a well-to-do businessman (*chaebŏl*) known as a devout evangelical himself—and in trouble with the law for illegally hoarding wealth outside the country. The controversy swirled around mutual accusations between the women as to who was guilty of initiating a bribe in the form of an expensive dress purchased from the clothier's shop. Although the court eventually found the businessman's wife guilty, in the course of the investigation the case evolved into something much more complicated and weighty—provoking accusations of a prosecutorial cover-up, revealing problems in the judiciary system, and compelling the government to introduce, for the first time in South Korean history, the office of special prosecutor. The case deeply embarrassed the government and the evangelicals, but especially the latter, as the women came across as hypocrites, mouthing pieties and lies in the same breath and directly contradicting each other in public hearings, even as they swore on the Bible.

These scandals were disconcerting and divisive enough, but in the 1990s the evangelicals also experienced another kind of conflict—between themselves and other religionists. Although the evangelicals provoked most of the friction, especially vis-à-vis the Buddhists, by the end of the decade they found themselves at the receiving end of provocation as well.

There is no question that much of this conflict stemmed from evangelicalism's exclusivist soteriology and the way it disparages the traditional religions of Korea. Pak Hyŏngnyong's stark view on this matter has already been mentioned—namely, his assertion that "Christianity's most appropriate relation to other religions is not compromise . . . but clash and conquest."[53]

Apparently, some evangelicals took Pak's message literally. In June 1998, for example, an evangelical man broke into a Zen center in Cheju Island and decapitated 750 granite Buddha statues and destroyed other religious objects. Under arrest, he confessed to attempting to convert the temple into a church. As disturbing as it was, this was not an isolated incident, nor was it the most heinous. On several occasions antagonistic evangelicals burnt entire Buddhist temples to the ground.[54]

It is to the Buddhists' credit that they did not retaliate in kind. However, incivility breeds incivility, and other religious or semireligious groups were quick to learn from the evangelicals' unilateral, uncivil tactics. A prime example is the conduct of the Korean Cultural Campaigns Association (Hanmunhwa undonghoe, or KCCA), a coalition of religious and semireligious organizations that erected a statue of Tan'gun, Korea's mythical founder, in 369 Korean public schools in 1998 and 1999 and declared its determination to erect one in every other public school in Korea.[55] The KCCA's rationale is that since all Koreans recognize—or should recognize—Tan'gun as their national founder, national unity would be enhanced if children grew up paying honor to his statues in their schools.

In reality, however, the Tan'gun statues have engendered division. The statues infuriated the evangelicals, who condemned them as idols, correctly pointing out that a number of indigenous religions worship Tan'gun as a deity.[56] They also questioned the constitutionality of the KCCA's action, since they believed that requiring students to pay obeisance to the statues amounted to infringing on the students' religious freedom. To the Tan'gunists' contention that because the statues were set in place with the principals' permission, due process had been observed, the evangelicals retorted that an endeavor as grave as the KCCA's should not have been left to the discretion of the principals. The evangelicals called on the government to remove the statutes immediately. Not getting satisfaction, some of them took matters into their own hands, assaulting and damaging many of the statues, thereby provoking an accusation from the Tan'gunists that the evangelicals were less than true patriots.[57]

Although denouncing the Tan'gunists, in the end the evangelicals oddly mirrored them. Like the evangelicals, the Tan'gunists were on a quest, but theirs was carried out in the name of Korean nationalism, rather than religion, and was aimed at solidifying a national identity that they alleged had become diluted because of alien influences like evangelicalism. Moreover, the Tan'gunists were similarly convinced of the rightness of their quest and were unwilling to relent. Hence, the evangelicals' beleaguerment in this regard persists.

The problems of conflict with other religionists, scandals that besmirched the church, and stagnation in membership growth, as well as successes of the 1990s—being the most influential religious institution and wielding preponderant influence in the economy, politics, and civil society—indicate that Korean evangelicalism started the twenty-first century in a very different mode from that at the start of the twentieth century. Then, Korean society was in shambles, and the church barely had a toehold in it. A great many Koreans sought a new moral order—a salvation—and expected to find it in the evangelical church. Evangelicals of today may want to ponder whether such expectation has been met. Whatever the result of such pondering, this much is clear: now evangelicalism is not only in Korean society but also of it.

Notes

Introduction

Epigraph. Joachim Wach, *Introduction to the History of Religions*, ed. Joseph M. Kitigawa (New York: Macmillan, 1988), 90.

1. The person most responsible for spreading such a view of Korea was probably William Elliot Griffis, whose book *Corea, the Hermit Nation* was one of the first comprehensive histories of Korea in a Western language. First published in 1882, it went through nine editions in thirty years and was must reading for missionaries going to Korea. Everett N. Hunt Jr., *Protestant Pioneers in Korea* (Maryknoll, NY: Orbis, 1980), 54.

2. L. George Paik, *The History of Protestant Missions in Korea, 1832–1910* (1929; reprint, Seoul: Yonsei University Press, 1987), 377.

3. *Sinanggye* (August 1988): 63. The revivals recorded a total attendance of about 1.5 million. Also see *Sinanggye* (November 1988): 77.

4. David Brudnoy, "Japan's Experiment in Korea," *Monumenta Nipponica* 2, no. 1 (1970): 155–195; Bruce Cumings, "The Legacy of Japanese Colonialism in Korea," in *The Japanese Colonial Empire, 1895–1945*, ed. Ramon H. Myers and Mark R. Peattie (Princeton, NJ: Princeton University Press, 1984), 478–496.

5. Bruce Cumings, *The Origins of the Korean War*, vol. 1, *Liberation and the Emergence of Separate Regimes, 1945–1947* (Princeton, NJ: Princeton University Press, 1981), 113, 121.

6. I recognize that a debate exists on the status of (neo-)Confucianism as a religion. Here I agree with John Duncan, who takes a Durkheimian position that Confucianism can be considered as "a commonly shared religious system that helps give definition to a large community." See his "Proto-nationalism in Premodern Korea," in *Perspectives on Korea*, ed. Sang-Oak Lee and Duk-Soo Park (Sydney: Wild Peony, 1998), 198–221.

7. According to a government census published in 1987, 483,366 South Koreans, or about one percent of the population, claimed Confucianism as their religion in 1985. This figure contrasted with 8,059,624 (20 percent) for Buddhism and 8,354,679 (21 percent) for Christianity (combining Catholics and Protestants). Minister of Economic Planning Board, *13th Population and Housing Census of the Republic of Korea*

(Seoul: Ministry of Economic Planning Board, 1985), 288, table 6. On (neo-)Confu-cianism's influence on Korea, see Martina Deuchler, *The Confucian Transformation of Korea: A Study of Society and Ideology* (Cambridge, MA: Council on East Asian Stud-ies, Harvard University, 1992); William Theodore de Bary and JaHyun Kim Haboush, eds., *The Rise of Neo-Confucianism in Korea* (New York: Columbia University Press, 1985); JaHyun Kim Haboush and Martina Deuchler, eds., *Culture and the State in Late Chosŏn Korea* (Cambridge, MA: Harvard University Asia Center, 1999); and John Duncan, "Confucian Social Values in Contemporary South Korea," in *Religion and So-ciety in Contemporary Korea*, ed. Lewis R. Lancaster and Richard K. Payne (Berkeley: Institute of East Asian Studies, University of California, Berkeley, 1997), 49–73.

8. James Huntley Grayson states that Korea's monastic Buddhism is especially dynamic, having no equal in East Asia. See his *Korea: A Religious History*, rev. ed. (London: RoutledgeCurzon, 2002), 1. See also Robert E. Buswell Jr., *The Zen Monastic Experience: Buddhist Practice in Contemporary Korea* (Princeton, NJ: Princeton Uni-versity Press, 1992); and Jaeryong Shim, *Korean Buddhism: Tradition and Transforma-tion* (Seoul: Jimoondang, 1999).

9. Yu Tongsik [Ryu Tong-shik], *Han'guk mugyo ŭi yŏksa wa kujo* (Seoul: Yonsei University Press, 1975); Hyun-key Kim Hogarth, *Korean Shamanism and Cultural Na-tionalism* (Seoul: Jimoondang, 1999); Chungmoo Choi, "Hegemony and Shamanism: The State, the Elite, and Shamans in Contemporary Korea," in *Religion and Society in Contemporary Korea*, ed. Lewis R. Lancaster and Richard K. Payne (Berkeley: Institute of East Asian Studies, University of California, Berkeley, 1997), 19–48.

10. By "Kim-Il-Sungism" I mean the set of beliefs (which incorporate some Marxism-Leninism but more significantly the North Korean ideology known as *juche*), practices, and aura of (quasi) sacrality that center around the person of Kim Il Sung (and later of his son Kim Jong Il). Granted, to some, Kim-Il-Sungism might not qualify as a religion. But if religion is defined in a functional sense as the organization of individual and/or societal lives in terms of realities that are considered sacred—and salvific—then Kim-Il-Sungism qualifies at least as what Paul Tillich has called a quasi religion. Regardless of what outsiders may think of it, for most North Koreans (at least till the death of the founder in 1994), Kim-Il-Sungism has loomed large as a salvific system that has provided them with a set of potent symbols and rituals for structur-ing their individual and societal lives. For religious aspects of this phenomenon, see Donald Baker's appendix "Spirituality in North Korea," in *Korean Spirituality* (Hono-lulu: University of Hawai'i, 2008), 145–151; Eun Hee Shin's chapter "The Sociopolitical Organism: The Religious Dimensions of Juche Philosophy," in *Religions of Korea in Practice*, ed. Robert E. Buswell Jr. (Princeton, NJ: Princeton University Press, 2007), 517–533; and Thomas J. Belke, *Juche: A Christian Study of North Korea's State Religion* (Bartlesville, OK: Living Sacrifice Book Co., 1999). Also see Kim Jong Il, *On the Juche Idea* (Pyongyang: Foreign Languages Publishing House, 1982); Byung Chul Koh, "The Cult of Personality and the Succession Issue," in *Journey to North Korea: Personal Per-ceptions*, ed. C. I. Eugene Kim and B. C. Koh (Berkeley: Institute of East Asian Studies, University of California, Berkeley, 1983), 25–41; Helen-Louise Hunter, *Kim Il-song's*

North Korea (London: Praeger, 1999); Dae-Sook Suh, *Kim Il Sung: The North Korean Leader* (New York: Columbia University Press, 1988); Bruce Cumings' chapter "Nation of the Sun King: North Korea, 1953–Present," in his *Korea's Place in the Sun: A Modern History*, updated ed. (New York: W. W. Norton, 2005), 299–341; Charles K. Armstrong's section "The Leader and the Masses: Origins and Dissemination of the 'Kim Cult,'" in his *North Korean Revolution, 1945–1950* (New York: Cornell University Press, 2003), 222–229; Ha Chongp'il, *Pukhan ŭi chonggyo munhwa* (Seoul: Sŏnin, 2003); Paul Tillich, *Dynamics of Faith* (New York: Harper and Row, Harper Torch books, 1958), 15; and Christel Lane, *The Rites of Rulers: Ritual in Industrial Society—the Soviet Case* (New York: Cambridge University Press, 1981).

11. The predominance of evangelicals in Korean Protestantism is discussed in chapter 4 and the epilogue.

12. Han Yŏngje, ed., *Han'guk kidokkyo sŏngjang 100-yŏn* (Seoul: Kidokkyo munsa, 1986), 198. The Eastern Orthodox Church also arrived in Korea in this period. It arrived in 1899 from Russia, but it never grew comparably to the other two communions, having been set back considerably by the Russo-Japanese War (1904–1905), the Russian Revolution (1917), and the Japanese colonial period (1910–1945). It claimed only a few thousand adherents at the end of the twentieth century. For a brief overview of the Orthodox Church's history in Korea, see Grayson, *Korea*, 169–170; and Kevin Baker, *A History of the Orthodox Church in China, Korea, and Japan* (Lewiston, NY: Edwin Mellen, 2006).

13. The National Statistical Office's figures for 1985 and 1995 are cited in Donald Baker, "Sibling Rivalry in Twentieth-Century Korea: Comparative Growth Rates of Catholic and Protestant Communities," in *Christianity in Korea*, ed. Robert E. Buswell Jr. and Timothy S. Lee, 283–308 (Honolulu: University of Hawai`i Press, 2006). For the 1991 figure, see National Statistical Office of Republic of Korea, *Han'guk ŭi sahoe chip'yo* (Seoul: National Statistical Office, 1993), 267. By contrast, the National Statistical Office found that the Buddhists constituted 20 percent and 23.2 percent of the South Korean population in 1985 and 1995, respectively. In the North, the government suppressed Christianity, barely allowing it to exist. In 1988, however, perhaps to soften its totalitarian image, it built two churches—one Protestant (P'yŏngyang Pongsu kyohoe [P'yŏngyang Pongsu Church]), the other Catholic (Changch'ung sŏngdang [Changch'ung Church]); in 1989, it built another Protestant church (Ch'ilgol kyohoe [Ch'ilgol Church]). In 2006, it also built a Russian Orthodox Church. *K'ŭrisŭch'yan t'udei*, August 17, 2006. An official North Korean report states that in 1988 the country's population was about 22 million; of this, about 11,000 were estimated to be Christians. See "North Korea Allows Religious Activities within Limits," *Han'guk ilbo*, Chicago edition, October 6, 1988; Kim Heung-soo, ed., *Haebanghu pukhan kyohoesa* (Seoul: Tasan kŭlpang, 1992); Paek Chunghyŏn, *Pukhan edo kyohoe ka inna yo?* (Seoul: Kung'min ilbo, 1998); Han'guk kidokkyo yŏksa yŏn'guso, *Pukhan kyohoesa* (Seoul: Han'guk kidokkyo yŏksa yŏn'guso, 1996).

14. Even in the 1990s, Christianity remains a numerically small religion in Japan, comprising about one percent of the population. See David Reid, *New Wine:*

The Cultural Shaping of Japanese Christianity (Berkeley, CA: Asian Humanities Press, 1991); and Mark R. Mullins, *Christianity Made in Japan: A Study of Indigenous Movements* (Honolulu: University of Hawai`i Press, 1998). In China, however, it has been a different story. There, since the late 1980s, Christianity—evangelical Protestantism in particular—has been growing rapidly. See Daniel H. Bays, ed., *Christianity in China: From the Eighteenth Century to the Present* (Stanford, CA: Stanford University Press, 1996); Tony Lamber, *The Resurrection of the Chinese Church* (Wheaton, IL: Harold Shaw, 1994); David Aikman, *Jesus in Beijing: How Christianity Is Transforming China and Changing the Global Balance of Power* (Washington, DC: Regnery, 2003); and Tony Lamber, *China's Christian Millions*, rev. and updated ed. (Oxford: Monarch, 2006).

15. Paul Freston, *Evangelicals and Politics in Asia, Africa and Latin America* (Cambridge: Cambridge University Press, 2001), 61. See also Philip Jenkins, *The Next Christendom: The Coming of Global Christianity* (Oxford: Oxford University Press, 2002).

16. George T. B. Davis, *Korea for Christ* (London: Christian Workers' Depot, 1910), 14.

17. Paul Ricoeur, *Hermeneutics and the Human Sciences*, ed. and trans. John B. Thompson (Cambridge: Cambridge University Press, 1981), 277.

18. Ibid., 278. Emphasis in original.

19. Ibid.

20. I am aware that some scholars dispute the usefulness of "evangelicalism" as a concept, contending that it has become amorphous. D. G. Hart makes this case in *Deconstructing Evangelicalism: Conservative Protestantism in the Age of Billy Graham* (Grand Rapids, MI: Baker Academic, 2004). But I am inclined to side with the mainstream scholarship on the issue, exemplified by works of scholars such as George M. Marsden, Mark Noll, Roger E. Olson, and Randall Balmer, who argue for its validity on historical and theological grounds. See Mark A. Noll, David W. Bebbington, and George A. Rawlyk, *Evangelicalism: Comparative Studies of Popular Protestantism in North America, the British Isles, and Beyond, 1700–1990* (Oxford: Oxford University Press, 1994); Randall Balmer, *Encyclopedia of Evangelicalism* (Waco, TX: Baylor University Press, 2004); Roger E. Olson, *Evangelical Theology* (Louisville, KY: Westminster John Knox Press, 2004); and two works by George M. Marsden, *Understanding Fundamentalism and Evangelicalism* (Grand Rapids, MI: Eerdmans, 1991) and *Fundamentalism and American Culture,* new ed. (Oxford: Oxford University Press, 2006). Also important are works of earlier scholars who preferred to call the phenomenon "Revivalism." See William G. McLoughlin Jr., *Modern Revivalism: Charles Grandison Finney to Billy Graham* (New York: Ronald Press, 1959); and the following works by Jerald C. Brauer: "Revivalism and Millenarianism in America," in *The Great Tradition*, ed. Joseph D. Ban and Paul R. Dekar, 147–159 (Valley Forge, PA: Judson, 1982); "Conversion: From Puritanism to Revivalism," in *Journal of Religion* 58 (July 1978): 227–243; and *Protestantism in America*, rev. ed. (Philadelphia: Westminster, 1965). Also apropos is the five-volume project on Fundamentalism edited by Martin E. Marty and R. Scott Appleby, including *Fundamentalism Observed* (Chicago: University of Chicago Press, 1991). Korean discussion on evangelicalism as such is limited, but see Ryu Dae Young,

"Ch'ogi han'guk kyohoe esŏ 'evangelical' ŭi ŭimiwa hyŏndaejŏk haesŏk ŭi munje," *Han'guk kidokkyo wa yŏksa* 15 (2001): 117–144; and Park Jong-Hyun, "Kim Insŏ ŭi 'pogŭmjuŭijŏk minjokchuŭi' sasang," *Han'guk kidokkyo wa yŏksa* 21 (2004):157–178.

1. Breakthrough for a New Moral Order, 1885–1919

Epigraph. Quoted by Reinhard Bendix in *Max Weber: An Intellectual Portrait* (Berkeley: University of California Press, 1960), 46–47. Emphasis mine.

1. By "cultural distortion," I mean the state of culture when its "elements are not harmoniously related but are mutually inconsistent and interfering." This is a concept developed by Anthony F. C. Wallace. See his "Revitalization Movements," *American Anthropologist* 58 (1956): 264–281.

2. Chin Young Choe notes, "Between 1782 and 1840 the country suffered a great famine or an epidemic on an average of once every two years, drastically increasing the number of the starving." Choe, *The Rule of the Taewongun, 1864–1873: Restoration in Yi Korea* (Cambridge, MA.: Harvard University Press, 1972), 11.

3. Woo-keun Han, *The History of Korea* (Honolulu: University of Hawai`i Press, 1971), 273.

4. On the idea of salvation, I am indebted to Joachim Wach, particularly his chapter "Salvation" in *Introduction to the History of Religions*, ed. Joseph M. Kitigawa (New York: Macmillan, 1988), 185–196. There he states, "The idea of salvation, which can be seen as constitutive of all religion, . . . arises from the conviction that human beings fundamentally stand in need of salvation, that is from the general experience of suffering, which may have many sources and causes, from accident and misfortune to an all-encompassing anxiety (*weltangst*)." (189) The term "nometic" derives from Peter Berger's "nomos, a socially constructed meaningful order." See his *Sacred Canopy: Elements of a Sociological Theory of Religion* (New York: Doubleday, 1967), 19. Also helpful is the work by Lewis R. Rambo: *Understanding Religious Conversion* (New Haven, CT: Yale University Press, 1993).

5. Chong-sik Lee, *The Politics of Korean Nationalism* (Berkeley: University of California Press, 1965), 125; Michael E. Robinson, *Cultural Nationalism in Korea, 1920–1925* (Seattle: University of Washington Press, 1988), 3.

6. Meredith B. McGuire, *Religion: The Social Context*, 3rd ed. (Belmont, CA: Wadsworth, 1992), 42.

7. James H. Grayson, *Korea: A Religious History*, rev. ed. (London: Routledge-Curzon, 2002), 205; Ki-baik Lee, *A New History of Korea* (Cambridge, MA: Harvard University Press, 1984), 223; Woo-keun Han, *History of Korea*, 354.

8. Han, *History of Korea*, 354; Grayson, *Korea*, 241, 242; Ki-baik Lee, *New History of Korea*, 258.

9. Keith Pratt and Richard Rutt, eds., *Korea: A Historical and Cultural Dictionary* (Surrey, UK: Curzon, 1999), s.v. "Sirhak." Also see the section on Sirhak in *Sourcebook of Korean Civilization*, vol. 2, ed. Peter H. Lee (New York: Columbia University Press, 1996), 337–338.

10. Ki-baik Lee, *New History of Korea*, 223. Also see the section "Wang Yang-ming in Korea," in Peter H. Lee, *Sourcebook of Korean Civilization*, 2:277–285.

11. *Han'guk kat'ollik sajŏn*, vol. 9 (Seoul: Research Institute for Korean Church History, 2005), s.v. "Yi Sŭnghun."

12. Till 1789, when they began to doubt the validity of their religious services, members of this protochurch elected their own priests, who not only baptized other Koreans but also administered Mass and extreme unction, as well as delivering homilies. Yu Hongnyŏl, *Han'guk chŏnju kyohoesa* (Seoul: Kat'ollik ch'ulp'ansa, 1962), 1: 93.

13. Ki-baik Lee, *New History of Korea*, 239.

14. William E. Henthorn, *A History of Korea* (New York: Free Press, 1971), 217.

15. Quoted in Donald Baker, "The Martyrdom of Paul Yun: Western Religion and Eastern Ritual in 18th Century Korea," *Transactions of the Royal Asiatic Society, Korea Branch* 54 (1979): 50. See also these other works by Donald Baker: "A Different Thread: Orthodoxy, Heterodoxy, and Catholicism in a Confucian World," in *Culture and the State in Late Chosŏn Korea*, ed. JaHyun Kim Haboush and Martina Deuchler (Cambridge, MA: Harvard University Press, 1999), 199–281; and "Tasan and His Brothers: How Religion Divided a Korean Confucian Family," in *Perspectives on Korea*, ed. Sang-Oak Lee and Duk-Soo Park (Sydney: Peony, 1998), 172–197.

16. Yu Hongnyŏl, *Han'guk chŏnju kyohoe yaksa* (Seoul: St. Joseph's Press, 1983), 56.

17. Kwang Cho, "The Meaning of Catholicism in Korean History," *Korea Journal* 24 (August 1984): 14–27. On the Koreans' reception of Catholic teachings, see Kwang Cho, "Human Relations as Expressed in Vernacular Catholic Writings of the Late Chosŏn Dynasty," in *Christianity in Korea*, ed. Robert E. Buswell Jr. and Timothy S. Lee (Honolulu: University of Hawai`i Press, 2006), 29–37. See also Hector Diaz, *A Korean Theology: Chu-gyo yo-ji: Essentials of the Lord's Teaching by Chŏng Yak-jong Augustine (1760–1801)* (Immensee, Switzerland: Neue Zeitschrift für Missionswissenschaft, 1986).

18. Yu Hongnyŏl, *Han'guk chŏnju kyohoe yaksa*, 164. On the extraordinary leadership displayed by a woman leader of the early Catholic community during the 1801 persecution, see Gari Ledyard, "Kollumba Kang Wansuk, an Early Catholic Activist and Martyr," in Buswell and Lee, *Christianity in Korea*, 38–71.

19. Suk-woo Choi, "Korean Catholicism Yesterday and Today" *Korea Journal* 24 (August 1984): 4–13; Peter H. Lee, "The Persecution of Catholicism," in his *Sourcebook of Korean Civilization*, 2:145–159; Jai-Keun Choi, *The Origins of the Roman Catholic Church in Korea: An Examination of Popular and Governmental Responses to Catholic Missions in the Late Chosŏn Dynasty* (Edinburgh, Scotland: Hermit Kingdom Press, 2006). For a glimpse of the life of Catholics in the underground, see Robert Sayer, "Potters and Christians: New Light on Korea's First Catholics," in *Korean Culture* 6, no. 2: 26–39.

20. In 1905, Tonghak's name was changed to Chŏndogyo (Religion of the Heavenly Way) by its Third Great Leader, Son Pyŏnghŭi. Up to the first half of the twentieth century, Chŏndogyo was a major religion in Korea. As late as the mid-1960s, it claimed 600,000 adherents, though its strength has weakened considerably since, with a 1986

census showing only 50,000 identifying themselves as adherents. See Grayson, *Korea*, 198, 236.

21. Peter H. Lee, *Sourcebook of Korean Civilization*, 2:313; Benjamin Weems, *Reform, Rebellion, and the Heavenly Way* (Tucson: University of Arizona Press, 1964), 7; Susan Shin, "The Tonghak Movement: From Enlightenment to Revolution," *Korean Studies Forum* 5 (1978–1979): 1–79.

22. Grayson, *Korea*, 198–200; Weems, *Reform, Rebellion, and the Heavenly Way*, 8.

23. See Donald Baker's chapter titled "The Great Transformation: Religious Practice in Chŏndogyo," in *Religions of Korea in Practice*, ed. Robert E. Buswell Jr. (Princeton, NJ: Princeton University Press, 2007), 449–463.

24. Weems, *Reform, Rebellion, and the Heavenly Way*, 11. See Peter H. Lee, *Sourcebook of Korean Civilization*, 2:314–315.

25. Ki-baik Lee, *New History of Korea*, 259.

26. Ibid., 283ff.

27. On Henry Appenzeller's vision of a new Korea, see Daniel M. Davies' "Building a City on a Hill in Korea: The Work of Henry G. Appenzeller," *Church History: Studies in Christianity and Culture* 61, no. 4 (1992): 422–435.

28. Min Kyoung-bae, *Han'guk kidokkyohoesa*, new rev. ed. (Seoul: Yonsei taehakkyo ch'ulp'ansa, 1993), 105; Peter H. Lee, *Sourcebook on Korean Civilization*, 2:309.

29. See Han Kyumu, "Chenŏrŏl syŏlmŏnho sakŏn kwa t'omas ŭi 'sun'gyo' munje kŏmt'o," *Han'guk kyohoe wa yŏksa* 1 (July 1997): 9–33. Also see the section "R. J. Thomas and the *General Sherman* Incident in 1865–6," in Sung Deuk Oak, ed., *Sources of Korean Christianity, 1832–1945* (Seoul: Institute for Korean Church History, 2004), 10–13. On Gutzlaff, see L. George Paik, *The History of Protestant Missions in Korea, 1832–1910* (1927; reprint, Seoul: Yonsei University Press, 1987), 43–47.

30. Han'guk kidokkyo yŏksa yŏn'guso, *Han'guk kidok kyohoe ŭi yŏksa I* (Seoul: Kidokkyo munsa, 1989), 117; Bruce Cumings, *Korea's Place in the Sun: A Modern History*, updated ed. (New York: W. W. Norton, 2005), 97; Han'guk kidokkyo yŏksa yŏn'guso, *Han'guk kidok kyohoe ŭi yŏksa II*, 119; Peter H. Lee, *Sourcebook of Korean Civilization*, 2:306.

31. Kang Mangil, *Koch'yŏssŭn han'guk kŭndaesa* (Seoul: Ch'angbi, 1994), 225; Martina Deuchler, *Confucian Gentlemen and Barbarian Envoys: The Opening of Korea, 1875–1885* (Seattle: University of Washington Press, 1977), 121.

32. Everett N. Hunt Jr., *Protestant Pioneers in Korea* (Maryknoll, NY: Orbis, 1980), 63.

33. Ki-baik Lee, *New History of Korea*, 276.

34. For an excellent study of Allen, see Fred Harvey Harrington, *God, Mammon and the Japanese* (New York: Arno Press, 1980).

35. Everett N. Hunt Jr., *Protestant Pioneers in Korea*, 82.

36. Paik, *History of Protestant Missions*, 164–165.

37. Ibid., 99; Han'guk kidokkyo yŏksa yŏn'guso, *Han'guk kidok kyohoe ŭi yŏksa I*, 243.

38. Ibid., 142.

39. Ibid., 146–152; Oak, *Sources of Korean Christianity*, 14.

40. The work was published by J. and R. Parlane, Paisley, of London. 1879). In 1880 the book was republished under the title, *Corea: Its History, Manners and Customs*. See Park Yong Kyu, *Han'guk kidokkyohoesa 1 (1784–1910)* (Seoul: Saengmyŏng ŭi malssŭmsa, 2004), 300; and Pratt and Rutt, *Korea*, s.v. "Ross, John."

41. Han'guk kidokkyo yŏksa yŏn'guso, *Han'guk kidok kyohoe ŭi yŏksa I*, 144–145; Oak, *Sources of Korean Christianity*, 14; Yi Tŏkchu [Rhie Deok-Joo], *Saero ssŭn kaejong iyaki* (Seoul: Han'guk kidokkyo yŏksa yŏn'guso, 2003), 18–19.

42. Yi Tŏkchu, *Saero ssŭn kaejong iyaki*, 23–24.

43. Ibid., 25. At this time in Korea, Hwanghae was one of the two provinces in the northwest, the other being P'yŏngan. The northwest region proved to be the most fertile ground for evangelical missions. See Chull Lee, "Social Sources of the Rapid Growth of the Christian Church in Northwest Korea: 1895–1910" (PhD diss., Boston University, 1997).

44. Yi Tŏkchu, *Saero ssŭn kaejong iyaki*, 26.

45. Ibid., 25–26.

46. H. G. Underwood to F. F. Ellinwood, January 22, 1887, in Oak, *Sources of Korean Christianity*, 24.

47. Oak, *Sources of Korean Christianity*, 25. This small congregation has grown into the Saemunan Presbyterian Church, the mother church of Korean Presbyterianism.

48. Paik, *History of Protestant Missions*, 168.

49. Arthur J. Brown, "The Rev. Horace Grant Underwood, D.D., LL.D.," *Korea Mission Field* (hereafter "*KMF*") 12 (February 1917): 32.

50. In the Taft-Katsura agreement of 1905, the United States recognized Japan's hegemonic interest in Korea, in exchange for Japan's recognition of American interest over the Philippines. Ki-baik Lee, *New History of Korea*, 309.

51. Professor Yi Mahn-yol makes the valid point that many Koreans joined the church partly to seek protection against feudalistic exploitation by Chosŏn officials. But such a reason alone is inadequate to account for the veritable rush of seekers the church faced. For one thing, the missionaries made it a policy not to meddle in local governments on behalf of their converts, precisely to discourage Koreans from coming to church for worldly motives. See Paik, *History of Protestant Missions*, 416. Moreover, converts like No Tosa and Sŏ Sangyun could not have joined the church out of such a motive, for when they were baptized, it was still unsafe to be known as a Christian. See Yi Mahn-yol, "Hanmal kidokkyoin ŭi minjok ŭisik hyŏngsŏng kwajŏng," in Yi Mahn-yol et al., *Han'guk kidokkyo wa minjok undong* (Seoul: Posŏng, 1986), 11ff.

52. J. R. Moose, "A Great Awakening," *KMF* 2 (January 1906): 51–52.

53. Han Yŏngje, ed., *Han'guk kidokkyo sŏngjang 100-yŏn* (Seoul: Kidokkyo munsa, 1986), 200.

54. The *Korea Mission Field* was an interdenominational journal dedicated to publicizing evangelistic needs and achievements of the Korean missions. It was published from November 1905 to November 1941.

55. "Current Notes," *KMF* 2 (November 1905): 10.

56. W. F. Bull, "No Need to Seek an Audience," *KMF* 2 (July 1906): 168–169.

57. W. G. Cram, "Revival Fires," *KMF* 2 (December 1905): 33.

58. "The Cry of the Church," *KMF* 4 (April 1908): 62.

59. Paik, *History of Protestant Missions*, 374.

60. Ibid., 367–368; Park Yong Kyu, *P'yŏngyang taebuhŭng undong, 1901–1910* (Seoul: Saengmyŏng ŭi malssŭmsa, 2000), 39–46.

61. Paik, *History of Protestant Missions*, 368.

62. "A Call to a Special Effort," *KMF* 2 (December 1905): 30. See also S. F. Moore, "The Revival in Seoul," *KMF* 2 (April 1906): 115–116. The General Council of Evangelical Missions in Korea was formed in 1905 to act as an advisory body to the Presbyterian and Methodist missions in Korea. Initially the council sought to create a united evangelical church in Korea, but this goal was not achieved. In 1912 the council changed to a federal council. Paik, *History of Protestant Missions*, 378–382.

63. Andre Schmid, *Korea between Empires, 1895–1919* (New York: Columbia University Press, 2002), 173.

64. Ibid., 173–174.

65. See John Duncan, "Proto-nationalism in Premodern Korea," in *Perspectives on Korea*, ed. Sang-Oak Lee and Duk-Soo Park (Sydney: Wild Peony, 1998), 198–221. Here the difficulty of using the concept "Korean nationalism" must be acknowledged more fully. Nationalism presupposes a nation, a collective identity. Much debate has occurred (and still occurs) as to what a Korean nation (*minjok*) is. The two dominant positions in this debate have been that of the primordialists, who regard the Korean *minjok* to have existed since time immemorial, even if the term itself was not coined till the turn of the twentieth century, and the modernists, who believe the Korean *minjok* to be an imaginary constructed by intellectuals such as Sin Ch'aeho in the modern era. Our purpose does not require us to take sides on this debate; here it suffices to affirm the prevalence of the proto-national sense indicated by the Duncan quotation. Complication continues, however. For even if Korean nationalism is defined generally—as *ch'ung'gun aeguksim*—at least three specific versions of it could be identified in the period: (1) that of the ultraconservative party *wijŏng ch'ŏksa* (Defend Orthodoxy, Reject Heterodoxy), which (rather like the regent Taewŏn'gun) sought to preserve intact the traditional order by sealing the borders; (2) that of the Tonghak, which sought to purify the state and keep out foreigners through an uprising; and (3) that of the *kaehwa* party (the progressives who staged the 1884 coup), which sought to keep Korea strong and independent by adopting modernizing measures much like those of Meiji Japan. Despite these variations, it is not untoward to use the term in the singular here, so long as it is taken to mean the general sentiments and representations that espoused the idea of "Korea of, by, and for Koreans," since, at least on this one important point, these three groups agreed. See Gi-Wook Shin, *Ethnic Nationalism in Korea: Genealogy, Politics, and Legacy* (Stanford, CA: Stanford University Press, 2006); Henry Em, "*Minjok* as a Modern and Democratic Construct: Sin Ch'aeho's Historiography," in *Colonial Modernity in Korea*, ed. Gi-Wook Shin and Michael E. Robinson (Cambridge, MA: Harvard University Asia Center, 1999), 336–361; Benedict Anderson, *Imagined Communities:*

Reflections on the Origin and Spread of Nationalism (London: Verso, 1983); Anthony D. Smith, *Nationalism and Modernism* (London: Routledge, 1998); Chai-sik Chung, *A Korean Confucian Encounter with the Modern World: Yi Hang-no and the West* (Berkeley: Institute of East Asian Studies, University of California, Berkeley, 1995); Young Ick Lew, "The Conservative Character of the 1894 Tonghak Peasant Uprising: A Reappraisal with Emphasis on Chŏn Pong-jun's Background and Motivation," *Journal of Korean Studies* 7 (1990): 149–177; Yong-ho Ch'oe, "The *Kapsin* Coup of 1884: A Reassessment," *Korean Studies* 6 (1982): 105–124; and Timothy S. Lee, "What Should Christians Do about a Shaman-Progenitor? Evangelicals and Ethnic Nationalism in Korea," *Church History: Studies in Christianity and Culture* 78, no. 1 (2009): 66–98.

66. Yi Mahn-yol, "Hanmal kidokkyoin ŭi minjok ŭisik hyŏngsŏng kwajŏng," 11–73. Also see Sŏng Paekkŏl, "Han'guk ch'ogi kaesingyoin dŭl ŭi kyohoe wa kukka ihae, 1884–1910)," *Han'guk kidokkyosa yŏn'gu* 21 (May 1988): 4–19.

67. Hyaeweol Choi, "Christian Modernity in the Missionary Discourse of Korea, 1905–1910," *East Asian History* 29 (2005): 42. Also see Kenneth M. Wells, *New God, New Nation: Protestants and Self-Reconstruction Nationalism in Korea, 1896–1937* (Honolulu: University of Hawai`i Press, 1990); Vipan Chandra, *Imperialism, Resistance, and Reform in Late Nineteenth-Century Korea: Enlightenment and the Independence Club* (Berkeley: Institute of East Asian Studies, University of California, Berkeley, 1988); and Chang Kyu-sik, *Ilcheha han'guk kidokkyo minjokchuŭi yŏn'gu* (Seoul: Haean, 2001).

68. Chang Kyu-sik, *Ilcheha han'guk kidokkyo minjokchuŭi yŏngu*, 74, 80.

69. *Missionary Review of the World* (March 1902): 188. See also Sŏ Chŏngmin's "Ch'ogi han'guk kyohoe taebuhŭng undong ihae," in Yi Mahn-yol et al., *Han'guk kidokkyo wa minjok undong*, 238. On the missionaries' views on Korean nationalism, see Cho Yŏngnyŏl, "Chaehan sŏn'gyosa wa han'guk tongnip undong," *Han'guk kidokkyo yŏksa yŏn'gu* 29 (January 1990): 4–12.

70. "The Time Opportune," *KMF* 2 (December 1905): 29–30.

71. For the background of some of these missionaries, see Everett N. Hunt Jr., *Protestant Pioneers in Korea*; and Elizabeth Underwood, *Challenged Identities: North American Missionaries in Korea, 1884–1934* (Seoul: Royal Asiatic Society, Korea Branch, 2003).

72. Cram, "Revival Fires," 33.

73. Moose, "Great Awakening," 51–52. Emphasis in original.

74. "Call to a Special Effort," 30. Emphasis in original.

75. Edith F. McRae, "For Thine Is the Power," *KMF* 2 (February 1906): 73; S. F. Moore, "Revival in Seoul," 115–116; "Revival at Ewa," *KMF* 2 (May 1906): 133; J. F. Preston, "The Need at Kwangju," *KMF* 2 (July 1906): 167.

76. William N. Blair, *Gold in Korea*, 2nd ed. (Topeka, KS: H. M. Ives and Sons, 1947): 57, 59.

77. Ibid., 63, 65.

78. Paik, *History of Protestant Missions*, 368.

79. Blair, *Gold in Korea*, 60.

80. Park Yong Kyu, *P'yŏngyang sanjŏnghyŏn kyohoe* (Seoul: Saengmyŏng ŭi malssŭmsa, 2006), 61–71.

81. Kil Sŏnju, a Presbyterian elder at the start of the revival, was ordained into ministry in July 1907. During the great revival, Kil was a significant lay revivalist and was instrumental in spreading the enthusiasm to Seoul. "Recent Work of the Holy Spirit in Seoul," *KMF* 3 (March 1907): 41.

82. W. B. Hunt, "Impressions of an Eye Witness," *KMF* 3 (March 1907): 37.

83. William N. Blair and Bruce F. Hunt, *The Korean Pentecost and the Sufferings Which Followed* (Carlisle, PA: Banner of Truth Trust, 1977), 69.

84. Blair, *Gold in Korea*, 62.

85. Graham Lee, "How the Spirit Came to Pyeng Yang," *KMF* 3 (March 1907): 33-37.

86. Blair and Hunt, *Korean Pentecost*, 75.

87. "The Spirit of Prayer," *KMF* 4 (June 1908): 84-85. See also Park Yong Kyu, *P'yŏngyang sanjŏnghyŏn kyohoe.*

88. Graham Lee, "How the Spirit Came to Pyeng Yang."

89. Ibid.

90. Mrs. W. M. [Annie Laurie Adams] Baird, "The Spirit among Pyeng Yang Students," *KMF* 3 (May 1907): 65-67.

91. W. L. Swallen, "God's Work of Grace in Pyeng Yang Classes," *KMF* 3 (May 1907): 77-80.

92. Ibid.

93. Ibid.

94. G. S. McCune, "Opening Days at the Theological Seminary," *KMF* 3 (June 1907): 89-90.

95. Swallen, "God's Work."

96. L. H. McCully, "Fruits of the Revival," *KMF* 3 (June 1907): 83-84.

97. H. M. Bruen, "The Spirit at Taiku," *KMF* 3 (April 1907): 51-53; W. G. Cram, "A Genuine Change," *KMF* 3 (May 1907): 67-68; C. A. Clark, "Seung dong Church of Seoul," *KMF* 3 (August 1907): 121-122.

98. "The Religious Awakening of Korea," *KMF* 4 (July 1908): 105-107.

99. Kenneth S. Latourette, *A History of Christian Missions to China* (New York: Macmillan, 1929), 574. Also see Yi Tŏkchu [Rhie Deok-Joo], "Ch'ogi kaesin'gyo e isŏsŏ han-jung kidokkyo kyoryu," *Han'guk kidokkyosa yŏn'gu* 1 (April–May 1985): 6.

100. George T. Davis, *Korea for Christ* (London: Christian Workers' Depot, 1910): 27.

101. "1,000,000 Souls This Year," *KMF* 5 (November 1909): 96-98; Davis, *Korea for Christ*, 7; Paik, *History of Protestant Missions*, 384.

102. Han Yŏngje, *Han'guk kidokkyo sŏngjang 100-yŏn*, 200; Paik, *History of Protestant Missions*, 385.

103. "The Million Movement and Its Results," *KMF* 7 (January 1911): 5-6.

104. Ibid.; "Statistics for 1910," *KMF* 7 (April 1911): 107; William N. Blair, "Report of Address to the Presbyterian Mission on the Million Movement," *KMF* 7 (November 1911): 310-311.

105. Samuel H. Moffett, *The Christians of Korea* (New York: Friendship Press, 1962), 54.

106. George Herber Jones, "The Korean Passion for Souls," *KMF* 5(January 1909): 10; F. S. Miller, "Some Thoughts about Women's Work in Chong Ju," *KMF* 8 (January 1912): 19–20; W. T. Cooke, "Korean Lad Walked 58 Miles to Attend a Bible Study Class Held at Chong Ju," *KMF* 5 (August 1909): 140; Davis, *Korea for Christ*, 10. In another issue, *KMF* notes a quip by an American visitor who witnessed an examination for membership to a Korean church: "The standard set by that church was so high that Mr. Ellis said. 'It is harder to get into the Korean Church than to enter the church at home.' Often this question is asked the applicant for church membership. 'Have you led a soul to Christ?' If this test were put to Christians in Christian lands how many would be able to stand?" Charles G. Hounshell, "Korea's Message to the World," *KMF* 8 (October 1912): 309–311.

107. Blair and Hunt, *Korean Pentecost*, 75.

108. G. Lee, "A Rigorous Moral Standard," *KMF* 2 (September 1906): 210.

109. In Korea, as late as the 1980s, a Protestant minister could not smoke in public without bringing opprobrium to himself. "From Growth to Maturity," *K'ŭrisŭch'yan sinmun*, June 22, 1985.

110. Blair and Hunt, *Korean Pentecost*, 75.

111. An Yongjun, *Sarang ŭi wŏnjat'an* (Seoul: Sŏnggwang munhwasa, 1972).

112. McRae, "For Thine Is the Power," 74. Emphasis in original.

113. John Z. Moore, "The Great Revival Year," *KMF* 3 (August 1907): 113–120.

114. John Z. Moore, "The Fullness of the Gospel," *KMF* 3 (December 1907): 178–180.

115. Paik notes a confession in which immoral conduct of a missionary was disclosed, forcing him to resign. Paik, *History of Protestant Missions*, 375n.

116. Blair and Hunt, *Korean Pentecost*, 73.

117. In Joachim Wach's *Sociology of Religion* (Chicago: University of Chicago Press, 1944), 39.

118. Mrs. W. M. Baird, "Spirit among Pyeng Yang Students," 67. On the missionary community, see Elizabeth Underwood, *Challenged Identities*.

119. H. H. Hamill, "God's Hand in Korea's Bible Study," *KMF* 4 (August 1908): 114–116.

120. George Herber Jones, "Native Religions," *KMF* 4 (February 1908): 26–29. See also Charles Allen Clark, *Religions of Old Korea* (1932; reprint, Seoul: Christian Literature Society of Korea, 1961). For an informed and sympathetic assessment of the missionaries' view on the subject, see Sung Deuk Oak, "The Indigenization of Christianity in Korea: North American Missionaries' Attitudes towards Korean Religions, 1884–1910" (PhD diss., Boston University, 2002). Also helpful in understanding the missionaries' theology of religions is Paul F. Knitter, *Introducing Theologies of Religions* (Maryknoll, NY: Orbis, 2002).

121. John Z. Moore, "Great Revival Year," 117.

122. "Field Notes," *KMF* 2 (September 1906): 215.

123. "The Dispensation of the Spirit," *KMF* 5 (June 1910): 146.

124. "Church Building," *KMF* 2 (September 1906): 219–220.

125. "The Campaigns in Syn Chen," *KMF* 7 (January 1911): 21–22.

126. C. E. Sharp, "Under Persecution," *KMF* 2 (April 1906): 123–124.

127. C. A. Clark, "Three Incidents," *KMF* 5 (January 1909): 18–20.

128. C. A. Clark, "Not Unpromising Now," *KMF* 2 (August 1906): 198–200.

129. F. S. Miller, "Gentleman and Commoner," *KMF* 3 (June 1907): 87.

130. "A Personal Report by Mrs. J. F. Preston," *KMF* 2 (April 1906): 126–128.

131. Wach, *Sociology of Religion*, 110.

132. "Keeping the Sabbath in Korea," *KMF* 4 (May 1908): 90.

133. Yu Hongnyŏl, *Han'guk chŏnju kyohoesa*, 2:434. The figure for Tonghak is an estimate based on the report that the church, at the time, claimed 150,000 families as its members. Seoul National University, Department of Religion, and Institute for the Study of Religious Culture, *Chŏnhwan'gi ŭi han'guk chonggyo* (Seoul: Chipmundang, 1986), 38. Also see Han Yŏngje, *Han'guk kidokkyo sŏngjang 100-yŏn*, 200.

134. Yu Hongnyŏl, *Han'guk chŏnju kyohoesa*, 2:434.

135. This is an approximation based on the estimate that 300,000 families composed the church at that time. Seoul National University, and Institute for the Study of Religious Culture, *Chŏnhwan'gi ŭi han'guk chonggyo*, 39.

136. Han Yŏngje, *Han'guk kidokkyo sŏngjang 100-yŏn*, 200; Alfred W. Wasson, *Church Growth in Korea* (New York: International Missionary Council, 1934), xi.

137. On Kil Sŏnju's motive for embracing evangelical Protestantism, see Kil Chingyŏng, *Yŏnggye Kil Sŏnju* (Seoul: Chongno sŏjŏk, 1980).

138. See Wells, *New God, New Nation*. Wells analyzes Korean nationalists' critique of their society and their rationale for endorsing Protestantism.

139. C. E. Sharpe, "Motive for Seeking Christ," *KMF* 2 (August 1906): 182–183; C. A. Clark, "Not Unpromising Now," *KMF* 2 (August 1906): 198–199.

140. Sharpe, "Motives for Seeking Christ."

141. E. M. Cable, "The Longing for Education," *KMF* 2 (June 1906): 144–145.

142. "Evangelistic Work at Kunsan," *KMF* 2 (April 1906): 106–107.

143. Han'guk kidokkyo yŏksa yŏn'guso, *Han'guk kidok kyohoe ŭi yŏksa I*, 303.

144. This stance was asserted in a *KMF* editorial of the time: "A strict neutrality has been maintained and a determination to keep hands out of politics is a well known fact to all who are acquainted with the missionary plans and policy of the Christian Church." *KMF* 3 (October 1907): 153–156.

145. Collaboration is a difficult and controversial issue in modern Korean historiography. Yun Ch'iho embodies many of these difficulties; a leading progressive patriot (and Protestant) at the end of the nineteenth century, he became a prominent collaborator after 1910. See the following works on him: Wells, *New God, New Nation*; Koen De Ceuster, "Through the Master's Eye: Colonized Mind and Historical Consciousness in the Case of Yun Ch'iho (1865–1945)," *Bochumer Jahrbuch zur Ostasienforschung* 27 (2003): 107–131; Yang Hyŏnhye, *Yun Ch'iho wa Kim Kyosin: Kŭndae chosŏn e issŏsŏ minjokchok aident'it'i wa kidokkyo* (Seoul: Hanul, 1994); and An Sin, "Chwa-ong Yun Ch'iho ŭi chonggyo kyŏnghŏm kwa chonggyoron: Chonggyo hyŏnsanghak chŏk haesŏk," *Han'guk kidokkyo wa yŏksa* 27 (2007): 45–69. Apropos here is the caution

voiced by Gi-Wook Shin and Michael E. Robinson against "the unitary focus, artificial unity, and binary-producing tendencies of older assumptions about nationalism that have too often dominated Korean historiography." Shin and Robinson, *Colonial Modernity in Korea*, 2.

146. W. M. Baird, "Pyeng Yang Academy," *KMF* 2 (October 1906): 221–224.

147. Ibid.

148. William Blair, "Report of an Address to the Presbyterian Mission on the Million Movement," *KMF* 7 (November 1911): 310–311.

149. "Editorial Notes," *KMF* 14 (January 1918): 1–3.

150. Han'guk kidokkyo yŏksa yŏn'guso, *Han'guk kidok kyohoe ŭi yŏksa I*, 308. The case was also known as the "105-person incident" (*105-in sakŏn*) for the number of principals put on trial for the alleged conspiracy, most of whom were Protestants. Occurring a year after the annexation, the incident was the governor-general's preemptive strike against nationalist leaders who might resist Japanese rule in Korea. In the trial, Yun Ch'iho was the main defendant. See Yun Kyŏngno, *Han'guk kŭndaesa ŭi kidokkyosa chŏk ihae* (Seoul: Yŏkminsa, 1992), especially the chapter titled "105-in sakŏn kwa kidokkyo sunan" [The 105-Person Incident and Ordeals of Christianity], 181–202; Wi Jo Kang, *Christ and Caesar in Modern Korea: A History of Christianity and Politics* (New York: State University of New York Press, 1997); and De Ceuster, "Through the Master's Eye," 107.

151. Min Kyoung-bae notes that An Ch'ang ho, a preeminent Korean nationalist and Christian, assaulted the missionaries Samuel A. Moffett and Graham Lee in broad daylight in P'yŏngyang for distracting Korean believers from the nation's political woes. Min Kyoung-bae, "Han'guk Kidokkyo e issŏsŏ minjok munje," in *Han'guk yŏksa wa kidokkyo*, ed. *Kidokkyo sasang* (Seoul: Literature Society of Korea, 1983), 111.

152. "Some Changes in the Korean Church," *KMF* 10 (March 1914): 69.

153. On nationalist Christians in Japan, see Irwin Scheiner, *Christian Converts and Social Protest in Japan* (Berkeley: University of California Press, 1970). For the same in China, see Philip West, "Christianity and Nationalism: The Career of Wu Lei-ch'uan at Yenching University," in *Missionary Enterprise in China and America*, ed. John Fairbank (Cambridge, MA: Harvard University Press, 1974), 226–246.

154. Paul Varg, *Missionary, Chinese, and Diplomats* (Princeton, NJ: Princeton University Press, 1958).

155. Kap-che Yip, *Religion, Nationalism and Chinese Students: The Anti-Christian Movement of 1922–1927* (Bellingham: Washington University Press, 1980), 2. On the conflict between missionaries and Chinese nationalism, also see Paul Cohen, *China and Christianity: The Missionary Movement and the Growth of Chinese Antiforeignism, 1860–1870* (Cambridge, MA: Harvard University Press, 1963); and Joseph W. Esherick, *The Origins of the Boxer Uprising* (Berkeley: University of California Press, 1987).

156. The Uchimura incident occurred when he, a Christian schoolteacher, refused to bow before the imperial rescript on education, whose "supercharged symbolic value exceeded by far the prestige and authority of anything but the emperor himself." As Helen Hardacre notes, "This celebrated incident became the occasion for renewed

invective against Christianity as an unpatriotic, foreign religion, incompatible with the 'the Japanese Way.' Uchimura was pilloried in the press and removed from his position by the minister of education." See Hardacre, *Shintō and the State, 1868–1988* (Princeton, NJ: Princeton University Press, 1989), 122–123.

157. Winburn Thomas, *Protestant Beginnings in Japan* (Rutland, VT: Charles E. Tuttle, 1959), 188.

158. For a detailed treatment of this event, see Frank Baldwin, Jr., "The March First Movement: Korean Challenge and Japanese Response" (PhD diss., Columbia University, 1969). See also Han'guk yŏksa yŏn'guso and Yŏksa munje yŏn'guhoe, eds., *3.1 minjok haebang undong yŏn'gu* (Seoul: Chŏngnyŏnsa, 1989).

159. "My thesis is that what we mean in naming certain texts, events, images, rituals, symbols and persons 'classic' is that here we recognize nothing less than the disclosure of a reality we cannot but name truth[;] . . . some disclosure of reality in a moment that must be called one of 'recognition' which surprises, provokes, challenges, shocks and eventually transforms us; an experience that upsets conventional opinions and expands the sense of the possible; indeed a realized experience of that which is essential, that which endures." David Tracy, *The Analogical Imagination: Christian Theology and the Culture of Pluralism* (New York: Crossroad, 1986), 108.

160. Michael E. Robinson, *Korea's Twentieth-Century Odyssey: A Short History* (Honolulu: University of Hawai'i Press, 2007), 47.

161. See Chong-shik Lee, "Anti-Japanese Struggles of the Korean Communists in Korea," in *The Korean Workers' Party: A Short History* (Stanford, CA: Hoover Institution Press), 58–72; Michael E. Robinson, *Cultural Nationalism in Colonial Korea, 1920–1925* (Seattle: University of Washington Press, 1988); and Ki-baik Lee, *New History of Korea*, 344.

162. Although written more than forty years ago, Baldwin's dissertation remains the best English-language (if not Western) treatment of the subject. Much more is available in Korean, but the Korean interpretations do not vary much from Baldwin's. Also see Yi Mahn-yol, "3.1 undong kwa kidokkyo," *Han'guk kidokkyo wa yŏksa* 7 (1997), 7–20; and "The March First Movement," in Chong-shik Lee, *Politics of Korean Nationalism* (Berkeley: University of California Press, 1965), 105–125.

163. North Korea has a very different view of the March First Movement. Its history books claim that the most important group that led the movement was a Korean People's Association (Chosŏn kungminhoe), which was led by Kim Il Sung's father. They also assert that the eight-year-old Kim Il Sung participated in a demonstration and that P'yŏngyang (not Seoul) was the center of this movement. These claims—and many others like them emanating from the North—are considered rank falsehoods by historians in the South. See Ko Sŏnghyŏn, "Pukhan ŭi han'guk kidokkyosa (Chosŏn hugi–ilche sidae) ihae e taehan yŏn'gu: Haebang hu palp'yo toen pukhan munhŏn ŭl chungsim ŭro," *Han'guk kidokkyo wa yŏksa* 10 (1999): 155–158.

164. The locus classicus of the Tan'gun myth is in the thirteenth-century work by Iryŏn: *Samguk Yusa: Legends and History of the Three Kingdoms of Korea*, trans. Tae-hung Ha and Grafton Mintz (Seoul: Yonsei University, 1972). Also see Peter H.

Lee, ed., *Sourcebook of Korean Civilization*, vol. 1, *From Early Times to the Sixteenth Century* (New York: Columbia University Press, 1993): 4–7.

165. Baldwin, "March First Movement," 12.

166. On the influence of the Paris Peace Conference on the March First Movement, see ibid., 14–51.

167. Ibid., 38, 39. Tokyo, as the metropolis of the Japanese empire, attracted young and ambitious people from Korea (and China and elsewhere in Asia). Once there, in an atmosphere much freer than that in Korea, they were exposed to streams of Japanese intellectual life, including communism, and instead of studying to be loyal imperial subjects, they strove to free Koreans.

168. By this time, the more radical members of the Korean independence movement were either imprisoned or exiled, prompting the moderate religionists to step forward.

169. Hugh Heung-Woo Cynn [Sin Hŭngu], *The Rebirth of Korea: The Reawakening of the People, Its Causes, and the Outlook* (New York: Abingdon, 1920), 24–25.

170. Ki-baik Lee, *New History of Korea*, 344. There is some dispute over the number of Korean participants in the uprising. Robinson cites the conservative figure of one million in *Korea's Twentieth-Century Odyssey*, 48. Baldwin cautiously endorses an estimate of two million. Using the conservative figure of one million, however, Baldwin makes some further estimates, given that in 1919 the Korean population was around sixteen million, and assuming that half of that number were women: "Of the remaining 8,000,000 Korean males, perhaps a quarter may be excluded as either too young, under fourteen years of age, or too old and infirm. Thus the one million demonstrators were from a potential 'pool' of six million. It appears then that approximately one out of six Korean males old enough to understand the meaning of the independence movement demonstrated against Japanese rule." Baldwin, "March First Movement," 231.

171. Baldwin, "March First Movement," 53.

172. Ibid., 91–96.

173. Ki-baik Lee, *New History of Korea*, 344; Baldwin, "March First Movement," 232–235.

174. Quoted in Cynn, *Rebirth of Korea*, 64.

175. U.S. State Department, State Department Record, Consular Bureau, *The Present Movement for Korean Independence*, report filed July 8, 1919, 44.

176. Frank P. Baldwin Jr., "Missionaries and the March First Movement: Can Moral Man Be Neutral?" in Andrew C. Nahm, ed., *Korea under Japanese Colonial Rule* (Kalamazoo: Western Michigan University Press, 1973), 193–219, 197. In this article, Baldwin argues that during the March First Movement the missionaries in fact remained neutral. But if neutrality required that the missionaries should not aid or hinder either the Koreans or the Japanese, they failed to be neutral, for the missionaries, as will be seen below, hindered the Japanese by helping to turn international opinion against their suppression of Korean demonstrations.

177. *The Journals of Mattie Wilcox Noble, 1892–1934* (Seoul: Han'guk kidokkyo yŏksa yŏn'guso, 1993), 275. The identity of "Mr. Tayler" is unclear. He is not listed

in *Naehan sŏngyosa chŏngnam, 1884–1984* (Seoul: Han'guk kidokkyo yŏksa yŏn'guso, 1994), compiled by Kim Sŭngt'ae and Pak Hyejin. Most likely, Noble meant to say "Mr. Taylor," perhaps referring to Henry C. Taylor, who was a Methodist missionary to Korea, serving in Seoul and the vicinity from 1908 till 1919. See ibid., 472.

178. Baldwin, "Missionaries," 197. Also see Wi Jo Kang, "Relation between the Japanese Colonial Government and the American Missionary Community in Korea, 1905–1945," in *One Hundred Years of Korean-American Relations, 1882–1982*, ed. Yurbok Lee and Wayne Patterson (Tuscaloosa: University of Alabama Press, 1986), 78.

179. Federal Council of the Churches of Christ of America, comp., *The Korean Situation: Authentic Accounts of Recent Events by Eye Witnesses* (New York: FCCCA, 1919), 30–31, 37, 33.

180. Baldwin, "March First Movement," 185.

181. One of the few Westerners, perhaps the only one, who had any inkling of the March First Movement before it erupted was Dr. Frank W. Scofield. He was a veterinarian and medical missionary from Canada and was asked to take pictures of the planned rallies. As the movement proceeded, he was one of the most vigorous advocates of Korean rights, speaking out against the violence of the Japanese, for example, at a conference of Far East missionaries in Tokyo in September 1919. But his most potent and enduring contribution to the movement was the photographs he took of its various aspects. These images, especially those of the Suwŏn and Cheamni massacres (discussed below in the text), played a role in galvanizing international pressure against Japan. In 1920 Scofield left Korea, but he returned when the country was liberated. His contributions to the March First Movement were appreciated by Koreans, who affectionately dubbed him the "thirty-fourth" signer of the Declaration of Independence. In 1960 Scofield was decorated with the Order of Cultural Merit by the South Korean government. Upon his death on February 20, 1970, his body was interred in the Tongnip yugonja section of the National Cemetery of the Republic of Korea, reserved for those who had rendered distinguished service for the independence of Korea. "Sunch'ŏn kyohoe panghwa-haksal sakŏn" [The Arson-Massacre Incident at the Sunch'ŏn Church], *K'ŭrisŭch'yan sinmun*, February 27, 1965; and "Sŏk'opi'ldŏ paksa" [Dr. Scofield], *K'ŭrisŭch'yan sinmun*, April 18, 1970.

182. Cynn, *Rebirth of Korea*, 15. Cynn was educated in a mission school and received a master's degree at the University of Southern California in 1911. He wrote this book while visiting the United States in May 1919 to participate in a Methodist conference.

183. Ibid., 187.

184. Ibid., 129.

185. Kim Sŭngt'ae, "Chonggyoin ŭi 3.1 undong ch'amyŏ wa kidokkyo ŭi yŏkhal," *Han'guk kidokkyosa yŏn'gu* 25 (April 1989): 17–24.

186. Ibid., 19.

187. Ibid.

188. *Kidokkyo taebaekkwa sajŏn*, s.v. "Cheamni kyohoe" [Cheamni church].

189. Wi Jo Kang, *Christ and Caesar*, 53–54.

190. Hong Sŏkch'ang, *Yu Kwansun-yang kwa maebong kyohoe* (Seoul: Tosŏ ch'ulp'an amen, 1989), 92.

191. Wasson, *Church Growth in Korea*, 98.

192. Ibid., 103.

2. Conflict, Introversion, and a Tradition of Korean Revivalists, 1920–1953

Epigraph. Ernst Troeltsch, *The Social Teachings of the Christian Churches*, vol. 1, trans. Olive Wyon (1911; reprints, New York: Macmillan, 1931; and Chicago: University of Chicago Press, Phoenix Books, 1981), 46–48.

1. Carter J. Eckert et al., *Korea Old and New: A History* (Seoul: published for the Korea Institute, Harvard University, by Ilchokak, 1990), 260.

2. Bruce Cumings, "The Legacy of Japanese Colonialism in Korea," in *The Japanese Colonial Empire, 1895–1945*, ed. Ramon H. Myers and Mark R. Peattie, 478–496 (Princeton, NJ: Princeton University Press, 1984); David Brudnoy, "Japan's Experiment in Korea," *Monumenta Nipponica* 2, no. 1 (1970): 155–195; Michael E. Robinson, *Cultural Nationalism in Colonial Korea, 1920–1925* (Seattle: University of Washington Press, 1988); Ki-baik Lee, *New History of Korea* (Cambridge, MA: Harvard University Press), 353; Andrew C. Nahm, ed., *Korea under Japanese Colonial Rule* (Kalamazoo: Western Michigan University Press, 1973). See also George Hicks, *The Comfort Women: Japan's Brutal Regime of Enforced Prostitution in the Second World War* (New York: W. W. Norton, 1994); Richard E. Kim, *Lost Names: Scenes from a Korean Boyhood* (Berkeley: University of California Press, 1998); and Linda Sue Park, *When My Name Was Keoko* (New York: Dell Yearling, 2002).

3. Han Kyumu, "Haebang chikhu namhan kyohoe ŭi tonghyang," *Han'guk kidokkyo wa yŏksa* 2 (1992): 39–54.

4. Bruce Cumings, *Korea's Place in the Sun: A Modern History*, updated ed. (New York: W. W. Norton, 2005), 154.

5. Bruce Cumings, *The Origins of the Korean War*, vol. 1, *Liberation and the Emergence of Separate Regimes, 1945–1947* (Princeton, NJ: Princeton University Press, 1981), 84. Also see Kang Mangil, *Koch'yŏssŭn han'guk hyŏndaesa* (Seoul: Ch'angbi, 1994), 254–259.

6. Bruce Cumings, *Two Koreas* (New York: Foreign Policy Association, 1984), 27.

7. Eckert et al., *Korea Old and New*, 343.

8. Ibid.; Kang Mangil, *Koch'yŏssŭn han'guk hyŏndaesa*, 279.

9. Kang Mangil, *Koch'yŏssŭn han'guk hyŏndaesa*, 279–285.

10. Peter Lowe, *The Origins of the Korean War* (London: Longman, 1986), 218; Korea Overseas Information Service, *Facts about Korea* (Seoul: Korea Overseas Information Service, 1991), 41.

11. For a sample of it, see Joint Publications Research Service, *Translations on North Korea*, no. 419 (August 6, 1975); and H. Edward Kim, "Rare Look at North Korea," *National Geographic*, August 1974, 252–277.

12. Chang Pyŏngwuk, *6.25 kongsan namch'im kwa kyohoe* (Seoul: Korean Educational Society, 1983), 265.

13. Another concern for evangelicalism in this period was the resurgence of traditional religions and the sprouting of new religions. *KMF* 27 (April 1927): 77.

14. Ki-baik Lee, *New History of Korea*, 305; Vipan Chandra, *Imperialism, Resistance, and Reform in Late Nineteenth-Century Korea: Enlightenment and the Independence Club* (Berkeley: Institute of East Asian Studies, University of California, Berkeley, 1988); Han'guk kŭnhyŏndae sahoe yŏn'guhoe, *Han'guk kŭndae kaehwa sasang kwa kaehwa undong* (Seoul: Sinsŏwŏn, 1998).

15. Cumings, *Origins of the Korean War*, 1:42; Chul-won Kang, "An Analysis of Japanese Policy and Economic Change in Korea," in *Korea under Japanese Colonial Rule*, ed. Andrew C. Nahm (Kalamazoo: Western Michigan University Press, 1973), 77–88.

16. Kim Hankyo, "The Japanese Colonial Administration in Korea: An Overview," in Nahm, *Korea under Japanese Colonial Rule*, 49; Eugene C. Kim, "Education in Korea," in Nahm, *Korea under Japanese Colonial Rule*, 137ff.

17. Cumings, *Two Koreas*, 24; Hatsue Shinohara, "Highway versus Development: Railroads in Korea under Japanese Colonial Rule," in *Chicago Occasional Papers on Korea*, ed. Bruce Cumings (Chicago: Center for East Asian Studies, University of Chicago, 1991), 6:33–57; Cumings, "Legacy of Japanese Colonialism."

18. Horace N. Allen, "Medical Notes," in *Things Korean* (New York: Fleming H. Revell, 1908), 188–208.

19. Margaret Best, "Fifty Years of Women's Work," in *The Fiftieth Anniversary Celebration of the Korea Mission of the Presbyterian Church in the U.S.A.* (1934; reprint, Seoul: Han'guk kidokkyo yŏksa yŏn'guso, 2000), 90.

20. Quoted in Chang Pyŏngwuk, *Han'guk kamnigyo yŏsŏngsa* [A History of Korean Methodist Women] (Seoul: Sŏnggwang munhwasa, 1979), cited in Yi Tŏkchu [Rhie Deok-Joo], *Han'guk kyohoe chŏŭm yŏsŏngdŭl* (Seoul: Kidokkyo munsa, 1990), 17. On the Bible women in Korea, see these two studies by Yang Migang: "Ch'ogi chŏndo puin ŭi sinang kwa hwaltong," *Han'guk kidokkyo wa yŏksa* 2 (1992): 91–109; and "Ch'amyŏ wa paeje ŭi kwanchŏm esŏ pon chŏndo puin e kwanhan yŏn'gu, 1910-yŏn–1930-yŏndae rŭl chungsim ŭro," *Han'guk kidokkyo wa yŏksa* 6 (1997): 139–179. Also see Donald N. Clark, "Mothers, Daughters, Biblewomen, and Sisters: An Account of 'Women's Work' in the Korea Mission Field," in *Christianity in Korea*, ed. Robert E. Buswell Jr. and Timothy S. Lee (Honolulu: University of Hawai`i Press), 167–192; and Kelly H. Chong, "In Search of Healing: Evangelical Conversion of Women in Contemporary South Korea," in Buswell and Lee, *Christianity in Korea*, 351–370.

21. Hyaeweol Choi, "An American Concubine in Old Korea: Missionary Discourse on Gender, Race, and Modernity," in *Frontier* 25, no. 3 (2004): 134–161. Also see Choi's "(En)Gendering a New Nation in Missionary Discourse: An Analysis of W. Arthur Noble's Ewa," in *Korea Journal* 46, no. 1 (2006): 139–169. On the New Woman movement in Korea, see Ch'oe Hyesil, *Sinyŏsongdŭl ŭn muŏt ŭl kkumkkuŏnnŭnga* (Seoul: Saenggak ŭi namu, 2002).

22. Arthur Judson Brown, a secretary of the Foreign Mission Board of the Northern Presbyterian Church, characterized the first generation of Protestant missionaries in Korea in a way that applies also to most of the second generation: "The typical

missionary of the first quarter century after the opening of the country was a man of the Puritan type. He kept the Sabbath as our New England forefathers did a century ago. He looked upon dancing, smoking, and card-playing as sins in which no true followers of Christ should indulge. In theology and biblical criticism he was strongly conservative, and he held as a vital truth the premillenarian view of the second coming of Christ. The higher criticism and liberal theology were deemed dangerous heresies. In most of the evangelical churches of America and Great Britain, conservatives and liberals have learned to live and work together in peace; but in Korea the few men who hold 'the modern view' have a rough road to travel, particularly in the Presbyterian group of missions." Quoted in L. George Paik, *History of Protestant Missions in Korea, 1832–1910* (1929; reprint, Seoul: Yonsei University Press, 1987), 424–425.

23. M. B. Stokes, "Some Thoughts about Revivals," *KMF* 27 (March 1932): 56.

24. Han'guk kidokkyo yŏksa yŏn'guso, *Han'guk kidok kyohoe ŭi yŏksa II, 1919–1945* (Seoul: Kidokkyo munsa, 1990), 155. In 1 Corinthians 11:3, Paul asserts, "Christ is the head of every man, and the husband is the head of his wife." In the same chapter, verses 8–9, he adds, "Indeed, man was not made from woman, but woman from man. Neither was man created for the sake of woman, but woman for the sake of man." First Timothy 2:11–12 states, "Let a woman learn in silence with full submission. I permit no woman to teach or to have authority over a man; she is to keep silent." New Revised Standard Version.

25. Ibid., 156. The first creed of the Korean Presbyterian church states, "The Old and New Testaments of the Bible are the correct and inerrant word of God, and they are the only guide for the faith and performance of one's duty." Taehan yesugyo chang-nohoe ch'onghoe, *Hŏnpŏp*, rev. ed. (Seoul: Taehan yesugyo changnohoe ch'onghoe, 1989), 17. My translation.

26. They included Han Kyŏngjik (trained in Princeton Theological Seminary), Ryu Hyŏnggi (Boston University), and Yang Chusam (Yale University).

27. Han'guk kidokkyo yŏksa yŏn'guso, *Han'guk kidok kyohoe ŭi yŏksa II*, 159.

28. D. A. MacDonald, "The Christian Message for the Korean of Today," *KMF* 18 (October 1922): 231.

29. Yi Kwangsu, "The Benefits Which Christianity Has Conferred on Korea," *KMF* 14 (February 1918): 34–36. Yi wrote this article and the December article in Korean; they were translated into English by Yun Ch'iho.

30. Yi Kwangsu, "Defects of the Korean Church Today," *KMF* 14 (December 1918): 253–257.

31. Sung C. Chun, *Schism and Unity in the Protestant Churches of Korea* (Seoul: Christian Literature Society of Korea, 1979).

32. See Young-suk Yi, "Liberal Protestant Leaders Working for Social Change: South Korea, 1957–1984" (PhD dissertation, University of Oregon, 1990); and Paul Yunshik Chang, "Carrying the Torch in the Darkest Hours: The Sociopolitical Origins of Minjung Protestant Movements," in Buswell and Lee, *Christianity in Korea*, 195–220.

33. See Helen Hardacre, *Shintō and the State, 1868–1988* (Princeton, NJ: Princeton University Press, 1989).

34. They were George S. McCune, Northern Presbyterian missionary and president of Sungsil (Union Christian) College in P'yŏngyang; H. M. Lee, Seventh-Day Adventist missionary and principal of an Adventist-sponsored school in Sunan; and Velma L. Snook, principal of Sungŭi Girls' High School in P'yŏngyang. Kim Sŭngt'ae, "1930-yŏndae kidokkyogye hakkyo ŭi 'sinsa munje,'" in *Han'guk kidokkyo wa sinsa ch'ambae munje*, ed. Kim Sŭngt'ae (Seoul: Han'guk kidokkyo yŏksa yŏn'guso, 1991), 365–391; William N. Blair, *Gold in Korea*, 2nd ed. (Topeka, KS: H. M. Ives and Sons, 1947), 94.

35. Wi Jo Kang, *Religion and Politics in Korea under Japanese Rule* (Lewiston, NY: Edwin Mellen, 1987), 36.

36. Kim Sŭngt'ae, "1930-yŏndae kidokkyogye hakkyo ŭi sinsa munje," 373; Wi Jo Kang, *Religion and Politics in Korea*, 36.

37. Wi Jo Kang, *Religion and Politics in Korea*, 37.

38. Han'guk kidokkyo yŏksa yŏn'guso, *Han'guk kidok kyohoe ŭi yŏksa II*, 300.

39. *Kidokkyo taebaekkwa sajŏn*, s.v. "Sinsa ch'ambae" [Paying obeisance at the Shintō shrine].

40. Though different Presbyterian missions worked in Korea, they and their Korean converts united in 1907 to found the independent Korean Presbyterian Church. Harry A. Rhodes, ed., *History of the Korea Mission: Presbyterian Church, USA, 1884–1934* (Seoul: Chosŏn Mission Presbyterian Church, USA, 1934), 386. An article titled "Protestant Christianity in Korea" presented these figures for 1937: "Of 410,000 Protestant Christians in Korea, 78% are Presbyterians, 14% Methodists and 8% of other denominations (English church, Seventh Day Adventists, Salvation Army and Holiness)." *KMF* 33 (June 1937): 111.

41. William N. Blair and Bruce F. Hunt, *The Korean Pentecost and the Sufferings Which Followed* (Carlisle, PA: Banner of Truth Trust, 1977), 92.

42. Ibid., 92.

43. Blair, *Gold in Korea*, 101; Kim Eŭihwan [Kim Ŭihwan], "The Korean Church under Japanese Occupation with Special Reference to the Resistance Movement within Presbyterianism" (PhD diss., Temple University, 1966).

44. Blair, *Gold in Korea*, 101.

45. Kim Eŭihwan, "Korean Church under Japanese Occupation," 182ff.

46. Donald N. Clark, *Living Dangerously in Korea: The Western Experience, 1900–1950* (Norwalk, CT: EastBridge, 2003), 243.

47. Kim Eŭihwan, "Korean Church under Japanese Occupation," 186.

48. Donald N. Clark, *Living Dangerously in Korea*, 248.

49. Blair, *Gold in Korea*, 105.

50. Kim Yangsun, *History of the Korean Church in the Ten Years since Liberation (1945–1955)*, trans. Allen D. Clark (n.p., [1964?]), 1.

51. *K'ŭrisŭch'yan sinmun*, September 8, 1984.

52. Kim Eŭihwan, "Korean Church under Japanese Occupation," 184; Yi Hyŏnggŭn, "Sinsa ch'ambae wa sun'gyo" [Shintō Worship and Martyrdom], *K'ŭrisŭch'yan sinmun*, September 8, 1984.

53. Kim Eŭihwan, "Korean Church under Japanese Occupation," 168, 185.

54. E. W. Koon, "A Survey of Withdrawal," *KMF* 37 (March 1941): 50.

55. Han'guk kidokkyo yŏksa yŏn'guso, *Han'guk kidok kyohoe ŭi yŏksa II*, 310ff.

56. Park Yong Kyu, *P'yŏngyang sanjŏnghyŏn kyohoe* (Seoul: Saengmyŏng ŭi malssŭmsa, 2006).

57. In 1963 the South Korean government posthumously awarded Chu the Order of Merit for National Foundation and placed Chu's cenotaph in the Ch'ungyŏl (Loyal) section of the National Cemetery (his tomb is in North Korea). It is also noteworthy in view of evangelicalism's conflict with communism (discussed below) that one of Chu's sons, a seminarian, was killed by North Korean communists in 1950. Kim Ch'ungnam, *Sun'gyoja Chu Kichŏl moksa saengae* (Seoul: Paekhap, 1991).

58. Kim Eŭihwan, "Korean Church under Japanese Occupation," 211; *Kidokkyo taebaekkwa sajŏn*, s.v. "Pak Kwanjun"; An Isuk, *Chugŭmyŏn chugŭ'ri'ra* (Seoul: Kidokkyo munsa, 1976).

59. Han'guk kidokkyo yŏksa yŏn'guso, *Han'guk kidok kyohoe ŭi yŏksa II*, 333; Kim Eŭihwan, "Korean Church under Japanese Occupation," 213; Bruce F. Hunt, *For a Testimony* (London: Banner of Truth Trust, 1966).

60. *Kidokkyo taebaekkwa sajŏn*, s.v. "Sinsa ch'ambae."

61. On the Decian and Diocletian persecutions, see W. H. C. Frend, *The Rise of Christianity* (Philadelphia: Fortress, 1984), 318–324.

62. For a detailed treatment of the conflict between compliers and resisters, see Han'guk kidokkyo yŏksa yŏn'guso and pukhan kyohoesa chipp'il wiwŏnhoe, *Pukhan kyohoesa* (Seoul: Han'guk kidokkyo yŏksa yŏn'guso, 1996).

63. *Kidokkyo taebaekkwa sajŏn*, s.v. "Koryŏp'a undong" [Koryŏ Faction Movement].

64. For an example of hard-line nationalist criticism of Korean evangelical leaders, see Kim Samung, ed., *Ch'inilp'a 100-in 100-mun* (Seoul: Tolbegae, 1995).

65. Cumings, *Origins of the Korean War*, 1:35.

66. Chul-won Kang, "Analysis of Japanese Policy," 77; Han Kyumu, *Ilcheha han'guk kidokkyo nongch'on undong, 1925–1937* (Seoul: Han'guk kidokkyo yŏksa yŏn'guso, 1997).

67. Eckert et al., *Korea Old and New*, 297; *Kidokkyo taebaekkwa sajŏn*, s.v. "Sahoejuŭi, han'guk kidokkyo wa" [Socialism, vis-à-vis Christianity in Korea].

68. Michael E. Robinson, *Korea's Twentieth-Century Odyssey: A Short Story* (Honolulu: University of Hawai'i Press), 69–70; Sawa Masahiko, "Han'guk kyohoe ŭi kongsanjuŭi e taehan t'aedo ŭi yŏksajŏk yŏn'gu," in Kim Heung-soo, *Ilcheha han'guk kidokkyo wa sahoejuŭi* (Seoul: Han'guk kidokkyo yŏksa yŏn'guso, 1992), 135–157.

69. Ki-baik Lee, *New History of Korea*, 361.

70. Victor W. Peters, "What Korean Young People Are Thinking," *KMF* 28 (May 1932): 94.

71. Sawa, "Han'guk kyohoe ŭi kongsanjuŭi e taehan t'aedo ŭi yŏksajŏk yŏn'gu," 141.

72. Dae-Sook Suh, *Documents of Korean Communism, 1918–1948* (Princeton, NJ: Princeton University Press, 1970), 8; Han Kyumu, "Yi Tonghwi wa kidokkyo sahoejuŭi,"

in Kim Heung-soo, *Ilcheha han'guk kidokkyo wa sahoejuŭi*, 173–191; Sŏ Chŏngmin, *Yi Tonghwi wa kidokkyo*; Kim Kwangsŏn, "Yŏ Unhyŏng ŭi saengae wa sasang ŭi hyŏngsŏng," in Kim Heung-soo, *Ilcheha han'guk kidokkyo wa sahoejuŭi*, 193–207.

73. Peter H. Lee, *Sourcebook of Korean Civilization*, vol. 2, *From the Seventeenth Century to the Modern Period* (New York: Columbia University Press, 1996), 456–457.

74. See Han Kyumu, "Yi Tonghwi wa kidokkyo sahoejuŭi"; Kim Kwangsŏn, "Yŏ Unhyŏng ŭi saengae wa sasang ŭi hyŏngsŏng"; Keith Pratt and Richard Rutt, *Korea: A Historical and Cultural Dictionary* (Surrey, UK: Curzon, 1999), s.v. "Yi Tonghwi" and "Yŏ Unhyŏng."

75. *Kidokkyo taebaekkwa sajŏn*, s.v. "Sin'ganhoe" [New Shoot Society].

76. Cited in Donald N. Clark, *Living Dangerously in Korea*, 100.

77. Karl Marx and Friedrich Engels, *On Religion* (Chico, CA: Scholars Press, 1964), 42; Kang In'gyu, "1920-yŏndae pan kidokkyo undong ŭl t'onghae pon kidokkyo," *Han'guk kidokkyosa yŏn'gu* 9 (August 1986): 12–15; Kim Heung-soo, *Ilcheha han'guk kidokkyo wa sahoejuŭi*.

78. Chang Pyŏngwuk, *6.25 kongsan namch'im kwa kyohoe*, 35.

79. "What Korean Young People Are Thinking," *KMF* 28 (June 1932): 129.

80. Min Kyoung-bae, *Han'guk kidokkyohoesa*, new rev. ed. (Seoul: Yonsei taehakkyo ch'ulp'ansa, 1993), 310; Kil Sŏnju, *Kil Sŏnju moksa yugojŏnjip*, ed. Kiel [Kil] Chin'gyŏng (Seoul: Chongno sŏjŏk, 1975), 302; *Kidokkyo taebaekkwa sajŏn*, s.v. "Kim Iktu."

81. Ibid.

82. At least until 1983 the South Korean government has designated November 23, the anniversary of this incident, as Student Anticommunist Day. *Kidokkyo taebaekkwa sajŏn*, s.v. "Sinŭiju haksaeng sakŏn" [Sinŭiju Student Incident].

83. Kim Yangsun, *History of the Korean Church*, 12.

84. Charles K. Armstrong, *North Korean Revolution, 1945–1950* (New York: Cornell University Press, 2003), 67.

85. Bruce Cumings, *The Origins of the Korean War*, vol. 2, *The Roaring of the Cataract, 1947–1950* (Princeton, NJ: Princeton University Press, 1990), 318.

86. Han'guk kidokkyo yŏksa yŏn'guso and Pukhan kyohoesa chipp'il wiwŏnhoe, *Pukhan kyohoesa*, 388–389; Robinson, *Korea's Twentieth-Century Odyssey*, 106–107. Armstrong, *North Korean Revolution*, 34.

87. Chang Pyŏngwuk, *6.25 kongsan namch'im kwa kyohoe*, 76ff., 89, 108.

88. Armstrong, *North Korean Revolution*, 120. Her correct name is Kang Pansŏk.

89. Han'guk kidokkyo yŏksa yŏn'guso and Pukhan kyohoesa chipp'il wiwŏnhoe, *Pukhan kyohoesa*, 387; Sawa Masahiko, "Haebang ihu pukhan chiyŏk ŭi kidokkyo: 1945.8–1950.6," in *Haebanghu pukhan kyohoesa*, ed. Kim Heung-soo, 13–51 (Seoul: Tasan kŭlpang, 1992).

90. Kim Yangsun, *History of the Korean Church*, 14; Han'guk kidokkyo yŏksa yŏn'guso and Pukhan kyohoesa chipp'il wiwŏnhoe, *Pukhan kyohoesa*, 398.

91. Chang Pyŏngwuk, *6.25 kongsan namch'im kwa kyohoe*, 44.

92. Kang Inch'ŏl, *Han'guk ŭi kaesin'gyo wa pangongjuŭi: Posujŏk kaesin'gyo ŭi chŏngch'ijŏk haendongjuŭi t'amgu* (Seoul: Chungsim, 2006), 410.

93. Ibid., 409. Kang finds the 300,000 figure the evangelical leaders mentioned in their petition to the communist regime to be inflated.

94. Ibid., 418.

95. Ibid., 496.

96. Ibid., 433.

97. This is an argument Kang Inch'ŏl persuasively makes in *Han'guk ŭi kaesin'gyo wa pangongjuŭi*, 496–502.

98. See Kim Heung-soo, *Han'guk chŏnjaeng kwa kiboksinang hwaksan yŏn'gu* (Seoul: Han'guk kidokkyo yŏksa yŏn'guso, 1999), 71–78.

99. Han Kyumu, "Haebang chikhu namhan kyohoe ŭi tonghyang," *Han'guk kidokkyo wa yŏksa* 2 (1992): 39–54; Kang Inch'ŏl, *Han'guk kidokkyohoe wa kukka-simin sahoe* (Seoul: Han'guk kidokkyo yŏksa yŏn'guso, 1996), 175–185.

100. Kang Inch'ŏl, *Han'guk kidokkyohoe wa kukka-simin sahoe*, 176. The 16,136,000 figure is the estimate given in a study by Tai Hwan Kwon et al. in *The Population of Korea* (Seoul: Population and Development Studies Center, Seoul National University, 1975), iv. Kang cites a figure of 19,190,877 for 1946, as stated in 1973 by Chungang sŏn'gŏ kwalli wiwŏnhoe (Central Committee for the Administration of Election), but this seems too high, given that the population for both North and South Korea in May 1944 was only 25,120,000.

101. Chang Pyŏngwuk, *6.25 kongsan namch'im kwa kyohoe*, 159.

102. Cumings, *Origins of the Korean War*, 2:198–203.

103. Chang Pyŏngwuk, *6.25 kongsan namch'im kwa kyohoe*, 159.

104. Kang Inch'ŏl, *Han'guk kidokkyohoe wa kukka-simin sahoe*, 216–220.

105. Kim Heung-soo, *Han'guk chŏnjaeng kwa kiboksinang hwaksan yŏn'gu*, 24.

106. Chang Pyŏngwuk, *6.25 kongsan namch'im kwa kyohoe*, 284. My translation.

107. Hwang So-kyong, *Sonnim* (Seoul: Ch'angjak kwa pip'yŏngsa, 2001). An English translation of the work is also available: *The Guest*, translated by Kyung-Ja Chun and Maya West (New York: Seven Stories Press, 2005). Also of relevance is Richard E. Kim's novel *The Martyred* (New York: George Braziller, 1964), published originally in English, to acclaim.

108. On the background and development of this rebellion, see Cumings, *Origins of the Korean War*, 2:259–267.

109. Chang Pyŏngwuk, *6.25 kongsan namch'im kwa kyohoe*, 144.

110. Kim Heung-soo, *Han'guk chŏnjaeng kwa kiboksinang hwaksan yŏn'gu*, 25–26.

111. Chang Pyŏngwuk, *6.25 kongsan namch'im kwa kyohoe*, 326.

112. *Kidokkyo taebaekkwa sajŏn*, s.v. "6.25 sabyŏn kwa kidokkyo" [The Korean War and Christianity].

113. Ibid.

114. Ibid.

115. Chang Pyŏngwuk, *6.25 kongsan namch'im kwa kyohoe*, 257.

116. Kang Inch'ŏl, *Han'guk ŭi kaesin'gyo wa pangongjuŭi*, 418. Kang estimates that 15,000 to 20,000 northern Catholics migrated to the South between 1945 and 1953, representing about 25 percent of the entire Catholic population in North Korea. Ibid., 410–412.

117. For an eyewitness account of Christians being persecuted in North Korea, see Soon Ok Lee, *Eyes of the Tailless Animals: Prison Memoirs of a North Korean Woman* (Bartlesville, OK: Living Sacrifice Book Co., 1999).

118. Kim himself used to attend this church when he was a child. Also see Han'guk kidokkyo yŏksa yŏn'guso and Pukhan kyohoesa chipp'il wiwŏnhoe, *Pukhan kyohoesa*, 478–479.

119. *Wŏlgan Choguk* is published by Chaeilbon chosŏnin ch'ongyŏnhaphoe/ Zainihon chōsenjin sōrengōkai (General Association of Korean Residents in Japan). The figures are taken from several articles published in the August 2004 issue of the journal, under the feature titled "Konghwaguk ŭi chonggyo sanghwang" [The State of Religions in the Republic]. These articles are also available at the online journal *Chosŏn sinbo* [The People's Korea], http://www.korea-np.co.jp; "Chwadamhoe, sinang ŭi chayunŭn ŏttŏke" [A Round Table: What of Religious Freedom?], http://www. korea-np.co.jp/news/ViewArticle.aspx?ArticleID=12132; "Chosŏn kŭrisŭdogyo rŏnmaeng chungangwiwŏnhoe o kyŏngwu sŏgichangegesŏ tŭnnŭnda" [Listening to O Kyŏngwu, Secretary of the Korean Christian Federation (the successor of North Korean Christian League)], http://www.korea-np.co.jp/news/ViewArticle. aspx?ArticleID=12131; "Changch'ung sŏngdang" [Changch'ung (Catholic) Church], http://www.korea-np.co.jp/news/ViewArticle.aspx?ArticleID=12130.

120. Donald N. Clark recognizes the centrality of P'yŏngyang for Korean Christianity in his book *Living Dangerously in Korea* by titling the chapter on the subject "The Jerusalem of the East." On Kim's Christian background, see Yongho Ch'oe, "Christian Background in the Early Life of Kim Il-Sŏng," *Asian Survey* 26, no. 10 (1986): 1082–1099.

121. The following excerpt published in a North Korean journal on an anniversary of the Korean War suggests the northern regime's typical attitude toward the United States at this time: "On the occasion of this day all of our youths and students, whose hearts are burning with a blazing hatred and feeling of hostility toward their inveterate enemy, the American imperialist aggressors, are tightening more firmly their revolutionary resolve to crush the American imperialists' maneuvering for the provocation of a new war." *Nodong ch'ongnyŏn* (June 25, 1975), trans. Joint Publications Research Service, *Translations on North Korea*, no. 419 (August 6, 1975), 1.

122. To offer a bit of anecdotal evidence, growing up as an elementary student in South Korea in the 1960s, I was so "indoctrinated" about the Ppalgaengi (the "Reds") that for some time I believed they were literally red. That my wife also felt this way suggests mine was not an atypical experience.

123. Chang Pyŏngwuk, *6.25 kongsan namch'im kwa kyohoe*, 262; "Kyohoe ŭi pangong kyoyuk: Kyohoe nŭn pangong ŭi poru" [The Church's Anticommunist Education: The Church Is a Stronghold of Anticommunism], *K'ŭrisŭch'yan sinmun*, June 21, 1969; Kang Inch'ŏl, *Han'guk ŭi kaesin'gyo wa pangongjuŭi*.

124. The reformative impulse was not unique to Korean evangelicalism. Timothy L. Smith shows how significant such an impulse was for American evangelicalism and the impact it had on antebellum America in his *Revivalism and Social Reform: American Protestantism on the Eve of the Civil War* (Nashville, TN: Abingdon, 1957).

125. Wells, *New God, New Nation*.

126. Walter R. Lambuth, "Korea Ripe for Evangelism," *KMF* 18 (February 1922): 25.

127. Frank T. Boreland, "The Rural Problem in Korea and Some Ways in Which It Is Being Faced," *KMF* 29 (July 1933): 133–134.

128. William N. Blair, "The Work of the Foreign Missionary in Korea Today," *KMF* 20 (January 1924): 5.

129. Kil Sŏnju, *Kil Sŏnju moksa yugojŏnjip*, 24.

130. On the millennial disposition of evangelicalism, see Jerald C. Brauer's "Revivalism and Millenarianism in America," in *The Great Tradition*, ed. Joseph D. Ban and Paul R. Dekar (Valley Forge, PA: Judson, 1982), 147–159.

131. The following synopsis of Kil's life is based mostly on a biography of Kil by his son Kil Chingyŏng, *Yŏnggye Kil Sŏnju* (Seoul: Chongno sŏjŏk, 1980).

132. Ibid., 72. See also the section on Kil Sŏnju in "Conversion Narratives in Korean Evangelicalism," by Timothy S. Lee in *Religions of Korea in Practice*, edited by Robert E. Buswell Jr. (Princeton, NJ: Princeton University Press, 2007), 393–408.

133. Kil Chingyŏng, *Yŏnggye Kil Sŏnju*, 326.

134. Charles F. Bernheisel, "Rev. Kil Sunju," *KMF* 32 (February 1936): 30.

135. Kil Chingyŏng, *Yŏnggye Kil Sŏnju*, 282. Kil was unable to publish this book in his lifetime, owing to Japanese proscription. Ibid., 254.

136. Ibid., 329.

137. Kil Sŏnju, *Kil Sŏnju moksa yugojŏnjip*, 70.

138. Kil Chingyŏng, *Yŏnggye Kil Sŏnju*, 282.

139. Bernheisel, "Rev. Kil Sunju," 29.

140. Brauer, "Revivalism and Millenarianism in America."

141. See, for example, Ronald L. Numbers et al., ed., *The Disappointed: Millerism and Millenarianism in the Nineteenth Century* (Knoxville: University of Tennessee Press, 1993).

142. On faith-healing movements among European and American Pentecostals, see Walter J. Hollenweger, *The Pentecostals* (London: SCM Press, 1972), 353ff. Also see Amanda Porterfield, *Healing in the History of Christianity* (Oxford: Oxford University Press, 2005).

143. Yi Tŏkchu [Rhie Deok-Joo], *Han'guk kŭristoin dŭl ŭi kaejong iyagi* (Seoul: Chŏnmangso, 1990), 354.

144. Park Yong Kyu, *Kim Iktu moksa chŏn'gi* (Seoul: Saengmyŏng ŭi malssŭmsa, 1991), 187.

145. Min Kyoung-bae, *Ilcheha ŭi han'guk kidokkyo* (Seoul: Christian Literature Society of Korea, 1991), 297.

146. Kim was not as actively involved in the March First Movement as was Kil, but the police suspected Kim of having instigated an independence demonstration in Sinch'ŏn. Yi Tŏkchu [Rhie Deok-Joo], *Han'guk kŭristoin dŭl ŭi kaejong iyagi*, 358.

147. Rhodes, *History of the Korea Mission*, 288.

148. Ibid., 288–289.

149. Ibid., 289–290.

150. Min, *Ilcheha ŭi han'guk kidokkyo*, 317.

151. *Kidokkyo taebaekkwa sajŏn*, s.v. "Kim Iktu."

152. Ibid.

153. Ibid.; Min, *Ilcheha ŭi han'guk kidokkyo*, 325.

154. Yi Tŏkchu [Rhie Deok-Joo], *Han'guk kŭristoin dŭl ŭi kaejong iyagi*, 360.

155. Pyŏn Chongho, *Yi Yongdo moksa chŏn*, in *Yi Yongdo moksa chŏnjip*, ed. Pyŏn Chongho (Seoul: Changan munhwasa, 1986), 30.

156. Min, *Ilcheha ŭi han'guk kidokkyo*, 338. Yi read of and admired Francis of Assisi. He also read Thomas A Kempis's *The Imitation of Christ*. Pyŏn, *Yi Yongdo moksa chŏn*.

157. Victor Wellington Peters, "Simeon, a Christian Korean Mystic," *KMF* 32 (September 1936): 196–198.

158. Mircea Eliade, *The Encyclopedia of Religion* (New York: Macmillan, 1987), s.v. "mysticism."

159. Yi Yongdo, *Yi Yongdo moksa ŭi ilgi* [The Diary of Reverend Yi Yongdo], in Pyŏn, *Yi Yongdo moksa chŏnjip*, 82. My translation.

160. Ibid., 118. My translation.

161. Yi Yongdo, *Yongdo sinang* [Yongdo Piety], in Pyŏn, *Yi Yongdo moksa chŏnjip*, 120.

162. Yi Yongdo, *Yi Yongdo moksa sŏganjip* [Collected Letters of Reverend Yi Yongdo], in Pyŏn, *Yi Yongdo moksa chŏnjip*, 198–199. My translation.

163. Victor Wellington Peters, "Simeon, a Christian Korean Mystic," *KMF* 32 (October 1936): 217.

164. Pyŏn, *Yi Yongdo moksa chŏn*, 101–102.

165. Min, *Han'guk kidokkyohoesa*, 441; "Isabel Murwi rŭl samgahara" [Avoid the Jezebel Gang], *Kidoksinbo*, December 14, 1932; *Kidokkyo taebaekkwa sajŏn*, s.v. "Yi Yongdo."

166. Pyŏn, a close friend and admirer of Yi while he was alive, took it as his life's mission to collect, interpret, and publish materials on Yi. His magnum opus is the ten-volume *Yi Yongdo moksa chŏnjip*.

167. Min, *Ilcheha ŭi han'guk kidokkyo*, 388. For more recent appraisals of Yi Yongdo, see P'yŏnjip wiwŏnhoe [Editorial Committee for Reverend Yi Yongdo's 100th Birthday Anniversary Festschrift], *Yi Yongdo ŭi saengae, sinhak, yŏngsŏng* [The Life, Theology, and Spirituality of Yi Yongdo] (Seoul: Handŭl ch'ulp'ansa, 2001); and Ryu Kŭmju, *Yi Yongdo ŭi sinbijuŭi wa han'guk kyohoe* [Yi Yongdo's Mysticism and the Korean Church] (Seoul: Taehan kidokkyo sŏhoe, 2005).

3. Evangelicalism Takes Off in South Korea, 1953–1988

Epigraph. Sidney E. Mead, *The Lively Experiment: The Shaping of Christianity in America* (New York: Harper and Row, 1963), 33.

1. Brainerd's remark is quoted in William R. Hutchison's *Errand to the World: American Protestant Thought and Foreign Missions* (Chicago: University of Chicago

Press, 1987), 30. Gale's is from George L. Paik, *The History of Protestant Missions in Korea, 1832–1910* (1929; reprint, Seoul: Yonsei University Press, 1987), 419. For a Native American view of Christian missionary work in North America, see George E. Tinker, *Missionary Conquest: The Gospel and Native American Cultural Genocide* (Minneapolis: Fortress, 1993).

2. Missionary statesmen were career mission leaders "known to the public and routinely associating with heads and ministers of state." See Valentin H. Rabe's "Evangelical Logistics: Mission Support and Resources to 1920," in *Missionary Enterprise in China and America*, ed. John Fairbank (Cambridge, MA: Harvard University Press, 1974), 56–90. The locus classicus of the movement to evangelize the world in a single generation is John R. Mott's *The Evangelization of the World in This Generation* (New York: Student Volunteer Movement for Foreign Missions, 1901).

3. For Speer's, Mott's, and Brown's quotations, see Paik, *History of Protestant Missions*, 273, 366.

4. One such leader was Han Kyŏngjik, who had escaped from the North before the Korean War and founded the Yŏngnak Presbyterian Church with other northern refugees, becoming one of the most respected Protestant leaders in the South. He wrote, "If the majority of Koreans in South Korea come to know and obey Christ, Korea will become a prosperous, democratic country where freedom and equality are enjoyed and human rights respected." See his article, "The Present and Future of the Korean Church," in *Korean Church Growth Explosion*, ed. Bong-rin Ro and Marlin L. Nelson (Korea: World of Life Press, 1983), 369. For a brief portrayal of Han, see Timothy S. Lee's section on him in "Conversion Narratives in Korean Evangelicalism," in *Religions of Korea in Practice*, ed. Robert E. Buswell Jr. (Princeton, NJ: Princeton University Press, 2007), 393–408.

5. Mead, *Lively Experiment*, 33.

6. The figures for 1950, 1960, and 1970 were estimated by Samuel H. Moffett, cited in *Han'guk kyohoe 100-yŏn chosa yŏn'gu*, by Han'guk kidokkyo sahoe munje yŏn'guwŏn (Seoul: Han'guk kidokkyo sahoe munje yŏn'guwŏn, 1982), 144. The figures for 1979 and 1985 were taken from government census reports, also quoted in *The Centennial Comprehensive Study*, 161. Also see Han Yŏngje, ed., *Kidokkyo taeyŏn'gam, 1991* (Seoul: Kidokkyo munsa, 1991), 6:233. A figure sometimes cited for 1980 is 7,180,627, which is the total calculated from the membership reports submitted by Protestant denominations in Korea. But this figure is inflated, due to the exaggeration in the reports and the failure to adjust for mobile churchgoers' multiple registrations. See Yi Chongyun, Chŏn Hojin, and Na Ilsŏn, eds., *Kyohoe sŏngjangnon* (Seoul: Emmaus, 1986), 262.

7. *K'ŭrisŭch'yan sinmun*, June 20, 1981.

8. John N. Vaughan, *The World's Twenty Largest Churches* (Grand Rapids, MI: Jordan, 1984) and *Absolutely Double* (Bolivar, MO: Megachurch Research Press, 1990). By 1993, South Korea also had the world's first- and second-largest Methodist churches: Kwangnim (Kwanglim) Methodist Church and Kŭmnan (Kumnan) Methodist Church, both of which had about 60,000 members. Sin Sŏngjong, *Irŏn kyohoe ka sŏngjang handa* (Seoul: Hana, 1993); *Chosŏn ilbo*, February 8, 1993.

9. *World*, cited in *Chosŏn ilbo*, February 8, 1993. The seventh-, ninth-, and tenth-largest churches were Kŭmnan Methodist Church (Seoul: 56,000), Sungŭi Methodist Church (Incheon: 48,000), and Chuan Presbyterian. Sin Sŏngjong, *Irŏn kyohoe ka sŏngjang handa*; and *Chosŏn ilbo*, February 8, 1993.

10. *Han'guk ilbo*, Chicago edition, July 31, 1986.

11. Carter J. Eckert et al., *Korea Old and New: A History* (Seoul: published for the Korea Institute, Harvard University, by Ilchokak, 1990), 347–387.

12. Kang Inch'ŏl, *Han'guk ŭi kaesin'gyo wa pangongjuŭi: Posujŏk kaesin'gyo ŭi chŏngch'ijŏk haendongjuŭi t'amgu* (Seoul: Chungsim, 2006).

13. See Don Oberdorfer, *The Two Koreas: A Contemporary History*, rev. and updated ed. (New York: Basic Books, 2001), 47–59, 184–186.

14. Eckert et al., *Korea Old and New*, 388.

15. T'onggye chŏng, *1990 ingu chut'aek ch'ong chosa chonghap punsŏk*, vol. 4–2, *Chiyŏkkan ingu pulgyunhyŏng punp'o ŭi wŏnin kwa kyŏlgwa* (Seoul: T'onggye chŏng, 1990), 5.

16. Ibid., 105.

17. Ibid.

18. Ibid., 19.

19. Ibid., 6.

20. Brian A. Wilson, "Values and Religion," in *A City in Transition: Urbanization in Taegu, Korea*, ed. Lee Mangap and Herbert R. Barringer (Seoul: Hollym, 1971), 383ff.

21. For example, see Kim Pyŏngsŏ, "Han'guk kyohoe hyŏnsang ŭi sahoehakjok ihae" [A Sociological Understanding of the Korean Church Phenomenon], *K'ŭrisŭch'yan sinmun*, November 21, 1981.

22. For such evidence in Japan, see David Reid's *New Wine: The Cultural Shaping of Japanese Christianity* (Berkeley, CA: Asian Humanities Press, 1991), 16; and F. C. Wallace, "Revitalization Movements," *American Anthropologist* 58 (1956): 264–281.

23. Spencer Palmer, ed., *The New Religions of Korea* (Seoul: Transactions of Royal Asiatic Society, Korea Branch, 1967); Kim Heung-soo, *Han'guk chŏnjaeng kwa kiboksinang hwaksan yŏn'gu*.

24. Han Yŏngje, ed., *Han'guk kidokkyo sŏngjang 100-yŏn* (Seoul: Kidokkyo munsa, 1986), 225.

25. Pak Chongsun, *Kyohoe sŏngjang kwa song'gŏng kongbu* (Seoul: Hyesŏn, 1980); "Han'guk kyohoe ŭi sŏngjangsang" [The Shape of Church Growth in Korea], *K'ŭrisŭch'yan sinmun*, November 20, 1976. Yonggi Cho, *Successful Home Cell Groups* (Seoul: Church Growth International, 1981); Alvin Sneller [Sin Naeri], *Han'guk kyohoe sŏngjang ŭi pigyŏl* (Seoul: Kyaehyŏkchuŭi sinhaeng hyŏphoe, 1992).

26. On the chaplaincy in the armed forces, police departments, and prisons, see Kang Inch'ŏl, *Han'guk ŭi kaesin'gyo wa pangongjuŭi*, 346–402.

27. "Sŏul chiphoe taesŏnghwang: Kŭraeham paksa yŏngnak kyohoe kangdan esŏ" [The Seoul Assembly a Big Success: Dr. Graham at Yŏngnak Church's Pulpit], *Han'guk kidok kongbo*, January 5, 1953; "Kyŏlsinja chŏnyŏmyŏng: Pŏlssŭn pŭhŭng chiphoe taejŏnsŏ sŏnghwang" [One Thousand or So New Believers: Pierson's Taejŏn Revival

a Success], *Han'guk kidok kongbo*, November 1, 1954. In Korea, Pierce also engaged in active humanitarian efforts such as raising funds to help war orphans, widows, and prisoners of war. For these efforts he was decorated by the Korean government in 1964. "Munhwa hunjang e pitnanŭn kongik" [The Public Service That Shines in the Cultural Order], *K'ŭrisŭch'yan sinmun*, October 10, 1964.

28. "Yuksimmanmyŏng chiphoe" [Six Hundred Thousand Gathered], *Han'guk kidok kongbo*, April 11, 1955. My translation.

29. Mun Sŏnmyŏng was another "heretic" who worried the Korean church leaders at this time. But his Unification Church was devoted to a global mission from very early on and had less direct impact on Korean evangelicalism than Pak's Chŏndogwan, which was confined to South Korea and thrived on the highly charged atmosphere that prevailed in the country in the wake of the Korean War. On Mun's movement, see George D. Chryssides, *The Advent of Sun Myung Moon: The Origins, Beliefs, and Practices of the Unification Church* (London: Macmillan, 1991); and Eileen Barker, *The Making of a Moonie: Choice or Brainwashing?* (Oxford: Basil Blackwell, 1984).

30. "Puhŭng chiphoe isang-itta" [There Is Something Wrong with Revival Meetings], *Han'guk kidok kongbo*, May 24, 1954.

31. "Puhŭngdan chŏtchiphoe sŏnghwan" [The Revivalists' Organization's First Gathering a Success], *Han'guk kidok kongbo*, June 20, 1955; "Puhŭngdan chiphoe sŏnghwang" [The Revivalists' Organizations' Gathering a Success], *Han'guk kidok kongbo*, July 4, 1955.

32. One reason for Graham's affinity for Korea had to do with his wife, Ruth Bell. She had attained her high school education at P'yŏngyang Foreign School in the 1930s, while her Presbyterian parents engaged in missionary work in China. Billy Graham recalls, "At that time, the Pyeng Yang Foreign School, established and run by American missionaries, was considered one of the finest boarding schools in Asia, with a reputation for sending more candidates on to earn medical degrees and doctorates than any other boarding school of its type in the world." Billy Graham, *Just as I Am: The Autobiography of Billy Graham* (New York: HarperCollins, 1997), 617. See also "Pilli kŭraeham paksa chŏndo kangyŏn" [Dr. Billy Graham's Revival Address], *Han'guk kidok kongbo*, March 5, 1956.

33. "Oroji han'guk kyohoega pŏnghwa manŭl pŏlsŏn chiphoega ŭimi hanŭngŏt" [The Pierson Gathering Only Signifies Peace in the Korean Church], *K'ŭrisŭch'yan sinmun*, October 11, 1960.

34. "Kŭllae tŭmun taechŏndo chiphoe" [A Huge Revival Gathering Rare in Modern Times], *K'ŭrisŭch'yan sinmun*, August 21, 1961.

35. Kim Chinhwan, *Han'guk kyohoe puhŭng undongsa*, rev. ed. (Seoul: Seoul sŏjŏk, 1993), 242.

36. Ibid.

37. Sung C. Chun, *Schism and Unity in the Protestant Churches of Korea* (Seoul: Christian Literature Society of Korea, 1979).

38. "Kŭristorŭl 14man siminega: Taesŏnghwangni chŏngjusi chipchung kaho chŏndo" [140,000 Citizens of Chŏngju to Christ: The Intensive House-to-House Evangelism in Chŏngju a Great Success], *K'ŭrisŭch'yan sinmun*, April 1, 1967; "Nasaret

chiphoe sŏnghwang" [A Nazarene Gathering a Success], *K'ŭrisŭch'yan sinmun*, August 2, 1969.

39. By this time, those Protestants who had been receptive to modern views during the Japanese occupation had become liberals, accepting the higher criticism and tending toward liberationist theology. See Young-suk Yi, "Liberal Protestant Leaders Working for Social Change: South Korea, 1957–1984" (PhD diss., University of Oregon, 1990); Commission on Theological Concerns of the Christian Conference of Asia, ed., *Minjung Theology: People as the Subjects of History* (Singapore: Christian Conference of Asia, 1981); and Andrew Sung Park, "*Minjung* and *Pungryu* Theologies in Contemporary Korea: A Critical and Comparative Examination" (PhD diss., Graduate Theological Union, 1985).

40. See George E. Ogle, *Liberty to the Captives: The Struggle against Oppression in South Korea* (Atlanta, GA: Westminster John Knox Press, 1977), and *How Long, O Lord: Stories of Twentieth Century Korea* (n.p.: Xlibris, 2002). Also see Donald N. Clark, "Growth and Limitation of Minjung Christianity in South Korea," in *South Korea's Minjung Movement: The Culture and Politics of Dissidence*, ed. Kenneth M. Wells (Honolulu: University of Hawai'i Press, 1995), 87–103; Harold Hakwon Sunoo, *Repressive State and Resisting Church: The Politics of CIA in South Korea* (Fayette, MO: Korean American Cultural Association, 1976); Cho Wha Soon [Cho Hwasun], *Let the Weak Be Strong: A Woman's Struggle for Justice*, ed. Lee Sun Ai and Ahn Sang Nim (Bloomington, IN: Meyer-Stone Books, 1988); Peggy Billings, *Fire Beneath the Frost: The Struggles of the Korean People and Church* (New York: Friendship Press, 1983); Jim Stentzel, ed., *More Than Witnesses: How a Small Group of Missionaries Aided Korea's Democratic Revolution* (Seoul: Korea Democracy Foundation, 2006); and Paul Yunshik Chang, "Carrying the Torch in the Darkest Hours: The Sociopolitical Origins of Minjung Protestant Movements," in *Christianity in Korea*, ed. Robert E. Buswell Jr. and Timothy S. Lee (Honolulu: University of Hawai'i Press, 2006), 195–220.

41. "Kwangjang meun 6 man inp'a" [The 60,000 Throng That Filled a Plaza], *K'ŭrisŭch'yan sinmun*, June 6, 1970; "Taechŏndo taehoe sŏngnyo" [A Huge Revival Meeting Ends Successfully], *K'ŭrisŭch'yan sinmun*, August 22, 1970; "Kisŏng namjŏndohoe simnyŏng puhŭnghoe" [A Spiritual Revival Meeting Led by the Men's Association of the Holiness Church], August 22, 1970. Sŏng'gyŏl kyohoe (literally "Holiness Church") is a major denomination in Korea and traces its roots to the Oriental Missionary Society. See Edward Erny and Esther Erny, *No Guarantee but God: The Story of the Founders of the Oriental Missionary Society* (Greenwood, IN: Oriental Missionary Society, 1969); Pak Myŏngsu [Park Myung Soo], *Ch'ogi han'guk sŏnggyŏl kyohoesa* (Seoul: Taehan kidokkyo sŏhoe, 2001); Meesang Lee Choi, *The Rise of the Korean Holiness Church in Relation to the American Holiness Movement: Wesley's "Scriptural Holiness" and the "Fourfold Gospel"* (Lanham, MD: Scarecrow Press, 2008).

42. "3,127 myŏng ege serye" [Baptism of 3,127], *K'ŭrisŭch'yan sinmun*, April 29, 1972.

43. "Pilli chibang taehoe k'ŭn sŏnggwa" [Billy (Graham's) Regional Rallies a Big Success], *K'ŭrisŭch'yan sinmun*, May 26, 1973; Kim Chinhwan, *Han'guk kyohoe puhŭng undongsa*, 250.

44. *Yahoo! Korea Paekkhwa sajŏn*, s.v. "Yŏŭido kwangjang" [Yŏŭido Plaza], http://kr.dictionary.search.yahoo.com/search/dictionaryp?pk=16168800&p=%BF%A9%C0%C7%B5%B5+%B1%A4%C0%E5&field=id&type=enc&subtype=enc; *New York Times*, "Pope, at Huge Mass in Seoul, Prays for a Reunified Korea," October 9, 1989.

45. "Pilli Kŭraeham chŏndo taehoe rŭl marhanda" [Talking about the Billy Graham Evangelistic Meeting], *Kidokkyo sasang* (July 1973): 80–91.

46. "Segi ŭi chŏndo taehoe p'yemak" [The Revival Meeting of the Century Closes], *K'ŭrisŭch'yan sinmun*, June 9, 1973; Ch'oe Namgyu"Kŭm ch'ottae ka han'guk e" [The Golden Candlestick Has Come to Korea], *Sinanggye* (July 1973): 80–83.

47. Kim Chinhwan, *Han'guk kyohoe puhŭng undongsa*, 250; "Segi ŭi chŏndo taehoe p'yemak," *K'ŭrisŭch'yan sinmun*, June 9, 1973. To determine how many people attended these assemblies with reasonable accuracy, organizers of the Billy Graham Crusade devised a scheme whereby about three square feet would be allotted to each person. Nonetheless, given the size of the crowd, and their mixing in the course of events, such accounting is at best an educated guess. Moreover, the figures released by the organizers of crusades often conflict with figures released by the police. On the last day of the BGC assembly, for example, the organizers reported 1.1 million people in attendance, whereas the police estimate was about half that. This does not necessarily mean that the organizers exaggerated the figures or that the police figures should be preferred over the organizers'. Although the police would have had less stake than the organizers in a high turnout for the events, it cannot be assumed that they had any more accurate way of estimating attendance. Thus these figures should be taken with a bit of skepticism. With this in mind, in the rest of this study I will quote attendance and other figures related to the BGC and other crusades as they were made public by their organizers, without second-guessing them. "Epochal Event: What God Did in Korea," *Christianity Today*, June 22, 1973.

48. "Pilli Kŭraeham chŏndo taehoe rŭl marhanda," 82.

49. "Han'guk pokŭmhwa undong ŭi sae chŏngi" [A Turning Point in Korea's Evangelization Movement], *K'ŭrisŭch'yan sinmun*, August 6, 1977.

50. "Osunjŏl segye taehoe kaech'oe" [The World Pentecostal Assembly Held], *K'ŭrisŭch'yan sinmun*, September 22, 1973.

51. "Kŭristo ŭi yongbyŏng tajim" [Pledging to Be Valiant Soldiers of Christ], *K'ŭrisŭch'yan sinmun*, November 3, 1973.

52. "Pokŭmhwa undong ŭn chŏn'guk e hwaktae toego itta" [The Evangelization Movement Is Expanding throughout the Country], *K'ŭrisŭch'yan sinmun*, June 8, 1974.

53. Kim Sŏngjin, "Saeroun hyŏngt'ae ŭi puhŭng undong (2)" [A New Form of Revival Movement (2)], *Kidokkyo sasang* (February 1973): 75–82.

54. Kim Chongnyŏl, "Minjok pogŭmhwa wa kunjung chiphoe" [Evangelization of the Nation and Mass Gatherings], *Kidokkyo sasang* (October 1974): 72–81.

55. "Yesu hyŏkmyŏng 'eksŭpullo74' taehoe kaech'oe" [The Jesus Revolution "Explo '74" to Be Held], *K'ŭrisŭch'yan sinmun*, August 17, 1974.

56. Ibid.; "Eksŭpullo 74 taehoe chunbi hwalbal" [Preparations for Explo '74 Active], *K'ŭrisŭch'yan sinmun*, July 13, 1974.

57. "Yesu hyŏkmyŏng 'eksŭpullo74' taehoe kaech'oe"; "Minjok ŭi kasŭme kŭristo simŏ" [To Plant Christ in the Heart of the Nation], K'ŭrisŭch'yan sinmun, August 24, 1974. Also see "70-yŏndae han'guk kyohoe wa taehyŏng chiphoe" [Massive Assemblies and the Korean Church in the '70s], Sinang segye (August–September 1980): 56–59.

58. "70-yŏndae han'guk kyohoe wa taehyŏng chiphoe"; "Minjok ŭi kasŭme kŭristo simŏ."

59. "Eksŭpŭllo 74, kŭ hyŏngjang e kada" [Explo '74: Visiting Its Venue], K'ŭrisŭch'yan sinmun, August 10, 1974; "1 paekman myŏngi hanjari e: Han'guk kyohoe chŏryŏk kwasi" [One Million Together at One Place: The Korean Church Displays Its Potential], K'ŭrisŭch'yan sinmun, December 15, 1979.

60. "Kusoktoen kyoyŏkja sŏnggŭm" [Donations for Arrested Ministers], K'ŭrisŭch'yan sinmun, March 16, 1974; "Eksŭpŭllo 74 rŭl malhanda" [Talking about Explo '74], Kidokkyo sasang, October 1974: 82–91; Kidokkyo taebaekkwa sajŏn, s.v. "Eksŭpŭllo taehoe."

61. "Konan kwa puhwal" [Suffering and Resurrection], K'ŭrisŭch'yan sinmun, March 30, 1974. See also "Eksŭp'ŭllo 74 rŭl marhanda," 82–91.

62. Kim Chongnyŏl, "Minjok pogŭmhwa wa kunjung chiphoe," 74. My translation.

63. Ibid. My translation.

64. "Eksŭp'ŭllo 74 rŭl marhanda," 86–87.

65. "Yesu hyŏkmyŏng 'eksŭp'ullo 74' taehoe kaemak" [The Jesus Revolution "Explo '74" Assembly Opens], K'ŭrisŭch'yan sinmun, August 17, 1974.

66. Max Weber, Sociology of Religion, trans. Ephraim Fischoff (Boston: Beacon, 1963), 190.

67. Sin Sŏngjong, Irŏn kyohoe ka sŏngjang handa, 196. My translation. Also see "Yangjŏk sŏngjanŭn tangbun kan kyesok" [Numerical Growth Will Continue for Some Time], K'ŭrisŭch'yan sinmun, June 4, 1983.

68. "Yuk Yŏngsu yŏsa kukminjang ŏmsu" [A National Funeral to Be Observed Strictly for Madam Yuk Yŏngsu], K'ŭrisŭch'yan sinmun, March 16 and August 24, 1974.

69. "Han'guk yesukyohoe e halmal itta" [Some Words for the Korean Council of Christian Churches], K'ŭrisŭch'yan sinmun, December 7, 1974.

70. Han Kyŏngjik, "Present and Future of the Korean Church," 369.

71. "Che 7 hoe taet'ongnyŏng choch'an kidohoe kŏhaeng" [The Seventh Presidential Prayer Breakfast Held], K'ŭrisŭch'yan sinmun, May 11, 1974.

72. "Chuil e sŏn'gŏ silsi paegyŏk: Pusan kidokkyoin 10 man kwŏlgi hangŭi" [A Denouncement of Holding an Election on Sunday: 10,000 Pusan Christians Hold a Protest Rally], Han'guk kidok kongbo, September 17, 1956. Syngman Rhee had ordered his government to avoid scheduling any official events on Sunday, but it had been difficult for such an order to trickle down to non-Christian officials in his government.

73. "Tan'gun sang kŏnnip pandae" [Opposition to Erecting the Tan'gun Statue], K'ŭrisŭch'yan sinmun, February 26, 1966. See Timothy S. Lee, "What Should Christians Do about a Shaman-Progenitor? Evangelicals and Ethnic Nationalism in South Korea," Church History: Studies in Christianity and Culture 78, no. 1 (2009): 66–98.

74. "Pulsang toan hwap'ye e pandae undong" [A Movement to Oppose a Buddhist Image for a Currency Design], *K'ŭrisŭch'yan sinmun*, April 22, 1972.

75. With the prolongation of the *yusin* rule, the government became suspicious and coercive toward the church, monitoring, for example, ministers' sermons. This practice eventually alienated even a great many conservatives, especially the moderates. "Minjusuho tansik kido" [A Fast to Protect Democracy], *K'ŭrisŭch'yan sinmun*, January 5, 1974; "Kim Kŏngnak moksa tŭng 10 myŏng kusok" [Rev. Kim Kŏngnak and Ten Other Ministers Arrested], *K'ŭrisŭch'yan sinmun*, January 26, 1975; "Mun Ikhwan, In Myŏngjin moksa tŭng yŏnhaeng" [Ministers Mun Ikhwan, In Myŏngjin, and Others under Police Custody], *K'ŭrisŭch'yan sinmun*, May 24, 1980. Also see a memoir by Kim Chinhong, *Hwangmuji ka changmi kkot katchi*, vol. 2 (Seoul: Hangilsa, 1999).

76. "Kukka suho t'ŭkpŏl kidohoe" [A Special Prayer Meeting for the Protection of the Nation], *K'ŭrisŭch'yan sinmun*, September 21, 1974; "Chŏngnyŏn yŏnhap kidohoe esŏdo 'sarang kwa chŏngŭi ŭi sŭngni' rŭl kan'gu" ["Love and Justice" Sought at a United Young Adults' Prayer Meeting As Well], *K'ŭrisŭch'yan sinmun*, October 26, 1974; "Chŏngnyŏn dŭl saesalm tajim: Chŏngnyŏn ch'ochŏng puhŭng sŏnghoe sŏngnyo" [Young Adults Dedicate Themselves to New Lives: Revival Gatherings with Invited Young Adults End Successfully], *K'ŭrisŭch'yan sinmun*, November 9, 1974.

77. From the time of his arrival in Korea in 1961, Ogle had helped pioneer urban industrial missions in Korea. Ogle denied the government's charge, stating that he was actually being deported for the critical remarks he had made about the Korean Central Intelligence Agency. For Ogle's account of this ordeal, see his *How Long, O Lord: Stories of Twentieth Century Korea* (n.p.: Xlibris, 2002); "O Myŏng'gŏl moksa e ch'ulguk ryŏng" [An Expulsion Order for Rev. O Myŏng'gŏl (George E. Ogle)], *K'ŭrisŭch'yan sinmun*, December 21, 1974; "Sŏkpang wihae sŏmyŏng undong: Kamnikyo kusokcha kidohoe kyŏlŭi" [A Signature-Gathering Campaign for Release: The Methodist Church Adopts a Resolution Regarding the Arrested], *K'ŭrisŭch'yan sinmun*, January 4, 1975. For other missionaries' contributions to South Korea's democratization, see Jim Stentzel, ed., *More Than Witnesses: How a Small Group of Missionaries Aided Korea's Democratic Revolution* (Seoul: Korea Democracy Foundation, 2006).

78. At the time, the T'onghap (Unity) Presbyterian Church was the largest Protestant denomination in Korea. "Saibi puhŭng undong chiyang: Yejang, puhŭng hyŏpŭihoe paljok" [To Counter False Revival Movements: Jesus Presbyterian Church Inaugurates Its Revivalist Association], *K'ŭrisŭch'yan sinmun*, January 11, 1975.

79. "100 man myŏng sindo sukuk kiwŏn" [One Million Believers Pray for the Protection of the Nation], *K'ŭrisŭch'yan sinmun*, June 28, 1975.

80. "50 man siminul kŭristo egero: Tae'jŏn-si pokŭmhwa chŏndo taehoe sŏngnyo" [500,000 Citizens for Christ: Gatherings to Evangelize Taejŏn End in Success], *K'ŭrisŭch'yan sinmun*, September 27, 1975.

81. Ibid.; "Sunsuhan kidok chŏngnyŏn undong kyŏlŭi: Chŏn'guk sŏ ch'okyop'a 5 chŏnyŏ myŏng ch'amga" [A Resolution for a Pure Christian Young Adult Movement: 5,000 Ecumenical Participants from All Over the Country], *K'ŭrisŭch'yan sinmun*, November 15, 1975.

82. "Kyohoe sŏngjang yŏn'gu suryŏnhoe" [Church Growth Training], *K'ŭrisŭch'yan sinmun*, July 10, 1976.

83. "Kangnŭng simin 5 man myŏng chiphoe" [Fifty Thousand Kangnŭng Citizens Gathered], *K'ŭrisŭch'yan sinmun*, September 4, 1976.

84. "Masan pokŭmhwa taehoe sŏngnyo" [Evangelistic Gatherings at Masan a Success] and "Wae pŭhŭngsa ka kŭrŏtke manŭnga" [Why are There So Many Revivalists?], *K'ŭrisŭch'yan sinmun*, September 4, 1976; "Ch'amho'e t'onghan sidaejŏk *samyong* tajim: Kamnigyo chŏnguk sŏn'gyo taehoe sŏngnyo" [Affirming the Mission of the Times through Repentance: The Methodist Church's National Evangelistic Gathering Ends Successfully], *K'ŭrisŭch'yan sinmun*, November 6, 1976.

85. "Han'guk kyohoe ŭi sŏngjang sang" [The Picture of the Korean Church's Growth], *K'ŭrisŭch'yan sinmun*, November 20, 1976.

86. In Korean, it was called 77-yŏn Minjok pogŭmhwa sŏnghoe.

87. "77-yŏn Minjok pogŭmhwa sŏnghoe k'auntŭdaun" [The Countdown for the '77 Holy Assembly for the Evangelization of the Nation], *K'ŭrisŭch'yan sinmun*, August 6, 1977. My translation.

88. Ibid. My translation. "Changdaehyŏn" was the Korean name of the P'yŏngyang (Presbyterian) Central Church, where the revival enthusiasm was ignited in 1907.

89. Eckert et al., *Korea Old and New*, 398.

90. "Chuhan migun chŏlsu pandae kidohoe yŏllŏ" [Holding a Prayer Meeting to Oppose the Withdrawal of American Troops Stationed in Korea], *K'ŭrisŭch'yan sinmun*, May 28, 1977; "Migun chŏlsu pandae siwi" [A Demonstration to Oppose the Withdrawal of American Troops], *K'ŭrisŭch'yan sinmun*, June 4, 1977; "Mijisanggun chŏlsu pandae: 100 manin sŏmyŏng undong" [Opposition to the Withdrawal of American Land Forces: 1 Million Signatures Gathering Movement], *K'ŭrisŭch'yan sinmun*, July 9, 1977.

91. Kim Tongil, chairman of the organizational subcommittee for the '77 Holy Assembly, "77-yŏn minjok pogŭmhwa sŏnghoe nŭn ŏdiro kal kŏsinga?" [Where Is the '77 Holy Assembly for the Evangelization of the Nation Headed?], *Sinang segye* (August 1977): 38–45. My translation.

92. Ibid., 40. My translation.

93. Ibid., 42.

94. "Yŏninwŏn 7 paekman myŏng ch'amsŏk" [A Total Attendance of 7 Million], *K'ŭrisŭch'yan sinmun*, August 27, 1977; "1 paekman myŏngi hanjari e."

95. "Yŏninwŏn 7 paekman myŏng ch'amsŏk." My translation.

96. Sin Hyŏnggyun, "Yŏnggwang ŭi hwoebok" [The Restoration of Glory], *Sinang segye* (August 1977): 46–49. Also see Ch'oe Namgyu, "Kŭm Ch'ottae ka han'guk e" [The Golden Candlestick Has Come to Korea], *Sinanggye* (July 1973): 80–83.

97. "Ch'ungbuk yŏnhap chŏndo taehoe sŏnghwang" [The Ch'ungbuk United Evangelistic Gathering a Success], *K'ŭrisŭch'yan sinmun*, June 10, 1978.

98. "'Han'guk kyohoe nŭn mobŭm chŏk': Syullŏ moksa kija hoekyŏnsŏ palkyŏ" [The Korean Church Is Exemplary: Rev. Schuller States at an Interview], *K'ŭrisŭch'yan sinmun*, July 15, 1978.

99. "Incheon pokŭmhwa sŏnghoe sŏnghwang" [The Holy Assembly to Evangelize Incheon a Success], *K'ŭrisŭch'yan sinmun*, July 22; "Haewae sŏn'gyosa tasu p'asongk'iro" [Resolved to Send Numerous Missionaries Abroad], *K'ŭrisŭch'yan sinmun*, October 21, 1978.

100. "Pukhan ŭi che 3 ttang'gul palgyŏn" [The Third North Korean Tunnel Found], *K'ŭrisŭch'yan sinmun*, November 4, 1978.

101. "Minjok pokŭmhwa sŏnghoe sŏnghwang" [A Holy Gathering to Evangelize the Nation a Success], *K'ŭrisŭch'yan sinmun*, November 4, 1978; "Chŏn ukpaek changbyŏng hapdong yebae" [1,600 Soldiers Baptized Together], *K'ŭrisŭch'yan sinmun*, December 23, 1978; "Changbyŏng 850 myŏng serye" [850 Soldiers Baptized], *K'ŭrisŭch'yan sinmun*, April 21, 1979.

102. "Kyoyŏkcha ŭi samyŏnggam saeropke tajim: Chŏnguk 3 chŏnyŏ kyoyŏkcha kŭmsik kido" [Ministers Recommit Themselves to Their Mission: Over 3,000 Ministers from All Over the Nation Gather for Fasting Prayer], *K'ŭrisŭch'yan sinmun*, June 30, 1979.

103. "Kin'gŭp choch'i wibanja 86 myŏng sŏkpang" [86 Violators of the Emergency Measures Released], *K'ŭrisŭch'yan sinmun* July 21, 1979; "Emnesŭti 8 wŏl yangsimsŭro mun ikhwan moksa sŏnjŏng" [Amnesty International Selects Rev. Mun Ikhwan as a Prisoner of Conscience of August], *K'ŭrisŭch'yan sinmun*, September 15, 1979.

104. "Taegu yŏnhap chŏndo taehoe sŏnghwang: Yŏninwŏn 15 man myŏng chamyŏ" [The United Taegu Evangelistic Gatherings a Great Success], *K'ŭrisŭch'yan sinmun*, October 6, 1979; "Sunbogŭm chungang kyohoe kyoinsu10 man myŏng tolp'a" [The Full Gospel Church's Membership Exceeds 100,000], *K'ŭrisŭch'yan sinmun*, November 10, 1979.

105. Oberdorfer, *Two Koreas*, 129. See also Henry Scott-Stokes and Lee Jai-eui, eds., *The Kwangju Uprising: Eyewitness Press Accounts of Korea's Tiananmen* (Armonk, NY: M. E. Sharpe, 2000); and Donald N. Clark, ed., *The Kwangju Uprising: Shadows over the Regime in South Korea* (Boulder, CO: Westview Press, 1988).

106. Arnold A. Peterson, "5.18: The Kwangju Incident," in *5.18 Kwangju sat'ae*, trans. Chŏng Tongsŏp (Seoul: P'ulpit, 1995), 189–190.

107. Eckert et al., *Korea Old and New*, 384.

108. Peterson, "5.18."

109. "Yŏsŏng chidoja kŭmsik kido" [Fasting Prayer of Women Leaders], *K'ŭrisŭch'yan raip'ŭ* (August–September 1980): 27. Ch'oe Chasil was Cho Yonggi's mother-in-law and a cofounder of Yoido Full Gospel Church. For a short portrayal of Ch'oe, see the section on her in Timothy S. Lee's "Conversion Narratives in Korean Evangelicalism."

110. "Minjok ŭi hwahoe wa Illyu sŏn'gyo ŭi pijŏn ŭro" [Through the Vision of National Reconciliation and Global Missions], *Sinang segye* (August–September 1980): 60–65. My translation.

111. "80 pokŭmhwa taesŏnghoe ŭi kyŏlsan" [Settling the Account on the '80 World Evangelization Crusade], *Kyohoe yŏnhap sinbo*, August 24, 1980.

112. "80 pokŭmhwa sŏnghoe naksu" [A Postmortem on the '80 World Evangelization Crusade], *Kyohoe yŏnhap sinbo*, August 17, 1980.

113. "80 pokŭmhwa taesŏnghoe ŭi kyŏlsan."

114. Ibid.

115. "'Nanŭn ch'ajatne': 80 segye pokŭmhwa taesŏnghoe p'yemak" ["I've Found It": The '80 World Evangelization Crusade Assembly Ends], *K'ŭrisŭch'yan raip'ŭ* (August–September 1980): 32-33.

116. "Segye pokŭmhwa ŭi chudo yŏkhwal tajim" [Committing to Take the Lead in the Evangelization of the World], *K'ŭrisŭch'yan sinmun*, August 23, 1980.

117. "80 pokŭmhwa taesŏnghoe ŭi kyŏlsan"; "'Nanŭn ch'ajatne.'" Also see Ro and Nelson, *Korean Church Growth Explosion*, 34.

118. "Sŏn'gyo taehoe kaemak: Yŏŭido sŏ 19 il kkaji" [The Evangelization Assembly Opens: At Yŏŭido till the 19th], *K'ŭrisŭch'yan sinmun*, August 18, 1984.

119. *Han'guk ilbo*, English edition, May 11, 1984; "I segi hyanghan hwahap ŭi myŏnmu kwasi: Han'guk kyohoe 100 chunyŏn kinyŏm sŏngyo taehoe sŏngnyo" [The Display of a Unity toward the Second Century: The 100th Anniversary Evangelistic Assembly Ends Successfully], *K'ŭrisŭch'yan sinmun*, August 25, 1984; "Paekchunyŏn sŏngyo taehoe p'yemak" [The Centenary Evangelistic Assembly Closes], *Kyohoe yŏnhap sinbo*, August 26, 1984.

120. Here it is important to note that at this stage the Korean revivalists' conception of their nation as a redeemer nation was only embryonic, in that their rhetoric—expressed chiefly in evangelistic terms—would find a receptive audience only within the Protestant community in Korea. This embryonic conception can be compared with the more fully developed version in the United States, where such rhetoric was embraced not only by the Protestants but by the whole nation. See Hutchison, *Errand to the World*; and Ernest Lee Tuveson, *Redeemer Nation: The Idea of America's Millennial Role* (Chicago: University of Chicago Press, 1968).

121. Segye pogŭmhwa undong chungang hyŏpŭihoe, *'88 segye pogŭmhwa taesŏnghoe kirok munjip: Sŏngnyŏng ŭi pŭlkir ŭl on segye ro* (Seoul: Segye pogŭmhwa undong chungang hyŏpŭihoe, 1988), 39. My translation. Of course, Koreans followed others in claiming a chosen or redeemer status for their nation. For Americans' take on this common tendency, see Tuveson, *Redeemer Nation*; and Conrad Cherry, ed., *God's New Israel: Religious Interpretation of American Destiny*, rev. and updated ed. (Chapel Hill: University of North Carolina Press, 1998).

122. Cho Yonggi, "Wae Sŏngnyŏng ŭl padaya hana?" in *'88 segye pogŭmhwa taesŏnghoe kirok munjip*, by Segye pogŭmhwa undong chungang hyŏpŭihoe, 75. My translation.

123. Kim Uyŏng, "Pŏn'yŏng kwa t'ongil ŭi hwansang," in *'88 segye pogŭmhwa taesŏnghoe kirok munjip*, by Segye pogŭmhwa undong chungang hyŏpŭihoe 89. My translation.

124. Kim Eŭihwan, "Sŏn'gyo ŭi tongyŏkcha," in *'88 segye pogŭmhwa taesŏnghoe kirok munjip*, by Segye pogŭmhwa undong chungang hyŏpŭihoe, 62. My translation.

125. Sin Hyŏnggyun, "Sŏngnyŏng ŭi pulkilŭr on segye ro," in *'88 Segye pogŭmhwa taesŏnghoe kirok munjip*, by Segye pogŭmhwa undong chungang hyŏpŭihoe, 119. My translation.

126. Yi Mansin, "Hananim ŭi sarang," in *'88 segye pogŭmhwa taesŏnghoe kirok munjip*, by Segye pogŭmhwa undong chungang hyŏpŭihoe, 85. My translation.

127. J. R. Moose, "A Great Awakening," *KMF* 2 (January 1906): 51–52.

4. The Intensely Practical and Devotional Character of Korean Evangelicalism

Epigraph. Arthur Judson Brown, *The Mastery of the Far East* (New York: Charles Scribner's Sons, 1919), 541.

1. *Mokhoe wa sinhak* (September 1990): 21.

2. Tae Chŏndŏk [Reuben A. Torrey], *San'koltchak esŏ on p'yŏnji*, vol. 2 (Seoul: Kungmin ilbo, 1985): 257.

3. As of 1990, the combined membership of Korea's high churches (Episcopalian and Lutheran churches) and that of the Taehan kijang changno kyohoe (Presbyterian Church in the Republic of Korea), the openly liberal denomination in South Korea, was 347,977, about 3 percent of the total number of Protestants for that year. The number of churches belonging to these three denominations was 1,359, or about 4 percent of the total number of Protestant churches. See Han Yŏngje, ed., *Kidokkyo taeyŏn'gam, 1991*, vol. 6 (Seoul: Kidokkyo munsa, 1991), 215–216.

4. One such conflict centered around charges of heresy leveled at Cho Yonggi and his Pentecostal church by the T'onghap Presbyterian Church, the second-largest Presbyterian denomination in Korea. See *K'ŭrisŭch'yan sinmun*, U.S. edition, October 25, 1993.

5. One study finds that between 1884 and 1945, the most formative years in the history of the Korean Protestant Church, 1,529 missionaries arrived in Korea. Of these, 1,059 (69.3 percent) were nationals of the United States. The next-largest group were British, numbering 199 (13 percent). Kim Sŭngt'ae and Pak Hyejin, comps., *Naehan sŏn'gyosa ch'ongnam, 1884–1984* (Seoul: Han'guk kidokkyo yŏksa yŏn'guso, 1994), 1–2.

6. Han'guk kidokkyo sahoe munje yŏn'guwŏn, *Han'guk kyohoe 100-yŏn chonghap chosa yŏn'gu* (Seoul: Han'guk kidokkyo sahoe munje yŏn'guwŏn, 1982); Hyŏndae sahoe yŏn'guso, *Han'guk kyohoe sŏngjang kwa sinang yangt'ae e kwanhan chosa yŏn'gu* (Seoul: Hyŏndae sahoe yŏn'guso, 1982).

7. In the case of IGRKC, *chŏndosa*s (literally, evangelists) were counted as ministers. *Chŏndosa*s are minister interns or unordained (but usually seminary-trained and paid) church leaders.

8. Hyŏndae sahoe yŏn'guso, *Hyŏndae kyohoe sŏngjang kwa sinang yangt'ae e kwanhan chosa yŏn'gu*, 77ff.

9. Han'guk kidokkyo sahoe munje yŏn'guwŏn, *Han'guk kyohoe 100-yŏn chonghap chosa yŏn'gu*, 63. As to what constitutes salvation, 74.6 percent of the ministers accepted the definition of it as each individual going to heaven after death, and 17.5 percent as the establishment of the kingdom of God on earth; 7.9 percent did not respond. The breakdown on the same question for the laypeople is as follows, in the same order: 66.9 percent, 29.4 percent, and 3.8 percent. Ibid., 64.

10. J. U. Selwyn Toms, "Our Weapon," *KMF* 10 (February 1914): 52.

11. C. Paul Dredge, "Korean Funerals: Ritual as Process," in *Religion and Ritual in Korean Society*, ed. Laurel Kendall and Griffin Dix (Berkeley: Institute of East Asian Studies, University of California, Berkeley, 1987), 71–92.

12. See Chong Bum Kim, "Christianity in Colonial Korea: The Culture and Politics of Proselytization" (PhD diss., Harvard University, 2004), 133–139.

13. These holidays are the Buddha's birthday, celebrated on the eighth day of the fourth month by the lunar calendar; Christmas, on December 25; and National Foundation Day, on October 3, which marks the traditional founding of Korea in 2333 BC by the mythic Tan'gun, the offspring of a bear and Son of the Lord of Heaven.

14. Pak Hyŏngnyong, "Igyo e taehan t'ahyŏp munje" [The Problem of Compromising with Other Religions], in *Sinhak chinam* [Theological Index], quoted in Kim Ch'angt'ae and Yu Tongsik [Ryu Tong-shik], *Han'guk chonggyo sasangsa* (Seoul: Yonsei University Press, 1986), 247.

15. Pak A-ron, "Kidokkyo pakkenŭn kuwŏn i ŏpta," *Wŏlgan mokhoe* (October 1977). For a helpful overview of how Christians have regarded other religions, see Paul Knitter, *Introducing Theologies of Religions* (Maryknoll, NY: Orbis, 2002).

16. "Survival-Syncretist," *Christian Century*, March 11, 1992. Eventually Chŏng left Korea and became a professor of systematic theology at Union Theological Seminary in New York City.

17. Mary Douglas, *Purity and Danger: An Analysis of the Concepts of Pollution and Taboo* (London: Routledge and Kegan Paul, 1966), 60.

18. Matthew 7:7.

19. Cho also has an English first name. It used to be Paul, but in the early 1990s he changed it to David. In this study, for the sake of clarity, only his Korean name is used. On May 17, 2006, in a Sunday sermon at Yoido Full Gospel Church, Cho explained his reason for dropping "Paul" in favor of "David." He said he was directed to do so in prayer: he was to be not a founder of churches himself (as was the apostle Paul) but the builder of a kingdom (as was David) that sent out church founders, with Yoido Full Gospel Church functioning as an analog of the Davidic kingdom. *K'ŭrisŭch'yan t'udei*, May 18, 2006, http://www.chtoday.co.kr/view.htm?code=cg&id=174549.

20. Yonggi Cho, *Salvation, Health, and Prosperity: Our Threefold Blessings in Christ* (Altamonte Springs, FL: Creation House, 1987), 11–12. On the development of Yoido Full Gospel Church, see Karen Hurston, *Growing the World's Largest Church* (Springfield, MO: Chrism, 1995); and Ig-Jin Kim, *History and Theology of Korean Pentecostalism: Sunbogeum (Pure Gospel) Pentecostalism* (Zoetermeer, The Netherlands: Boekencentrum, 2003).

21. Oral Roberts, foreword to *Salvation, Health, and Prosperity*, by Yonggi Cho, 9.

22. *K'ŭrisŭch'yan sinmun*, U.S. edition, October 25, 1993.

23. Han Wansang, "Kyohoe yangchŏk kŭpsŏngjang e taehan sahoehakchŏk koch'al," in *Han'guk kyohoe sŏngnyŏng undong ŭi hyŏnsang kwa kujo*, ed. Kim Kwangil et al. (Seoul: Korea Christian Academy, 1981), 165–231.

24. Bong-ho Son, "Some Dangers of Rapid Growth," in *Korean Church Growth Explosion*, ed. Bong-rin Ro and Marlin L. Nelson (Seoul: World of Life Press, 1983), 337–339.

25. Kukche sinhak yŏn'guwŏn, *Yŏŭido sunbogŭm kyohoe ŭi sinang kwa sinhak* (Seoul: Seoul sŏjŏk, 1993), 303.

26. Yonggi Cho, *Salvation, Health, and Prosperity*, 54.

27. Ibid., 68.

28. Ibid.

29. Ibid., 126.

30. Allan Anderson, *An Introduction to Pentecostalism: Global Charismatic Christianity* (Cambridge: University of Cambridge Press, 2004), 2. Also see Walter J. Hollenweger, *The Pentecostals* (London: SCM Press, 1972).

31. The church with most multiple services is probably Yoido Full Gospel Church, which, in my visit to it in 1995, held seven services each Sunday (including an evening service), all of which were packed.

32. Han'guk kidokkyo sahoe munje yŏn'guwŏn, *Han'guk kyohoe 100-yŏn chonghap chosa yŏn'gu*, 68.

33. The scriptural warrants often invoked to justify the tithe are Genesis 14:20 and Malachi 3:8–11.

34. *Mokhoe wa sinhak* (October 1989): 136–145.

35. *K'ŭrisŭch'yan sinmun*, October 10, 1989.

36. See Timothy S. Lee, "Korea, the Movement," in *The Encyclopedia of the Stone-Campbell Movement*, ed. Douglas A. Foster, Paul M. Blowers, Anthony L. Dunnavant, and D. Newell Williams (Grand Rapids, MI: Eerdmans, 2004), 447–448.

37. Han'guk kidokkyo sahoe munje yŏn'guwŏn, *Han'guk kyohoe 100-yŏn chonghap chosa yŏn'gu*, 64.

38. *KMF* 7 (June 1911), 163.

39. *K'ŭrisŭch'yan sinmun*, March 4, 1995.

40. This record is a letter from the Roman governor Pliny to Emperor Trajan. Pliny had been sent to Bithynia to investigate alleged disturbances caused by Christians, who then were a group obscure to most Romans and were under the suspicion of practicing immoral acts in their gatherings. In the letter, Pliny states that "the sum of their [i.e., Christians of Bithynia] guilt or error had amounted only to this, that on an appointed day they had been accustomed to meet before daybreak, and to recite a hymn antiphonally to Christ; as to a god, and to bind themselves by an oath." See Henry Bettenson and Chris Maunder, eds., *Documents of the Christian Church*, 3rd ed. (Oxford: Oxford University Press, 1999), 4.

41. Im T'aekchin, "Han'guk kyohoe wa saebyŏk kido," *Kido*, January 1986; and Kim Myŏnghyŏk, "Han'guk kyohoe kido ŭi sŭpkwan" [Prayer Habits of the Korean (Protestant) Church], *Kido*, January 1987.

42. *Kido*, July 1987; *K'ŭrisŭch'yan sinmun*, October 10, 1989.

43. *Han'guk kidok kongbo*, November 22, 1954. My translation.

44. "Chŏrya kido-hoe rŭl ch'ajasŏ" [In Search of Nightlong Devotional], *Kido*, February 1987, 26–27.

45. Ibid.

46. Ibid.

47. Tae Chŏndŏk, *San'koltchak esŏ on p'yŏnji*, 2:261. My translation. Reuben A. Torrey (whose Korean name was Tae Chŏndŏk) was a respected Anglican priest with an affinity for Pentecostalism. The namesake grandson of the famous American fundamentalist who helped found the Moody Bible Institute in Chicago, Torrey was born in China of missionary parents and educated in America, England, and Korea. He lived for four decades in Korea and operated a prayer retreat in Kangwŏn Province. Torrey cut an exceptional figure among foreigners in Korea, becoming a kind of guru to many Christians there. He took pains to be fluent in Korean and published his four-volume series, *Letters from a Mountain Valley*, in the language. Based on the correspondence he had had with numerous Korean Christians who sought his advice on issues of faith, they deal with issues ranging from the Holy Spirit to real estate speculation and Christian faith. Torrey died in Korea in 2002.

48. See, for example, "T'ŭgpŏl taedam: Han'guk kyohoe kido rŭl tŭrŏbonda" [A Special Discussion: Hearing about Prayer in the Korean Church], *Wŏlgan mokhoe* (July–August 1983): 22–37; Im Yongsu, "Kŭrisŭdo ŭi 40-il kŭmsik kido ka uri ege chunŭn kyohun" [The Lesson Given to Us by Christ's Forty-Day Fasting-Prayer], *Kido*, July–August 1986, 22–25. See also, in the same issue of *Kido*, by the editors, "Kŭmsik kido kaidŭ" [A Guide to Fasting-Prayer], 26–29.

49. For more empathetic and informed treatments of Korean Shamanism, see Laura Kendall, *Shamans, Housewives, and Other Restless Spirits* (Honolulu: University of Hawai'i Press, 1985); and Chai-shin Yu and R. Guisso, eds., *Shamanism: The Spirit World of Korea* (Berkeley, CA: Asian Humanities Press, 1988). See also Youngsook Kim Harvey, "The Korean Shaman and the Deaconess: Sisters in Different Guises," in *Religion and Ritual in Korean Society*, ed. Laurel Kendall and Griffin Dix (Berkeley: Institute of East Asian Studies, University of California, Berkeley, 1987): 149–170; and Sun Soon-Hwa, "Women, Religion, and Power: A Comparative Study of Korean Shamans and Women Ministers" (PhD diss., Drew University, 1991).

50. Jashil Choi [Ch'oe Chasil], *Korean Miracles* (Seoul: Seoul Book, 1978), 1, 3.

51. "Kŭmsik kido ron" [An Argument for Fasting Prayer], *Wŏlgan mokhoe* (April 1980): 101.

52. Kim Chun'gon, "CCC an esŏ ŭi kido undong," *Wŏlgan mokhoe* (July 1986): 68.

53. Jashil Choi, *Korean Miracles*, 2.

54. See Williston Walker et al., *A History of the Christian Church*, 4th ed. (New York: Charles Scribner's Sons, 1985), 588; and Philip Jacob Spener, *Pia Desideria* (Minneapolis: Fortress, 1964).

55. "Uri kyohoe kuyŏk ŭi changchŏm" [The Strengths of Our Church's Class Meeting], *Wŏlgan mokhoe* (July 1978).

56. There are two types of evangelists, or *chŏndosa*s, in Korean Protestant churches. One type is a minister intern, a seminarian undergoing field training who usually conducts Sunday school or youth programs. The other is an unordained but usually

seminary-trained leader, most often a woman. Her duties may consist of conducting Sunday school, visiting members, and leading cell-group Bible studies.

57. It was called Chŏrwŏn taehan kidowŏn, built by Pak Kyŏngnyŏng, the pastor of Changhŭngni Church, and Yi Sŏnghae, a deacon of the church. Yi Tŏkchu [Rhie Deok-Joo], "Han'guk kyohoe kido undong paljach'wi," *Kido*, November 1986, 22–25. Also see Pak Manyong, *Kidowŏn undong kwa sinang sŏngjang* (Seoul: K'umnan ch'ulpansa, 1998).

58. "Kidowŏn," *K'ŭrisŭch'yan sinmun*, August 29, 1981. Also see *Yahoo! Korea Paekkhwa sajŏn* s.v. "Kidowŏn" [Prayer House], http://kr.dic.yahoo.com/search/enc/result.html?pk=11587800&p=%EA%B8%B0%EB%8F%84%EC%9B%90&field=id&type=enc.

59. For example, Yoido Full Gospel Church's Osanni Prayer Mountain, the largest "prayer House" in Korea, is built on eighty-one acres of hilly land and is able to accommodate up to twenty thousand people at one time. *K'ŭrisŭch'yan sinmun*, July 9, 1983.

60. "The Great Present Need of Korea," *KMF* 7 (April 1911): 104–106. Emphasis in original.

61. Han'guk kidokkyo yŏksa yŏn'guso, *Han'guk kidok kyohoe ŭi yŏksa I, 16C–1918* (Seoul: Kidokkyo munsa, 1989), 369.

62. Mrs. F. S. Miller, "Some Thoughts about Women's Work in Hong Ju," in *KMF* 8 (January 1912): 19.

63. They read, for example, the nationalist newspaper *Tongnip sinmun* [Independent], the first vernacular Korean newspaper, published between 1896 and 1899; it was published in both *han'gŭl* and English versions. Vipan Chandra, *Imperialism, Resistance, and Reform in Late Nineteenth-Century Korea: Enlightenment and the Independence Club* (Berkeley: Institute of East Asian Studies, University of California, Berkeley, 1988), 104–125.

64. William N. Blair, *Gold in Korea*, 2nd ed. (Topeka, KS: H. M. Ives and Sons, 1947), 60.

65. *KMF* 11 (February 1915): 35.

66. "A Missionary Letter," in *KMF* 7 (April 1911), 115. Emphasis in original.

67. "Reading the Bible from Cover to Cover, Milk Line to the Reformation of the Church," *Mokhoe wa sinhak* (April 1994): 212–221. Also see *Wŏlgan mokhoe* (September 1985): 162–163.

Epilogue

Epilogue. Joachim Wach, *The Comparative Study of Religions* (New York: Columbia University Press, 1958): 31.

1. David B. Barrett, George T. Kurian, and Todd M. Johnson, *World Christian Encyclopedia*, 2nd ed., vol. 1 (Oxford and New York: Oxford University Press, 2002), 682.

2. The 1995 census report by the South Korean National Statistics Office finds 23.2 percent of South Korean to be Buddhists, 19.7 percent Protestant, and 6.6 percent Roman Catholic. See T'onggye chŏng, *1995 ingu chut'aek ch'ong chosa: Ch'oejong chŏnsu*

chipkye kyŏlgwa (Seoul: T'onggye chŏng, 1995). The number of Orthodox Christians was too small to be detected by the census.

3. See Andrew Sung Park, "*Minjung* and *Pungryu* Theologies in Contemporary Korea: A Critical and Comparative Examination" (PhD diss., Graduate Theological Union, 1985); and Paul Yunshik Chang, "Carrying the Torch in the Darkest Hours: The Sociopolitical Origins of Minjung Protestant Movements," in *Christianity in Korea*, ed. Robert E. Buswell Jr. and Timothy S. Lee (Honolulu: University of Hawai`i Press, 2006), 195–220.

4. Han'guk kidokkyo sahoe munje yŏn'guwŏn, *Han'guk kyohoe 100-yŏn chonghap chosa yŏn'gu* (Seoul: Han'guk kidokkyo sahoe munje yŏn'guwŏn, 1982); Hyŏndae sahoe yŏn'guso, *Han'guk kyohoe sŏngjang kwa sinang yangt'ae e kwanhan chosa yŏn'gu* (Seoul: Hyŏndae sahoe yŏn'guso, 1982).

5. Gallup Korea, *Han'guk kaesin'gyoin ŭi kyohoe hwaltong kwa sinang ŭisik* (Seoul: Turano, 1999). The study was commissioned by Hanmijun, an organization of Korean Protestant ministers.

6. Ibid., 57.

7. That this question is not addressed may puzzle an American scholar of religion, since it seems so basic to understanding Protestantism in the United States, but it may also say something about the nature of Protestantism (or, for that matter, Christianity) in South Korea. Due to the prevalence of the evangelical ethos, and the lack of a comparable "mainline" tradition, there is little occasion for such a question to arise as a serious matter. Furthermore, given the evangelicals' numerical superiority over the Catholics and non-evangelicals, and given their exclusionist theology, there is a sharper distinction between evangelicals (Protestants) and Catholics in Korea than in the West. A telling example is that because the standard Korean translation for Christianity, *kidokkyo*, has been monopolized by evangelicals, Catholics do not use the term to refer to themselves, preferring instead *chŏnjugyo*. The word *kaesin'gyo* specifically means Protestantism, but the evangelicals do not use it as commonly as *kidokkyo* to refer to themselves.

8. This could mean that in the late 1990s there were more non-evangelicals in the church than in the 1980s. It could also mean that a higher percentage of Koreans attended the churches primarily for social, rather than religious, reasons. Or it could mean both.

9. This point is supported by the fact that these denominations had 347,977 members, about 3 percent of the total Korean Protestant population for that year. Han Yŏngje, ed., *Han'guk kidokkyo sŏngjang 100-yŏn* (Seoul: Kidokkyo munsa, 1986), 215–216. In 2001, Korean Computer Missions conducted an informal online study, based on its website visitors' response to the question "Have you had a Holy Spirit experience?" Of 1,440 visitors, 77 percent (1,110) responded yes. Since 2001 was not far from the 1990s, this finding, albeit ad hoc, supports the estimate that evangelicals constituted at least 75 percent of Korean Protestants in the 1990s. *Kungmin ilbo*, August 2, 2001.

10. Gallup Korea, 1997 survey, 147.

11. *Random House Webster's Unabridged Dictionary*, 2nd ed., s.v. "success."

12. Gallup Korea, 1997 survey, 462.

13. Larry Diamond, "Rethinking Civil Society: Toward Democratic Consolidation," *Journal of Democracy* 5, no. 3 (1994): 6, quoted by Sunhyuk Kim, "Civil Society in South Korea: From Grand Democracy Movements to Petty Interest Groups?" *Journal of Northeast Asian Studies* 15:2 (Summer 1996): 82–83.

14. Munhwabu (Ministry of Culture), *Han'guk ŭi chonggyo hyŏnhwang, 1990* [The State of Korean Religions], cited in Han'guk chonggyo sahoe yŏn'guso, ed., *Han'guk chonggyo yŏn'gam, 1993* (Seoul: Korea hallimŏn, 1993), 208.

15. The figures are those reported by the denominations as of December 31, 1996. Cited by Gallup Korea, *Han'gugin ŭi chonggyo wa chonggyo ŭisik: '84-yŏn, '89-yŏn, '97-yŏn chosa kyŏlgwa wa pigyohan chonggyo yŏn'guso*, 198.

16. Munhwa kwan'gwangbu, chongmusil, *Han'guk ŭi chonggyo hyŏnhwang, 1999* (Seoul: Munhwa kwan'gwangbu, chongmusil, 1999).

17. Figures from *Han'guk chonggyo hyŏnhwang* [The State of Religions in Korea], quoted in *K'ŭrisŭch'yan sinmun*, November 30, 1996.

18. Buddhists had 9; Wŏn Buddhists, 57; and Catholics, 180. Kwŏn O'hyŏn, "Han'guk chonggyo hyŏnhwang pogo" [A Report on the State of Korean Religion], in *Midŭm kwa silchŏn—onŭl ŭi chwap'yo* [Faith and Practice—Coordinates for Today] (Seoul: Taewŏnjŏngsa, 1985), cited in No Ch'ijun, *Han'guk ŭi kyohoe chojik* (Seoul: Minyŏngsa, 1995), 124. *Kungmin ilbo*, July 25, 2001.

19. *Kungmin ilbo*, July 25, 2001.

20. The most effective of these organizations is named Han'guk kidokkyo pukhan tongp'o huwŏn yŏnhaphoe, which literally means "the United Association of the Korean Christian Church for the Support of North Korean Brothers and Sisters." On its website (http://www.sharing.net), it is simply called Nambuk nanum [North-South Sharing]. The exact value of the aid is 59,199,030,138 won, which is roughly $59,1999,000, assuming $1 equals 1,000 won.

21. *Pulgyo sinmun*, March 21, 2000.

22. *K'ŭrisŭch'yan sinmun*, January 11, 1997.

23. *Pulgyo sinmun*, March 21, 2000.

24. *Chungang ilbo*, U.S. edition, August 4, 2000.

25. *Pulgyo sinmun*, June 16, 1998.

26. In that election 81.9 percent of the 29,422,658 registered voters cast their ballots. Of these, 9,977,332 (41 percent) voted for Kim Young Sam; 8,041,285 (33 percent), for Kim Dae Jung; and 3,880,067 (16 percent), for Chŏng Chuyŏng, who professed no religion. Andrew C. Nahm, *Introduction to Korean History and Culture* (Seoul and Elizabeth, NJ: Hollym, 1993), 318.

27. This should not be taken to mean that the evangelicals were narrow-minded politically, that they voted for Kim Young Sam simply because he was an evangelical. Given his formidable record as a pro-democracy leader of the 1970s and 1980s, he would have been a strong candidate regardless. But then, Kim Dae Jung was just as well regarded, if not more so, for his pro-democracy leadership during those decades and had an even tighter lock on his region, the Chŏlla provinces, than Kim Young Sam had

on his. That the former was a Catholic and the latter an evangelical was likely a decisive factor among the evangelical voters outside the Chŏlla provinces.

28. *K'ŭrisŭch'yan sinmun*, February 2, 1998.

29. By saying this, Kim meant that, if elected, he would make the presidential residence available for regular evangelical services. When he took office, he attempted to live up to this promise, only to encounter a fierce Buddhist protest, which caused him to backpedal; this waffling, in turn, soured his relationship with many of his evangelical supporters.

30. *K'ŭrisŭch'yan sinmun*, February 2, 1998.

31. In contrast, non-evangelical Protestants came out in full support of Kim Dae Jung, and some of them ended up in high positions in Kim's administration. Consequently, from 1998 onward, it would be more accurate to say that Protestants, rather than evangelicals, stood out in South Korean politics. It is difficult to tell how many of the Protestants in Kim's administration were evangelical or non-evangelical. Even so, if the full spectrum of South Korean politics is considered, including the religious makeup of the National Assembly, there is no question that the evangelicals wielded strong influence.

32. *K'ŭrisŭch'yan sinmun*, May 31 and August 4, 1997; *Chungang ilbo*, December 8, 1997.

33. *K'ŭrisŭch'yan sinmun*, August 25 and September 1, 1997.

34. *K'ŭrisŭch'yan sinmun*, March 2, 1998.

35. By 1990 nearly 75 percent of South Koreans were urban dwellers. T'onggye chŏng, *1990 ingu chut'aek ch'ong chosa chonghap punsŏk*, vol. 4-2, *Chiyŏkkan ingu pulgyunhyŏng punp'o ŭi wŏnin kwa kyŏlgwa*, 5. The 1995 census study results can be found in *Kungmin ilbo*, May 27, 1997; also see *K'ŭrisŭch'yan sinmun*, March 4, 1995.

36. These were adherents of Confucianism (17), Wŏn Buddhism (15), the Unification Church (2), Chŏlligyo (1), and Chŏndogyo (1). *Weekly Economist*, March 29, 1995, 17.

37. Ibid.

38. *Pulgyo sinmun*, May 9, 2000.

39. Lee Won Gue, "A Sociological Study on the Factors of Church Growth and Decline in Korea," *Korea Journal* (Winter 1999): 238.

40. No Ch'ijun, *K'ŭrisŭch'yan sinmun*, March 1, 1997.

41. Lee Won Gue, "Sociological Study," 238.

42. The 2005 census is cited in "Han'guk kidokkyoin 1300 man i anin 862 man" [Not 13 Million but 862,000 Korean Protestants], *News N Joy*, March 25, 2006, http://www.newsnjoy.co.kr. See also "Chŏsŏngjang sidae, mokhoe chŏllyak ŭi saeroun p'aerŏdaim yoch'ŏng" [Low Growth Period: A New Paradigm for Ministerial Strategy Requested], *K'ŭrisŭch'yan sinmun*, March 2, 1998. A 2004 study by Gallup Korea offers a more positive result. It finds the number of Korean Protestants to have increased from 20.3 percent in 1997 to 21.4 percent in 2004. Gallup Korea, *Han'gugin ŭi chonggyo wa chonggyo ŭisik: '84-yŏn, '89-yŏn, '97-yŏn, '04-yŏn chosa kyŏlgwa rŭl pigyohan chonggy yŏn'guso* (Seoul: Gallup Korea, 2004). However, the study done by the national census in 2005 is usually given more credence by scholars than this one.

43. *WEF Theological News*, January–March 1995, 6.

44. See Patrick Johnstone and Jason Mandryk, eds., *Operation World: 21st Century Edition* (Harrisonburg, VA: Paternoster, 2001), 388; Rob Moll, "Mission Incredible: South Korea Sends More Missionaries Than Any Country but the U.S. and It Won't Be Long Before It's Number One," *Christianity Today* 50, no. 3 (2006): 28–35; and Sangkeun Kim, "Sheer Numbers Do Not Tell the Entire Story: The Challenges of the Korean Missionary Movement from an Ecumenical Perspective," *Ecumenical Review* 57, no. 4 (2005): 463–473.

45. See No Ch'ijun's incisive article "Mokhoeja kwa'ing paech'ul" [Overproduction of Ministers], *K'ŭrisŭch'yan sinmun*, March 1, 1997. Also see "Mokhoejadŭl ŭi kyŏngjaeng sidae ka watta" [The Age of Competition Has Come for the Ministers], *K'ŭrisŭch'yan sinmun*, February 9, 1998.

46. Cited by Korea Computer Missions, http://kcm.co.kr/statistics/5/s013.html.

47. *Han'guk ilbo*, September 25, 1992.

48. "Samp'ung paekkhwajŏm punggoe sago p'ihae posang i mamuri tan'gye e chŏbŏ tŭrŏtta" [Compensation Case Related to the Collapse of the Sampung Department Store Nearing Its End], *Kyŏnghyang sinmun*, May 24, 2006.

49. See "Kim Hyŏnch'ŏl kukchŏng nongdan piri sagŏn" [A Corruption Case Involving Kim Hyŏnch'ŏl Assuming Exclusive Privileges in National Affairs], *Yahoo! Korea Paekkhwa sajŏn*, http://kr.dic.yahoo.com/search/enc/result.html?pk= 11795500&field=id&type=enc&p=??????????.

50. *K'ŭrisŭch'yan sinmun*, February 2, 1998.

51. See "'Chŏngguk noegwan' Kwŏn Yŏnghae X pail" ["A Detonator for the Political Situation" Kwŏng Yŏnghae's X File], http://www.donga.com/fbin/news_ plus?d=news127&f=np127aa020.html.

52. *K'ŭrisŭch'yan sinmun*, April 6, 1998.

53. Pak Hyŏng-nyong, "Igyo e taehan t'ahyŏp munje" [The Problem of Compromising with Other Religions], in *Sinhak chinam*, quoted in Kim Ch'angt'ae and Yu Tongsik [Ryu Tong-shik], *Han'guk chonggyo sasangsa* (Seoul: Yonsei University Press, 1986), 247.

54. "Buddhism under Siege in Korea," http://www.buddhapia.com/eng/tedesco/3. html, 3.

55. "Nuga tan'gun ŭi mok ŭl pennŭn'ga?" [Who Is Decapitating Tan'gun?], *Sunday Seoul*, April 29, 2000, E-26. See also Timothy S. Lee, "What Should Christians Do about a Shaman-Progenitor? Evangelicals and Ethnic Nationalism in South Korea," *Church History: Studies in Christianity and Culture* 78, no. 1 (2009): 66–98.

56. See Yi Mahn-yol, "Tan'gun sinhwa munje e taehan kidokkyohoe ŭi ipchang" [The Christian [Protestant] Church's Position on the Tan'gun Myth Problem], in his *Han'guk kidokkyosa yŏngu: Han'guk kidokkyo wa minjok t'ongil undong* (Seoul: Han'guk kidokkyo yŏksa yŏn'guso, 2001).

57. By April 2000 thirty-seven more Tan'gun statues had been either stolen or damaged, with some of the culprits being identified as evangelicals. "Nuga Tan'gun ŭi Mogŭl Pennŭn'ga?" *Kidok sinmun*, April 12, 2000.

Bibliography

Aikman, David. *Jesus in Beijing: How Christianity Is Transforming China and Changing the Global Balance of Power*. Washington, DC: Regnery, 2003.

Allen, Horace N. *Things Korean*. New York: Fleming H. Revell, 1908.

An Isuk. *Chugŭmyŏn chugŭ'ri'ra* [If I die, I die]. Seoul: Kidokkyo munsa, 1976.

An Sin. "Chwa-ong Yun Ch'iho ŭi chonggyo kyŏnghŏm kwa chonggyoron: Chonggyo hyŏnsanghak chŏk haesŏk" [Yun Ch'iho's Religious Experience and Thought: A Religious-Phenomenological Interpretation]. *Han'guk kidokkyo wa yŏksa* [Korean Christianity and History] 27 (2007): 45–67.

An Yongjun. *Sarang ŭi wŏnjat'an* [The Atomic Bomb of Love: Life and Martyrdom of Pastor Son Yangwŏn]. Seoul: Sŏnggwang munhwasa, 1972.

Anderson, Allan. *An Introduction to Pentecostalism: Global Charismatic Christianity*. Cambridge: University of Cambridge Press, 2004.

Anderson, Benedict. *Imagined Communities: Reflections on the Origin and Spread of Nationalism*. London: Verso, 1983.

Armstrong, Charles K. *North Korean Revolution, 1945–1950*. New York: Cornell University Press, 2003.

Baker, Donald. "A Different Thread: Orthodoxy, Heterodoxy, and Catholicism in a Confucian World." In JaHyun Kim Haboush and Martina Deuchler, eds., *Culture and the State in Late Chosŏn Korea*, 199–230.

———. *Korean Spirituality*. Honolulu: University of Hawai'i Press, 2008.

———. "The Martyrdom of Paul Yun: Western Religion and Eastern Ritual in 18th Century Korea." *Transactions of the Royal Asiatic Society, Korea Branch* 54 (1979): 33–58.

———. "Sibling Rivalry in Twentieth-Century Korea: Comparative Growth Rates of Catholic and Protestant Communities." In Robert E. Buswell, Jr., and Timothy S. Lee, eds., *Christianity in Korea*, 243–308.

———. "Tasan and His Brothers: How Religion Divided a Korean Confucian Family." In Sang-Oak Lee and Duk-Soo Park, eds., *Perspectives on Korea*, 172–197. Sydney: Peony, 1998.

Baker, Kevin. *A History of the Orthodox Church in China, Korea, and Japan*. Lewiston, NY: Edwin Mellen, 2006.

Baldwin, Frank, Jr. "The March First Movement: Korean Challenge and Japanese Response." PhD diss., Columbia University, 1969.

———. "Missionaries and the March First Movement: Can Moral Man Be Neutral?" In Andrew C. Nahm, ed., *Korea under Japanese Colonial Rule*, 193–219.

Balmer, Randall. *Encyclopedia of Evangelicalism*. Waco, TX: Baylor University Press, 2004.

Barker, Eileen. *The Making of a Moonie: Choice or Brainwashing?* Oxford: Basil Blackwell, 1984.

Barrett, David B., George T. Kurian, and Todd M. Johnson. *World Christian Encyclopedia*. 2nd ed. Vol. 1. Oxford and New York: Oxford University Press, 2002.

Bays, Daniel H., ed. *Christianity in China: From the Eighteenth Century to the Present*. Stanford, CA: Stanford University Press, 1996.

Bebbington, D. W. *Evangelicalism in Modern Britain: A History for the 1730s to the 1980s*. London: Routledge, 1989.

Belke, Thomas J. *Juche: A Christian Study of North Korea's State Religion*. Bartlesville, OK: Living Sacrifice Book Co., 1999.

Bendix, Reinhard. *Max Weber: An Intellectual Portrait*. Berkeley: University of California Press, 1960.

Berger, Peter. *Sacred Canopy: Elements of a Sociological Theory of Religion*. New York: Doubleday, 1967.

Best, Margaret. "Fifty Years of Women's Work." In *The Fiftieth Anniversary Celebration of the Korea Mission of the Presbyterian Church in the U.S.A.* 1934; reprint, Seoul: Han'guk kidokkyo yŏksa yŏn'guso, 2000.

Bettenson, Henry, and Chris Maunder, eds. *Documents of the Christian Church*. 3rd ed. Oxford: Oxford University Press, 1999.

Billings, Peggy. *Fire Beneath the Frost: The Struggles of the Korean People and Church*. New York: Friendship Press, 1983.

Blair, William N. *Gold in Korea*. 2nd ed. Topeka, KS: H. M. Ives and Sons, 1947.

Blair, William N., and Bruce F. Hunt. *The Korean Pentecost and the Sufferings Which Followed*. Carlisle, PA: Banner of Truth Trust, 1977.

Brauer, Jerald C. "Conversion: From Puritanism to Revivalism." *Journal of Religion* 58 (July 1978): 227–243.

———. *Protestantism in America*. Rev. ed. Philadelphia: Westminster, 1965.

———. "Revivalism and Millenarianism in America." In Joseph D. Ban and Paul R. Dekar, eds., *The Great Tradition*, 147–159. Valley Forge, PA: Judson, 1982.

Brown, Arthur Judson. *The Mastery of the Far East*. New York: Charles Scribner's Sons, 1919.

Brudnoy, David. "Japan's Experiment in Korea." *Monumenta Nipponica* 2, no. 1 (1970): 155–195.

Buswell, Robert E., Jr., ed. *Religions of Korea in Practice*. Princeton, NJ: Princeton University Press, 2007.

———. *The Zen Monastic Experience: Buddhist Practice in Contemporary Korea*. Princeton, NJ: Princeton University Press, 1992.

Buswell, Robert E., Jr., and Timothy S. Lee, eds. *Christianity in Korea*. Honolulu: University of Hawai'i Press, 2006.

Chandra, Vipan. *Imperialism, Resistance, and Reform in Late Nineteenth-Century Korea: Enlightenment and the Independence Club*. Berkeley: Institute of East Asian Studies, University of California, Berkeley, 1988.

Chang Kyusik. *Ilcheha han'guk kidokkyo minjokchuŭi yŏn'gu* [A Study of Korean Christian (Protestant) Nationalism in the Japanese Colonial Period]. Seoul: Haean, 2001.

Chang, Paul Yunshik. "Carrying the Torch in the Darkest Hours: The Sociopolitical Origins of Minjung Protestant Movements." In Robert E. Buswell, Jr., and Timothy S. Lee, eds., *Christianity in Korea*, 195–220.

Chang Pyŏngwuk. *6.25 kongsan namch'im kwa kyohoe* [The Church and the June 25 Communist Invasion of the South]. Seoul: Korean Educational Society, 1983.

Cherry, Conrad, ed. *God's New Israel: Religious Interpretations of American Destiny*. Rev. and updated ed. Chapel Hill: University of North Carolina Press, 1998.

Cho, Kwang. "Human Relations as Expressed in Vernacular Catholic Writings of the Late Chosŏn Dynasty." In Robert E. Buswell, Jr., and Timothy S. Lee, eds., *Christianity in Korea*, 29–37.

———. "The Meaning of Catholicism in Korean History." *Korea Journal* 24 (August 1984): 14–27.

Cho, Wha Soon [Cho Hwasun]. *Let the Weak Be Strong: A Woman's Struggle for Justice*. Edited by Lee Sun Ai and Ahn Sang Nim. Bloomington, IN: Meyer-Stone Books, 1988.

Cho, Yonggi. *Salvation, Health, and Prosperity: Our Threefold Blessings in Christ*. Altamonte Springs, FL: Creation House, 1987.

———. *Successful Home Cell Groups*. Seoul: Church Growth International, 1981.

———. "Wae Sŏngnyŏng ŭl padaya hana?" [Why Do We Have to Receive the Holy Spirit?]. In Segye pogŭmhwa undong chungang hyŏpŭihoe, '88 *segye pogŭmhwa taesŏnghoe kirok munjip*, 72–75.

Cho Yŏngnyŏl. "Chaehan sŏn'gyosa wa han'guk tongnip undong" [Korea Missionaries and the Korean Independence Movement]. *Han'guk kidokkyo yŏksa yŏn'gu* 29 (January 1990): 4–12.

Choe, Ching Young. *The Rule of the Taewongun, 1864–1873: Restoration in Yi Korea*. Cambridge, MA: Harvard University Press, 1972.

Ch'oe Hyesil. *Sinyŏsongdŭl ŭn muŏt ŭl kkumkkuŏnnŭnga* [What Did the New Women Dream Of?]. Seoul: Saenggak ŭi namu, 2002.

Ch'oe Namgyu. "Kŭm ch'ottae ka han'guk e" [The Golden Candlestick Has Come to Korea]. *Sinanggye* [Spiritual Realm] (July 1973): 80–83.

Ch'oe, Yongho. "Christian Background in the Early Life of Kim Il-Sŏng." *Asian Survey* 26, no. 10 (1986): 1082–1099.

———. "The *Kapsin* Coup of 1884: A Reassessment." *Korean Studies* 6 (1982): 105–124.

Choi, Chungmoo. "Hegemony and Shamanism: The State, the Elite, and Shamans in Contemporary Korea." In Lewis R. Lancaster and Richard K. Payne, eds., *Religion and Society in Contemporary Korea*, 19–48. Berkeley: Institute of East Asian Studies, University of California, Berkeley, 1997.

Choi, Hyaeweol. "An American Concubine in Old Korea: Missionary Discourse on Gender, Race, and Modernity." *Frontier* 25, no. 3 (2004): 134–161.

———. "Christian Modernity in the Missionary Discourse of Korea, 1905–1910." *East Asian History* 29 (2005): 39–68.

———. "(En)Gendering a New Nation in Missionary Discourse: An Analysis of W. Arthur Noble's Ewa." *Korea Journal* 46, no. 1 (2006): 139–169.

Choi, Jai-Keun. *The Origins of the Roman Catholic Church in Korea: An Examination of Popular and Governmental Responses to Catholic Missions in the Late Chosŏn Dynasty.* Edinburgh, Scotland: Hermit Kingdom Press, 2006.

Choi, Jashil [Ch'oe Chasil]. *Korean Miracles.* Seoul: Seoul Book, 1978.

Choi, Meesang Lee. *The Rise of the Korean Holiness Church in Relation to the American Holiness Movement: Wesley's "Scriptural Holiness" and the "Fourfold Gospel."* Lanham, MD: Scarecrow Press, 2008.

Choi, Suk-woo. "Korean Catholicism Yesterday and Today." *Korea Journal* 24 (August 1984): 4–13.

Chong, Kelly H. *Deliverance and Submission: Evangelical Women and the Negotiation of Patriarchy in South Korea.* MA: Harvard University Asia Center, 2008.

———. "In Search of Healing: Evangelical Conversion of Women in Contemporary South Korea." In Robert E. Buswell, Jr., and Timothy S. Lee, eds., *Christianity in Korea,* 351–370.

Chryssides, George D. *The Advent of Sun Myung Moon: The Origins, Beliefs, and Practices of the Unification Church.* London: Macmillan, 1991.

Chun, Sung C. *Schism and Unity in the Protestant Churches of Korea.* Seoul: Christian Literature Society of Korea, 1979.

Chung, Chai-sik. *A Korean Confucian Encounter with the Modern World: Yi Hang-no and the West.* Berkeley: Institute of East Asian Studies, University of California, Berkeley, 1995.

Chung, David. *Syncretism: The Religious Context of Christian Beginnings in Korea.* Edited by Kang-nam Oh. New York: State University of New York Press, 2001.

Clark, Allen D. *A History of the Church in Korea.* 1961; rev., Seoul: Christian Literature Society of Korea, 1986.

Clark, Charles Allen. *The Korean Church and the Nevius Method.* New York: Fleming H. Revell, 1930.

———. *Religions of Old Korea.* 1932; reprint, Seoul: Christian Literature Society of Korea, 1961.

Clark, Donald N. *Christianity in Modern Korea.* America's Asian Agenda Series, no. 5. Lanham, MD: University Press of America/Asia Society, 1986.

———. "Growth and Limitation of Minjung Christianity in South Korea." In Kenneth M. Wells, ed., *South Korea's Minjung Movement: The Culture and Politics of Dissidence,* 87–103. Honolulu: University of Hawai'i Press, 1995.

———. ed. *The Kwangju Uprising: Shadows over the Regime in South Korea.* Boulder, CO: Westview Press, 1988.

———. *Living Dangerously in Korea: The Western Experience, 1900–1950.* Norwalk, CT: EastBridge, 2003.

Cohen, Paul. *China and Christianity: The Missionary Movement and the Growth of Chinese Antiforeignism, 1860–1870.* Cambridge, MA: Harvard University Press, 1963.

Commission on Theological Concerns of the Christian Conference of Asia. *Minjung Theology: People as the Subjects of History.* Singapore: Christian Conference of Asia, 1981.

Cumings, Bruce. *Korea's Place in the Sun: A Modern History.* Updated ed. New York: W. W. Norton, 2005.

———. "The Legacy of Japanese Colonialism in Korea." In Ramon H. Myers and Mark R. Peattie, eds., *The Japanese Colonial Empire, 1895–1945,* 478–496. Princeton, NJ: Princeton University Press, 1984.

———. *The Origins of the Korean War.* Vol. 1, *Liberation and the Emergence of Separate Regimes, 1945–1947.* Princeton, NJ: Princeton University Press, 1981.

———. *The Origins of the Korean War.* Vol. 2, *The Roaring of the Cataract, 1947–1950.* Princeton, NJ: Princeton University Press, 1990.

———. *Two Koreas.* New York: Foreign Policy Association, 1984.

Cynn, Hugh Heung-Woo [Sin Hŭnghu]. *The Rebirth of Korea: The Reawakening of the People, Its Causes, and the Outlook.* New York: Abingdon, 1920.

Dallet, Charles. *Histoire de l'Église de Corée.* 2 vols. 1874; reprint, Seoul: Royal Asiatic Society, Korea Branch, 1975.

Davies, Daniel M. "Building a City on a Hill in Korea: The Work of Henry G. Appenzeller." *Church History* 61, no. 4 (1992): 422–435.

———. *The Life and Thought of Henry Gerhard Appenzeller (1858–1902), Missionary to Korea.* Lewiston, NY: Edwin Mellen, 1988.

Davis, George T. B. *Korea for Christ.* London: Christian Workers' Depot, 1910.

Dayton, Donald W., and Robert K. Johnston, eds. *The Variety of American Evangelicalism.* Knoxville: University of Tennessee Press, 1991.

de Bary, William Theodore, and JaHyun Kim Haboush, eds. *The Rise of Neo-Confucianism in Korea.* New York: Columbia University Press, 1985.

De Ceuster, Koen. "Through the Master's Eye: Colonized Mind and Historical Consciousness in the Case of Yun Ch'iho (1865–1945)." *Bochumer Jahrbuch zur Ostasienforschung* 27 (2003): 107–131.

Deuchler, Martina. *Confucian Gentlemen and Barbarian Envoys: The Opening of Korea, 1875–1885.* Seattle: University of Washington Press, 1977.

———. *The Confucian Transformation of Korea: A Study of Society and Ideology.* Cambridge, MA: Council on East Asian Studies, Harvard University, 1992.

Diaz, Hector. *A Korean Theology: Chu-gyo yo-ji; Essentials of the Lord's Teaching by Chŏng Yak-jong Augustine (1760–1801).* Immensee, Switzerland: Neue Zeitschrift für Missionswissenschaft, 1986.

Douglas, Mary. *Purity and Danger: An Analysis of the Concepts of Pollution and Taboo.* London: Routledge and Kegan Paul, 1966.

Dredge, C. Paul. "Korean Funerals: Ritual as Process." In Laurel Kendall and Griffin Dix, eds., *Religion and Ritual in Korean Society,* 71–92.

Duncan, John. "Confucian Social Values in Contemporary South Korea." In Lewis R. Lancaster and Richard K. Payne, eds., *Religion and Society in Contemporary*

Korea, 49–73. Berkeley: Institute of East Asian Studies, University of California, Berkeley, 1997.

———. "Proto-nationalism in Premodern Korea." In Sang-Oak Lee and Duk-Soo Park, eds., *Perspectives on Korea*, 198–221. Sydney: Wild Peony, 1998.

Eckert, Carter J., Ki-baik Lee, Young Ick Lew, Michael Robinson, and Edward W. Wagner. *Korea Old and New: A History*. Seoul: published for the Korea Institute, Harvard University, by Ilchokak, 1990.

Eliade, Mircea, ed. *The Encyclopedia of Religion*. New York: Macmillan, 1987.

Em, Henry. "*Minjok* as a Modern and Democratic Construct: Sin Ch'aeho's Historiography." In Gi-Wook Shin and Michael E. Robinson, eds., *Colonial Modernity in Korea*, 336–361. Cambridge, MA: Harvard University Asia Center, 1999.

Erny, Edward, and Esther Erny. *No Guarantee but God: The Story of the Founders of the Oriental Missionary Society*. Greenwood, IN: Oriental Missionary Society, 1969.

Esherick, Joseph W. *The Origins of the Boxer Uprising*. Berkeley: University of California Press, 1987.

Fairbank, John, ed. *Missionary Enterprise in China and America*. Cambridge, MA: Harvard University Press, 1974.

Federal Council of the Churches of Christ of America (FCCCA), comp. *The Korean Situation: Authentic Accounts of Recent Events by Eye Witnesses*. New York: FCCCA, 1919.

Frend, W. H. C. *The Rise of Christianity*. Philadelphia: Fortress, 1984.

Freston, Paul. *Evangelicals and Politics in Asia, Africa and Latin America*. Cambridge: Cambridge University Press, 2001.

Gale, James S. *Korea in Transition*. New York: Young People's Missionary Movement of the United States and Canada, 1909.

Gallup Korea. *Han'gugin ŭi chonggyo wa chonggyo ŭisik: '84-yŏn, '89-yŏn, '97-yŏn chosa kyŏlgwa wa pigyohan chonggyo yŏn'guso* [Koreans' Religions and Religious Consciousness: A Study of Religions Based on Comparisons of Survey Results of '84, '89, and '97]. Seoul: Gallup Korea, 1998.

———. *Han'gugin ŭi chonggyo wa chonggyo ŭisik: '84-yŏn, '89-yŏn, '97-yŏn, '04-yŏn chosa kyŏlgwa rŭl pigyohan chonggy yŏn'guso* [Koreans' Religions and Religious Consciousness: A Study of Religions Based on Comparisons of Survey Results from '84, '89, '97, and '04]. Seoul: Gallup Korea, 2004.

———. *Han'guk kaesin'gyoin ŭi kyohoe hwaltong kwa sinang ŭisik* [Korean Protestants' Churchly Activities and Religious Consciousness]. Seoul: Turano, 1999.

Graham, Billy. *How to Be Born Again*. Dallas: Word Publishing, 1977.

———. *Just as I Am: The Autobiography of Billy Graham*. New York: HarperCollins, 1997.

Grayson, James Huntley. "Cultural Encounter: Korean Protestantism and Other Religious Traditions." *International Bulletin of Missionary Research* 25, no. 2 (2001): 66–72.

———. *Korea: A Religious History*. Rev. ed. London: RoutledgeCurzon, 2002.

Griffis, William Elliot. *Corea, the Hermit Nation*. New York: Charles Scribner's Sons, 1882.

Ha Chongp'il. *Pukhan ŭi chonggyo munhwa* [North Korea's Religious Culture]. Seoul: Sŏnin, 2003.

Haboush, JaHyun Kim, and Martina Deuchler, eds. *Culture and the State in Late Chosŏn Korea*. Cambridge, MA: Harvard University Asia Center, 1999.

Han Kyumu. "Chenŏrŏl syŏlmŏnho sakŏn kwa t'omas ŭi 'sun'gyo' munje kŏmt'o" [Examining the *General Sherman* Incident and the Problem of Thomas' "Martyrdom"]. *Han'guk kyohoe wa yŏksa* [Korean Church and History] 1 (July 1997): 9–33.

———. "Haebang chikhu namhan kyohoe ŭi tonghyang" [The Southern Church's Trends after Liberation]. *Han'guk kidokkyo wa yŏksa* [Korean Christianity and History], 2 (1992): 39–54.

———. *Ilcheha han'guk kidokkyo nongch'on undong, 1925–1937* [Korean Christians' Rural Movement under Japanese Rule, 1925–1937]. Seoul: Han'guk kidokkyo yŏksa yŏn'guso, 1997.

———. "Yi Tonghwi wa kidokkyo sahoejuŭi" [Yi Tonghwi and Korean Christian Socialism]. In Kim Heung-soo, *Ilcheha han'guk kidokkyo wa sahoejuŭi* [Christianity and Socialism in Korea under Japanese Rule], 173–191. Seoul: Han'guk kidokkyo yŏksa yŏn'guso, 1992.

Han, Kyung-Chik [Han Kyŏngjik]. "The Present and Future of the Korean Church." In Bong-rin Ro and Marlin L. Nelson, ed., *Korean Church Growth Explosion*, 348–370.

Han Wansang. "Kyohoe yangchŏk kŭpsŏngjang e taehan sahoehakchŏk koch'al" [A Sociological Examination of the Rapid Quantitative Growth in the Korean (Protestant) Church]. In Kim Kwangil et al., *Han'guk kyohoe sŏngnyŏng undong ŭi hyŏnsang kwa kujo*, 165–231.

Han, Woo-keun. *The History of Korea*. Honolulu: University of Hawai'i Press, 1971.

Han Yŏngje, ed. *Han'guk kidokkyo sŏngjang 100-yŏn* [One Hundred Years of the Korean Church's Growth]. Seoul: Kidokkyo munsa, 1986.

———, ed. *Kidokkyo taeyŏn'gam, 1991* [The Christian Yearbook of Korea, 1991]. Vol. 6. Seoul: Kidokkyo munsa, 1991.

Han'guk chonggyo sahoe yŏn'guso [Korea Research Institute for Religion and Society], ed. *Han'guk chonggyo yŏn'gam, 1993* [A Yearbook of Korean Religions, 1993]. Seoul: Korea Hallimŏn, 1993.

Han'guk kat'ollik sajŏn [Korean Catholic Encyclopedia]. Seoul: Research Institute for Korean Church History, 2005.

Han'guk kidokkyo sahoe munje yŏn'guwŏn [Christian Institute for the Study of Justice and Development]. *Han'guk kyohoe 100-yŏn chonghap chosa yŏn'gu* [Centennial Comprehensive Study of the Korean (Protestant) Church]. Seoul: Han'guk kidokkyo sahoe munje yŏn'guwŏn, 1982.

Han'guk kidokkyo yŏksa yŏn'guso [Institute of Korean Church History Studies]. *Han'guk kidok kyohoe ŭi yŏksa I, 16 segi–1918* [A History of the Korean Church, vol. 1, 16th Century to 1918]. Seoul: Kidokkyo munsa, 1989.

———. *Han'guk kidok kyohoe ŭi yŏksa II, 1919–1945* [A History of the Korean Church, vol. 2, 1919–1945]. Seoul: Kidokkyo munsa, 1990.

———. *Pukhan kyohoesa* [North Korean Church History]. Seoul: Han'guk kidokkyo yŏksa yŏn'guso, 1996.

Han'guk kidokkyo yŏksa yŏn'guso [Institute of Korean Church History Studies] and Pukhan kyohoesa chipp'il wiwŏnhoe [Committee of North Korean Church History Writers]. *Pukhan kyohoesa* [North Korean Church History]. Seoul: Han'guk kidokkyo yŏksa yŏn'guso, 1996.

Han'guk kŭnhyŏndae sahoe yŏn'guhoe [Institute for the Study of Modern and Contemporary Korean Society]. *Han'guk kŭndae kaehwa sasang kwa kaehwa undong* [Enlightenment Thought and Enlightenment Movements in Modern Korea]. Seoul: Sinsŏwŏn, 1998.

Han'guk yŏksa yŏn'guso [Institute for the Study of Korean History] and Yŏksa munje yŏn'guhoe [Institute for the Study of Historical Problems], eds. *3.1 minjok haebang undong yŏn'gu* [A Study of the March First National Liberation Movement]. Seoul: Chŏngnyŏnsa, 1989.

Hardacre, Helen. *Shintō and the State, 1868–1988*. Princeton, NJ: Princeton University Press, 1989.

Harrington, Fred Harvey. *God, Mammon and the Japanese*. New York: Arno Press, 1980.

Hart, D. G. *Deconstructing Evangelicalism: Conservative Protestantism in the Age of Billy Graham*. Grand Rapids, MI: Baker Academic, 2004.

———. *That Old-Time Religion in Modern America: Evangelical Protestantism in the Twentieth Century*. Chicago: Ivan R. Dee, 2002.

Harvey, Youngsook Kim. "The Korean Shaman and the Deaconess: Sisters in Different Guises." In Laurel Kendall and Griffin Dix, eds., *Religion and Ritual in Korean Society*, 149–170.

Henthorn, William E. *A History of Korea*. New York: Free Press, 1971.

Hicks, George Hicks. *The Comfort Women: Japan's Brutal Regime of Enforced Prostitution in the Second World War*. New York: W. W. Norton, 1994.

Hogarth, Hyun-key Kim. *Korean Shamanism and Cultural Nationalism*. Seoul: Jimoondang, 1999.

Hollenweger, Walter J. *The Pentecostals*. London: SCM Press, 1972.

Hong, Sŏkch'ang. *Yu Kwansun-yang kwa maebong kyohoe* [Yu Kwansun and Maebong Church]. Seoul: Tosŏ ch'ulp'an amen, 1989.

Hulbert, Homer B. *The Passing of Korea*. London: William Heinemann, 1906.

Hunt, Bruce F. *For a Testimony*. London: Banner of Truth Trust, 1966.

Hunt, Everett N., Jr. *Protestant Pioneers in Korea*. Marynoll, NY: Orbis, 1980.

Hunter, Helen-Louise. *Kim Il-song's North Korea*. London: Praeger, 1999.

Huntley, Martha. *Caring, Growing, Changing: A History of the Protestant Mission in Korea*. New York: Friendship Press, 1984.

Hurston, Karen Hurston. *Growing the World's Largest Church*. Springfield, MO: Chrism, 1995.

Hutchison, William R. *Errand to the World: American Protestant Thought and Foreign Missions*. Chicago: University of Chicago Press, 1987.

Hwang, So-kyong [Hwang Sŏgyŏng]. *The Guest*. Translated by Kyung-Ja Chun and Maya West. New York: Seven Stories Press, 2005.

———. *Sonnim*. Seoul: Ch'angjak kwa pip'yŏngsa, 2001.

Hyŏndae sahoe yŏn'guso [Institute for the Study of Modern Society]. *Han'guk kyohoe sŏngjang kwa sinang yangt'ae e kwanhan chosa yŏn'gu* [Investigation into the Growth and Religiosity of the Korean (Protestant) Church]. Seoul: Hyŏndae sahoe yŏn'guso, 1982.

Im T'aekchin. "Han'guk kyohoe wa saebyŏk kido" [The Korean (Protestant) Church and Daybreak Prayer]. *Kido* [Prayer], January 1986, 18–21.

Im Yongsu. "Kŭrisŭdo ŭi 40-il kŭmsik kido ka uri ege chunŭn kyohun" [The Lesson Given to Us by Jesus' Forty-Day Fasting-Prayer]. *Kido* [Prayer], July–August 1986, 22–25.

Iryŏn. *Samguk Yusa: Legends and History of the Three Kingdoms of Korea*. Translated by Tae-hung Ha and Grafton Mintz. Seoul: Yonsei University, 1972.

Jenkins, Philip. *The Next Christendom: The Coming of Global Christianity*. Oxford: Oxford University Press, 2002.

Johnstone, Patrick, and Jason Mandryk, eds. *Operation World: 21st Century Edition*. Harrisonburg, VA: Paternoster, 2001.

Joint Publications Research Service. *Translations on North Korea*. No. 419 (August 6, 1975).

Kang, Chul-won. "An Analysis of Japanese Policy and Economic Change in Korea." In Andrew C. Nahm, ed., *Korea under Japanese Colonial Rule*, 77–88.

Kang Inchŏl. *Han'guk kidokkyohoe wa kukka-simin sahoe* [The Korean Christian Church, the State, and the Civil Society]. Seoul: Han'guk kidokkyo yŏksa yŏn'guso, 1996.

———. *Han'guk ŭi kaesin'gyo wa pangongjuŭi: Posujŏk kaesin'gyo ŭi chŏngch'ijŏk haendongjuŭi t'amgu* [Korean Protestantism and Anticommunism: An Examination of Conservative Protestants' Political Behaviorism]. Seoul: Chungsim, 2006.

Kang In'gyu. "1920-yŏndae pan kidokkyo undong ŭl t'onghae pon kidokkyo" [Christianity Seen through the Anti-Christian Movements of the 1920s]. *Han'guk kidokkyosa yŏn'gu* [Journal of the Institute of Korean Church History Studies] 9 (August 1986): 12–15.

Kang Mangil. *Koch'yŏssŭn han'guk hyŏndaesa* [A Revised History of Contemporary Korea]. Seoul: Ch'angbi, 1994.

———. *Koch'yŏssŭn han'guk kŭndaesa* [A Revised History of Modern Korea]. Seoul: Ch'angbi, 1994.

Kang, Wi Jo. *Christ and Caesar in Modern Korea: A History of Christianity and Politics*. New York: State University of New York Press, 1997.

———. "Relation between the Japanese Colonial Government and the American Missionary Community in Korea, 1905–1945." In Yur-bok Lee and Wayne Patterson, eds, *One Hundred Years of Korean-American Relations, 1882–1982*, 68–107.

———. *Religion and Politics in Korea under Japanese Rule*. Lewiston, NY: Edwin Mellen, 1987.

Kendall, Laurel. *Shamans, Housewives, and Other Restless Spirits*. Honolulu: University of Hawai`i Press, 1985.

Kendall, Laurel, and Griffin Dix, eds. *Religion and Ritual in Korean Society*. Berkeley: Institute of East Asian Studies, University of California, Berkeley, 1987.

Kerr, Edith A., and George Anderson. *The Austrian Presbyterian Mission in Korea, 1889–1941*. Sydney: Australian Presbyterian Board of Missions, 1970.

Kidokkyo taebaekkwa sajŏn [Christian Encyclopedia]. Seoul: Kidokkyo munsa, 1980.

Kil Chingyŏng. *Yŏnggye Kil Sŏnju* [Kil Sŏnju, the Spiritual Stream]. Seoul: Chongno sŏjŏk, 1980.

Kil Sŏnju. *Kil Sŏnju moksa yugojŏnjip* [Posthumous Collection of Works by Reverend Kil Sŏnju]. Edited by Kiel [Kil] Chin'gyŏng. Seoul: Chongno sŏjŏk, 1975.

Kim Ch'angt'ae and Yu Tongsik [Ryu Tong-shik]. *Han'guk chonggyo sasangsa* [A History of Korean Religious Thought]. Seoul: Yonsei University Press, 1986.

Kim Chinhong. *Hwangmuji ka changmi kkot katchi* [Till Wasteland Becomes a Rose]. Vol. 2. Seoul: Hangilsa, 1999.

Kim Chinhwan. *Han'guk kyohoe puhŭng undongsa* [A History of Revival Movements in the Korean Church]. Rev. ed. Seoul: Seoul sŏjŏk, 1993.

Kim, Chong Bum. "Christianity in Colonial Korea: The Culture and Politics of Proselytization." PhD diss., Harvard University, 2004.

———. "Preaching the Apocalypse in Colonial Korea: The Protestant Millennialism of Kil Sŏn-ju." In Robert E.Buswell, Jr., and Timothy S. Lee, eds., *Christianity in Korea*, 149–166.

Kim Chongnyŏl. "Minjok pogŭmhwa wa kunjung chiphoe" [Evangelization of the Nation and Mass Gatherings]. *Kidokkyo sasang* [Christian Thought] (October 1974): 72–81.

Kim Ch'ungnam. *Sun'gyoja Chu Kichŏl moksa saengae* [The Life of the Martyred Reverend Chu Kichŏl; English title, He Left When the Azalea Bloomed]. Seoul: Paekhap, 1991.

Kim Chun'gon. "CCC an esŏ ŭi kido undong" [Prayer Movement in the CCC]. *Wŏlgan mokhoe* [Pastoral Monthly] (July 1986): 62–71.

———. "Minjok ŭi hwahoe wa illyu sŏn'gyo ŭi pijŏn ŭro" [Through the Vision of National Reconciliation and Global Missions]. *Sinang segye* [Spiritual World] (August–September 1980): 60–65.

Kim, Eugene C. "Education in Korea." In Andrew C. Nahm, ed., *Korea under Japanese Colonial Rule*, 137–145.

Kim, Eŭihwan [Kim Ŭihwan]. "The Korean Church under Japanese Occupation with Special Reference to the Resistance Movement within Presbyterianism." PhD diss., Temple University, 1966.

———. "Sŏn'gyo ŭi tongyŏkcha" [Partners in Missions]. In Segye pogŭmhwa undong chungang hyŏpŭihoe, *'88 segye pogŭmhwa taesŏnghoe kirok munjip*, 62–63.

Kim, H. Edward. "Rare Look at North Korea." *National Geographic*, August 1974, 252–277.

Kim, Hankyo. "The Japanese Colonial Administration in Korea: An Overview." In Andrew C. Nahm, *Korea under Japanese Colonial Rule*, 41–53.

Kim Heung-soo [Kim Hŭngsu], ed. *Haebanghu pukhan kyohoesa* [A History of the North Korean Church since Liberation]. Seoul: Tasan kŭlpang, 1992.

———. *Han'guk chŏnjaeng kwa kiboksinang hwaksan yŏn'gu* [A Study of the Korean War and the Spread of the Health-and-Prosperity Gospel]. Seoul: Han'guk kidokkyo yŏksa yŏn'guso, 1999.

———. *Ilcheha han'guk kidokkyo wa sahoejuŭi* [Christianity and Socialism in Korea under Japanese Rule]. Seoul: Han'guk kidokkyo yŏksa yŏn'guso, 1992.

Kim, Ig-Jin. *History and Theology of Korean Pentecostalism: Sunbogeum (Pure Gospel) Pentecostalism*. Zoetermeer, The Netherlands: Boekencentrum, 2003.

Kim Jong Il. *On the Juche Idea*. Pyongyang: Foreign Languages Publishing House, 1982.

Kim Kwangil et al. *Han'guk kyohoe sŏngnyŏng undong ŭi hyŏnsang kwa kujo* [A Study of the Pentecostal Movement in Korea]. Seoul: Korea Christian Academy, 1981.

Kim Kwangsŏn. "Yŏ Unhyŏng ŭi saengae wa sasang ŭi hyŏngsŏng" [Yŏ Unhyŏng's Life and the Formation of His Thought]. In Kim Heung-soo, *Ilcheha han'guk kidokkyo wa sahoejuŭi* [Christianity and Socialism in Korea under Japanese Rule], 193–207. Seoul: Han'guk kidokkyo yŏksa yŏn'guso, 1992.

Kim Myŏnghyŏk. "Han'guk kyohoe kido ŭi sŭpkwan" [Prayer Habits of the Korean (Protestant) Church]. *Kido* [Prayer], January 1987, 48–51.

Kim, Nyung. "The Politics of Religion in South Korea, 1974–89: The Catholic Church's Political Opposition to the Authoritarian State." PhD diss., University of Washington, 1993.

Kim Pyŏngsŏ. *Han'guk sahoe wa kaesin'gyo: Chonggyosahoe chŏk chŏpkŭn* [Korean Society and Protestantism: A Sociology of Religion Approach]. Seoul: Hanul ak'ademi, 1995.

Kim, Richard E. *Lost Names: Scenes from a Korean Boyhood*. Berkeley: University of California Press, 1998.

———. *The Martyr*. New York: George Braziller, 1964.

Kim Samung, ed. *Ch'inilp'a 100-in 100-mun* [One Hundred Documents of One Hundred Collaborators with the Japanese]. Seoul: Tolbegae, 1995.

Kim, Sangkeun. "Sheer Numbers Do Not Tell the Entire Story: The Challenges of the Korean Missionary Movement from an Ecumenical Perspective." *Ecumenical Review* 57, no. 4 (2005): 463–473.

Kim Sŏngjin. "Saeroun hyŏngt'ae ŭi puhŭng undong (2)" [A New Form of Revival Movement (2)]. *Kidokkyo sasang* [Christian Thought] (February 1973): 75–82.

Kim Sŭngt'ae. "Chonggyoin ŭi 3.1 undong ch'amyŏ wa kidokkyo ŭi yŏkhal" [Religionists' Participation in the March First Movement and the Role of Christianity]. *Han'guk kidokkyosa yŏn'gu* [Journal of the Institute of Korean Church History Studies], 25 (April 1989): 17–24.

———. "1930-yŏndae kidokkyogye hakkyo ŭi 'sinsa munje'" [The "Shintō Rites" Problem among Korean Christian Schools in the 1930s]. In Kim Sŭngt'ae, ed., *Han'guk kidokkyo wa sinsa ch'ambae munje* [The Korean Church and the Shinto Shrine Issue], 361–391. Seoul: Han'guk kidokkyo yŏksa yŏn'guso, 1991.

Kim Sŭngt'ae and Pak Hyejin, comps. *Naehan sŏn'gyosa ch'ongnam, 1884–1984* [A Survey of Korea Missionaries]. Seoul: Han'guk kidokkyo yŏksa yŏn'guso, 1994.

Kim, Sunhyuk. "Civil Society in South Korea: From Grand Democracy Movements to Petty Interest Groups?" *Journal of Northeast Asian Studies* 15:2 (Summer 1996): 81–98.

———. *The Politics of Democratization in Korea: The Role of Civil Society.* Pittsburgh, PA: University of Pittsburgh Press, 2000.

Kim Tongil. "77-yŏn minjok pogŭmhwa sŏnghoe nŭn ŏdiro kal kŏsinga?" [Where Is the '77 Holy Assembly for the Evangelization of the Nation Headed?]. *Sinang segye* [Spiritual World] (August 1977): 38–45.

Kim Uyŏng. "Pŏn'yŏng kwa t'ongil ŭi hwansang" [A Vision of Prosperity and Unification]. In Segye pogŭmhwa undong chungang hyŏpŭihoe, *'88 segye pogŭmhwa taesŏnghoe kirok munjip,* 88–91.

Kim, Yangsun. *History of the Korean Church in the Ten Years since Liberation (1945–1955).* Translated by Allen D. Clark. N.p., [1964?].

Knitter, Paul F. *Introducing Theologies of Religions.* Maryknoll, NY: Orbis, 2002.

Ko Sŏnghyŏn. "Pukhan ŭi han'guk kidokkyosa (Chosŏn hugi–ilche sidae) ihae e taehan yŏn'gu: Haebang hu palp'yo toen pukhan munhŏn ŭl chungsim ŭro" [A Study on North Korea's Understanding of Korean Christian History (Late Chosŏn–Japanese Colonial Period): Focusing on the North Korean Literature Published after Liberation]. *Han'guk kidokkyo wa yŏksa* [Korean Christianity and History] 10 (1999): 155–158.

Koh, Byung Chul. "The Cult of Personality and the Succession Issue." In C. I. Eugene Kim and B. C. Koh, eds., *Journey to North Korea: Personal Perceptions,* 25–41. Berkeley: Institute of East Asian Studies, University of California, Berkeley, 1983.

Korea Overseas Information Service. *Facts about Korea.* Seoul: Korea Overseas Information Service, 1991.

Kukche sinhak yŏn'guwŏn [International Theological Institute]. *Yŏŭido sunbogŭm kyohoe ŭi sinang kwa sinhak* [Theology and Faith of the Yoido Full Gospel Church]. Seoul: Seoul sŏjŏk, 1993.

Kwon, Tai Hwan, Hae Young Lee, Yunshik Chang, and Eui-Young Yu. *The Population of Korea.* Seoul: Population and Development Studies Center, Seoul National University, 1975.

Lamber, Tony. *China's Christian Millions.* Rev. and updated ed. Oxford: Monarch, 2006.

———. *The Resurrection of the Chinese Church.* Wheaton, IL: Harold Shaw, 1994.

Lane, Christel. *The Rites of Rulers: Ritual in Industrial Society—the Soviet Case.* New York: Cambridge University Press, 1981.

Latourette, Kenneth S. *A History of Christian Missions to China.* New York: Macmillan, 1929.

Ledyard, Gari. "Kollumba Kang Wansuk, an Early Catholic Activist and Martyr." In Robert E. Buswell, Jr., and Timothy S. Lee, eds., *Christianity in Korea,* 38–71.

Lee, Chong-shik. *The Korean Workers' Party: A Short History.* Stanford, CA: Hoover Institution Press.

———. *The Politics of Korean Nationalism.* Berkeley: University of California Press, 1965.

Lee, Chull. "Social Sources of the Rapid Growth of the Christian Church in Northwest Korea: 1895–1910." PhD diss., Boston University, 1997.

Lee, Graham. "How the Spirit Came to Pyeng Yang." *Korea Mission Field* 3 (March 1907): 33–37.

Lee, Ki-baik. *New History of Korea.* Cambridge, MA: Harvard University Press, 1984.

Lee, Man-gap, and Herbert R. Barringer, eds. *A City in Transition: Urbanization in Taegu, Korea.* Seoul: Hollym, 1971.

Lee, Peter H., ed. *Sourcebook of Korean Civilization.* Vol. 1, *From Early Times to the Sixteenth Century.* New York: Columbia University Press, 1993.

———. *Sourcebook of Korean Civilization.* Vol. 2, *From the Seventeenth Century to the Modern Period.* New York: Columbia University Press, 1996.

Lee, Soon Ok. *Eyes of the Tailless Animals: Prison Memoirs of a North Korean Woman.* Bartlesville, OK: Living Sacrifice Book Co., 1999.

Lee, Timothy S. "Beleaguered Success: Korean Evangelicalism in the Last Decade of the Twentieth Century." In Robert E. Buswell, Jr., and Timothy S. Lee, eds., *Christianity in Korea*, 330–350.

———. "Conversion Narratives in Korean Evangelicalism." In Robert E. Buswell, ed., *Religions of Korea in Practice*, 393–408.

———. "Devotional Practices in Korean Evangelicalism." In Robert E. Buswell, ed., *Religions of Korea in Practice*, 421–433.

———. "The Great Revival of 1907 in Korea: Its Evangelical and Political Background." *Criterion: A Publication of the Divinity School of the University of Chicago* 40, no. 2 (2001): 10–17.

———. "Han'guk kaesin'gyo ŭi kŭpsŏngjang wŏnin, 1950–1988" [Accounting for the Rapid Growth of South Korean Protestant Church since the Korean War, 1950–1988]. *Han'guk kidokkyo yŏksa yŏn'guso sosik* [News of the Institute of Korean Church History Study] 20 (July 1995).

———. "Korea, the Movement." In Douglas A. Foster, Paul M. Blowers, Anthony L. Dunnavant, and D. Newell Williams, eds., *The Encyclopedia of the Stone-Campbell Movement*, 447–448. Grand Rapids, MI: Eerdmans, 2004.

———. "A Political Factor in the Rise of Protestantism in Korea: Protestantism and the March First Movement." *Church History: Studies in Christianity and Culture* 69, no. 1 (2000): 116–142.

———. "Two Aspects of Evangelical Quest to Christianize Korea: Mammoth Crusades and Sectarian Incivility." *Acta Koreana* 5, no. 2 (2002): 27–43.

———. "What Should Christians Do about a Shaman-Progenitor? Evangelicals and Ethnic Nationalism in South Korea." *Church History: Studies in Christianity and Culture* 78, no. 1 (2009): 66–98.

Lee, Won Gue. "A Sociological Study on the Factors of Church Growth and Decline in Korea." *Korea Journal* 39, no. 4 (1999): 235–269.

Lee, Yur-bok, and Wayne Patterson, eds. *One Hundred Years of Korean-American Relations, 1882–1982.* Tuscaloosa: University of Alabama Press, 1986.

Lew, Young Ick. "The Conservative Character of the 1894 Tonghak Peasant Uprising: A Reappraisal with Emphasis on Chŏn Pong-jun's Background and Motivation." *Journal of Korean Studies* 7 (1990): 149–177.

Lowe, Peter. *The Origins of the Korean War*. London: Longman, 1986.

Marsden, George M. *Fundamentalism and American Culture*. New ed. Oxford: Oxford University Press, 2006.

———. *Understanding Fundamentalism and Evangelicalism*. Grand Rapids, MI: Eerdmans, 1991.

Marty, Martin. *The Christian World: A Global History*. New York: Modern Library, 2007.

———. *A Nation of Behaviors*. Chicago: University of Chicago Press, 1976.

———. *The Public Church: Mainline-Evangelical-Catholic*. New York: Crossroad, 1981.

———. *Righteous Empire: The Protestant Experience in America*. New York: Dial Press, 1970.

Marty, Martin E., and R. Scott Appleby, eds. *Fundamentalism Observed*. Chicago: University of Chicago Press, 1991.

Marx, Karl, and Friedrich Engels. *On Religion*. Chico, CA: Scholars Press, 1964.

McGuire, Meredith B. *Religion: The Social Context*. 3rd ed. Belmont, CA: Wadsworth, 1992.

McLoughlin, William G., Jr. *Modern Revivalism: Charles Grandison Finney to Billy Graham*. New York: Ronald Press, 1959.

———. *Revivals, Awakenings, and Reform: An Essay on Religion and Social Change in America, 1607–1977*. Chicago: University of Chicago Press, 1978.

Mead, Sidney E. *The Lively Experiment: The Shaping of Christianity in America*. New York: Harper and Row, 1963.

Min Kyoung-bae. *Han'guk kidokkyohoesa* [A History of the Korean Christian Church]. New rev. ed. Seoul: Yonsei taehakkyo ch'ulp'ansa, 1993.

———. "Han'guk kidokkyo e issŏsŏ minjok munje" [The Problem of the Nation in Korean Christianity]. In *Han'guk yŏksa wa kidokkyo* [Korean History and Christianity], edited by *Kidokkyo sasang*, 104–123. Seoul: Literature Society of Korea, 1983.

———. *Ilcheha ŭi han'guk kidokkyo* [The Korean Church under Japanese Imperialism]. Seoul: Christian Literature Society of Korea, 1991.

Ministry of Economic Planning Board. *13th Population and Housing Census of the Republic of Korea*. Seoul: Ministry of Economic Planning Board, 1985.

Moffett, Samuel H. *The Christians of Korea*. New York: Friendship Press, 1962.

———. *A History of Christianity in Asia*. Vol. 2, *1500–1900*. Maryknoll, NY: Orbis, 2005.

Moose, J. R. "A Great Awakening." *Korea Mission Field* 2 (January 1906): 51–52.

Mott, John R. *The Evangelization of the World in This Generation*. New York: Student Volunteer Movement for Foreign Missions, 1901.

Mullins, Mark R. *Christianity Made in Japan: A Study of Indigenous Movements*. Honolulu: University of Hawai'i Press, 1998.

Munhwa kwan'gwangbu, chongmusil [Ministry of Culture and Tourism, Religious Affairs]. *Han'guk ŭi chonggyo hyŏnhwang, 1999* [The State of Korean Religions, 1999]. Seoul: Munhwa kwan'gwangbu, chongmusil, 1999.

Nahm, Andrew C., ed. *Introduction to Korean History and Culture.* Seoul and Elizabeth, NJ: Hollym, 1993.

————. *Korea under Japanese Colonial Rule.* Kalamazoo: Western Michigan University Press, 1973.

National Statistics Office of the Republic of Korea. *Han'guk ŭi sahoe chip'yo* [Social Indicators in Korea]. Seoul: National Statistics Office, 1993.

No Ch'ijun. *Han'guk ŭi kyohoe chojik* [The Organization of Korean Churches]. Seoul: Minyŏngsa, 1995.

Noble, Mattie Wilcox. *The Journals of Mattie Wilcox Noble, 1892–1934.* Seoul: Han'guk kidokkyo yŏksa yŏn'guso, 1993.

Noll, Mark A. *American Evangelical Christianity: An Introduction.* Oxford: Blackwell, 2001.

————. *The Rise of Evangelicalism: The Age of Edwards, Whitefield, and the Wesleys.* Downers Grove, IL: Inter-Varsity Press, 2003.

————. *The Scandal of the Evangelical Mind.* Grand Rapids, MI: Eerdmans, 1994.

Noll, Mark A., David W. Bebbington, and George A. Rawlyk. *Evangelicalism: Comparative Studies of Popular Protestantism in North America, the British Isles, and Beyond, 1700–1990.* Oxford: Oxford University Press, 1994.

Numbers, Ronald L., et al., eds. *The Disappointed: Millerism and Millenarianism in the Nineteenth Century.* Knoxville: University of Tennessee Press, 1993.

Oak, Sung Deuk. "The Indigenization of Christianity in Korea: North American Missionaries' Attitudes towards Korean Religions, 1884–1910." PhD diss., Boston University, 2002.

————, ed. *Sources of Korean Christianity, 1832–1945.* Seoul: Institute for Korean Church History, 2004.

Oberdorfer, Don. *The Two Koreas: A Contemporary History.* Rev. and updated ed. New York: Basic Books, 2001.

Ogle, George E. *How Long, O Lord: Stories of Twentieth Century Korea.* N.p.: Xlibris, 2002.

————. *Liberty to the Captives: The Struggle against Oppression in South Korea.* Atlanta, GA: Westminster John Knox Press, 1977.

Olson, Roger E. *Evangelical Theology.* Louisville, KY: Westminster John Knox Press, 2004.

Paek Chunghyŏn. *Pukhan edo kyohoe ka inna yo?* [Is There a Church in North Korea?]. Seoul: Kung'min ilbo, 1998.

Paik, L. George. *The History of Protestant Missions in Korea, 1832–1910.* 1929; reprint, Seoul: Yonsei University Press, 1987.

Pak A-ron. "Kidokkyo pakkenŭn kuwŏn i ŏpta" [There Is No Salvation outside Christianity]. *Wŏlgan mokhoe* [Pastoral Monthly] (October 1977): 58–64.

Pak Chongsun. *Kyohoe sŏngjang kwa sŏnggŏng kongbu* [Church Growth and Bible Study]. Seoul: Hyesŏn, 1980.

Pak Manyong. *Kidowŏn undong kwa sinang sŏngjang* [The Prayer House Movement and the Growth of the Faith]. Seoul: K'umnan ch'ulpansa, 1998.

Pak Myŏngsu [Park Myung Soo]. *Ch'ogi han'guk sŏnggyŏl kyohoesa* [Early History of the Korean Holiness Church: Its Background and Early Development]. Seoul: Taehan kidokkyo sŏhoe, 2001.

Palmer, Spencer. *Korea and Christianity: The Problem of Identification with Tradition.* Seoul: Hollym, 1967.

———, ed. *The New Religions of Korea.* Seoul: Transactions of the Royal Asiatic Society, Korea Branch, 1967.

Park, Andrew Sung. "*Minjung* and *Pungryu* Theologies in Contemporary Korea: A Critical and Comparative Examination." PhD diss., Graduate Theological Union, 1985.

———. *The Wounded Heart of God: The Asian Concept of Han and the Christian Doctrine of Sin.* Nashville, TN: Abingdon, 1993.

Park, Chung-Shin. *Protestantism and Politics in Korea.* Seattle: University of Hawai`i Press, 2003.

Park Jong-Hyun. "Kim Insŏ ŭi 'pogŭmjuŭijŏk minjokchuŭi' sasang" [Kim Insŏ's "Evangelical Christian Nationalism"]. *Han'guk kidokkyo wa yŏksa* [Korean Christianity and History], 21 (2004): 157–178.

Park, Linda Sue. *When My Name Was Keoko.* New York: Dell Yearling, 2002.

Park, Seong-Won. *Worship in the Presbyterian Church in Korea: Its History and Implications.* Frankfurt: Peter Lang, 2001.

Park Yong Kyu. *Han'guk kidokkyohoesa 1 (1784–1910)* [History of the Korean Church, vol. 1, 1784–1910]. Seoul: Saengmyŏng ŭi malssŭmsa, 2004.

———. *Kim Iktu moksa chŏn'gi* [A Biography of Reverend Kim Iktu]. Seoul: Saengmyŏng ŭi malssŭmsa, 1991.

———. *P'yŏngyang sanjŏnghyŏn kyohoe* [P'yŏngyang's Sanjŏnghyŏn Church]. Seoul: Saengmyŏng ŭi malssŭmsa, 2006.

———. *P'yŏngyang taebuhŭng undong, 1901–1910* [The Great Revivalism in Korea: Its History, Character, and Impact, 1901–1910]. Seoul: Saengmyŏng ŭi malssŭmsa, 2000.

Peterson, Arnold A. *5.18 Kwangju sat'ae* [The May Eighteenth Kwangju Incident]. Translated by Chŏng Tongsŏp. Seoul: P'ulpit, 1995.

Porterfield, Amanda. *Healing in the History of Christianity.* Oxford: Oxford University Press, 2005.

Pratt, Keith, and Richard Rutt, eds. *Korea: A Historical and Cultural Dictionary.* Surrey, UK: Curzon, 1999.

Pyŏn Chongho. *Yi Yongdo moksa chŏn* [The Life of Reverend Yi Yongdo]. Vol. 2 of Pyŏn, *Yi Yongdo moksa chŏnjip.*

———, ed. *Yi Yongdo moksa chŏnjip* [The Complete Works of Reverend Yi Yongdo]. Seoul: Changan munhwasa, 1986.

P'yŏnjip wiwŏnhoe [Editorial Committee for Reverend Yi Yongdo's 100th Birthday Anniversary Festschrift]. *Yi Yongdo ŭi saengae, sinhak, yŏngsŏng* [The Life, Theology, and Spirituality of Yi Yongdo]. Seoul: Handŭl ch'ulp'ansa, 2001.

Rabe, Valentin H. "Evangelical Logistics: Mission Support and Resources to 1920." In John Fairbank, *Missionary Enterprise in China and America,* 56–90.

Rambo, Lewis R. *Understanding Religious Conversion.* New Haven, CT: Yale University Press, 1993.

Reid, David. *New Wine: The Cultural Shaping of Japanese Christianity.* Berkeley, CA: Asian Humanities Press, 1991.

Rhodes, Harry A., ed. *History of the Korea Mission: Presbyterian Church, USA, 1884–1934.* Seoul: Chosŏn Mission Presbyterian Church, USA, 1934.

Ricoeur, Paul. *Hermeneutics and the Human Sciences.* Edited and translated by John B. Thompson. Cambridge: Cambridge University Press, 1981.

Ro, Bong-rin, and Marlin L. Nelson. *Korean Church Growth Explosion.* Seoul: World of Life Press, 1983.

Robinson, Michael E. *Cultural Nationalism in Colonial Korea, 1920–1925.* Seattle: University of Washington Press, 1988.

———. *Korea's Twentieth-Century Odyssey: A Short History.* Honolulu: University of Hawai`i Press, 2007.

Ryu Dae Young. "Ch'ogi han'guk kyohoe esŏ 'evangelical' ŭi ŭimiwa hyŏndaejŏk haesŏk ŭi munje" [The Meaning of "Evangelical" in the Early Korean (Protestant) Church and the Problems It Poses for Modern Interpretation]. *Han'guk kidokkyo wa yŏksa* [Korean Christianity and History] 15 (2001): 117–144.

———. "The Origin and Character of Evangelical Protestantism in Korea at the Turn of the Twentieth Century." *Church History: Studies in Christianity and Culture* 77, no. 2 (2008): 337–398.

Ryu Kŭmju. *Yi Yongdo ŭi sinbijuŭi wa han'guk kyohoe* [Yi Yongdo's Mysticism and the Korean Church]. Seoul: Taehan kidokkyo sŏhoe, 2005.

Sauer, Charles August. *Methodists in Korea, 1930–1960.* Seoul: Christian Literature Society of Korea, 1973.

Sawa Masahiko. "Haebang ihu pukhan chiyŏk ŭi kidokkyo: 1945.8–1950.6" [Christianity in Northern Korea after Liberation: August 1945–June 1950]. In Kim Heung-soo, ed., *Haebanghu pukhan kyohoesa,* 13–51.

———. "Han'guk kyohoe ŭi kongsanjuŭi e taehan t'aedo ŭi yŏksajŏk yŏn'gu" [A Historical Study of the Korean Church's Attitude toward Communism]. In Kim Heung-soo, ed., *Ilcheha han'guk kidokkyo wa sahoejuŭi* [Christianity and Socialism in Korea under Japanese Rule]. Seoul: Han'guk kidokkyo yŏksa yŏn'guso, 1992.

Sayer, Robert. "Potters and Christians: New Light on Korea's First Catholics." *Korean Culture* 6, no. 2 (1985): 26–35.

Scheiner, Irwin. *Christian Converts and Social Protest in Japan.* Berkeley: University of California Press, 1970.

Schmid, Andre. *Korea between Empires, 1895–1919.* New York: Columbia University Press, 2002.

Schmidt, Jean Miller. *Souls or the Social Order: The Two-Party System in American Protestantism.* New York: Carlson, 1991.

Scott-Stokes, Henry, and Lee Jai-eui, eds. *The Kwangju Uprising: Eyewitness Press Accounts of Korea's Tiananmen.* Armonk, NY: M. E. Sharpe, 2000.

Segye pogŭmhwa undong chungang hyŏpŭihoe [World Evangelistic Movement Central Association]. '88 segye pogŭmhwa taesŏnghoe kirok munjip: Sŏngnyŏng ŭi pŭlkir ŭl on segye ro [Record of the '88 World Evangelization Crusade: Spread the Fire of the Holy Spirit throughout the World]. Seoul: Segye pogŭmhwa undong chungang hyŏpŭihoe, 1988.

Seoul National University, Department of Religion, and Institute for the Study of Religious Culture. Chŏnhwan'gi ŭi han'guk chonggyo [Korean Religions at a Turning Point]. Seoul: Chipmundang, 1986.

Shim, Jaeryong. Korean Buddhism: Tradition and Transformation. Seoul: Jimoondang, 1999.

Shin, Eun Hee. "The Sociopolitical Organism: The Religious Dimensions of Juche Philosophy." In Robert E. Buswell, Jr., Religions of Korea in Practice, 517–533.

Shin, Gi-Wook. Ethnic Nationalism in Korea: Genealogy, Politics, and Legacy. Stanford, CA: Stanford University Press, 2006.

Shin, Gi-Wook, and Michael E. Robinson, eds. Colonial Modernity in Korea. Cambridge, MA: Harvard University Asia Center, 1999.

Shin, Susan. "The Tonghak Movement: From Enlightenment to Revolution." Korean Studies Forum 5 (Winter–Spring 1978–1979): 1–79.

Shinohara, Hatsue. "Highway versus Development: Railroads in Korea under Japanese Colonial Rule." In Bruce Cumings, ed., Chicago Occasional Papers on Korea, 6:33–57. Chicago: Center for East Asian Studies, University of Chicago, 1991.

Sin Hyŏnggyun. "Sŏngnyŏng ŭi pulkilŭr on segye ro" [Spread the Fire of the Holy Spirit throughout the World]. In Segye pogŭmhwa undong chungang hyŏpŭihoe, '88 segye pogŭmhwa taesŏnghoe kirok munjip.

———. "Yŏnggwang ŭi hwoebok" [The Restoration of Glory]. Sinang segye [Spiritual World] (August 1977).

Sin Sŏngjong. Irŏn kyohoe ka sŏngjang handa [This Is the Kind of Church That Grows]. Seoul: Hana, 1993.

Smith, Anthony D. Nationalism and Modernism. London: Routledge, 1998.

Smith, Timothy L. Revivalism and Social Reform: American Protestantism on the Eve of the Civil War. Nashville, TN: Abingdon, 1957.

Sneller, Alvin [Sin Naeri]. Han'guk kyohoe sŏngjang ŭi pigyŏl [Secrets of the Korean Church's Growth]. Seoul: Kyaehyŏkchuŭi sinhaeng hyŏphoe, 1992.

Sŏ Chŏngmin. "Ch'ogi han'guk kyohoe taebuhŭng undong ihae" [Understanding the Great Revival Movement in the Early Korean (Protestant) Church]. In Yi Mahnyol et al., eds., Han'guk kidokkyo wa minjok undong, 233–283.

———. Yi Tonghwi wa kidokkyo [Yi Tonghwi and Christianity]. Seoul: Yonsei taehakkyo ch'ulp'anbu, 2007.

Son, Bong-ho. "Some Dangers of Rapid Growth." In Bong-rin Ro and Marlin L. Nelson, eds., Korean Church Growth Explosion, 333–348.

Sŏng Paekkŏl. "Han'guk ch'ogi kaesingyoin dŭl ŭi kyohoe wa kukka ihae, 1884–1910." [Early Korean Protestants' Understanding of the Church and the State, 1884–1910]. Han'guk kidokkyosa yŏn'gu [Journal of the Institute of Korean Church History Studies] 21 (May 1988): 4–19.

Soon-Hwa, Sun. "Women, Religion, and Power: A Comparative Study of Korean Shamans and Women Ministers." PhD diss., Drew University, 1991.

Spener, Philip Jacob. *Pia Desideria*. Minneapolis: Fortress, 1964.

Stentzel, Jim, ed. *More Than Witnesses: How a Small Group of Missionaries Aided Korea's Democratic Revolution*. Seoul: Korea Democracy Foundation, 2006.

Stromberg, Peter G. *Language and Self-Transformation: A Study of the Christian Conversion Narrative*. Cambridge: University of Cambridge, 1993.

Suh, Dae-Sook. *Documents of Korean Communism, 1918–1948*. Princeton, NJ: Princeton University Press, 1970.

———. *Kim Il Sung: The North Korean Leader*. New York: Columbia University Press, 1988.

Sunoo, Harold Hakwon. *Repressive State and Resisting Church: The Politics of CIA in South Korea*. Fayette, MO: Korean American Cultural Association, 1976.

Tae Chŏndŏk [Reuben A. Torrey]. *San'koltchak esŏ on p'yŏnji* [Letters from a Mountain Valley]. Vol. 2. Seoul: Kungmin ilbo, 1985.

Taehan yesugyo changnohoe ch'onghoe [General Assembly of the Presbyterian Church of Korea]. *Hŏnpŏp* [Constitution]. Rev. ed. Seoul: Taehan yesugyo changnohoe ch'onghoe, 1989.

Thomas, Winburn. *Protestant Beginnings in Japan*. Rutland, VT: Charles E. Tuttle, 1959.

Tillich, Paul. *Dynamics of Faith*. New York: Harper and Row, Harper Torch Books, 1958.

Tinker, George E. *Missionary Conquest: The Gospel and Native American Cultural Genocide*. Minneapolis: Fortress, 1993.

T'onggye ch'ŏng [National Statistics Office of the Republic of Korea]. *1990 ingu chut'aek ch'ong chosa chonghap punsŏk* [Comprehensive Analysis of the 1990 Population Census]. Vol. 4-2, *Chiyŏkkan ingu pulgyunhyŏng punp'o ŭi wŏnin kwa kyŏlgwa* [Causes and Effects of Uneven Distribution of Population in Regions]. Seoul: T'onggye ch'ŏng, 1990.

———. *1995 ingu chut'aek ch'ong chosa: Ch'oejong chŏnsu chipkye kyŏlgwa* [Comprehensive Investigation of Population and Housing for 1995: Results of the Final Enumeration]. Seoul: T'onggye ch'ŏng, 1995.

Tracy, David. *The Analogical Imagination: Christian Theology and the Culture of Pluralism*. New York: Crossroad, 1986.

Troeltsch, Ernst. *The Social Teachings of the Christian Churches*. Vol. 1. Translated by Olive Wyon. 1911; reprints, New York: Macmillan, 1931; and Chicago: University of Chicago Press, Phoenix Books, 1981.

Tuveson, Ernest Lee. *Redeemer Nation: The Idea of America's Millennial Role*. Chicago: University of Chicago Press, 1968.

Underwood, Elizabeth. *Challenged Identities: North American Missionaries in Korea, 1884–1934*. Seoul: Royal Asiatic Society, Korea Branch, 2003.

Underwood, Horace G. *The Call of Korea*. New York: Fleming H. Revell, 1908.

Underwood, Lillias H. *Underwood of Korea*. 1918; reprint, Seoul: Yonsei University Press, 1983.

U.S. State Department. State Department Record, Consular Bureau. *The Present Movement for Korean Independence*. Report filed July 8, 1919.

Varg, Paul. *Missionary, Chinese, and Diplomats.* Princeton, NJ: Princeton University Press, 1958.

Vaughan, John N. *Absolutely Double.* Bolivar, MO: Megachurch Research Press, 1990.

———. *The World's Twenty Largest Churches.* Grand Rapids, MI: Jordan, 1984.

Wach, Joachim. *The Comparative Study of Religions.* New York: Columbia University Press, 1958.

———. *Introduction to the History of Religions.* Edited by Joseph M. Kitigawa. New York: Macmillan, 1988.

———. *Sociology of Religion.* Chicago: University of Chicago Press, 1944.

Walker, Williston, et al. *A History of the Christian Church.* 4th ed. New York: Charles Scribner's Sons, 1985.

Wallace, F. C. "Revitalization Movements." *American Anthropologist* 58 (1956): 264–281.

Wasson, Alfred W. *Church Growth in Korea.* New York: International Missionary Council, 1934.

Weber, Max. *Sociology of Religion.* Translated by Ephraim Fischoff. Boston: Beacon, 1963.

Weems, Benjamin. *Reform, Rebellion, and the Heavenly Way.* Tucson: University of Arizona Press, 1964.

Wells, Kenneth M. *New God, New Nation: Protestants and Self-Reconstruction Nationalism in Korea, 1896–1937.* Honolulu: University of Hawai'i Press, 1990.

Wilson, Brian A. "Values and Religion." In Lee Mangap and Herbert R. Barringer, eds., *A City in Transition: Urbanization in Taegu, Korea.* Seoul: Hollym, 1971.

Yang Hyŏnhye. *Yun Ch'iho wa Kim Kyosin: Kŭndae chosŏn e issŏsŏ minjokchŏk aident'it'i wa kidokkyo* [Yun Ch'iho and Kim Kyosin: National Identity and Christianity in Modern Korea]. Seoul: Hanul, 1994.

Yang Migang. "Ch'amyŏ wa paeje ŭi kwanchŏm esŏ pon chŏndo puin e kwanhan yŏn'gu 1910-yŏn–1930-yŏndae rŭl chungsim uro" [A Study of the Bible Women from the Perspective of Their Participation and Exclusion, Focusing on the 1910s through the 1930s]. *Han'guk kidokkyo wa yŏksa* [Korean Christianity and History] 6 (1997): 139–179.

———. "Ch'ogi chŏndo puin ŭi sinang kwa hwaltong" [The Piety and Activity of Early Bible Women]. *Han'guk kidokkyo wa yŏksa* [Korean Christianity and History] 2 (1992): 91–109.

Yi Chongyun, Chŏn Hojin, and Na Ilsŏn. *Kyohoe sŏngjangnon* [Theories of Church Growth]. Seoul: Emmaus, 1986.

Yi, Kwangsu. "The Benefits Which Christianity Has Conferred on Korea." *Korea Mission Field* 14 (February 1918): 34–36.

———. "Defects of the Korean Church Today." *Korea Mission Field* 14 (December 1918): 253–257.

Yi Mahn-yol. *Han'guk kidokkyosa yŏngu: Han'guk kidokkyo wa minjok t'ongil undong* [Studies in Korean Christianity: Korean Christianity and a Movement for National Unification]. Seoul: Han'guk kidokkyo yŏksa yŏn'guso, 2001.

———. "Hanmal kidokkyoin ŭi minjok ŭisik hyŏngsŏng kwajŏng" [The Formation of National Consciousness among Korean Christians near the End of the Han Empire]. In Yi Mahn-yol et al., eds., *Han'guk kidokkyo wa minjok undong*, 11–73.

———. "3.1 undong kwa kidokkyo" [The March First Movement and Christianity]. *Han'guk kidokkyo wa yŏksa* [Korean Christianity and History] 7 (1997): 7–20.

Yi Mahn-yol, Pak Hyosaeng, Yi Tŏkchu [Rhie Deok-Joo], Yi Hwŭihwan, Sŏ Chŏngmin, Yun Kyŏngno, Kim Hyŏngsŏk, and Sŏ Kwoengil. *Han'guk kidokkyo wa minjok undong* [Korean Christianity and Nationalist Movement]. Seoul: Posŏng, 1986.

Yi Mansin. "Hananim ŭi sarang" [God's Love]. In Segye pogŭmhwa undong chungang hyŏpŭihoe, *'88 segye pogŭmhwa taesŏnghoe kirok munjip*, 84–87.

Yi Tŏkchu [Rhie Deok-Joo]. "Ch'ogi kaesin'gyo e isŏsŏ han-jung kidokkyo kyoryu" [Early Interaction between the Christian Churches of Korea and China]. *Han'guk kidokkyosa yŏn'gu* [Journal of the Institute of Korean Christian History Studies] 1 (April–May) 1985.

———. *Han'guk kŭristoin dŭl ŭi kaejong iyagi* [Conversion Stories of Korean Christians]. Seoul: Chŏnmangsa, 1990.

———. *Han'guk kyohoe chŏŭm yŏsŏngdŭl* [Early Christian Women in Korea]. Seoul: Kidokkyo munsa, 1990.

———. "Han'guk kyohoe kido undong paljach'wi" [Footprints of the Korean Protestant Churches' Prayer Movement]. *Kido* [Prayer], November 1986, 22–25.

———. *Saero ssŭn kaejong iyaki* [Newly Written Conversion Stories of Korean Christians]. Seoul: Han'guk kidokkyo yŏksa yŏn'guso, 2003.

Yi, Young-suk. "Liberal Protestant Leaders Working for Social Change: South Korea, 1957–1984." PhD diss., University of Oregon, 1990.

Yip, Kap-che. *Religion, Nationalism and Chinese Students: The Anti-Christian Movement of 1922–1927*. Bellingham: Washington University Press, 1980.

Yoo, Young-sik. "The Impact of Canadian Missionaries in Korea: A Historical Survey of Early Canadian Mission Work, 1888–1898." PhD diss., University of Toronto, 1996.

Yu, Chai-Shin, ed. *The Founding of Catholic Tradition in Korea*. Mississauga, Ontario: Korea and Related Studies Press, 1996.

———, ed. *Korea and Christianity*. Seoul: Korean Scholar Press, 1996.

Yu, Chai-shin, and R. Guisso, eds. *Shamanism: The Spirit World of Korea*. Berkeley, CA: Asian Humanities Press, 1988.

Yu Hongnyŏl. *Han'guk chŏnju kyohoe yaksa* [A Concise History of Korean Catholicism]. Seoul: St. Joseph's Press, 1983.

———. *Han'guk chŏnju kyohoesa* [A History of the Korean Catholic Church]. Vol. 1. Seoul: Kat'ollik ch'ulp'ansa, 1962.

———. *Han'guk chŏnju kyohoesa* [A History of the Korean Catholic Church]. Vol. 2. Seoul: Kat'ollik ch'ulp'ansa, 1964.

Yu Tongsik [Ryu Tong-shik]. *Han'guk mugyo ŭi yŏksa wa kujo* [The History and Structure of Korean Shamanism]. Seoul: Yonsei University Press, 1975.

———. *Han'guk sinhak ŭi kwangmaek* [Veins in Korean Theology]. Seoul: Chŏnmangsa, 1982.

Yun Kyŏngno. *Han'guk kŭndaesa ŭi kidokkyosa chŏk ihae* [A Christian Interpretation of Modern Korean History]. Seoul: Yŏkminsa, 1992.

Periodicals and Web sites

Bulgyo sinmun [Buddhist News] (Seoul)

Chosŏn ilbo [Chosun ilbo] (Seoul)

Christian Century (Chicago)

Christianity Today (Carol Stream, IL)

Chungang ilbo [Joong ang ilbo; Joong ang Daily] (Seoul)

Han'guk ilbo [Hankook ilbo; Korea Times] (Seoul)

Han'guk kidok kongbo [Christian News] (Seoul)

Kido [Prayer]

Kidok sinmun [Christian Newspaper] (Seoul)

Kidokkyo sasang [Christian Thought] (Seoul)

Kidoksinbo [Christian News] (Seoul)

Korea Computer Missions, http://kcm.co.kr/statistics/5/s013.html

Korea Mission Field (*KMF*) (Seoul), published from November 1905 to November 1941

Kungmin ilbo [Kookmin ilbo] (Seoul)

K'ŭrisŭch'yan raip'ŭ [Christian Life] (Seoul)

K'ŭrisŭch'yan sinmun [Christian Press] (Seoul)

K'ŭrisŭch'yan t'udei [Christian Today] (Seoul), http://www.chtoday.co.kr

Kyohoe yŏnhap sinbo [Church Union News] (Seoul)

Kyŏnghyang sinmun [Kyunghyang Daily] (Seoul)

Missionary Review of the World

Mokhoe wa sinhak [Ministry and Theology] (Seoul)

Nambuk nanum [North-South Sharing], http://www.sharing.net

New York Times

News N Joy (Seoul), http://www.newsnjoy.co.kr

Pulgyo sinmun [Buddhist News] (Seoul)

Sinang segye [Spiritual World] (Seoul)

Sinanggye [Shinangge; Spiritual Realm] (Seoul)

Sunday Seoul (Seoul)

Weekly Economist (Seoul)

WEF Theological News (Seoul)

Wŏlgan choguk [Monthly Fatherland], available at *Chosŏn sinbo* [People's Korea], http://www.korea-np.co.jp

Wŏlgan mokhoe [Pastoral Monthly] (Seoul)

Yahoo Korea! Paekkhwa sajŏn [Yahoo! Korea Encyclopedia], http://kr.dictionary .search.yahoo.com

Index

Allen, Horace N., 9, 11
An Isuk, 59
Ancestor worship, 55
ansu kido (laying-on-of-hands prayer),
130
anticommunism, xiv, 69, 86–87, 114.
See also communism/communists
Appenzeller, Henry G., vi, 7–12, 32, 85,
118, 136, 159n. 27
Armstrong, Charles K., 64, 155n. 10
Assemblies of God, 124

Baird, Annie Laurie Adams (Mrs. W.
M.), 21, 29
Baker, Don, 154n. 10, 155n. 13, 158n.
15, 159n. 23
Baptists, 58, 86, 91, 106–107, 109
Beyerhaus, Peter, 109
Bible: and blessings, 125;
bowdlerization of, 58; Chinese
translations in Korea, 8, 11; Cho
Yonggi's interpretation of, 122; and
higher criticism, 53; inerrancy of,
117–118, 140; and Kil Sŏnju, 73,
74; Kim Chun'gon's interpretation,
99; New Testament, 11, 121, 136,
172n. 25; Old Testament (Hebrew
Bible), 73, 136, 149; translation
of, 10, 11, 53, 136; vis-à-vis

authorities, 34. *See also* Bible study;
Gospels
Bible study: and cell meeting, 134–135;
and church growth, 89–90; and
devotional, 25, 126, 130; in the
great revival, 15, 19–23; and Kil
Sŏnju, 73; and Kim Iktu, 76–77;
137–138; in mammoth crusades,
108, 109
Bible women, 51, 171n. 20
Blair, William N., 18, 20, 28, 73
born-again (new birth) experience, 17,
21–22, 25–26, 85, 103, 124, 140.
See also conversion
Brauer, Jerald C., ix, 156n. 20, 178n.
130
Bright, Bill R., 86, 96–96, 109
Brown, Arthur J., 12, 60, 85, 112, 115,
160n. 49, 171n. 22, 190 epigraph
Buddhism (Buddhists) in Korea, xii–
xiv, 5, 38, 43, 69, 72, 120, 135, 139,
142–144,153n. 7, 154n. 8

Campus Crusade for Christ (CCC), 86,
96, 97, 102, 134
Catholicism (Catholics) in Korea,
xii–xiii, 3–5, 7, 9, 31–32, 44, 55, 69,
89, 139, 142–147, 149–150, 153n.
7, 155n. 13, 176n. 116

About the Author

TIMOTHY S. LEE received his doctorate in the history of Christianity from the University of Chicago Divinity School. He has received grants from the Social Science Research Council and the Fulbright Program and served as a Henry Luce Postdoctoral Fellow in Korean Christianity at the University of California, Los Angeles (2001–2002), and was visiting assistant professor at the University of Chicago, Department of East Asian Studies. He has published numerous works on Korean Christianity. An ordained minister of the Christian Church (Disciples of Christ) and co-chair of the Korean Group of the American Academy of Religion, Professor Lee teaches the history of Christianity at Brite Divinity School, Texas Christian University.

Production notes for Lee / *Born Again*
Jacket design by Julie Matsuo-Chun
Interior design by the University of Hawai'i Press production staff
Display type in Papyrus; text in Minion Pro
Printing and binding by The Maple-Vail Book Manufacturing Group